3c⊥
3JT

9⁵⁰
12⁰⁰

D0886548

Sigmund Freud

PSYCHOLOGICAL WRITINGS AND LETTERS

The German Library: Volume 59

Volkmar Sander, General Editor

Sigmund Freud

PSYCHOLOGICAL WRITINGS AND LETTERS

Edited by Sander L. Gilman

CONTINUUM · NEW YORK

1995

The Continuum Publishing Company
370 Lexington Avenue, New York, NY 10017

The German Library
is published in cooperation with Deutsches Haus,
New York University.
This volume has been supported by Inter Nationes, and a grant
from the funds of Stifterverband für die Deutsche Wissenschaft.

Printed in the United States of America

Library of Congress Cataloging-in-Publication Data

Freud, Sigmund, 1856–1939.
    [Selections. English. 1995]
    Psychological writings and letters / Sigmund Freud ;
edited by Sander L. Gilman.
        p.   cm. — (The German library ; v. 59)
    Includes bibliographical references.
    ISBN 0-8264-0722-6 (alk. paper) — ISBN 0-8264-0723-4
(pbk. : alk. paper)
    1. Psychoanalysis. 2. Freud, Sigmund, 1856–1939—Correspondence.
3. Psychoanalysts—Austria—Correspondence. I. Gilman, Sander L.
II. Title. III. Series.
BF109.F74A25   1995
150.19′52—dc20   93-47191
                                                              CIP

Acknowledgments will be found on page 282,
which constitutes an extension of the copyright page.

Contents

Introduction

Sigmund Freud (1856–1939) was one of the shapers of twentieth-century consciousness through his development of the concept of the unconscious and the therapy that he evolved based on this discovery. Trained as a neurologist at the University of Vienna, his creation "psychoanalysis" presented a threefold approach to understanding the human psyche: it was a therapeutic method; a method in inquiry, a way of exploring a subject matter, collecting data; a theory, a scientific structure, a body of knowledge. All three were intimately linked in his understanding of his innovations in the field of psychotherapy. Freud's work built on an ongoing tradition of psychotherapy as it evolved in Western civilization.[1]

Psychotherapy is the noninvasive treatment of those mental or emotional states, understood by the patient and the therapist as pathological or maladaptive. It may be used independently of or in addition to somatic procedures and psychopharmacology (somatotherapy). (The "therapist" may or may not be a physician; the "patient" may or may not manifest the symptoms that are defined as "mental illness" in the various standard nosological handbooks such as the *Diagnostic and Statistical Manual of the American Psychiatric Association.*)

Psychotherapy presupposes a specific relationship between therapist and patient and more or less clearly defined roles for both; it is undertaken in a physical space labeled as a therapeutic context; it presumes that therapy can be effective and so sets an optimistic prognosis; it is so structured that both therapist and patient have specific, assigned tasks that permit the therapist's interventions.[2]

While the term, *psychotherapy*, is recorded in English as early as 1853, it comes into common medical use only in the late 1880s through French-language publications.[3] The tradition of an interpersonal, physically noninvasive psychotherapy, however, has long roots in Western culture.[4] It is possible to speak of the sacrament of confession within the Catholic church as a model for the overall practice of psychotherapy.[5] Present within the rhetoric of the Gospels is the image of "Christ as the physician." The Church, using this biblical metaphor of healing, saw confession (the verbal articulation of sins by the parishioner to the priest within the confessional and the priest's absolution through the assignment of specific ritual tasks) as healing the soul of those ailments that caused both physical and psychic distress. In addition to the confessional, "healing miracles," such as those experienced by the Jansenists in the seventeenth and early eighteenth centuries, like other forms of faith healing, led to cures of both somatic as well as psychological disorders through such religious practices. Such interventions were believed to be the result of the intervention of the divinity through the action of saints represented by relics. But it is clear, if the Jansenist accounts are read, that such cures took place through the active intervention of the clergy and the participation through assigned roles of those undertaking to be healed. In all cases in the definition of roles of patient and therapist, in the determination of the place of healing, the potential for intervention was present.

With the medicalization of specific practices of psychotherapy in the course of the late eighteenth century, a secular definition of psychotherapy evolved. Given its secular nature, the roots of this new psychotherapy were within—but often combated by—the traditional medical establishment of the late Enlightenment. The European asylum tradition of the eighteenth century had established a specific model for treating those mental and emotional states that rendered an individual unable to function within the increasingly urbanized and industrial society of Europe. Using the traditional pharmacopoeia, diet, baths (especially popular in the latter half of the nineteenth century), and other forms of somatic intervention, physicians attempted to treat debilitating emotional or psychological states with greater or lesser success. With the medicalization of animal magnetism or what comes to be called "mesmeric treatment," the path to a psychological procedure that seemed overtly different enough from both conventional medicine as well as religious tradition was introduced. It was in the theory and practice of the Viennese physician Franz Anton Mesmer (1734–1815), but even more in the work of his disciple, Armand-Marie-Jacques de Chastenet, marquis de Puységur (1751–1825), that the theory of animal magnetism was applied as a healing tool. They both used the rhetoric of the high science of the eighteenth century, such as chemistry and physiology, to provide a "scientific" veneer for their treatment.[6] The very name, *animal magnetism,* reflects the Enlightenment interest in concrete forms of physical science, such as electricity and magnetism. The procedure was one of suggestion, but its outward trappings were that of physical science. The use of a *baquet,* the object that was to gather the body "fluid" to be magnetized by the physician and thus cure the patient, was a clear replica of one of the most avant-garde pieces of scientific instrumentation of the day, the Leyden jar. (One of the more accepted forms of treatment for a wide range of psychological and emotional disorders during the nineteenth century was low-voltage electrolization.) The magnetizer's power over the patients did not rely solely on these scientific substitutes for religious relics.[7] Rather Mesmer stressed that the power of healing lay solely with the magnetizer and the special relationship, the "rapport," that the magnetizer had with the patient. While individual treatment soon gave way to mass treatment, the relationship between the magnetizer and the patient was a personalized one of trust and belief.

Mesmer's patients were often suffering from what seemed to be physical symptoms and yet were healed by Mesmer's noninvasive procedures. Such a blanket claim for the efficacy of mesmerism placed it in direct competition with all forms of institutionalized medicine. The scientific establishment quickly came to view animal magnetism, both in its theoretical as well as its applied form, as bad science and as a dangerous quackery. The preeminent commission appointment by the king of France in 1784 (the astronomer Jean-Sylvain Bailly, the chemist Antoine-Laurent Lavoisier, the physician Joseph-Ignace Guillotin and the American ambassador to France, Benjamin Franklin) to examine Mesmer's approach to healing totally rejected the existence of any fluid that could explain animal magnetism. But it also pointed out the dangers that might lie in the sexual exploitation of the suggestible subject through the special "rapport" that was evidently generated through the act of mesmeric healing. There is a tension between the tradition of psychotherapy as practiced by marginalized physicians such as Mesmer and the mainstream practice of a medicine that defined itself in terms of the high science of its time.

In the German Enlightenment pre-Romantic writers and thinkers such as Karl Philipp Moritz (1757–93) concerned themselves with the social and cultural context of aberrant emotional states, their relationship to physical ailments, and to language and its use as a means of therapy. In practice the treatments for such states were often as not through mesmerism or suggestion. Academic physicians in Germany such as Dietrich Georg Kieser (1779–1862) continued to stand in this tradition in their treatment of the mentally ill and the poet-physician Justinus Kerner (1786–1862) used a baquet in his treatment of psychological, emotional, and physical disorders well into the 1850s. Because of the rapport between therapist and patient, such an approach was understood to be more humane than alternative treatment. Advocates of what came to be called "moral treatment" of the mentally ill elsewhere in Europe, such as the Quaker reformer of the British asylum William Tuke (1732–1822) in England, while advocating very different approaches to psychotherapy, adapted the close, personal sense of "rapport" that marked the tradition of mesmerism without the overt use of mesmeric treatment. Like the German Romantic therapists, they spoke and interacted with their charges in terms of accepted social convention, had specific places where treatment took place, and assigned specific tasks to both therapist and patient in the course of the treatment.

With the medicalization of the treatment of the mentally ill in the mid–nineteenth century, certain modes of therapy, such as mesmerism, came to be understood as having some basis in the science of that time. In the 1850s, the work of James Braid (1795–1860) had restored mesmerism as an accepted form of therapy through his realization that pure suggestion rather than instruments such as the *baquet* could be used to place patients in a trance. Braid relabeled mesmerism with the more "scientific" and less pejorative name: *neurohypnotism* or *hypnotism*. However he did this in the context of his interest in phrenology, another "new" science of the mind in the mid–nineteenth century, as he discussed in his principal work, *Neurypnology; or, The Rationale of Nervous Sleep, Considered in Relation with Animal Magnetism* (1843). Braid's interest in phrenology and hypnotism was branded as unscientific by the materialists of his day, such as the German neurologist Wilhelm

Griesinger (1817–68) who reduced "mind illness to brain illness." This epiphenomenalism made the study of the psyche as an independent or dominant phenomenon impossible for those "mainstream" physicians who dealt with the mentally and emotionally ill. Dominated by this view during the latter half of the nineteenth century, the study of human physiology and anatomy came to be the sole manner of exploring all those mental and emotional states that were labeled as pathological.

Thus it was only within the new scientific rhetoric of brain localization, the search for the place within the structure of the brain where the lesions that caused specific forms of mental or emotional illness were to be located, that psychotherapy was able to reappear within mainstream medicine. Given the search for the material basis for the mind, access to the mind (and therefore to the brain) through its psychological manifestations, such as the hypnotic state, again became of interest. Auguste Ambroise Liébeault (1823–1904) in Nancy began, like Mesmer, to treat all of the ills of the poor through the means of hypnosis. Liébeault, in his *Concerning Sleep and Analogous States, Considered from the Angle of the Mind-Body Relationship* (1866), explained hypnotism to be a natural state, analogous to normal sleep, but induced in the subject by the suggestion of the physician. For Liébeault this accounted for the special relationship between the patient and the hypnotizer. Liébeault's work influenced the approach of Hippolyte Bernheim (1840–1919), the professor of internal medicine at the new University of Nancy. Bernheim's work was based on a broad application of the implications of his findings concerning hypnotism. In his *Suggestive Therapeutics: A Treatise on the Nature and Uses of Hypnotism* (1886) he suggested that everyone—both the "ill" and the "normal"—has the potential to be hypnotized and that this universal aspect of the psyche permitted not only a therapeutics (of negative as well as positive suggestion) but also a research agenda concerning the normal structure of the psyche independent of any material structures within the brain.

Bernheim's furtherance of Liébeault's work was in the light of the dominance of French neurology by Jean-Martin Charcot (1825–93), the first professor of clinical diseases of the nervous system (as of 1882) at the University of Paris. (Psychiatry was not yet an independent specialty, as all aberrant psychological phenomena were understood to be physical and therefore "nervous" dis-

eases.) Charcot too employed hypnotism or "Braidism" to treat
the seemingly organic problems of one category of mental illness,
hysteria. He understood his ability to place these subjects into a
trance as a further symptom of their illness. For Charcot suggest-
ibility was itself a symptom of the functional deficit of the hysteric.

The conflict between the "Parisian" and the "Nancy" schools
could be summarized in their self-definition of the efficacy of therapy. Charcot's work became more and more rooted in his understanding of the physiological state that he saw mirrored in the
symptoms of "his" hysterics. He understood this state as the direct
result of some physically traumatic shock on the nervous system.
His lack of long-term success in treating the symptoms of his hysterical patients through hypnotism became a further proof of the
constitutional nature of their disease. Bernheim, on the other hand,
came more and more to abandon hypnosis as the primary mode
of therapeutic treatment, relying on direct suggestion. This mode
of treatment came to be labeled as *psychotherapy* (a term employed
by Bernheim in the title of his *Hypnotism, Suggestion, Psychotherapy* [1891]).

Into the midst of this debate between Bernheim and Charcot
concerning the treatment of specific forms of mental illness the
Viennese neurologist Sigmund Freud came to Paris (1885–86),
where he attended Charcot's lectures and through them became
interested in the question of hysteria.[8] He subsequently visited
Bernheim in 1889 in order to further his facility in hypnotism.
Freud eventually translated works by both Charcot and Bernheim
into German. His personal exposure to both schools, as well as his
own biological training in the laboratories of the University of
Vienna, led him to evolve a three-pronged approach that he came
to call *psychoanalysis:* a therapeutics of psychopathology initially
based on hypnosis but quickly evolving to the use of Bernheim's
suggestive psychotherapy; a theory of the mind employing the
model of hidden or subconscious levels taken from German Romantic psychiatry and philosophy; and a research agenda concerning the impact of history on the mind and of the mind on history
that reflected the importance of anthropological models as well as
biological models to fin-de-siècle medicine.[9]

All of these cultural factors were in turn shaped by Freud's self-
understanding as an outsider, specifically a Viennese Jew. This marginal role helped shape Freud's sense of the need for a new disci-

pline, first within medicine, then outside of it, that could place the Jewish physician in a very different relationship to the patient. The demands of nineteenth-century medical science placed Jews (like women and homosexuals) in the position of the observed. They were understood as the object of treatment as much as they were seen as the physicians able to give treatment. This epistemological double bind meant that the subject position of the Jewish physician was central to his (and these physicians were male into the twentieth century) self-definition. It is of little surprise that Freud soon found his own psyche at the center of his new science. He began by using his patients as his material, but because of the social stratification of Viennese society, these patients were, for the greater part, middle-class Jews. In *The Interpretation of Dreams,* Freud provided a detailed reading of what he labels the model dream. Freud's sense of the growing importance of his identity as a Jew (in the biological or racial terms of the medical science of the turn of the century) can be measured in his autobiography of 1924 that begins with a genealogical statement that places his ancestors in the center of German Jewry on the Rhine rather than in the peripheries of the outmost reaches of the Austro-Hungarian Empire, Moravia, where Freud was born.

Freud's initial work in the area of the therapeutics of hysteria was undertaken together with his somewhat older and more established Viennese colleague Josef Breuer (1842–1925).[10] Their jointly authored *Studies in Hysteria* (1895) was the initial statement of both the theoretical basis of their approach as well as their therapeutic innovations. These essays and case studies outlined three areas of investigation in terms of vocabularies of science taken from other fields. The "economic" aspect described the quantity of excitation of the nervous system that, in the normal state was released in order to create pleasure. In the hysteric it was dammed up and created symptoms. This "dynamic" aspect was evoked to explain the creation of specific symptoms by specific emotionally charged experiences. They argued that all hysterical symptoms were the product of the memory of real events forgotten by the conscious mind but retained elsewhere in the psyche. For Freud, these were recent events of a sexual nature that evoked memories of early sexual experiences of seduction. The "topographic" aspect of the theory locates where these events take place: the unconscious, a powerful area of the mind not directly accessible to the conscious mind. Later Freud refines this aspect of his theory. Between the conscious and the unconscious mind stands the preconscious, the screen that stands between the conscious and the unconscious. It is here that neuroses arise as preconscious material is repressed into the unconscious.

Freudian theory evolves during the first decade of the twentieth century, but its contours follow these initial categories. Initially Freud and Breuer (as had Bernheim) substituted a form of suggestion for the hypnotic trance when they found that their patient's experiences were not sufficiently resolved through posthypnotic suggestion. Their therapy for hysterical neurosis, free association, was developed in concert with their patients, especially the patient Breuer called "Anna O," Bertha Pappenheim (1859–1936). (She later in life became one of the founders of modern German social work.) She evolved a system of what she labeled as *chimney sweeping*. In discussing with Breuer the meaning and origin of each symptom, the underlying cause of the symptom was articulated and the symptom vanished. "Anna O," like many of Freud's and Breuer's patients, was middle class and well-educated.[11] They entered into the therapeutic situation with a sense of having or needing some control over the therapeutic situation not offered through traditional medicine. Indeed, Freud's own record of those patients who terminated treatment abruptly is a sign of the overall sense of autonomy granted to the patient within the psychoanalytic milieu as opposed to that of establishment psychiatry of the fin de siècle.

Of Freud's contributions to the *Studies in Hysteria* perhaps the most revealing is his case of Katharina. (See this selection, pp. 1–10) Freud recorded the case of "Katherina," actually Aurelia Clothide Catherina Kronich, during the summer of 1893.[12] Kronich is the only non-Jewish, nonurban, non-middle-class patient whose case is recorded in the *Studies in Hysteria*. There he ironically expressed his amazement that hysteria (and its cause, incest) could "exist at over six thousand feet?"[13] Here the question of the biology of race and the substantial role that racial science played in directing the interests of the fin-de-siècle Jewish physician can be noted. For the charge of Jewish "incest," based on the notion of the Jews as a chosen people, was omnipresent in the medical discourse of the time. For Freud, it is not only the Jews in the city, but even the peasants in the countryside who develop hysterical symptoms when they are exposed to traumatic events. Underlying Freud's reading of this case is the charge of inbreeding and incest that is lodged against the Jews. The source of Katherina's illness is her attempted rape by her father (disguised in the original report under the identity of her uncle) who had already seduced or raped her cousin. The theme of the case study is the ubiquity of such sexual contacts within the extended (in the initial case report) or the nuclear family (according to a note to the case written in 1924). Auguste Forel represented such incestuousness as a quality of life both in the mountains and the city (1905):

> The most severe cases of incest occur particularly between parents and children. Most commonly, their cause lies in familiar mental abnormalities, alcoholism, working-class promiscuity, or in the remote isolation of a family from the rest of the world. Incest occurs with relative frequency in Switzerland among the occupants of remote Alpine farm-cottages.[14]

Freud's mountain peasants seem to be the antithesis of the Jews. They are not urban, but rural; not middle but working class; not Jewish but Christian; not inherently endogenous but exogenous. Indeed, Freud selects Katherina exactly because of this dichotomy. But why do they commit incest—Forel provides a "geographical" or "class" explanation but avoids any yet hint of "taint." Freud needs to have the case of Katherina in the *Studies in Hysteria* just as he needed to be able to evoke the specter of a male hysteria separate from the category of Jewish male in his initial lecture on hysteria in Vienna. It is the very beginning of the universalizing process of seeing those qualities ascribed to the Jews as a universal quality—not merely projection on to a subgroup of Jews but to all human beings. And the individual who can describe and treat such an illness is the neutral physician. For Katherina, according to Freud's account, sees him as that. She is unencumbered by modesty because Freud is a doctor: "One can, for sure, tell everything to a doctor" (SE 2:125). There is no qualification here. She does not see him in his role as a Jew or a Jewish doctor—only as a physician. This is another truly universalizing moment in which the association between the role of the physician's gaze and the object of analysis is clearly defined. The doctor treats and the patient is treated. No confusion is permitted, especially here in the mountains where the roles are most clear-cut. The underlying message of this case is itself complicated for, even though Freud "abandons" the trauma theory of hysteria (which sought the source of all hysteria in real sexual seduction in 1897) in a 1924 footnote to the case of Katherina in *The Studies on Hysteria,* he observed that her hysterical symptoms were the result of a real seduction (SE 2:134). In the mountains real incest takes place, unlike in the mythmaking about the Jews.

The centrality of human sexuality, while clear to Freud in his initial work with Josef Breuer in the 1890s, was most clearly expressed in his work of the fin de siècle. The force repressed in the hysteric, the experiences that are shaped by the fantasy over the first few years of life, is sexual—the underlying driving force of human instincts (libido). Freud's model for the id is male sexuality. While he recognized the existence of models of male and female sexuality, reflecting cognitive as well as anatomical difference, he departed from an explicit model of aggressive male sexuality. The Oedipus complex is a clear expression of this male model—it is the successful or unsuccessful renunciation of the attraction to the mother and the concomitant fear of punishment through castration by the father that determines the psychological health or pathology of the male child. The female child must not only abandon her attraction to the mother but must also deal with the sudden awareness of her own physical incompleteness, her envy of the penis. Freud's discussion of the fantasies of female anatomy reflected a male fantasy of castration rather than potential female fantasies of fecundity and childbirth. Likewise, Freud's use of the categories of "active" and "passive" to represent the male and female character reflect his presumption about the definition of gender.

By 1897 Freud transcended his initial view that all neuroses were the result of real events and came to understand that the origins of neurosis were in universal psychological drives and the fantasies of sexually arousing events. (See his letters to Wilhelm Fliess in this selection, pp. 11–16) And the source for all of these fantasies was the nature of the unconscious. The unconscious was the space where all the basic libidinal drives were housed. This would include the sexual, but also drives such as hatred and shame. It is the place within the psyche that the repressed incestuous desires of the child were hidden. Freud in no way excluded the possibility that real disturbing events, in the form of childhood sexual experience, could exist. To examine the underlying processes that structure human fantasy in the unconscious, Freud turned to universal experiences that he saw as revealing unconscious processes—dreaming, slips of the tongue, errors of memory, and jokes. In *The Interpretation of Dreams* (1900), he set out a model for interpreting the underlying structure of the unconscious "dream work." The primary source for his work in this period was his analysis of his own experiences and dreams. He illustrated how the manifest content of the dream (its overt story) employed aspects of daily experience to both mask and expose the underlying sexual fantasies of early childhood. He thus saw the analysis of dreams by the psychoanalyst and the analysand as a central means of psychotherapy. Freud thus completely abandoned hypnotism as a means of accessing the psyche for therapy and developed the "cathartic" method that Breuer had begun to evolve in his treatment of "Anna O." (On Freud's understanding of his method at the turn of the century see this selection, pp. 114–19)

The analysis of all aspects of the analysand's mental life— dreams, memories, thoughts, preoccupations—presented the key to the underlying tension between the social demands of the world (represented in the psyche as the superego) and the immediate demands of libidinous instincts (the id). It is in the ego, the realm of reason and balance, that there is an attempt to resolve these conflicts. What occurs in therapy is transference, an intense "rapport" (which may take the positive form of love but may also take the negative form of hate) with the neutral figure of the analyst who comes to replace that "object" (parent, authority figure). The means of therapy is the free association of ideas, thoughts, images and feelings.

The rapport that Mesmer had described between the subject and the magnetizer, the suggestion that Bernheim (and unconsciously Charcot) had seen between the patient and the physician, evolved within the psychoanalytic model as the transference between the analyst and the analysand. The therapeutic dimension thus rested on the relationship between the analyst and the analysand as well as on the roles that they accepted as part of the therapy. The "talking cure" was not merely the secular confession of failings. The analysand is to tell the analyst "what he knows and conceals from other people; he is to tell us too what he does not know. . . . He is to tell us not only what he can say intentionally and willingly, what will give him relief like a confession, but everything else that

his self-observation yields him" (SE 23:174). Freud's central therapeutic approach, which impacts either positively or negatively on
virtually all forms of psychotherapy, arises to no little degree out
of the social milieu in which he and Breuer found themselves. They
were not psychiatrists dealing with the institutionalized mentally
ill. As neurologists they dealt with what was perceived as somatic
illnesses. They thus spoke with their patients, asking them about
their experience as well as their symptoms. For physicians with a
mainly middle- and upper-middle-class, educated clientele there
were few problems in finding a common language about more or
less common experiences. And as Jews treating a mainly Jewish
patient population they could lay claim to an immediate rapport
between themselves and their patients, as all found themselves in
an extremely hostile environment. They themselves bore the stigma
of difference while being part of the select world of medical power.

Sigmund Freud and his collaborator at the turn of the century
Wilhelm Fliess (1853–1928), a Berlin ear-nose-and-throat specialist, with whom he collaborated at the turn of the century, transformed this difference into a universal sign of human nature in a
successful form of resistance to the racist substructure of European
medicine. It is from the intellectual and emotional relationship with
Wilhelm Fliess, as is generally acknowledged, that Freud began to
evolve the basic theories of psychoanalysis. But this relationship
was played out against the cultural context that medical science is
always a part of. For Freud, the idea of friendship is always un-
stable and is linked to the image of betrayal of friendship. In 1892,
Freud was developing the first clinical procedures for the treatment
of hysteria. He began to work many of the theoretical presuppositions behind these approaches in his correspondence with Fliess.
In an early letter of May 25, 1892, to Fliess, Freud appended a
footnote: "By the way and since nothing more intelligent occurs
to me, let me inform you that I was startled to read on your last
card a W. Ch. I realized only later that you write your first name
equivocally."[15] This is a classic remark—one of Freud's first accounts of his own misreading, accounts that will become more and
more important as he collects materials for his work on dreams as
well as on the errors of everyday life. And this misreading evokes
the image of his new friend Wilhelm Fliess as a convert. If Freud's
own view of the meaningfulness of such misreadings is correct,
what does this misreading mean?

Freud had rebelled, in 1882, against the "Christian views of a few *Hofräte* who have long forgotten what work is like"[16] dominating the medical society of which he was a member. These included a number of Jewish converts to Christianity, who had made major careers for themselves in the Viennese medical establishment. It is clear that Freud had been greatly concerned with the question of conversion: his own professional academic life, he believed, depended on his overcoming his Jewish identity. By June 1892 Freud's relationship with Fliess had developed substantially. This was indeed the last letter in which Freud addressed Fliess with the more formal "Sie." By the end of June 1892 he was addressing him with the familiar "Du." Thus Freud was clearly beginning to see Fliess as a close friend. Here, in the moment he is deciding to see his new acquaintance as a friend, he misreads the signature as "W. Ch." rather than "Wlhm." The signature is that of one who had been baptized and who was given the ubiquitous baptismal name of "Christian." Suddenly Freud sees in his acquaintance perhaps a potential convert, one who would betray his own reality. And this is the same letter in which Freud acknowledges Fliess's new marriage. His conversion is related to the ostensible subject of this letter to Fliess—the first meeting with Fliess and his new bride Ida on holiday at Reichenau. Freud's sense of betrayal is manifest in this "slip." To this point he and his friend had created the illusion of a scientific academy, writing papers and holding regular congresses by themselves. All of the illusion of science in its neutrality negates any sense of the powerful emotional bonds that link Freud (in his own later estimation) to Fliess. Freud's powerful cathexis now seems in danger of being revealed, for Fliess has introduced the question of sexuality into the equation. His honeymoon with his wife forces Freud to bring his own wife along. What had been a celebration of the discovery of the new science is converted into a social meeting. The only image powerful enough to evoke this betrayal of their scientific twinning is that of the convert who betrays his faith. Converts abandon their faith and the institutions that bear them. But a religious conversion out of the Jewish "race" (as Jews were defined within the science at the turn of the century) is impossible—and Freud knows that. So this misreading is double-edged. It is an acknowledgment of the betrayal of their intellectual relationship but a sign of the immutability of that relationship. Freud placed the onus of the misreading on Fliess. He cannot read

Fliess's bad handwriting. It is Fliess who is at fault, not Freud. This ambivalence is articulated in Freud's "slip." (On the nature of the slip as a clue to self-analysis in Freud's *Psychopathology of Everyday Life* (1901) written during the end of his relationship with Fliess, see this selection, pp. 154–58) But Freud's ambivalence seems to be repressed until some three years later.

Fliess actually acted on his medical theories of the relationship between the nose and the genitalia, undertaking surgical procedures on the nose to relieve sexual problems. As is well-known, his surgical ineptitude almost killed Freud's patient Emma Eckstein. He left a wad of surgical dressing in the nasal cavity that caused massive bleeding and infection. Fliess operated on Freud's nose during the same stay in Vienna in February 1895 in which he operated on Emma Eckstein. Fliess's action, as Max Schur stated when he first revealed this material, must have negatively influenced Freud's image of the implications of science both in the ineptitude it revealed and the fact that Fliess had been placed on an intellectual plane by Freud that clearly paralleled the level that he himself wished to attain. Fliess's assumed role as a "surgeon," the highest of the medical specialties, was only disguised by his label as a "nose" doctor. His actions were those of medical practitioners whose status was clearly higher than that permitted him by the society in which he lived. This denial was based on Fliess's racial identity.

On July 23–24, 1895, while Freud was completing his work *The Studies on Hysteria* with Josef Breuer, he had "the dream of Irma's injection" of the night of July 24, 1895, which served him as the central, exemplary dream for his 1900 *Interpretation of Dreams*.[17] (See this selection, pp. 17–42) This dream, to which Freud gave extraordinary importance, came in the midst of his struggle with Fliess's role as scientist and friend. The dream recounts a medical consultation, an injection, the discovery of a botched medical procedure, and the scientific rationale for this. Freud retells the dream twice in his text. The first is his unbroken narrative of the dream; the second version stresses the central aspects of the dream. The first version of the Irma's Injection Dream is as follows:

> A large hall—numerous guests, whom we are receiving.—
> Among them was Irma. I at once took her on one side, as though
> to answer her letter and to reproach her for not having accepted

my "solution" yet. I said to her: "If you still get pains, it's really only your fault." She replied: "If you only knew what pains I've got now in my throat and stomach and abdomen—it's choking me"—I was alarmed and looked at her. She looked pale and puffy. I thought to myself that after all I must be missing some organic trouble. I took her to the window and looked down her throat, and she showed signs of recalcitrance, like women with artificial dentures. I thought to myself that there was really no need for her to do that.—She opened her mouth properly and on the right I found a big white patch; at another place I saw extensive whitish gray scabs upon some remarkable curly structures which were evidently modeled on the turbinal bones of the nose.—I at once called in Dr. M., and he repeated the examination and confirmed it. . . . Dr. M. looked quite different from usual; he was very pale, he walked with a limp and his chin was clean-shaven. . . . My friend Otto was now standing beside her as well, and my friend Leopold was percussing her through her bodice and saying: "She has a dull area low down on the left." He also indicated that a portion of the skin on the left shoulder was infiltrated. (I noticed this, just as he did, in spite of her dress.) . . . M. said: "There's no doubt it's an infection, but no matter; dysentery will supervene and the toxin will be eliminated." . . . We were directly aware, too, of the origin of the infection. Not long before, when she was feeling unwell, my friend Otto had given her an injection of a preparation of propyl, propyls . . . propionic acid . . . trimethylamine (and I saw before me the formula for this printed in heavy type). . . . Injections of that sort ought not to be made so thoughtlessly. . . . And probably the syringe had not been clean. (SE 4:107)

The day residue of the dream seems clear. Irma is a composite figure. On one level Irma, the patient depicted in the dream, is one of his favorite patients, Anna Lichtheim, the daughter of his religion teacher Samuel Hammerschlag, the woman after whom Freud will name his youngest child. Part of the character of Irma is also Emma Eckstein. But if this is the tale of Fliess and the botched operation, where is Fliess? The other actors in the dream are "Dr. M" (Josef Breuer); "my friend Otto" (Oskar Rie, Freud's family pediatrician) and "Leopold" (Dr. Ludwig Rosenberg).[18] Wilhelm Fliess seems to have been completely repressed in Freud's dream-memory of the events.

The only mention of Fliess is in Freud's interpretation. His appearance is keyed in the second version of the dream by the word "trimethylamine ... the chemical formula ... [of which] was printed in heavy type, as though there had been a desire to lay emphasis on some part of the context as being of quite special importance."[19] In Freud's interpretation he is mentioned as "another friend" who had associated the genitalia and the nose, but who was at the time himself suffering from suppurative rhinitis, a disease of the nose. In the fragmentary retelling of the dream, which is selected so that Freud can interpret what seemed to him to be the most important aspects of the dream, the centrality of the disease and the chemical is stressed. What is the disease that Irma has and what function does this chemical have in unraveling the story present in the dream?

Freud was quizzed on this aspect of his analysis by Karl Abraham, who queried whether what Irma suffered from was not syphilis: "I find that trimethylamine leads to the most important part, to sexual allusions which became more distinct in the last lines. After all everything points to the suspicion of syphilitic infection in the patient; the spot in her mouth is the plaque representing the infection, the injection of trimethylamine which has been carelessly given, the dirty syringe (??) Is not this the organic illness for whose continued persistence you cannot be made responsible, because syphilis or a nervous disease originating from it cannot be influenced by psychological treatment."[20] Freud denied in his answer that the dream has anything to do with syphilis. Rather he answers that hidden behind the dreams is his own "sexual megalomania," his sexual cure for the anxiety neurosis that he diagnosed in three women patients (Mathilde Breuer, Sophie Paneth, Anna Lichtheim).[21] Freud's view at the time was that such anxiety neurosis was the product of the collection of sexual toxins such as trimethylamine in the body. But the true sexual anxiety in this case was that of Freud and his intense relationship with Fliess. In his exchange with Abraham he stands as the "doctor" curing these female patients; in his dream, he is the feminized patient as well.

In the dream, Irma is given an injection of a preparation of propionic acid—proponesin, a clear, seemingly pleasant liquid. This narcotic is simply a "scientific place holder" according to Freud but leads to the visualization of the formula. This is one of the basic means of symbolization in the dream, according to

Freud's dream theory. One often sees visual images rather than events and these visual images have a symbolic value. "Dreams," according to Freud, "think predominantly in visual images" (SE 4:49). Now, it is clear that the power of seeing has a major component in Freud's awareness of the way that science as well as the mind works. His training with Jean-Martin Charcot was a training in seeing the patient and the signs and symptoms that the patient exhibited as the central key to diagnosis.[22] The nosology of the "categories" of difference are really quite analogous to Charcot's construction of the visual pattern of the actions of the hysteric. One can argue that Freud's intellectual as well as analytic development in the 1890s was a movement away from the "meaning" of visual signs (a skill that he ascribes to Charcot in his obituary of 1893) and to the interpretation of verbal signs, from the "crudity" of seeing to the subtlety of hearing (SE 1:17). Charcot conceived the realism of the image to transcend the crudity of the spoken word. In a letter to Freud on November 23, 1891, he commented concerning the transcription of his famed Tuesday lectures that "the stenographer is not a photographer."[23] The assumption of the inherent validity of the gaze and its mechanical reproduction forms the image of the hysteric. The central argument that can be brought is that this vocabulary of seeing remains embedded in Freud's interpretation of the hysteric, who must be seen to be understood. This is not present in the earliest papers on hysteria written directly under Charcot's influence, such as Freud's differential diagnosis of organic and hysterical paralysis written in 1886.[24] For Freud, the rejection of Charcot's mode of "seeing" the hysteric is also a rejection of the special relationship that the Jew has with the disease. The theme of the specific, inherited risk of the Jew for hysteria (and other forms of mental illness) was reflected in the work of Charcot that Freud translated.[25] But even more so this general claim about the hereditary risk of the Jew was linked to a diagnostic system rooted in belief of external appearance as the source of knowledge about the pathological. For the "seeing" of the Jew as different was a topos of the world in which Freud lived. Satirical caricatures were to be found throughout the German-speaking world that stressed the Jew's physical difference and in the work of Charcot (and his contemporaries) these representations took on pathological significance. The model of seeing that Freud evokes in the *Interpretation of Dreams* is, however, not that of Jean-Martin

Charcot, but of the eugenist Francis Galton, whose fin-de-siècle multiple exposures attempted to capture the essential gaze of the Jew. And the very idea of the composite central character, Irma, with specific qualities taken from a number of identifiable figures, is a Galtonian mode of seeing.

Yet, Freud does not let the reader see what he sees in the dream. He describes all of the sights he "sees" in the dream in detail except for one. Freud does not supply the visual image; he does not supply the formula for trimethylamine $(CH_3)_3N$, which is found to be in vaginal secretions. The source of Irma's disease is thus in the sexuality of the Jewish female, the widowed Anna Lichtheim and Emma Eckstein, according to Freud. But hidden within the diseased nasal cavity that has been shown to be interchangeable with the vagina by Fliess is the symbolic reference to the person who betrayed Freud, to the "convert" who reveals himself by his action: it is CH, written bold for all to see, but unprinted in the text, a scientific text in which a formula could well have appeared. It is Wilhelm Fliess—hidden within the formula—the CH is the evocation of the earlier doubt about Fliess. It is the sign of "Christian," the convert, himself diseased. Freud refuses to print the formula for it would have revealed more than he would have wanted it to. This violated one of the premises that Freud presented in his mode of interpreting dreams. For visualization has a central role in creating the symbolic vocabulary of the dream. To deny the gaze of the Jew within the dream—a dream that is filled with the doctor's act of seeing and diagnosing, represses Freud's inability to deal with his own sense of betrayal and justified anxiety about Fliess's medical practices. For it is the Jew Freud who would have been seeing the convert Fliess revealed in the visualized formula. This entire aspect vanishes as long as the formula remains unseen for the author and his reader. Just as the figures are robbed of any racial identity, none is mentioned as a Jew, the "quack" Fliess vanishes, only to appear in the sign of the betrayer, the convert. Male sexuality becomes female sexuality, race is effaced only to reappear within the rules of interpretation that Freud outlines in his own text. The anxiety about Irma is a displacement of two fears. The first appears in the explanation—the death of Freud's patient Mathilde and the parallel that Freud draws with Josef Breuer's agreement about her treatment with sulfonal that led to her death and Freud's consultation of him in the case of Irma. Unstated is the analogous role that Fliess played in the treatment of Eckstein that was all the more terrifying for Freud, as he too had been Fliess's patient on that ill-fated trip to Vienna. To "see" Fliess Freud must overcome his anxiety about his own body and its vulnerability. This is repressed and displaced onto the image of the woman and her sexuality. As readers we must metamorphose the written word into the visual image that Freud denies us and this reveals to us the hidden "convert." It is at this moment that the relationship between Freud and Fliess becomes strained and finally dissolves over the work of another Jew, Otto Weininger, a convert and a neurotic, whom Fliess accuses of plagiarizing his work with Freud's help. For it is indeed in a conflict about the work on bisexuality, that Freud's friendship with Fliess ceased. But it is within the specimen dream, that central document in Freud's scientific life, the central text of *The Interpretation of Dreams,* that Fliess's betrayal is inscribed. In recording his memory of the dream, Freud repressed the visualization of the formula. These are the formulas of inscribed conversion that haunt Weininger's work, which haunt the pseudoscience of Freud's day and which Freud uses in his unpublished papers, such as those that accompanied his letters to Fliess. (The most notable of these is the so-called "Project for a Scientific Psychology" [1895] that Freud quickly abandoned.)[26] For the type of visualization that Weininger evoked was linked to the betrayal of the neurotic, of the neurotic who was both convert and homosexual. And it is this that vanished in *The Interpretation of Dreams* along with the figure of Wilhelm Fliess.

Freud's Jewish identity was a formative element in his understanding of his undertaking within psychoanalysis. Freud is, of course, exactly such an Eastern Jew, a fact that he can articulate in public only in the 1920s. He introduced his short autobiography written in 1925 as a contribution to a series in the contemporary history of medicine, which was widely circulated among fellow professionals with the statement:

> I was born on May 6, 1856, at Freiburg in Moravia, a small town in what is now Czechoslovakia. My parents were Jews, I have remained a Jew myself. I have reason to believe that my father's family were settled for a long time on the Rhine (at Cologne), that as a result of persecution of the Jews during the fourteenth or fifteenth century, they fled eastwards, and that,

they migrated back from Lithuania through Galicia into German Austria. (SE 20:7–8)

Freud acknowledged in his autobiography that he is not only a Jew, but a specific subspecies of Jew, an Eastern Jew, as he himself noted, out of his appropriate place (and class) and living now in the center of Austrian culture, Vienna. And yet, according to this account, he is not truly an Eastern Jew. Just as Theodor Herzl imagined his ancestors coming from an idealized medieval Spain, so too Freud saw his family moving from one cultural landscape (Germany) through the barbaric East and returning eventually to another cultural sphere (Austria). It is this tension between the perception of belonging and yet not belonging to any given culture that mirrors the position of the acculturated Jew in late nineteenth-century Europe. It is the Jew as the great unknown. In 1926, Freud stated in an address to the B'nai B'rith on the occasion of being honored on his seventieth birthday, that being Jewish is sharing "many obscure emotional forces [*viele dunkle Gefühlsmächte*], which were the more powerful the less they could be expressed in words, as well as a clear consciousness of inner identity, the safe privacy of a common mental construction [*die Heimleichkeit der gleichen seelischen Identität*]." (See pp. 266–68 in this volume) His contemporaries, such as Theodor Reik (along with Freud and Eduard Hintschmann the only psychoanalysts to be members of the B'nai B'rith), "were especially struck" by these very words as the appropriate central definition of the Jew. Jewishness added a new dimension to the complexity of being a medical scientist at the turn of the century. For it marked Freud as potentially the unknown subject that demanded examination and investigation. This was the great epistemological problem of the Jewish medical scientist of the time, one that is then worked out in the discourse of psychoanalysis.

In 1905, Freud published his descriptive study on the theory of sexuality (*Three Essays on the Theory of Sexuality*). Freud evolved a model of phases of psychosexual development. The infant's early experiences revolved about its oral activity with its focus on the mouth; then the anal stage, which evolves with the appearance of teeth; then the phallic stage (from three to seven), with the Oedipus phase for males and the Electra phase for females (the attraction to the opposite-sex parent and fear of the same-sex parent); a latency stage (with a strong identification with the same-sex parent); and finally the genital stage. Here in the greatest detail Freud laid out the relationship between psychosexual development and neurotic symbol formation. (See this selection, pp. 80–113 for Freud's detailed and complex analysis of infantile sexuality) Freud evolved this model in complex and new directions. By 1914 he had used the model of psychosexual development in early childhood as a means of generating an understanding of narcissism and the initial resistance to psychotherapy. (See his popular paper on this topic, "A Difficulty in the Path of Psycho-Analysis" (1917) in this selection, pp. 269–76)

Freud's cultural criticism was shaped by his readings of those works that defined "high culture" at the turn of the century. It was sharing in this high culture that allowed Jews to enter the mainstream of Viennese life. Thus Freud's extraordinarily influential essay on "The Uncanny" (1919) not only defines a major psychological problem of the late nineteenth century, the meaning of "false memory" or "déjà vu," but places it within the arena of high culture. Likewise, Freud's error of memory on the Acropolis (See this selection, pp. 158–68) reflects the high-culture status, not only of Greek culture in Germany and Austria, but also of Freud's relationship with the notable French writer Romain Rolland to whom he dedicated this memory. Freud's readings from the German Romantics, an essential part of late nineteenth-century high culture, is at the very center of this work. Freud also applied the development model taken from nineteenth-century biology to the study of "primitive" societies. In a series of anthropological works from *Totem and Taboo* (1913) to his final work *Moses and Monotheism* (1938) (See this selection, pp. 277–81), Freud used the mythic embryological model of "ontogeny recapitulating phylogeny" (the development of the species repeating in the development of the individual) to trace the historical impact of the model of psychosexual development he evolved. He returned to a model of trauma, but a model of historical trauma, in which he saw an earlier act— the murder of the "primitive" father by the sons or the murder of Moses by the Jews—as historical realities that come to be implanted in the memory of the group or race and that provided a model for human action. Freud's debt to nineteenth-century anthropology for the materials and approaches to these questions was certainly as great as his debt to nineteenth-century neurology for the talking cure and to nineteenth-century biology for his underlying views of the structures of the psyche.

Belonging to the mainstream of Freudian theory and practice, from the fin de siècle to the present, meant following the general therapeutic milieu of the talking cure, holding to the centrality of the sexual origin of neurosis, and seeing a parallel between development and historical or cultural manifestations of the psyche. The orthodoxy of psychoanalysis was challenged by many of those who had been Freud's closest followers during the beginnings of the organization of the psychoanalytic movement. A major role in mainstream Freudian psychotherapy during the very beginnings of the movement was played by the Hungarian-Jewish psychoanalyst Sándor Ferenczi (1873–1933), whose innovations both in theory and therapy altered the primary Freudian model of the neutral stance of the psychoanalyst. Initially Ferenczi was much more rigid than Freud in terms of forbidding any release of the analysand's libido, hoping that the damming of libidinous drives would be released within the therapeutic setting. He came to reject this position and evolved an intensive interactive therapy based on his view that the analysand's neurosis was the result of not having had enough love as a child. Freud's neutral analyst was replaced by Ferenczi. Likewise Otto Rank (1884–1939), whose cultural history of incest, *The Incest Motif in Poetry and Legend* (1912), was the prototype of all later psychoanalytic approaches to cultural artifacts, broke with Freud, among other reasons, over the question of the length of the therapy. He advocated a specific, preset time limit rather than an open-ended therapy. Rank's theoretical emphasis was on the manner by which each person separated from the mother and became a "self-realized" individual. This was initially seen through his focus on "birth trauma." For Rank, the anxiety of the birth trauma becomes a means of understanding all of the later developments of the adult, as separation is necessary for the individual fully to mature. Thus Rank's planning of the length of therapy was a means of introducing the anxiety of separation as part of the psychotherapeutic method.

Without a doubt the most orthodox follower of the second generation of psychoanalysts was Freud's youngest child, Anna Freud (1895–1982).[27] Her work on child analysis, begun with a paper in 1926, developed the ego psychology outlined by her father. Especially in her *Ego and the Mechanisms of Defence* (1936) she outlined the means (repression and projection) by which the ego protected itself from unpleasant ideas and emotions. She escaped with her father from Nazi-occupied Vienna in 1938, and settled in England where she founded the Hampstead nurseries for wartime children.[28] Out of that experience came a series of studies of the mental lives of children in institutional settings.

Anna Freud's great opponent within the London psychoanalytic community was Melanie Klein (1882–1960), an analysand of Sándor Ferenczi, who had come to London from Vienna in 1926.[29] Like Anna Freud, her initial interest lay in the area of child development. Her focus on the meaning of play in the mental world of the child and its symbolic language was best outlined in her *Psychoanalysis of Children* (1932). She expanded Freud's discussion of the formation of the ego and focused on the internalization of the representation of those objects in the world, such as the mother, which the child first understands as different from itself. She described introjection, the process by which internal representations of good and evil, of control or lack of control, are generated by the developing psyche of the child.

The number of psychoanalytic schismatics is extensive. The primary figures who came to found independent psychoanalytic schools were also the first major disciples of Freud who were seen by him as his potential successors within the psychoanalytic movement: Alfred Adler and Carl Gustav Jung. Both broke with Freud over the question of the centrality of sexuality in the structure and treatment of the human psyche. Adler (1870–1937) stressed the physical nature of the individual as the source of mental illness.[30] As early as his 1907 *Study of Organ Inferiority and Its Psychical Compensation,* Adler emphasized the attempts of children to compensate for their physical inferiority by producing specific pathological character structures that lead to specific "lifestyles." Adler expressly rejected Freud's sexual theory in his *Neurotic Constitution* (1912). He was the first of Freud's major followers to break with him (in 1911). Adler's creation of "individual psychology" emphasized the fictions through which the individual created and achieved life goals. The central tenet of Adlerian psychotherapy reflected the individual's creation of socially meaningful, personal goals. This was to be achieved through the analysis of early memories as the source of an understanding of the patient's social maladaption. Adler's approach became the primary model for psychotherapy among psychotherapeutic social workers in the 1920s and 1930s.

Jung (1875–1961), the first important non-Jewish follower of Freud, was trained in Switzerland as well as in Paris. He was a colleague of the Swiss academic psychiatrist Eugen Bleuler (1857–1939), the first major figure in academic psychiatry to accept and apply Freud's therapeutic methods. Basing his work on the mental association methods of Wilhelm Wundt (1832–1920), Jung developed a word-association test that was initially employed to explore the unconscious following Freud's model. Through the analysis of the test results, Jung was able to describe the "complexes" of the individual. For Jung, however, the unconscious that was to be so explored came more and more to be a historical rather than a sexual unconscious. What for Freud was sexual libido became for Jung "life force." Jung stressed the inheritance of psychological models of the world, archetypes. Jung broke with Freud in 1912. He saw these as inherent and motivating, rather than (as did Freud) the articulation of the repression of instinct. Sexuality was thus relegated to a minor feature within Jung's system. Central to Jung's therapeutics was the image of "coming to selfhood" or "self-realization." This was the integration of the various "persona," of social and individual personalities, into a whole. Where Freud departed from the pathological in order to present an understanding of the human psyche, for Jung normal psychic development stood at the center of his system.

Jung's archetypes were not bound by time and space; they were truly universal. Jung generated a series of images, restructuring the Freudian vocabulary of sexuality into a vocabulary of archetypes. Thus the Freudian image of bisexuality (the view that all individuals contained the potential for "masculine" as well as "feminine" qualities) became the syzygy, the anima, or feminine quality of the male and the animus, the male quality of the female. These became asexual driving forces, Jung's libido, existing as part of the collective unconscious. This is the origin of all creativity, but also all mental illness. It is the balance between psychic forces within the collective unconscious that structured the human being's manner of relating to the world. The domination of one pole created the "introvert"; of the other, the "extrovert."

Alfred Adler had set a social agenda only peripheral to Freud's own interest: how does the experience of the self in society structure the psyche. The question of the social context of the individual and its role in creating circumstances that could be labeled as pathogenic became the agenda of the neo-Freudian or culturally oriented psychoanalysts in the 1930s and 1940s. For Erich Fromm (1900–1980), the organization of society provides the structure for definition of the self. He visualized a political choice for the individual that also shaped and gave form to the psyche: either the productive use of freedom to fulfill the individual or the flight from individual freedom into the control of totalitarianism. His categories of ego formation (relatedness, transcendence, rootedness, identity, and orientation) all stressed the social factor in the shaping of the psyche.

It is in the work of the neo-Freudian psychoanalyst Karen Horney (1885–1952) that Freud's analysis of feminine psychology has its first and most intensive critique.[31] While some female followers of Freud had supported Freud's male-oriented model of sexuality, Horney challenged Freud over this question.[32] Beginning in a series of papers in 1924 (on the "Dissolution of the Oedipus Complex"), she saw feminine psychology as a process parallel to but different from the development of male sexuality. Rather than being robbed of the penis, the woman's fecundity, she argues in a 1926 paper ("The Flight from Womanhood"), becomes an object of envy for men—the ability to conceive and bear. Horney's neo-Freudian work extended into her American experience after she came to the University of Chicago from Berlin in 1932. Her interest in the question of feminine psychology gave way to broader questions about the cultural context of neurosis. In the late 1930s she broke with orthodox Freudian theory over the primacy of Freud's libido theory. Her most important work of the American period was *The Neurotic Personality of Our Time* (1937). For her, the origin of neurosis is not the articulation of the Oedipus complex but basic existential anxiety common to all human beings. Other psychoanalysts who dealt with the question of the psychology of women and their therapy, Edith Jacobson (1897–1978) and Melanie Klein, were of central importance during this period in drawing attention to social as well as to the biological specificity of the woman's experience.[33]

In the United States, Freudian theory and therapy had had a powerful beginning in the first decade of the twentieth century. The attraction and support of established psychologists such as

William James (1842–1910) (Harvard University) and G. Stanley Hall (1844–1924) (Clark University) for psychoanalysis opened the doors for the wide dissemination of this therapy after Freud's visit to the United States in 1909. Of all the American reinterpreters of Freud, none were more influential than Harry Stack Sullivan (1892–1949), who, like Horney, stressed the central role of anxiety in the shaping of maladaptive behavior. Sullivan carried on the interests of Ferenczi in anxiety. Ferenczi's work had been brought to the United States by his analysand Clara Thompson (1893–1958), with whom Sullivan in turn worked.[34] For Sullivan, this anxiety is transferred empathetically from mother to child. Psychotherapy is the interpersonal process of alleviating the psychic tension that is the result of this anxiety, and, if successful, it results in equilibrium. Sullivan's therapeutic model was widely influential in the 1940s and 1950s. But it was not only within the Americanization of the "talking cure" that psychotherapy found its therapeutic tools. It was also in the United States that hypnosis was reintroduced after World War II within mainstream psychology by Milton H. Erickson (1901–80).[35]

In France, following World War II, it was in the work of Jacques Lacan (1901–81) that Freudian theory had its most controversial representative.[36] Lacan, like the Freudo-Marxist Herbert Marcuse (1898–1979) in the United States, placed psychoanalysis at the center of political change during the 1960s and 1970s. Lacan laid claim to the revolutionary history of psychoanalysis and saw it as a force of eventual social change. Central to Lacan's views was a developmental model in which the process of acquiring language and the internalization of symbols shaped the inner structure of the psyche. Lacan argued for the universality of transference into all spheres of social interaction. Lacanian psychoanalysis came to structure and focus French (and to a limited extent Anglo-American) cultural life during this period. But Lacan also developed a strikingly innovative mode of psychotherapy. His introduction of very short session therapy, with its intense moment of transference, related to certain developments by Sándor Ferenczi in the field of brief (short-term) psychotherapy.[37] In the United States and Western Europe, the open-ended therapeutic model of traditional psychoanalysis came to be restructured into the needs of a more mobile patient population, the cost of whose therapy was no longer born personally but by third parties (such as the state or private insurance).

In Great Britain psychoanalysis acquired an established place in traditional medical establishment through the work of Ernest Jones (1879–1958), the founder of the British Psychoanalytic Society (1919).[38] Jones had invited Melanie Klein to England and was helpful in relocating both Sigmund and Anna Freud there when they were forced to leave Vienna by the Nazis in 1938. He was also able to maintain a working relationship between the dominant groups within British psychoanalysis during the 1940s and 1950s. This was quite unlike the experience in the United States, where schism after schism fragmented the various organized Freudian groups. In Britain the conflict between Melanie Klein and Anna Freud reflected itself in the therapeutic milieu as well as in the protagonists' theoretical positions. Both groups were concerned with child therapy. The "Kleinians," however, were quite willing to intercede earlier and more rigorously in the therapy of the child than the "Freudians" and employed free-association play therapy with very young children rather than those verbal methods that could only be effective with slightly older children. Anna Freud's impact on the wider culture in the United States and Western Europe came with her collaboration in the 1950s and 1960s in a series of studies that defined the legal framework for societies' treatment of children.

The impact of Melanie Klein was felt within psychotherapy with the rise of object-relationship theory, the theory of how the developing child related to the earliest and most intense relationship with the caregiver or mother.[39] This work departed from Freud's 1914 paper "On Narcissism," in which he described how the infant differentiated itself from the world in which it found itself. The continuation of Freud's interest in ego psychology in the United States was furthered by Margaret Mahler (1897–1985), who had come from Vienna to New York in 1938.[40] Her interest, best expressed in her *On Human Symbiosis* (1968), focused on the problems of the process of individuation in severely mentally disturbed infants as well as in normal development. Donald Woods Winnicott (1896–1971) in Great Britain, Hans Kohut (1913–81) (at the University of Chicago) and Otto Kemberg (1928–) (at Cornell University) all contributed to the discussions of how the child differentiates itself from the world and constructs an ego and superego.[41] The reflection of this view in therapy surfaced with the renewed emphasis on very early childhood, pre-Oedipal development at the core of the formation of psychopathology, such as the "borderline" or "narcissistic" personality.

The psychotherapists who radically departed from Freudian theory and evolved their own models of psychotherapy range widely across the therapeutic field. The Freudo-Marxist Wilhelm Reich (1897–1951), who had begun as a traditional, if politically radical follower of Freud in the 1920s, evolved a theory of mass neurosis and its origin in sexual repression.[42] Reich stressed the meaning of body position and contact. Out of this theoretical view came the "orgone box," a device developed by him in the 1940s to harness psychic energy as a treatment for neurosis, as well as "vegetotherapy." Such devices are the exception within mainstream psychotherapy, but they hark back to the tradition of Mesmer's *baquet*. Reich's work assumed that psychological maladaption reflected itself in the structure of the body. He saw the development of a "character armor" that was mirrored in the very musculature of the body. Reich's followers evolved various therapies out of his basic views.

Alternative therapies such as the reenactment of lived experience, "psychodrama," in groups rather than in individual sessions with a therapist had been developed in the 1920s. Jacob Levy Moreno (1892–1974) evolved a role-playing structure in which aspects of the patient's life were reenacted in order to come to a clinical resolution.[43] It was Moreno who introduced the term *group therapy* in 1932. A standard feature of Moreno's therapy was "role reversal" in which the patients reversed their antagonistic social roles, each playing the others. Such group treatments had begun with patients suffering from pulmonary tuberculosis at the turn of the century. Frederick Perls (1894–1970) developed "Gestalt Therapy" as a means of allowing the patients to make a creative adjustment to their present situation.[44] The patient constructs a dialogue by which the warring aspects of the personality are reunited into a single "Gestalt" or structure. Through Perls's institute at Esalen (in California), Gestalt therapy had a disproportionate influence on the antipsychoanalytic views of the 1960s. Family therapy arose after World War II with the attempt to treat the entire family unit through psychotherapy rather than only the patient. The Wisconsin psychiatrist Christian Frederick Midelfort

(1906–) developed the view that there were compensatory and opposing psychopathologies within every family that may well only manifest themselves overtly with any given member. Treating the family unit was necessary in treating the individual. Ronald David Laing (1927–89) also postulated a reenactment of childhood and a retraining of the mentally ill individual in his therapeutic community at Philadelphia House (in London).[45] Alexander Wolf (1907–) evolved a means of treatment for large groups, and group therapy spread widely in specific environments (such as public hospitals) during the 1950s.[46] The psychologist Carl Ransom Rogers (1902–87) evolved a variation of the group—the encounter group, which is a client-centered therapy based on existentialist philosophy.[47] Related to this were the "T-groups" that evolved from the work of Kurt Lewin (1890–1947). There the rules of the group demanded complete self-disclosure. These groups had the quasireligious parallel in the twelve-step movement of group psychotherapy, initially developed by William G. Wilson (1895–1971), known as "Bill W," for the treatment of alcoholism (Alcoholics Anonymous), but evolving during the 1960s and 1970s to cover a wide range of addictive or assumed addictive behaviors (including food-related disorders, codependency, tobacco addiction, as well as the impact of addictive behavior on family members [Al-Anon]).[48] These movements are all extensions of the idea of a total therapy to combat a total illness. Their dynamics were shaped more by religious models (such as the Protestant tradition of bearing testimony) than by strictly medical ones, but they have come to be a major adjunct to the treatment of various addictions, tendencies, and habits. The stress in these movements, as in Clifford Beers's (1876–1943) "Mental Hygiene Movement" begun in the 1920s, is on patient self-identification and self-help.[49]

While there was a lowering of the prestige of traditional psychoanalysis in the United States and Western Europe without the introducing of psychoactive drugs, such as lithium, for the treatment of manic-depressive psychosis, during the 1960s, psychoanalysis retained its importance in certain areas such as feminist therapy. The continuation and abridgment of traditional psychotherapy through the feminist model can be best seen in the 1970s in the work of the British psychoanalytic theorist Juliet Mitchell (1940–).[50] Mitchell's work synthesized streams coming from France (Jacques Lacan) and Britain (D. W. Winnicott). She stressed the underlying unconscious forces depicted in Freud's theory and Freud's rejection of biologically based instinct theories. Her reading of Freud's work as a more abstract and symbolic system made Freudian psychoanalysis not only a central feature of feminist theory of the 1970s and 1980s, but also provided the intellectual background for the development of a feminist psychotherapy. Parallel trends can be seen in the work of Hélène Cixous (1937–   ) in France and Margarete Mitscherlich-Nielsen (1917–   ) in Germany.[51]

By the 1980s, psychotherapy had become so complex and fragmented that no single approach could be understood as primary.[52] With the rise of psychopharmacological treatments for psychosis, neurosis, as well as behavioral problems beginning in the 1960s, many of the forms of psychotherapy were adapted as supportive psychotherapy both within and beyond the clinical setting. Indeed, one of the ironies is that Freudian psychotherapy, stripped of its theoretical basis, comes by the 1970s and 1980s to be a substantial addition to the chemotherapy of emotional and psychic illness as "supportive psychotherapy." Psychotherapy in the 1990s is extraordinarily diverse and holds an important position within both medical and nonmedical aspects of culture.

S. L. G.

Notes

1. See Richard D. Chessick, *Great Ideas in Psychotherapy* (New York: Jason Aronson, 1977); Jan Ehrenwald, ed., *The History of Psychotherapy: From Healing Magic to Encounter* (New York: Jason Aronson, 1976); Henri F. Ellenberger, *The Discovery of the Unconscious: The History and Evolution of Dynamic Psychiatry* (New York: Basic Books, 1970); Reuben Fine, *A History of Psychoanalysis* (New York: Columbia University Press, 1979); Sander L. Gilman, ed., *Introducing Psychoanalytic Theory* (New York: Brunner/Mazel, 1982); Robert A. Harper, *Psychoanalysis and Psychotherapy: Thirty-Six Systems* (New York: Jason Aronson, 1974); David Healy, *The Suspended Revolution: Psychiatry and Psychotherapy Re-examined* (London: Faber and Faber, 1990); Ernest R. Hilgard, *Psychology in America: A Historical Survey* (San Diego, CA: Harcourt Brace Jovanovich, 1987); David Hothersall, *History of Psychology* (Philadelphia: Temple University Press, 1984); Edith Kurzweil, *The Freudians: A Comparative Perspective* (New Haven, CT: Yale University Press, 1990).

2. This definition is based on the discussion of Jerome Frank, *Persuasion and Healing: A Comparative Study of Psychotherapy* (Baltimore: Johns Hopkins University Press, 1961).

3. Walter Cooper Dendy, "Psychotherapeia; or, The Remedial Influence of Mind," *Journal of Psychological Medicine and Mental Pathology* (1853): 268. The first modern use of the term seems to be in the work of A. W. van Renterghem and F. van Eeden, *Clinique de Psychothérapie Suggestive fondée à Amsterdam le 15 août 1887 . . .* (Brussels: A. Manceaux, 1889). See I. N. Bulhof, "From Psychotherapy to Psychoanalysis: Frederik van Eeden and Albert Willem van Renterghem," *Journal of the History of the Behavioral Sciences* 17 (1981): 209–21; D. Pivnicki, "The Beginnings of Psychotherapy," *Journal of the History of the Behavioral Sciences* 5 (1969): 238–47; and E. Harms, "Historical Background of Psychotherapy as a New Scientific Field," *Diseases of the Nervous System* 31 (1970): 116–18.

4. On classical ideas of psychotherapy see C. Gill, "Ancient Psychotherapy," *Journal of the History of Ideas* 46 (1985): 307–25, and on a case of psychotherapy that would meet our definition during the Middle Ages see J. P. Williman and R. G. Kvarnes, "A Medieval Example of Psychotherapy," *Psychiatry* 47 (1984): 93–95.

5. Hanna Wolff, *Jesus als Psychotherapeut: Jesu Menschenbehandlung als Modell moderner Psychotherapie* (Stuttgart: Radius, 1986).

6. Robert Darnton, *Mesmerism and the End of the Enlightenment in France* (Cambridge, MA: Harvard University Press, 1968), and Leon Chertok and Raymond de Saussure, *The Therapeutic Revolution, from Mesmer to Freud* (New York: Brunner Mazel, 1979).

7. As for example in the Jansenist healings. See Louis Basile Carré de Montgeron, *La verité des miracles operés par l'intercession de M. de Pâris et autres appellans demontrée contre* M. L'archevêque de Sens . . . 3 vols. (Cologne: Chez les libraires de la Campagnie, 1745–47).

8. Peter Gay, *Sigmund Freud: A Life for Our Time* (New York: Norton, 1988).

9. Edwin Wallace IV, *Freud and Anthropology: A History and Reappraisal* (New York: International Universities Press, 1983).

10. Albrecht Hirschmüller, *The Life and Work of Josef Breuer: Physiology and Psychoanalysis* (New York: New York University Press, 1989).

11. E. Jones, "Social Class and Psychotherapy: A Critical Review of Research," *Psychiatry* 37 (1974): 307–20.

12. Jeffrey Moussaieff Masson, ed., *The Complete Letters of Sigmund Freud to Wilhelm Fliess, 1887–1904* (Cambridge, MA: Harvard University Press, 1985), p. 54. In letter to Fliess 20 August 1893 notes that he "was consulted by the daughter of the innkeeper on the Rax: it was a lovely case for me."

13. All of the quotations and texts from Freud's works in this volume, unless otherwise noted, are to Sigmund Freud, *Standard Edition of the Complete*

Psychological Works of Sigmund Freud, ed. and trans., J. Strachey, A. Freud, A. Strachey, and A. Tyson, 24 vols. (London: Hogarth, 1955–74). (Referred to in the notes as SE.) Here SE 2:125. While I have (and continue to) critique the existing English translation, it is the most widely available one and is the format in which Freud is best known in the English-speaking world. See "Reading Freud in English: Problems, Paradoxes, and a Solution," *International Review of Psycho-Analysis* 18 (1991): 331–44.

14. Auguste Forel, *Die sexuelle Frage* (Munich: Ernst Reinhardt, 1906), p. 435; *The Sexual Question,* trans. C. F. Marshall (New York: Medical Art Agency, 1922), p. 402.

15. Freud-Fliess, p. 30.

16. Freud-Fliess, p. 19.

17. A good survey of the various readings of this dream is given by Didier Anzieu, *Freud's Self-analysis,* trans. Peter Graham (London: Hogarth Press, 1986), pp. 131–40.

18. On the identity of the persons appearing in the dream see Alexander Grinstein, *On Sigmund Freud's Dreams* (Detroit: Wayne State University Press, 1989), pp. 21–24.

19. On the complexity of reading this dream see Jeffrey Mehlman, "Trimethylamine: Notes on Freud's Specimen Dream," in Robert Young, ed., *Untying the Text: A Post-Structuralist Reader* (Boston: Routledge & Kegan Paul, 1981), pp. 177–88.

20. Letter from Abraham to Freud 8 January 1908: *Sigmund Freud–Karl Abraham, Briefe, 1907–1926,* ed. Hilda C. Abraham and Ernst L. Freud (Frankfurt a. M.: S. Fischer, 1980), p. 32; translation here is from *A Psycho-Analytic Dialogue: The Letters of Sigmund Freud and Karl Abraham, 1907–1926,* trans. Bernard Marsh and Hilda Abraham (London: Hogarth, 1965), p. 18.

21. Abraham-Freud, 9 January 1908, p. 34, the translation is from *A Psycho-Analytic Dialogue,* trans. Marsh and Abraham, p. 20.

22. J. Aguayo, "Charcot and Freud: Some Implications of Late Nineteenth-Century French Psychiatry and Politics for the Origins of Psychoanalysis," *Psychoanalysis and Contemporary Thought* 9 (1986): 223–60.

23. Toby Gelfand, "'Mon Cher Docteur Freud': Charcot's Unpublished Correspondence to Freud, 1888–1893," *Bulletin of the History of Medicine* 62 (1988): 563–88; here 571.

24. SE 26:29–43. While this paper was published only in 1893 it was conceptualized if not written before Freud left Paris in 1886.

25. Toby Gelfand, "Charcot's Response to Freud's Rebellion," *Journal of the History of Ideas* 50 (1989): 293–307.

26. K. H. Pribram and M. M. Gill, *Freud's "Project" Re-assessed: Preface to Contemporary Cognitive Theory and Neuropsychology* (New York: Basic

Books, 1976); M. Sirkin and M. Fleming, "Freud's 'Project' and Its Relationship to Psychoanalytic Theory," *Journal of the History of the Behavioral Sciences* 18 (1982): 230–41; J. Friedman and J. Alexander, "Psychoanalysis and Natural Science: Freud's 1895 Project Revisited," *International Review of Psychoanalysis* 10 (1983): 303–18; I. F. Knight, "Freud's 'Project': A Theory for Studies on Hysteria," *Journal of the History of the Behavioral Sciences* 20 (1984): 340–58.

27. Elisabeth Young-Bruehl, *Anna Freud: A Biography* (New York: Summit Books, 1988).

28. On the tradition of psychotherapy under the Nazis see Geoffrey Cocks, *Psychotherapy in the Third Reich: the Göring Institute* (New York: Oxford University Press, 1985).

29. Phyllis Grosskurth, *Melanie Klein: Her World and Her Work* (New York: Knopf, 1986).

30. Paul E. Stepansky, *In Freud's Shadow: Adler in Context* (Hillsdale, NJ: Analytic Press, 1983); B. Handlbauer, *Die Entstehungsgeschichte der Individualpsychologie Alfred Adlers* (Wien: Geyer-Edition, 1984).

31. Susan Quinn, *A Mind of Her Own: The Life of Karen Horney* (New York: Summit Books, 1987).

32. Janet Sayers, *Mothers of Psychoanalysis: Helene Deutsch, Karen Horney, Anna Freud, and Melanie Klein* (New York: W. W. Norton, 1991).

33. Otto Kernberg, "The Contributions of Edith Jacobson: An Overview," *Journal of the American Psychoanalytic Association* 27 (1979): 793–819.

34. R. Moulton, "Clara Thompson, M.D.: Unassuming Leader," L. J. Dickstein and C. C. Nadelson, eds., *Women Physicians in Leadership Roles* (Washington, DC: American Psychiatric Press, 1986), pp. 87–93, and H. S. Perry, "Clara Mabel Thompson," *Notable American Women: The Modern Period* (Cambridge, MA: Belknap-Harvard University Press, 1980).

35. J. D. Beahrs, "The Hypnotic Psychotherapy of Milton H. Erickson," *American Journal of Clinical Hypnosis* 14 (1971): 73–90.

36. Sherry Turkle, *Psychoanalytic Politics: Freud's French Revolution* (Cambridge, MA: MIT Press, 1981); Michael Clark, *Jacques Lacan: An Annotated Bibliography* (New York: Garland, 1988); Shoshana Felman, *Jacques Lacan and the Adventure of Insight: Psychoanalysis in Contemporary Culture* (Cambridge, MA: Harvard University Press, 1987).

37. P. E. Sifneos, "Short-term Dynamic Psychotherapy: Its History, Its Impact, and Its Future," *Psychotherapy and Psychosomatic Medicine* 35 (1981): 224–29.

38. Gregorio Kohon, ed., *The British School of Psychoanalysis: The Independent Tradition* (London: Free Association Books, 1986).

39. Jay R. Greenberg and Stephen A. Mitchell, *Object Relations in Psychoanalytic Theory* (Cambridge, MA: Harvard University Press, 1983).

40. In general on the relationship between Viennese and American psycho-analysis see A. Schick, "Psychotherapy in Old Vienna and New York: Cultural Comparisons," *Psychoanalytic Review* 60 (1973): 111–26. On Mahler see J. R. Smith, "Margaret S. Mahler, M.D.: Original Thinker, Exceptional Woman," in L. J. Dickstein and C. C. Nadelson, ed., *Women Physicians in Leadership Roles* (Washington, DC: American Psychiatric Press, 1986), pp. 109–19.

41. A. Phillips, *Winnicott* (Cambridge, MA: Harvard University Press, 1989), and F. R. Rodman, *The Spontaneous Gesture: Selected Letters of D. W. Winnicott* (Cambridge, MA: Harvard University Press, 1987).

42. M. Sharaf, *Fury on Earth: A Biography of Wilhelm Reich* (New York: St. Martin's Press/Marek, 1983); Erwin H. Ackerknecht, "Wilhelm Reich (1897–1957)," in K. Ganzinger, et al., eds., *Festschrift für Erna Lesky zum 70. Geburtstag* (Vienna: Bruder Hollinek, 1981), pp. 5–12; Paul A. Robinson, *The Freudian Left: Wilhelm Reich, Geza Roheim, Herbert Marcuse* (Ithaca, NY: Cornell University Press, 1990).

43. Jacob Levy Moreno, "Psychodrama," in *American Handbook of Psychiatry*, ed. Silvano Arieti (New York: Basic Books, 1959), pp. 1375–96.

44. Martin Shepard, *Fritz* (New York: Saturday Review Press, 1975).

45. A. Collier, *R. D. Laing: The Philosophy and Politics of Psychotherapy* (New York: Pantheon, 1977), and Richard I. Evans, *R. D. Laing: The Man and His Ideas* (New York: Dutton, 1976).

46. M. F. Ettin, "'Come on, Jack, Tell Us about Yourself': The Growth Spurt of Group Psychotherapy," *International Journal of Group Psychotherapy* 39 (1989): 35–57 and his "'By the Crowd They Have Been Broken, by the Crowd They Shall Be Healed': The Advent of Group Psychotherapy," *International Journal of Group Psychotherapy* 38 (1988): 139–67. See also H. Papanek, "Adler's Psychology and Group Psychotherapy," *American Journal of Psychiatry* 127 (1970): 783–86.

47. Richard I. Evans, *Carl Rogers: The Man and His Ideas* (New York: Dutton, 1975).

48. Bill W., *Twelve Steps and Twelve Traditions* (New York: Alcoholics Anonymous, 1953). See also Robert Thomsen, *Bill W* (New York, Harper & Row, 1975), and H. M. Trice and W. J. Staudenmeier, "A Sociocultural History of Alcoholics Anonymous," *Recent Developments in Alcoholism* 7 (1989): 11–35.

49. Norman Dain, *Clifford W. Beers: Advocate for the Insane* (Pittsburgh: University of Pittsburgh Press, 1980).

50. Juliet Mitchell, *Psychoanalysis and Feminism* (New York: Pantheon Books, 1974). See also Hannah Lerman, Natalie Porter, eds., *Feminist Ethics in Psychotherapy* (New York: Springer Pub. Co., 1990); Toni Ann Laidlaw, Cheryl Malmo, and associates, *Healing Voices: Feminist Approaches to Therapy with Women* (San Francisco: Jossey-Bass, 1990).

51. Elaine Marks and Isabelle de Courtivron, eds., *New French Feminisms: An Anthology* (New York: Schocken Books, 1981), and Edith Hoshino Altbach, et. al., eds., *German Feminism: Readings in Politics and Literature* (Albany, NY: SUNY Press, 1984).

52. Yehuda Fried and Joseph Agassi, *Psychiatry as Medicine: Contemporary Psychotherapies* (The Hague/Boston: Nijhoff, 1983).

1

Katharina

In the summer vacation of the year 189– I made an excursion into the Hohe Tauern[1] so that for a while I might forget medicine and more particularly the neuroses. I had almost succeeded in this when one day I turned aside from the main road to climb a mountain which lay somewhat apart and which was renowned for its views and for its well-run refuge hut. I reached the top after a strenuous climb and, feeling refreshed and rested, was sitting deep in contemplation of the charm of the distant prospect. I was so lost in thought that at first I did not connect it with myself when these words reached my ears: "Are you a doctor, sir?" But the question was addressed to me, and by the rather sulky-looking girl of perhaps eighteen who had served my meal and had been spoken to by the landlady as "Katharina." To judge by her dress and bearing, she could not be a servant, but must no doubt be a daughter or relative of the landlady's.

Coming to myself I replied: "Yes, I'm a doctor: but how did you know that?"

"You wrote your name in the Visitors' Book, sir. And I thought if you had a few moments to spare. . . . The truth is, sir, my nerves are bad. I went to see a doctor in L—— about them and he gave me something for them; but I'm not well yet."

So there I was with the neuroses once again—for nothing else could very well be the matter with this strong, well-built girl with her unhappy look. I was interested to find that neuroses could flourish in this way at a height of over six thousand feet; I questioned her further therefore. I report the conversation that followed

---

1. One of the highest ranges in the Eastern Alps.

between us just as it is impressed on my memory and I have not altered the patient's dialect.[2]

"Well, what is it you suffer from?"

"I get so out of breath. Not always. But sometimes it catches me so that I think I shall suffocate."

This did not, at first sight, sound like a nervous symptom. But soon it occurred to me that probably it was only a description that stood for an anxiety attack: she was choosing shortness of breath out of the complex of sensations arising from anxiety and laying undue stress on that single factor.

"Sit down here. What is it like when you get 'out of breath'?"

"It comes over me all at once. First of all it's like something pressing on my eyes. My head gets so heavy, there's a dreadful buzzing, and I feel so giddy that I almost fall over. Then there's something crushing my chest so that I can't get my breath."

"And you don't notice anything in your throat?"

"My throat's squeezed together as though I were going to choke."

"Does anything else happen in your head?"

"Yes, there's a hammering, enough to burst it."

"And don't you feel at all frightened while this is going on?"

"I always think I'm going to die. I'm brave as a rule and go about everywhere by myself—into the cellar and all over the mountain. But on a day when that happens I don't dare to go anywhere; I think all the time someone's standing behind me and going to catch hold of me all at once."

So it was in fact an anxiety attack, and introduced by the signs of a hysterical "aura"[3]—or, more correctly, it was a hysterical attack the content of which was anxiety. Might there not probably be some other content as well?

"When you have an attack do you think of something? and always the same thing? or do you see something in front of you?"

"Yes. I always see an awful face that looks at me in a dreadful way, so that I'm frightened."

Perhaps this might offer a quick means of getting to the heart of the matter.

---

2. No attempt has been made in the English translation to imitate this dialect.
3. The premonitory sensations preceeding an epileptic or hysterical attack.

"Do you recognize the face? I mean, is it a face that you've really seen some time?"

"No."

"Do you know what your attacks come from?"

"No."

"When did you first have them?"

"Two years ago, while I was still living on the other mountain with my aunt. (She used to run a refuge hut there, and we moved here eighteen months ago.) But they keep on happening."

Was I to make an attempt at an analysis? I could not venture to transplant hypnosis to these altitudes, but perhaps I might succeed with a simple talk. I should have to try a lucky guess. I had found often enough that in girls anxiety was a consequence of the horror by which a virginal mind is overcome when it is faced for the first time with the world of sexuality.[4]

So I said: "If you don't know, I'll tell you how *I* think you got your attacks. At that time, two years ago, you must have seen or heard something that very much embarrassed you, and that you'd much rather not have seen."

"Heavens, yes!" she replied, "that was when I caught my uncle with the girl, with Franziska, my cousin."

"What's this story about a girl? Won't you tell me all about it?"

"You can say *anything* to a doctor, I suppose. Well, at that time, you know, my uncle—the husband of the aunt you've seen here—kept the inn on the —— kogel.[5] Now they're divorced, and it's my fault they were divorced, because it was through me that it came out that he was carrying on with Franziska."

"And how did you discover it?"

"This way. One day two years ago some gentlemen had climbed the mountain and asked for something to eat. My aunt wasn't at

---

4. I will quote here the case in which I first recognized this causal connection. I was treating a young married woman who was suffering from a complicated neurosis and, once again, was unwilling to admit that her illness arose from her married life. She objected that while she was still a girl she had had attacks of anxiety, ending in fainting fits. I remained firm. When we had come to know each other better she suddenly said to me one day: "I'll tell you now how I came by my attacks of anxiety when I was a girl. At that time I used to sleep in a room next to my parents"; the door was left open and a night-light used to burn on the table. So more than once I saw my father get into bed with my mother and heard sounds that greatly excited me. It was then that my attacks came on."

5. The name of the "other" mountain.

home, and Franziska, who always did the cooking, was nowhere to be found. And my uncle was not to be found either. We looked everywhere, and at last Alois, the little boy, my cousin, said: 'Why, Franziska must be in Father's room!' And we both laughed; but we weren't thinking anything bad. Then we went to my uncle's room but found it locked. That seemed strange to me. Then Alois said: 'There's a window in the passage where you can look into the room.' We went into the passage; but Alois wouldn't go to the window and said he was afraid. So I said: 'You silly boy! I'll go. I'm not a bit afraid.' And I had nothing bad in my mind. I looked in. The room was rather dark, but I saw my uncle and Franziska; he was lying on her."

"Well?"

"I came away from the window at once, and leaned up against the wall and couldn't get my breath—just what happens to me since. Everything went blank, my eyelids were forced together and there was a hammering and buzzing in my head."

"Did you tell your aunt that very same day?"

"Oh no, I said nothing."

"Then why were you so frightened when you found them together? Did you understand it? Did you know what was going on?"

"Oh no. I didn't understand anything at that time. I was only sixteen. I don't know what I was frightened about."

"Fräulein Katharina, if you could remember now what was happening in you at that time, when you had your first attack, what you thought about it—it would help you."

"Yes, if I could. But I was so frightened that I've forgotten everything."

(Translated into the terminology of our "Preliminary Communication," this means: "The affect itself created a hypnoid state, whose products were then cut off from associative connection with the ego-consciousness.")

"Tell me, Fräulein. Can it be that the head that you always see when you lose your breath is Franziska's head, as you saw it then?"

"Oh no, she didn't look so awful. Besides, it's a man's head."

"Or perhaps your uncle's?"

"I didn't see his face as clearly as that. It was too dark in the room. And why should he have been making such a dreadful face just then?"

"You're quite right."

(The road suddenly seemed blocked. Perhaps something might turn up in the rest of her story.)

"And what happened then?"

"Well, those two must have heard a noise, because they came out soon afterwards. I felt very bad the whole time. I always kept thinking about it. Then two days later it was a Sunday and there was a great deal to do and I worked all day long. And on the Monday morning I felt giddy again and was sick, and I stopped in bed and was sick without stopping for three days."

We [Breuer and I] had often compared the symptomatology of hysteria with a pictographic script which has become intelligible after the discovery of a few bilingual inscriptions. In that alphabet being sick means disgust. So I said: "If you were sick three days later, I believe that means that when you looked into the room you felt disgusted."

"Yes, I'm sure I felt disgusted," she said reflectively, "but disgusted at what?"

"Perhaps you saw something naked? What sort of state were they in?"

"It was too dark to see anything; besides they both of them had their clothes on. Oh, if only I knew what it was I felt disgusted at!"

I had no idea either. But I told her to go on and tell me whatever occurred to her, in the confident expectation that she would think of precisely what I needed to explain the case.

Well, she went on to describe how at last she reported her discovery to her aunt, who found that she was changed and suspected her of concealing some secret. There followed some very disagreeable scenes between her uncle and aunt, in the course of which the children came to hear a number of things which opened their eyes in many ways and which it would have been better for them not to have heard. At last her aunt decided to move with her children and niece and take over the present inn, leaving her uncle alone with Franziska, who had meanwhile become pregnant. After this, however, to my astonishment she dropped these threads and began to tell me two sets of older stories, which went back two or three years earlier than the traumatic moment. The first set related to occasions on which the same uncle had made sexual advances to her herself, when she was only fourteen years old. She described how she had once gone with him on an expedition down into the valley in the winter and had spent the night in the inn there. He sat in the bar drinking and playing cards, but she felt sleepy and went up to bed early in the room they were to share on the upper floor. She was not quite asleep when he came up; then she fell asleep again and woke up suddenly "feeling his body" in the bed. She jumped up and remonstrated with him: "What are you up to, Uncle? Why don't you stay in your own bed?" He tried to pacify her: "Go on, you silly girl, keep still. You don't know how nice it is."—"I don't like your 'nice' things; you don't even let one sleep in peace." She remained standing by the door, ready to take refuge outside in the passage, till at last he gave up and went to sleep himself. Then she went back to her own bed and slept till morning. From the way in which she reported having defended herself it seems to follow that she did not clearly recognize the attack as a sexual one. When I asked her if she knew what he was trying to do to her, she replied: "Not at the time." It had become clear to her much later on, she said; she had resisted because it was unpleasant to be disturbed in one's sleep and "because it wasn't nice."

I have been obliged to relate this in detail, because of its great importance for understanding everything that followed.—She went on to tell me of yet other experiences of somewhat later date: how she had once again had to defend herself against him in an inn when he was completely drunk, and similar stories. In answer to a question as to whether on these occasions she had felt anything resembling her later loss of breath, she answered with decision that she had every time felt the pressure on her eyes and chest, but with nothing like the strength that had characterized the scene of discovery.

Immediately she had finished this set of memories she began to tell me a second set, which dealt with occasions on which she had noticed something between her uncle and Franziska. Once the whole family had spent the night in their clothes in a hayloft and she was woken up suddenly by a noise; she thought she noticed that her uncle, who had been lying between her and Franziska, was turning away, and that Franziska was just lying down. Another time they were stopping the night at an inn at the village of N——; she and her uncle were in one room and Franziska in an adjoining one. She woke up suddenly in the night and saw a tall white figure by the door, on the point of turning the handle: "Goodness, is that you, Uncle? What are you doing at the door?"—"Keep quiet. I was only looking for something."—"But the way out's by the *other* door,"—"I'd just made a mistake" . . . and so on.

I asked her if she had been suspicious at that time. "No, I didn't think anything about it; I only just noticed it and thought no more about it." When I enquired whether she had been frightened on these occasions too, she replied that she thought so, but she was not so sure of it this time.

At the end of these two sets of memories she came to a stop. She was like someone transformed. The sulky, unhappy face had grown lively, her eyes were bright, she was lightened and exalted. Meanwhile the understanding of her case had become clear to me. The later part of what she had told me, in an apparently aimless fashion, provided an admirable explanation of her behavior at the scene of the discovery. At that time she had carried about with her two sets of experiences which she remembered but did not understand, and from which she drew no inferences. When she caught sight of the couple in intercourse, she at once established a connection between the new impression and these two sets of recollections, she began to understand them and at the same time to fend them off. There then followed a short period of working-out, of "incubation,"[6] after which the symptoms of conversion set in, the vomiting as a substitute for moral and physical disgust. This solved the riddle. She had not been disgusted by the sight of the two people but by the memory which that sight had stirred up in her. And, taking everything into account, this could only be the memory of the attempt on her at night when she had "felt her uncle's body."

So when she had finished her confession I said to her: "I know now what it was you thought when you looked into the room. You thought: 'Now he's doing with her what he wanted to do with me that night and those other times.' That was what you were disgusted at, because you remembered the feeling when you woke up in the night and felt his body."

"It may well be," she replied, "that that was what I was disgusted at and that that was what I thought."

"Tell me just one thing more. You're a grown-up girl now and know all sorts of things. . . ."

"Yes, now I am."

---

6. Cf. below, p. 10.

"Tell me just one thing. What part of his body was it that you felt that night?"

But she gave me no more definite answer. She smiled in an embarrassed way, as though she had been found out, like someone who is obliged to admit that a fundamental position has been reached where there is not much more to be said. I could imagine what the tactile sensation was which she had later learned to interpret. Her facial expression seemed to me to be saying that she supposed that I was right in my conjecture. But I could not penetrate further, and in any case I owed her a debt of gratitude for having made it so much easier for me to talk to her than to the prudish ladies of my city practice, who regard whatever is natural as shameful.

Thus the case was cleared up.—But stop a moment! What about the recurrent hallucination of the head, which appeared during her attacks and struck terror into her? Where did it come from? I proceeded to ask her about it, and, as though *her* knowledge, too, had been extended by our conversation, she promptly replied: "Yes, I know now. The head is my uncle's head—I recognize it now—but not from *that* time. Later, when all the disputes had broken out, my uncle gave way to a senseless rage against me. He kept saying that it was all my fault: if I hadn't chattered, it would never have come to a divorce. He kept threatening he would do something to me; and if he caught sight of me at a distance his face would get distorted with rage and he would make for me with his hand raised. I always ran away from him, and always felt terrified that he would catch me some time unawares. The face I always see now is his face when he was in a rage."

This information reminded me that her first hysterical symptom, the vomiting, had passed away; the anxiety attack remained and acquired a fresh content. Accordingly, what we were dealing with was a hysteria which had to a considerable extent been abreacted. And in fact she had reported her discovery to her aunt soon after it happened.

"Did you tell your aunt the other stories—about his making advances to you?"

"Yes. Not at once, but later on, when there was already talk of a divorce. My aunt said: 'We'll keep that in reserve. If he causes trouble in the Court, we'll say that too.'"

I can well understand that it should have been precisely this last period—when there were more and more agitating scenes in the house and when her own state ceased to interest her aunt, who was entirely occupied with the dispute—that it should have been this period of accumulation and retention that left her the legacy of the mnemic symbol [of the hallucinated face].

I hope this girl, whose sexual sensibility had been injured at such an early age, derived some benefit from our conversation. I have not seen her since.

Discussion

If someone were to assert that the present case history is not so much an analyzed case of hysteria as a case solved by guessing, I should have nothing to say against him. It is true that the patient agreed that what I interpolated into her story was probably true; but she was not in a position to recognize it as something she had experienced. I believe it would have required hypnosis to bring that about. Assuming that my guesses were correct, I will now attempt to fit the case into the schematic picture of an "acquired" hysteria on the lines suggested by Case 3. It seems plausible, then, to compare the two sets of erotic experiences with "traumatic" moments and the scene of discovering the couple with an "auxiliary" moment. The similarity lies in the fact that in the former experiences an element of consciousness was created which was excluded from the thought-activity of the ego and remained, as it were, in storage, while in the latter scene a new impression forcibly brought about an associative connection between this separated group and the ego. On the other hand there are dissimilarities which cannot be overlooked. The cause of the isolation was not, as in Case 3, an act of will on the part of the ego but *ignorance* on the part of the ego, which was not yet capable of coping with sexual experiences. In this respect the case of Katharina is typical. In every analysis of a case of hysteria based on sexual traumas we find that impressions from the presexual period which produced no effect on the child attain traumatic power at a later date as memories, when the girl or married woman has acquired an understanding of sexual life.[7] The splitting-off of psychical groups may be said to be a normal process in adolescent development; and it is easy to see that their later reception into the ego affords frequent opportunities for psy-

---

7. Freud discussed this at considerable length in the later sections of part 2 of his 1895 "Project" (Freud, 1950a) and expressed the same view in section 1 of his second paper on "The Neuro-Psychoses of Defense" (1896b). It was not until some years later that he came to recognize the part played in the production of neuroses

chical disturbances. Moreover, I should like at this point to express a doubt as to whether a splitting of consciousness due to ignorance is really different from one due to conscious rejection, and whether even adolescents do not possess sexual knowledge far oftener than is supposed or than they themselves believe.

A further distinction in the physical mechanism of this case lies in the fact that the scene of discovery, which we have described as "auxiliary," deserves equally to be called "traumatic." It was operative on account of its own content and not merely as something that revived previous traumatic experiences. It combined the characteristics of an "auxiliary" and a "traumatic" moment. There seems no reason, however, why this coincidence should lead us to abandon a conceptual separation which in other cases corresponds also to a separation in time. Another peculiarity of Katharina's case, which, incidentally, has long been familiar to us, is seen in the circumstance that the conversion, the production of the hysterical phenomena, did not occur immediately after the trauma but after an interval of incubation. Charcot liked to describe this interval as the "period of psychical working-out" [*élaboration*].[8]

The anxiety from which Katharina suffered in her attacks was a hysterical one; that is, it was a reproduction of the anxiety which had appeared in connection with each of the sexual traumas. I shall not here comment on the fact which I have found regularly present in a very large number of cases—namely, that a mere suspicion of sexual relations calls up the affect of anxiety in virginal individuals.[9] [Cf. p. 3, *n*. 4]

Translated by James Strachey,
in collaboration with Anna Freud, et al.

---

by sexual impulses already present in early childhood. Cf. the editor's note to the *Three Essays* (1905*d*), *Standard Ed.*, 7, 127–29.

8. See Charcot 1888, *1*, 99.

9. (*Footnote added* 1924:) I venture after the lapse of so many years to lift the veil of discretion and reveal the fact that Katharina was not the niece but the daughter of the landlady. The girl fell ill, therefore, as a result of sexual atttempts on the part of her own father. Distortions like the one which I introduced in the present instance should be altogether avoided in reporting a case history. From the point of view of understanding the case, a distortion of this kind is not, of course, a matter of such indifference as would be shifting the scene from one mountain to another.

2

Letters to Fliess

Letter 70[1]

... [October 3] Very little is still happening to me externally, but internally something most interesting. For the last four days my self-analysis, which I consider indispensable for throwing light upon the whole problem, has proceeded in dreams and has presented me with the most valuable inferences and clues. At some points I have a feeling of being at the end, and so far, too, I have always known where the dream of the next night would take things up. To describe it in writing is more difficult than anything else, and also it would be far too diffuse. I can only say shortly that *der Alte* [my father] played no active part in my case, but that no doubt I drew an inference by analogy from myself on to him; that the "prime originator" [of my troubles] was a woman, ugly, elderly, but clever, who told me a great deal about God Almighty and Hell and who gave me a high opinion of my own capacities;[2] that later (between the ages of two and two-and-a-half) my libido was stirred up towards *matrem,* namely on the occasion of a journey with her from Leipzig to Vienna, during which we must have spent the night together and I must have had an opportunity of seeing her *nudam*[3]—you drew the conclusion from this long ago for your own son, as a remark of yours revealed to me—; that I greeted my

---

1. Dated Vienna, October 3 and 4, 1897.

2. This old nurse is referred to in *The Interpretation of Dreams* (1900a), *Standard Ed.*, 4, 247–48 and in *The Psychopathology of Everyday Life* (1901b), ibid., 6, 50–51. But these do not include the account of Freud's reconstruction of her behavior from his dreams and its verification, which only appears here.

3. Freud seems in fact to have been four years old at the time of this journey.

brother (who was a year my junior and died after a few months) with ill wishes and genuine childish jealousy, and that his death left the germ of self-reproaches in me. I have also long known the companion in my evil deeds between the ages of one and two. It was my nephew, a year older than myself, who is now living in Manchester and who visited us in Vienna when I was fourteen. The two of us seem occasionally to have behaved in a cruel fashion to my niece, who was a year younger. This nephew and this younger brother have determined what is neurotic, but also what is intense, in all my friendships.[4] You yourself have seen my travel anxiety in full swing.

I have not yet found out anything about the scenes which underlie the whole business. If they come to light and if I succeed in resolving my own hysteria, I shall be grateful to the memory of the old woman who provided me at such an early age with the means for living and going on living. As you see, my old liking for her is breaking through again. I can give you no idea of the intellectual beauty of the work. . . .

October 4. . . . Today's dream has produced what follows, under the strangest disguises.

She was my teacher in sexual matters and scolded me for being clumsy and not being able to do anything. (This is always how neurotic impotence comes about; it is thus that fear of incapacity at school obtains its sexual substratum.) At the same time I saw the skull of a small animal and in the dream I thought "Pig!" But in the analysis I associated it with your wish two years ago that I might find a skull on the Lido to enlighten me, as Goethe once did. But I failed to find one. So I was a little fool.[5] The whole dream was full of the most mortifying allusions to my present powerlessness as a therapist. Perhaps this is where an inclination to believe that hysteria is incurable has its start. Besides this, she washed me in

4. Freud's relations with his nephew John and his niece Pauline are further explained and discussed in *The Interpretation of Dreams*, ibid., *4*, 198 and 231, and *5*, 423–25 and 483–87, and in the disguised autobiographical episode in "Screen Memories" (1899*a*), ibid., *3*, 309 ff.

5. *"Ein kleiner Schafskopf,"* literally "a little sheep's-head."—The reference is to the story that Goethe found the skull of a sheep on the Lido, which gave him the idea of the so-called vertebral theory of the skull. This story makes its appearance again in *On Dreams* (1901*a*) as an association to another dream (*Standard Ed.*, *5*, 664).

reddish water, in which she had previously washed herself. (The interpretation is not difficult; I find nothing like this in the chain of my memories, so I regard it as a genuine ancient discovery.) And she made me carry off *"zehners"* (ten kreuzer pieces)[6] and give them to her. There is a long chain from these first silver *zehners* to the heap of paper ten-florin notes which I saw in the dream as Martha's housekeeping money. The dream can be summed up as "bad treatment." Just as the old woman got money from me for her bad treatment of me, so today I get money for my bad treatment of my patients. A special part was played by Frau Qu., whose remark you reported to me: I ought not to take anything from her as she was the wife of a colleague. (Of course he made it a condition that I should.)

A severe critic might say of all this that it was retrogressively phantasied and not progressively determined. *Experimenta crucis* [crucial experiments] would have to decide against him. The reddish water seems to be one such already. Where do all patients get the frightful perverse details which are often as remote from their experience as from their knowledge?

Letter 71[7]

... My self-analysis is in fact the most essential thing I have at present and it promises to become of the greatest value to me if it reaches its end. In the middle of it, it suddenly ceased for three days and I had the feeling of being tied up inside which patients complain of so much, and I was really inconsolable. ...

It is an uncanny fact that my practice still allows me a great deal of time.

The whole thing is all the more valuable for my purposes since I have succeeded in finding a few real points of reference for the story. I asked my mother whether she still recollected the nurse. "Of course," she said, "an elderly person, very clever. She was always taking you to church: when you came back afterwards you used to preach sermons and tell us all about God Almighty. During my confinement when Anna was born" (she is two and a half years my junior) "it was discovered that she was a thief, and all the shiny

---

6. Silver coins worth about two-pence at that time.
7. Dated Vienna, October 15, 1897.

new kreuzers and zehners and all the toys that had been given to you were found in her possession. Your brother Philipp [see below] himself went for the policeman and she was given ten months in prison." Now just see how this confirms the conclusions of my dream-interpretation. I have found a simple explanation of my own possible mistake. I wrote to you that she led me into stealing zehners and giving them to her. The dream really meant that she stole them herself. For the dream-picture was a memory of my taking money from the mother of a doctor—that is, wrongfully. The correct interpretation is: I = she, and the mother of a doctor equals my mother. So far was I from knowing that she was a thief that I made a wrong interpretation.

I also made inquiries about the doctor we had in Freiberg, because a dream showed a great deal of resentment against him. In the analysis of the figure in the dream behind which he was concealed I thought also of a Professor von K., who was my history master at school. He did not seem to fit in at all, as my relations with him were indifferent or, rather, agreeable. My mother then told me that the doctor in my childhood had only one eye, and of all my schoolmasters Professor K. too was the only one with that same defect.[8]

The evidential value of these coincidences might be invalidated by the objection that on some occasion in my later childhood I had heard that the nurse was a thief, and that I had then apparently forgotten it till it finally emerged in the dream. I think myself that that is so. But I have another unexceptionable and amusing piece of evidence. I said to myself that if the old woman disappeared so suddenly, it must be possible to point to the impression this made on me. Where is that impression, then? A scene then occurred to me which, for the last twenty-nine years, has occasionally emerged in my conscious memory without my understanding it. My mother was nowhere to be found: I was screaming my head off. My brother Philipp, twenty years older than me, was holding open a cupboard [*Kasten*] for me, and, when I found that my mother was not inside it either, I began crying still more, till, looking slim and beautiful, she came in by the door. What can this mean? Why was

---

8. The episode of the one-eyed doctor is mentioned in *The Interpretation of Dreams* (1900a), *Standard Ed.*, 4, 17 and in Lecture XIII of the *Introductory Lectures* (1916–17), ibid., 16, 201.

my brother opening the cupboard, though he knew that my mother was not in it, so that this could not pacify me? And then suddenly I understood. I had asked him to do it. When I missed my mother, I had been afraid she had vanished from me just as the old woman had a short time before. Now I must have heard that the old woman had been locked up and consequently I must have thought that my mother had been too—or rather had been "boxed up" [*"eingekastelt"*];[9] for my brother Philipp, who is sixty-three now, is fond to this very day of talking in this punning fashion. The fact that it was to him in particular that I turned proves that I knew quite well of his share in the nurse's disappearance.[10]

Since then I have got much further, but have not yet reached any real stopping point. Communicating what is unfinished is so diffuse and laborious that I hope you will excuse me from it and content yourself with a knowledge of the portions that are established with certainty. If the analysis contains what I expect from it, I will work it over systematically and put it before you afterwards. So far I have found nothing completely new, only complications, to which I am ordinarily[11] accustomed. It is not quite easy. To be completely honest with oneself is good practice. One single thought of general value has been revealed to me. I have found, in my own case too, falling in love with the mother and jealousy of the father, and I now regard it as a universal event of early childhood, even if not so early as in children who have been made hysterical. (Similarly with the romance of parentage in paranoia—heroes, founders of religions.) If that is so, we can understand the riveting power of *Oedipus Rex*, in spite of all the objections raised by reason against its presupposition of destiny; and we can understand why the later "dramas of destiny" were bound to fail so miserably. Our feelings rise against any arbitrary, individual compulsion [of fate], such as is presupposed in [Grillparzer's] *Die Ahnfrau*, etc. But the Greek legend seizes on a compulsion which everyone recognizes because he feels its existence within himself. Each member of the audience

---

9. Literally, "put in a *Kasten* (or cupboard)."
10. The story of the screen memory about the cupboard was included at greater length in Chapter IV of *The Psychopathology of Everyday Life* (1901b), *Standard Ed.*, 6, 49–51. In a footnote added to that passage in 1924 Freud pointed out the womb symbolism of the cupboard, and pursued the whole analysis further.
11. *"Sonst"* in the MS. *"Bis jetzt"* ("hitherto") in *Anf.*, 237.

was once, in germ and in fantasy, just such an Oedipus, and each one recoils in horror from the dream-fulfillment here transplanted into reality, with the whole quota of repression which separates his infantile state from his present one.

A fleeting idea has passed through my head of whether the same thing may not lie at the bottom of *Hamlet* as well. I am not thinking of Shakespeare's conscious intention, but I believe rather that here some real event instigated the poet to his representation, in that the unconscious in him understood the unconscious in his hero. How can Hamlet the hysteric justify his words "Thus conscience does make cowards of us all," how can he explain his hesitation in avenging his father by the murder of his uncle—he, the same man who sends his courtiers to their death without a scruple and who is positively precipitate in killing Laertes? How better could he justify himself than by the torment he suffers from the obscure memory that he himself had meditated the same deed against his father from passion for his mother, and—"use every man after his desert, and who should 'scape whipping?" His conscience is his unconscious sense of guilt. And is not his sexual alienation in his conversation with Ophelia typically hysterical? and his rejection of the instinct[12] which seeks to beget children? and, finally, his transferring the deed from his own father to Ophelia's? And does he not in the end, in the same remarkable way as my hysterical patients, bring down punishment on himself by suffering the same fate as his father of being poisoned by the same rival?[13]

Translated by Eric Mosbacher and James Strachey

---

12. *"Instinkt"* in the original.

13. This is the first explicit introduction of the Oedipus complex, hinted at above on p. 255. Its first published appearance was in *The Interpretation of Dreams* (1900a), *Standard Ed.*, 4, 260–66. The application of the idea to *Oedipus Rex* and to *Hamlet* is to be found in the same passage.

3

The Method of Interpreting Dreams: An Analysis of a Specimen Dream

The title that I have chosen for my work makes plain which of the traditional approaches to the problem of dreams I am inclined to follow. The aim which I have set before myself is to show that dreams are capable of being interpreted; and any contributions I may be able to make toward the solution of the problems dealt with in the last chapter will only arise as byproducts in the course of carrying out my proper task. My presumption that dreams can be interpreted at once puts me in opposition to the ruling theory of dreams and in fact to every theory of dreams with the single exception of Scherner's; for "interpreting" a dream implies assigning a "meaning" to it—that is, replacing it by something which fits into the chain of our mental acts as a link having a validity and importance equal to the rest. As we have seen, the scientific theories of dreams leave no room for any problem of interpreting them, since in their view a dream is not a mental act at all, but a somatic process signalizing its occurrence by indications registered in the mental apparatus. Lay opinion has taken a different attitude throughout the ages. It has exercised its indefeasible right to behave inconsistently; and, though admitting that dreams are unintelligible and absurd, it cannot bring itself to declare that they have no significance at all. Led by some obscure feeling, it seems to assume that, in spite of everything, every dream has a meaning, though a hidden one, that dreams are designed to take the place of some other process of thought, and that we have only to undo the substitution correctly in order to arrive at this hidden meaning.

Thus the lay world has from the earliest times concerned itself with "interpreting" dreams and in its attempts to do so it has made use of two essentially different methods.

The first of these procedures considers the content of the dream as a whole and seeks to replace it by another content which is intelligible and in certain respects analogous to the original one. This is *"symbolic"* dream-interpreting; and it inevitably breaks down when faced by dreams which are not merely unintelligible but also confused. An example of this procedure is to be seen in the explanation of Pharaoh's dream propounded by Joseph in the Bible. The seven fat kine followed by seven lean kine that ate up the fat kine—all this was a symbolic substitute for a prophecy of seven years of famine in the land of Egypt which should consume all that was brought forth in the seven years of plenty. Most of the artificial dreams constructed by imaginative writers are designed for a symbolic interpretation of this sort: they reproduce the writer's thoughts under a disguise which is regarded as harmonizing with the recognized characteristics of dreams.[1] The idea of dreams being chiefly concerned with the future and being able to foretell it—a remnant of the old prophetic significance of dreams—provides a reason for transposing the meaning of the dream, when it has been arrived at by symbolic interpretation, into the future tense. It is of course impossible to give instructions upon the *method* of arriving at a symbolic interpretation. Success must be a question of hitting on a clever idea, of direct intuition, and for that reason it was possible for dream-interpretation by means of symbolism to be exalted into an artistic activity dependent on the possession of peculiar gifts.[2]

---

1. [*Footnote added* 1909:] I found by chance in *Gradiva*, a story written by Wilhelm Jensen, a number of artificial dreams which were perfectly correctly constructed and could be interpreted just as though they had not been invented but had been dreamt by real people. In reply to an enquiry, the author confirmed the fact that he had no knowledge of my theory of dreams. I have argued that the agreement between my researches and this writer's creations is evidence in favor of the correctness of my analysis of dreams. (See Freud, 1907a.)

2. [*Footnote added* 1914:] Aristotle [*De divinatione per somnum*, II (Trans., 1935, 383)] remarked in this connection that the best interpreter of dreams was

The second of the two popular methods of interpreting dreams is far from making any such claims. It might be described as the *"decoding"* method, since it treats dreams as a kind of cryptography in which each sign can be translated into another sign having a known meaning, in accordance with a fixed key. Suppose, for instance, that I have dreamt of a letter and also of a funeral. If I consult a "dream-book," I find that "letter" must be translated by "trouble" and "funeral" by "betrothal." It then remains for me to link together the keywords which I have deciphered in this way and, once more, to transpose the result into the future tense. An interesting modification of the process of decoding, which to some extent corrects the purely mechanical character of its method of transposing, is to be found in the book written upon the interpretation of dreams [*Oneirocritica*] by Artemidorus of Daldis.[3] This method takes into account not only the content of the dream but

---

the man who could best grasp similarities; for dream-pictures, like pictures on water, are pulled out of shape by movement, and the most successful interpreter is the man who can detect the truth from the misshapen picture. (Büchsenschütz, 1868, 65.)

3. [*Footnote added* 1914:] Artemidorus of Daldis, who was probably born at the beginning of the second century A.D., has left us the most complete and painstaking study of dream-interpretation as practiced in the Graeco-Roman world. As Theodor Gomperz (1866, 7 f.) points out, he insisted on the importance of basing the interpretation of dreams on observation and experience, and made a rigid distinction between his own art and others that were illusory. The principles of his interpretative art, according to Gomperz, is identical with magic, the principle of association. A thing in a dream means what it recalls to the mind—to the dream-interpreter's mind, it need hardly be said. An insuperable source of arbitrariness and uncertainty arises from the fact that the dream-element may recall *various* things to the interpreter's mind and may recall something different to different interpreters. The technique which I describe in the pages that follow differs in one essential respect from the ancient method: it imposes the task of interpretation upon the dreamer himself. It is not concerned with what occurs to the *interpreter* in connection with a particular element of the dream, but with what occurs to the *dreamer*.—Recent reports, however, from a missionary, Father Tfinkdji (1913, [516–17 and 523]), show that modern dream-interpreters in the East also make free use of the dreamer's collaboration. He writes as follows of dream-interpreters among the Arabs of Mesopotamia: "Pour interpréter exactement un songe, les oniromanciens les plus habiles s'informent de ceux qui les consultent de toutes les circonstances qu'ils regardent nécessaires pour la bonne explication. . . . En un mot, nos oniromanciens ne laissent aucune circonstance leur échapper et ne donnent l'interprétation désirée avant d'avoir parfaitement saisi et reçu toutes les interrogations désirables." [In order to give a precise interpretation of a dream, the most skillful dream-diviners find out from those who consult them all the circumstances

also the character and circumstances of the dreamer; so that the same dream-element will have a different meaning for a rich man, a married man, or, let us say, an orator, from what it has for a poor man, a bachelor, or a merchant. The essence of the decoding procedure, however, lies in the fact that the work of interpretation is not brought to bear on the dream as a whole but on each portion of the dream's content independently, as though the dream were a geological conglomerate in which each fragment of rock required a separate assessment. There can be no question that the invention of the decoding method of interpretation was suggested by disconnected and confused dreams.[4]

It cannot be doubted for a moment that neither of the two popular procedures for interpreting dreams can be employed for a scien-

---

which they consider essential in order to arrive at a right explanation. . . . In short, these dream-diviners do not allow a single point to escape them and only give their interpretation after they have completely mastered the replies to all the necessary enquiries.] Among these enquiries are habitually included questions as to the dreamer's closest family relations—his parents, wife, and children—as well as such a typical formula as: "Habuistine in hac nocte copulam conjugalem ante vel post somnium?" [Did you copulate with your wife that night before or after you had the dream?]—"L'idée dominante dans l'interprétation des songes consiste à expliquer le rêve par son opposée." [The principal idea in interpreting dreams lies in explaining a dream by its opposite.]

4. [*Footnote added* 1909:] Dr. Alfred Robitsek has pointed out to me that the oriental "dream-books" (of which ours are wretched imitations) base the greater number of their interpretations of dream-elements upon similarity of sounds and resemblance between words. The fact that these connections inevitably disappear in translation accounts for the unintelligibility of the renderings in our own popular dream-books. The extraordinarily important part played by punning and verbal quibbles in the ancient civilizations of the East may be studied in the writings of Hugo Winckler [the famous archaeologist].—[*Added* 1911:] The nicest instance of a dream-interpretation which has reached us from ancient times is based on a play upon words. It is told by Artemidorus [book 4, chap. 24; Krauss's translation, 1881, 255]: "I think too that Aristander gave a most happy interpretation to Alexander of Macedon when he had surrounded Tyre [Τύρος] and was besieging it but was feeling uneasy and disturbed because of the length of time the siege was taking. Alexander dreamt he saw a satyr [σάτυρος] dancing on his shield. Aristander happened to be in the neighborhood of Tyre, in attendance on the king during his Syrian campaign. By dividing the word for satyr into σά and τύρος he encouraged the king to press home the siege so that he became master of the city." (σὰ Τύρος = Tyre is thine.)— Indeed, dreams are so closely related to linguistic expression that Ferenczi [1910] has truly remarked that every tongue has its own dream-language. It is impossible as a rule to translate a dream into a foreign language and this is equally true, I fancy, of a book such as the present one. [*Added* 1930:] Nevertheless, Dr. A. A.

tific treatment of the subject. The symbolic method is restricted in its application and incapable of being laid down on general lines. In the case of the decoding method everything depends on the trustworthiness of the "key"—the dream-book, and of this we have no guarantee. Thus one might feel tempted to agree with the philosophers and the psychiatrists and, like them, rule out the problem of dream-interpretation as a purely fanciful task.[5]

But I have been taught better. I have been driven to realize that here once more we have one of those not infrequent cases in which an ancient and jealously held popular belief seems to be nearer the truth than the judgment of the prevalent science of today. I must affirm that dreams really have a meaning and that a scientific procedure for interpreting them is possible

My knowledge of that procedure was reached in the following manner. I have been engaged for many years (with a therapeutic aim in view) in unraveling certain psychopathological structures— hysterical phobias, obsessional ideas, and so on. I have been doing so, in fact, ever since I learned from an important communication by Josef Breuer that as regards these structures (which are looked on as pathological symptoms) unraveling them coincides with removing them.[6] (Cf. Breuer and Freud, 1895). If a pathological idea of this sort can be traced back to the elements in the patient's mental life from which it originated, it simultaneously crumbles away and the patient is freed from it. Considering the impotence of our other therapeutic efforts and the puzzling nature of these disorders, I felt tempted to follow the path marked out by Breuer, in spite of every difficulty, till a complete explanation was reached. I shall have on another occasion to report at length upon the form finally taken by this procedure and the results of my labors. It was in the course of these psychoanalytic studies that I came upon dream-interpretation. My patients were pledged to communicate

---

Brill of New York, and others after him, have succeeded in translating *The Interpretation of Dreams*.

5. After I had completed my manuscript I came across a work by Stumpf (1899) which agrees with my views in seeking to prove that dreams have a meaning and can be interpreted. He effects his interpretations, however, by means of a symbolism of an allegorical character without any guarantee of the general validity of his procedure.

6. *"Auflösung"* and *"Lösung"* in the original.

to me every idea or thought that occurred to them in connection with some particular subject; amongst other things they told me their dreams and so taught me that a dream can be inserted into the psychical chain that has to be traced backwards in the memory from a pathological idea. It was then only a short step to treating the dream itself as a symptom and to applying to dreams the method of interpretation that had been worked out for symptoms.

This involves some psychological preparation of the patient. We must aim at bringing about two changes in him: an increase in the attention he pays to his own psychical perceptions and the elimination of the criticism by which he normally sifts the thoughts that occur to him. In order that he may be able to concentrate his attention on his self-observation it is an advantage for him to lie in a restful attitude and shut his eyes.[7] It is necessary to insist explicitly on his renouncing all criticism of the thoughts that he perceives. We therefore tell him that the success of the psychoanalysis depends on his noticing and reporting whatever comes into his head and not being misled, for instance, into suppressing an idea because it strikes him as unimportant or irrelevant or because it seems to him meaningless. He must adopt a completely impartial attitude to what occurs to him, since it is precisely his critical attitude which is responsible for his being unable, in the ordinary course of things, to achieve the desire unraveling of his dream or obsessional idea or whatever it may be.

I have noticed in my psychoanalytical work that the whole frame of mind of a man who is reflecting is totally different from that of a man who is observing his own psychical processes. In reflection there is one more psychical activity at work than in the most attentive self-observation, and this is shown amongst other things by the tense looks and wrinkled forehead of a person pursuing his reflections as compared with the restful expression of a self-observer. In both cases attention must be concentrated, but the man who is reflecting is also exercising his *critical* faculty; this leads him to reject some of the ideas that occur to him after perceiving them, to cut short others without following the trains of

---

7. The stress upon the advisability of shutting the eyes (a remnant of the old hypnotic procedure) was very soon dropped. See, for instance, the account of psychoanalytic technique in Freud (1904a), where it is specifically mentioned that the analyst does *not* ask the patient to shut his eyes.

thought which they would open up to him, and to behave in such a way toward still others that they never become conscious at all and are accordingly suppressed before being perceived. The self-observer on the other hand need only take the trouble to suppress his critical faculty. If he succeeds in doing that, innumerable ideas come into his consciousness of which he could otherwise never have got hold. The material which is in this way freshly obtained for his self-perception makes it possible to interpret both his pathological ideas and his dream-structures. What is in question, evidently, is the establishment of a psychical state which, in its distribution of psychical energy (that is, of mobile attention), bears some analogy to the state before falling asleep—and no doubt also to hypnosis. As we fall asleep, "involuntary ideas" emerge, owing to the relaxation of a certain deliberate (and no doubt also critical) activity which we allow to influence the course of our ideas while we are awake. (We usually attribute this relaxation to "fatigue.") As the involuntary ideas emerge they change into visual and acoustic images. (Cf. the remarks by Schleiermacher and others quoted above on pp. 49 f. [and 71 f.].)[8] In the state used for the analysis of dreams and pathological ideas, the patient purposely and deliberately abandons this activity and employs the psychical energy thus saved (or a portion of it) in attentively following the involuntary thoughts which now emerge, and which—and here the situation differs from that of falling asleep—retain the character of ideas. *In this way the "involuntary" ideas are transformed into "voluntary" ones.*

The adoption[9] of the required attitude of mind toward ideas that seem to emerge "of their own free will" and the abandonment of the critical function that is normally in operation against them seem to be hard of achievement for some people. The "involuntary thoughts" are liable to release a most violent resistance, which seeks to prevent their emergence. If we may trust that great poet and philosopher Friedrich Schiller, however, poetic creation must demand an exactly similar attitude. In a passage in his correspon-

---

8. [*Footnote added* 1919:] Silberer (1909, 1910, and 1912) has made important contributions to dream-interpretation by directly observing this transformation of ideas into visual images.

9. This paragraph was added in 1909, and the first sentence of the next paragraph modified accordingly.

dence with Körner—we have to thank Otto Rank for unearthing it—Schiller (writing on December 1, 1788) replies to his friend's complaint of insufficient productivity: "The ground for your complaint seems to me to lie in the constraint imposed by your reason upon your imagination. I will make my idea more concrete by a simile. It seems a bad thing and detrimental to the creative work of the mind if Reason makes too close an examination of the ideas as they come pouring in—at the very gateway, as it were. Looked at in isolation, a thought may seem very trivial or very fantastic; but it may be made important by another thought that comes after it, and, in conjunction with other thoughts that may seem equally absurd, it may turn out to form a most effective link. Reason cannot form any opinion upon all this unless it retains the thought long enough to look at it in connection with the others. On the other hand, where there is a creative mind, Reason—so it seems to me—relaxes its watch upon the gates, and the ideas rush in pell-mell, and only then does it look them through and examine them in a mass.—You critics, or whatever else you may call yourselves, are ashamed or frightened of the momentary and transient extravagances which are to be found in all truly creative minds and whose longer or shorter duration distinguishes the thinking artist from the dreamer. You complain of your unfruitfulness because you reject too soon and discriminate too severely."

Nevertheless, what Schiller describes as a relaxation of the watch upon the gates of Reason, the adoption of an attitude of uncritical self-observation, is by no means difficult. Most of my patients achieve it after their first instructions. I myself can do so very completely, by the help of writing down my ideas as they occur to me. The amount of psychical energy by which it is possible to reduce critical activity and increase the intensity of self-observation varies considerably according to the subject on which one is trying to fix one's attention.

Our first step in the employment of this procedure teaches us that what we must take as the object of our attention is not the dream as a whole but the separate portions of its content. If I say to a patient who is still a novice: "What occurs to you in connection with this dream?," as a rule his mental horizon becomes a blank. If, however, I put the dream before him cut up into pieces, he will give me a series of associations to each piece, which might be described as the "background thoughts" of that particular part of the dream. Thus the method of dream-interpretation which I practice already differs in this first important respect from the popular, historic, and legendary method of interpretation by means of symbolism and approximates to the second or "decoding" method. Like the latter, it employs interpretation *en détail* and not *en masse;* like the latter, it regards dreams from the very first as being of a composite character, as being conglomerates of psychical formations.[10]

In the course of my psychoanalyses of neurotics I must already have analyzed over a thousand dreams; but I do not propose to make use of this material in my present introduction to the technique and theory of dream-interpretation. Apart from the fact that such a course would be open to the objection that these are the dreams of neuropaths, from which no valid inferences could be made as to the dreams of normal people, there is quite another reason which forces this decision upon me. The subject to which these dreams of my patients lead up is always, of course, the case history which underlies their neurosis. Each dream would therefore necessitate a lengthy introduction and an investigation of the nature and etiological determinants of the psychoneuroses. But these questions are in themselves novelties and highly bewildering and would distract attention from the problem of dreams. On the contrary, it is my intention to make use of my present elucidation of dreams as a preliminary step toward solving the more difficult problems of the psychology of the neuroses.[11] If, however, I forego my principal material, the dreams of my neurotic patients, I must not be too particular about what is left to me. All that remains are such dreams as have been reported to me from time to time by normal persons of my acquaintance, and such others as have been

---

10. The technique of dream-interpretation is further discussed below. See also the first two sections of Freud (1923c). The quite other question of the part played by dream-interpretation in the technique of therapeutic psychoanalysis is considered in Freud (1911e).

11. At the beginning of section E of chapter 7, Freud reflects upon the difficulties imposed upon his exposition of the subject by this program, which is already laid down in his preface to the first edition. As he points out on p. 146 and again on p. 151 *n.*, he is often led into disregarding it. In spite of his declared intention, he makes use of many of his patients' dreams, and more than once enters into a discussion of the mechanism of neurotic symptoms.

quoted as instances in the literature dealing with dream-life. Un-luckily, however, none of these dreams are accompanied by the analysis without which I cannot discover a dream's meaning. My procedure is not so convenient as the popular decoding method which translates any given piece of a dream's content by a fixed key. I, on the contrary, am prepared to find that the same piece of content may conceal a different meaning when it occurs in various people or in various contexts. Thus it comes about that I am led to my own dreams, which offer a copious and convenient material, derived from an approximately normal person and relating to multifarious occasions of daily life. No doubt I shall be met by doubts of the trustworthiness of "self-analyses" of this kind; and I shall be told that they leave the door open to arbitrary conclu-sions. In my judgment the situation is in fact more favorable in the case of *self*-observation than in that of other people; at all events we may make the experiment and see how far self-analysis takes us with the interpretation of dreams. But I have other difficulties to overcome, which lie within myself. There is some natural hesitation about revealing so many intimate facts about one's mental life; nor can there be any guarantee against misinterpretation by strangers. But it must be possible to overcome such hesitations. "Tout psycho-logiste," writes Delbœuf [1885], "est obligé de faire l'aveu même de ses faiblesses s'il croit par là jeter du jour sur quelque problème obscur."[12] And it is safe to assume that my readers too will very soon find their initial interest in the indiscretions which I am bound to make replaced by an absorbing immersion in the psychological problems upon which they throw light.[13]

Accordingly I shall proceed to choose out one of my own dreams and demonstrate upon it my method of interpretation. In the case of every such dream some remarks by way of preamble will be necessary.—And now I must ask the reader to make my interests his own for quite a while, and to plunge, along with me, into the minutest details of my life; for a transference of this kind is peremptorily demanded by our interest in the hidden meaning of dreams.

---

12. Every psychologist is under an obligation to confess even his own weak-nesses, if he thinks that it may throw light upon some obscure problem.

13. I am obliged to add, however, by way of qualification of what I have said above, that in scarcely any instance have I brought forward the *complete* interpreta-

Preamble

During the summer of 1895 I had been giving psychoanalytic treatment to a young lady who was on very friendly terms with me and my family. It will be readily understood that a mixed relationship such as this may be a source of many disturbed feelings in a physician and particularly in a psychotherapist. While the physician's personal interest is greater, his authority is less; any failure would bring a threat to the old-established friendship with the patient's family. This treatment had ended in a partial success; the patient was relieved of her hysterical anxiety but did not lose all her somatic symptoms. At that time I was not yet quite clear in my mind as to the criteria indicating that a hysterical case history was finally closed, and I proposed a solution to the patient which she seemed unwilling to accept. While we were thus at variance, we had broken off the treatment for the summer vacation.—One day I had a visit from a junior colleague, one of my oldest friends, who had been staying with my patient, Irma, and her family at their country resort. I asked him how he had found her and he answered: "She's better, but not quite well." I was conscious that my friend Otto's words, or the tone in which he spoke them, annoyed me. I fancied I detected a reproof in them, such as to the effect that I had promised the patient too much; and, whether rightly or wrongly, I attributed the supposed fact of Otto's siding against me to the influence of my patient's relatives, who, as it seemed to me, had never looked with favor on the treatment. However, my disagreeable impression was not clear to me and I gave no outward sign of it. The same evening I wrote out Irma's case history, with the idea of giving it to Dr. M. (a common friend who as at that time the leading figure in our circle) in order to justify myself. That night (or more probably the next morning) I had the following dream, which I noted down immediately after waking.[14]

---

tion of one of my own dreams, as it is known to me. I have probably been wise in not putting too much faith in my readers' discretion.

14. [*Footnote added* 1914:] This is the first dream which I submitted to a detailed interpretation. [Freud describes some first groping attempts at the analysis of his own dreams in *Studies on Hysteria* (Breuer and Freud, 1895). They will be found mentioned in the course of the long footnote attached to the entry of May 15 in the Case History of Frau Emmy von N.]

Dream of July 23rd–24th, 1895

A large hall—numerous guests, whom we were receiving.—Among them was Irma. I at once took her on one side, as though to answer her letter and to reproach her for not having accepted my "solution" yet. I said to her: "If you still get pains, it's really only your fault." She replied: "If you only knew what pains I've got now in my throat and stomach and abdomen—it's choking me"—I was alarmed and looked at her. She looked pale and puffy. I thought to myself that after all I must be missing some organic trouble. I took her to the window and looked down her throat, and she showed signs of recalcitrance, like women with artificial dentures. I thought to myself that there was really no need for her to do that.—She then opened her mouth properly and on the right I found a big white[15] patch; at another place I saw extensive whitish grey scabs upon some remarkable curly structures which were evidently modeled on the turbinal bones of the nose.—I at once called in Dr. M., and he repeated the examination and confirmed it. . . . Dr. M. looked quite different from usual; he was very pale, he walked with a limp and his chin was clean-shaven. . . . My friend Otto was now standing beside her as well, and my friend Leopold was percussing her through her bodice and saying: "She has a dull area low down on the left." He also indicated that a portion of the skin on the left shoulder was infiltrated. (I noticed this, just as he did, in spite of her dress.) . . . M. said: "There's no doubt it's an infection, but no matter; dysentery will supervene and the toxin will be eliminated." . . . We were directly aware, too, of the origin of the infection. Not long before, when she was feeling unwell, my friend Otto had given her an injection of a preparation of propyl, propyls . . . propionic acid . . . trimethylamin (and I saw before me the formula for this printed in heavy type). . . . Injections of that sort ought not to be made so thoughtlessly. . . . And probably the syringe had not been clean.

This dream has one advantage over many others. It was immediately clear what events of the previous day provided its starting-point. My preamble makes that plain. The news which Otto had given me of Irma's condition and the case history which I had been

---

15. The word *white* is omitted, no doubt accidentally, in the 1942 edition only.

engaged in writing till far into the night continued to occupy my mental activity even after I was asleep. Nevertheless, no one who had only read the preamble and the content of the dream itself could have the slightest notion of what the dream meant. I myself had no notion. I was astonished at the symptoms of which Irma complained to me in the dream, since they were not the same as those for which I had treated her. I smiled at the senseless idea of an injection of propionic acid and at Dr. M.'s consoling reflections. Toward its end the dream seemed to me to be more obscure and compressed than it was at the beginning. In order to discover the meaning of all this it was necessary to undertake a detailed analysis.

Analysis

The hall—numerous guests, whom we were receiving. We were spending that summer at Bellevue, a house standing by itself on one of the hills adjoining the Kahlenberg.[16] The house had formerly been designed as a place of entertainment and its reception-rooms were in consequence unusually lofty and hall-like. It was at Bellevue that I had the dream, a few days before my wife's birthday. On the previous day my wife had told me that she expected that a number of friends, including Irma, would be coming out to visit us on her birthday. My dream was thus anticipating this occasion: it was my wife's birthday and a number of guests, including Irma, were being received by us in the large hall at Bellevue.

I reproached Irma for not having accepted my solution; I said: "If you still get pains, it's your own fault." I might have said this to her in waking life, and I may actually have done so. It was my view at that time (though I have since recognized it as a wrong one) that my task was fulfilled when I had informed a patient of the hidden meaning of his symptoms: I considered that I was not responsible for whether he accepted the solution or not—though this was what success depended on. I owe it to this mistake, which I have now fortunately corrected, that my life was made easier at a time when, in spite of all my inevitable ignorance, I was expected to produce therapeutic successes.—I noticed, however, that the words which I spoke to Irma in the dream showed that I was

---

16. A hill which is a favorite resort in the immediate neighborhood of Vienna.

specially anxious not to be responsible for the pains which she still had. If they were her fault they could not be mine. Could it be that the purpose of the dream lay in this direction?

Irma's complaint: pains in her throat and abdomen and stomach; it was choking her. Pains in the stomach were among my patient's symptoms but were not very prominent; she complained more of feelings of nausea and disgust. Pains in the throat and abdomen and constriction of the throat played scarcely any part in her illness. I wondered why I decided upon this choice of symptoms in the dream but could not think of an explanation at the moment.

She looked pale and puffy. My patient always had a rosy complexion. I began to suspect that someone else was being substituted for her.

I was alarmed at the idea that I had missed an organic illness. This, as may well be believed, is a perpetual source of anxiety to a specialist whose practice is almost limited to neurotic patients and who is in the habit of attributing to hysteria a great number of symptoms which other physicians treat as organic. On the other hand, a faint doubt crept into my mind—from where, I could not tell—that my alarm was not entirely genuine. If Irma's pains had an organic basis, once again I could not be held responsible for curing them; my treatment only set out to get rid of *hysterical* pains. It occurred to me, in fact, that I was actually *wishing* that there had been a wrong diagnosis; for, if so, the blame for my lack of success would also have been got rid of.

I took her to the window to look down her throat. She showed some recalcitrance, like women with false teeth. I thought to myself that really there was no need for her to do that. I had never had any occasion to examine Irma's oral cavity. What happened in the dream reminded me of an examination I had carried out some time before of a governess: at a first glance she had seemed a picture of youthful beauty, but when it came to opening her mouth she had taken measures to conceal her plates. This led to recollections of other medical examinations and of little secrets revealed in the course of them—to the satisfaction of neither party. *"There was really no need for her to do that"* was no doubt intended in the first place as a compliment to Irma; but I suspected that it had another meaning besides. (If one carries out an analysis attentively, one gets a feeling of whether or not one has exhausted all the background thoughts that are to be expected.) The way in which

Irma stood by the window suddenly reminded me of another experience. Irma had an intimate woman friend of whom I had a very high opinion. When I visited this lady one evening I had found her by a window in the situation reproduced in the dream, and her physician, the same Dr. M., had pronounced that she had a diphtheritic membrane. The figure of Dr. M. and the membrane reappear later in the dream. It now occurred to me that for the last few months I had had every reason to suppose that this other lady was also a hysteric. Indeed, Irma herself had betrayed the fact to me. What did I know of her condition? One thing precisely: that, like my Irma of the dream, she suffered from hysterical choking. So in the dream I had replaced my patient by her friend. I now recollected that I had often played with the idea that she too might ask me to relieve her of her symptoms. I myself, however, had thought this unlikely, since she was of a very reserved nature. She was *recalcitrant,* as was shown in the dream. Another reason was that *there was no need for her to do it:* she had so far shown herself strong enough to master her condition without outside help. There still remained a few features that I could not attach either to Irma or to her friend: *pale; puffy; false teeth.* The false teeth took me to the governess whom I have already mentioned; I now felt inclined to be satisfied with *bad* teeth. I then thought of someone else to whom these features might be alluding. She again was not one of my patients, nor should I have liked to have her as a patient, since I had noticed that she was bashful in my presence and I could not think she would make an amenable patient. She was usually pale, and once, while she had been in specially good health, she had looked puffy.[17] Thus I had been comparing my patient Irma with two other people who would also have been recalcitrant to treatment. What could the reason have been for my having exchanged her in the dream for her friend? Perhaps it was that I should have *liked* to exchange her: either I felt more sympathetic toward her friend or had a higher opinion of her intelligence. For

---

17. The still unexplained complaint about *pains in the abdomen* could also be traced back to this third figure. The person in question was, of course, my own wife; the pains in the abdomen reminded me of one of the occasions on which I had noticed her bashfulness. I was forced to admit to myself that I was not treating either Irma or my wife very kindly in this dream; but it should be observed by way of excuse that I was measuring them both by the standard of the good and amenable patient.

Irma seemed to me foolish because she had not accepted my solution. Her friend would have been wiser, that is to say she would have yielded sooner. She would then have *opened her mouth properly,* and have told me more than Irma.[18]

What I saw in her throat: a white patch and turbinal bones with scabs on them. The white patch reminded me of diphtheritis and so of Irma's friend, but also of a serious illness of my eldest daughter's almost two years earlier and of the fright I had had in those anxious days. The scabs on the turbinal bones recalled a worry about my own state of health. I was making frequent use of cocaine at that time to reduce some troublesome nasal swellings, and I had heard a few days earlier that one of my women patients who had followed my example had developed an extensive necrosis of the nasal mucous membrane. I had been the first to recommend the use of cocaine, in 1885,[19] and this recommendation had brought serious reproaches down on me. The misuse of that drug had hastened the death of a dear friend of mine. This had been before 1895 [the date of the dream].

I at once called in Dr. M., and he repeated the examination. This simply corresponded to the position occupied by M. in our circle. But the *"at once"* was sufficiently striking to require a special explanation. It reminded me of a tragic event in my practice. I had on one occasion produced a severe toxic state in a woman patient by repeatedly prescribing what was at that time regarded as a harmless remedy (sulfonal), and had hurriedly turned for assistance and support to my experienced senior colleague. There was a subsidiary detail which confirmed the idea that I had this incident in mind. My patient—who succumbed to the poison—had the same name as my eldest daughter. It had never occurred to me before,

---

18. I had a feeling that the interpretation of this part of the dream was not carried far enough to make it possible to follow the whole of its concealed meaning. If I had pursued my comparison between the three women, it would have taken me far afield.—There is at least one spot in every dream at which it is unplumbable—a navel, as it were, that is its point of contact with the unknown.

19. This is a misprint (which occurs in every German edition) for "1884," the date of Freud's first paper on cocaine. A full account of Freud's work in connection with cocaine will be found in chapter 6 of the first volume of Ernest Jones's life of Freud. From this it appears that the "dear friend" was Fleischl von Marxow (see p. 482 *n.*). Further indirect allusions to this episode will be found on pp. 170f., 206, 216f. and 484.

but it struck me now almost like an act of retribution on the part of destiny. It was as though the replacement of one person by another was to be continued in another sense: this Mathilde for that Mathilde, an eye for an eye and a tooth for a tooth. It seemed as if I had been collecting all the occasions which I could bring up against myself as evidence of lack of medical conscientiousness.

Dr. M. was pale, had a clean-shaven chin and walked with a limp. This was true to the extent that his unhealthy appearance often caused his friends anxiety. The two other features could only apply to someone else. I thought of my elder brother, who lives abroad, who is clean-shaven and whom, if I remembered right, the M. of the dream closely resembled. We had had news a few days earlier that he was walking with a limp owing to an arthritic affection of his hip. There must, I reflected, have been some reason for my fusing into one the two figures in the dream. I then remembered that I had a similar reason for being in an ill-humor with each of them: they had both rejected a certain suggestion I had recently laid before them.

My friend Otto was now standing beside the patient and my friend Leopold was examining her and indicated that there was a dull area low down on the left. My friend Leopold was also a physician and a relative of Otto's. Since they both specialized in the same branch of medicine, it was their fate to be in competition with each other, and comparisons were constantly being drawn between them. Both of them acted as my assistants for years while I was still in charge of the neurological outpatients' department of a children's hospital.[20] Scenes such as the one represented in the dream used often to occur there. While I was discussing the diagnosis of a case with Otto, Leopold would be examining the child once more and would make an unexpected contribution to our decision. The difference between their characters was like that between the bailiff Bräsig and his friend Karl:[21] one was distinguished for his quickness, while the other was slow but sure. If in the dream I was contrasting Otto with the prudent Leopold, I was evidently doing

---

20. For details of this hospital see section 2 of Kris's introduction to the Fliess correspondence (Freud, 1950a).

21. The two chief figures in the once popular novel, *Ut mine Stromtid*, written in Mecklenburg dialect, by Fritz Reuter (1862–64). There is an English translation, *An Old Story of My Farming Days* (London, 1878).

so to the advantage of the latter. The comparison was similar to the one between my disobedient patient Irma and the friend whom I regarded as wiser than she was. I now perceived another of the lines along which the chain of thought in the dream branched off: from the sick child to the children's hospital.—*The dull area low down on the left* seemed to me to agree in every detail with one particular case in which Leopold had struck me by his thoroughness. I also had a vague notion of something in the nature of a metastatic affection; but this may also have been a reference to the patient whom I should have liked to have in the place of Irma. So far as I had been able to judge, she had produced an imitation of a tuberculosis.

A portion of the skin on the left shoulder was infiltrated. I saw at once that this was the rheumatism in my own shoulder, which I invariably notice if I sit up late into the night. Moreover, the wording in the dream was most ambiguous: "*I noticed this, just as he did. . . .*" I noticed it in my own body, that is. I was struck, too, by the unusual phrasing: "a portion of the skin was infiltrated." We are in the habit of speaking of "a left upper posterior infiltration," and this would refer to the lung and so once more to tuberculosis.

In spite of her dress. This was in any case only an interpolation. We naturally used to examine the children in the hospital undressed: and this would be a contrast to the manner in which adult female patients have to be examined. I remembered that it was said of a celebrated clinician that he never made a physical examination of his patients except through their clothes. Further than this I could not see. Frankly, I had no desire to penetrate more deeply at this point.

Dr. M. said: "It's an infection, but no matter. Dysentery will supervene and the toxin will be eliminated." At first this struck me as ridiculous. But nevertheless, like all the rest, it had to be carefully analyzed. When I came to look at it more closely it seemed to have some sort of meaning all the same. What I discovered in the patient was a local diphtheritis. I remembered from the time of my daughter's illness a discussion on diphtheritis and diphtheria, the latter being the general infection that arises from the local diphtheritis. Leopold indicated the presence of a general infection of this kind from the existence of a dull area, which might thus be regarded as a metastatic focus. I seemed to think, it is true, that metastases like this do not in fact occur with diphtheria: it made me think rather of pyemia.

No matter. This was intended as a consolation. It seemed to fit into the context as follows. The content of the preceding part of the dream had been that my patient's pains were due to a severe organic affection. I had a feeling that I was only trying in that way to shift the blame from myself. Psychological treatment could not be held responsible for the persistence of diphtheritic pains. Nevertheless I had a sense of awkwardness at having invented such a severe illness for Irma simply in order to clear myself. It looked so cruel. Thus I was in need of an assurance that all would be well in the end, and it seemed to me that to have put the consolation into the mouth precisely of Dr. M. had not been a bad choice. But here I was taking up a superior attitude toward the dream, and this itself required explanation.

And why was the consolation so nonsensical?

Dysentery. There seemed to be some remote theoretical notion that morbid matter can be eliminated through the bowels. Could it be that I was trying to make fun of Dr. M.'s fertility in producing far-fetched explanations and making unexpected pathological connections? Something else now occurred to me in relation to dysentery. A few months earlier I had taken on the case of a young man with remarkable difficulties associated with defecating, who had been treated by other physicians as a case of "anemia accompanied by malnutrition." I had recognized it as a hysteria, but had been unwilling to try him with my psychotherapeutic treatment and had sent him on a sea voyage. Some days before, I had had a despairing letter from him from Egypt, saying that he had had a fresh attack there which a doctor declared was dysentery. I suspected that the diagnosis was an error on the part of an ignorant practitioner who had allowed himself to be taken in by the hysteria. But I could not help reproaching myself for having put my patient in a situation in which he might have contracted some organic trouble on top of his hysterical intestinal disorder. Moreover, "dysentery" sounds not unlike "diphtheria"—a word of ill omen which did not occur in the dream.[22]

---

22. The German words *Dysenterie* and *Diphtherie* are more alike than the English ones.

Yes, I thought to myself, I must have been making fun of Dr. M. with the consoling prognosis "Dysentery will supervene, etc.": for it came back to me that, years before, he himself had told an amusing story of a similar kind about another doctor. Dr. M. had been called in by him for consultation over a patient who was seriously ill, and had felt obliged to point out, in view of the very optimistic view taken by his colleague, that he had found albumen in the patient's urine. The other, however, was not in the least put out: "*No matter,*" he had said, "the albumen will soon be eliminated!"—I could no longer feel any doubt, therefore, that this part of the dream was expressing derision at physicians who are ignorant of hysteria. And, as though to confirm this, a further idea crossed my mind: "Does Dr. M. realize that the symptoms in his patient (Irma's friend) which give grounds for fearing tuberculosis also have a hysterical basis? Has he spotted this hysteria? or has he been taken in by it?"

But what could be my motive for treating this friend of mine so badly? That was a very simple matter. Dr. M. was just as little in agreement with my "solution" as Irma herself. So I had already revenged myself in this dream on two people: on Irma with the words "If you still get pains, it's your own fault," and on Dr. M. by the wording of the nonsensical consolation that I put into his mouth.

We were directly aware of the origin of the infection. This direct knowledge in the dream was remarkable. Only just before we had had no knowledge of it, for the infection was only revealed by Leopold.

When she was feeling unwell, my friend Otto had given her an injection. Otto had in fact told me that during his short stay with Irma's family he had been called in to a neighboring hotel to give an injection to someone who had suddenly felt unwell. These injections reminded me once more of my unfortunate friend who had poisoned himself with cocaine. I had advised him to use the drug internally [i.e., orally] only, while morphia was being withdrawn; but he had at once given himself cocaine *injections.*

A preparation of propyl . . . propyls . . . propionic acid. How could I have come to think of this? During the previous evening, before I wrote out the case history and had the dream, my wife had opened a bottle of liqueur, on which the word *Ananas*[23] ap-

---

23. I must add that the sound of the word *Ananas* bears a remarkable resemblance to that of my patient Irma's family name.

peared and which was a gift from our friend Otto: for he has a habit of making presents on every possible occasion. It was to be hoped, I thought to myself, that some day he would find a wife to cure him of the habit.[24] This liqueur gave off such a strong smell of fusel oil that I refused to touch it. My wife suggested our giving the bottle to the servants, but I—with even greater prudence—vetoed the suggestion, adding in a philanthropic spirit that there was no need for *them* to be poisoned either. The smell of fusel oil (amyl . . .) evidently stirred up in my mind a recollection of the whole series—propyl, methyl, and so on—and this accounted for the propyl preparation in the dream. It is true that I carried out a substitution in the process: I dreamt of propyl after having smelt amyl. But substitutions of this kind are perhaps legitimate in organic chemistry.

Trimethylamin. I saw the chemical formula of this substance in my dream, which bears witness to a great effort on the part of my memory. Moreover, the formula was printed in heavy type, as though there had been a desire to lay emphasis on some part of the context as being of quite special importance. What was it, then, to which my attention was to be directed in this way by trimethylamin? It was to a conversation with another friend who had for many years been familiar with all my writings during the period of their gestation, just as I had been with his.[25] He had at that time confided some ideas to me on the subject of the chemistry of the sexual processes, and had mentioned among other things that he believed that one of the products of sexual metabolism was trimethylamin. Thus this substance led me to sexuality, the factor to which I attributed the greatest importance in the origin of the nervous disorders which it was my aim to cure. My patient Irma was a young widow; if I wanted to find an excuse for the failure of my treatment in her case, what I could best appeal to would no doubt be this fact of her widowhood, which her friends would be so glad to see changed. And how strangely, I thought to myself, a

24. [*Footnote added* 1909, but omitted again from 1925 onwards:] In this respect the dream did not turn out to be prophetic. But in another respect it *was*. For my patient's "unsolved" gastric pains, for which I was so anxious not to be blamed, turned out to be the forerunners of a serious disorder caused by gallstones.

25. This was Wilhelm Fliess, the Berlin biologist and nose and throat specialist, who exercised a great influence on Freud during the years immediately preceding the publication of this book, and who figures frequently, though as a rule anonymously, in its pages. See Freud (1950*a*).

dream like this is put together! The other woman, whom I had as a patient in the dream instead of Irma, was also a young widow.

I began to guess why the formula for trimethylamin had been so prominent in the dream. So many important subjects converged upon that one word. Trimethylamin was an allusion not only to the immensely powerful factor of sexuality, but also to a person whose agreement I recalled with satisfaction whenever I felt isolated in my opinions. Surely this friend who played so large a part in my life must appear again elsewhere in these trains of thought. Yes. For he had a special knowledge of the consequences of affections of the nose and its accessory cavities; and he had drawn scientific attention to some very remarkable connections between the turbinal bones and the female organs of sex. (Cf. the three curly structures in Irma's throat.) I had had Irma examined by him to see whether her gastric pains might be of nasal origin. But he suffered himself from suppurative rhinitis, which caused me anxiety; and no doubt there was an allusion to this in the pyaemia which vaguely came into my mind in connection with the metastases in the dream.[26]

Injections of that sort ought not to be made so thoughtlessly. Here an accusation of thoughtlessness was being made directly against my friend Otto. I seemed to remember thinking something of the same kind that afternoon when his words and looks had appeared to show that he was siding against me. It had been some such notion as: "How easily his thoughts are influenced! How thoughtlessly he jumps to conclusions!"—Apart from this, this sentence in the dream reminded me once more of my dead friend who had so hastily resorted to cocaine injections. As I have said, I had never contemplated the drug being given by injection. I noticed too that in accusing Otto of thoughtlessness in handling chemical substances I was once more touching upon the story of the unfortunate Mathilde, which gave grounds for the same accusation against myself. Here I was evidently collecting instances of my conscientiousness, but also of the reverse.

And probably the syringe had not been clean. This was yet another accusation against Otto, but derived from a different source.

---

26. The analysis of this part of the dream is further elaborated below. It had already been used by Freud as an example of the mechanism of displacement in section 21 of part 1 of his very early "Project for a Scientific Psychology," written in the autumn of 1895 and printed as an appendix to Freud (1950a).

I had happened the day before to meet the son of an old lady of eighty-two, to whom I had to give an injection of morphia twice a day.[27] At the moment she was in the country and he told me that she was suffering from phlebitis. I had at once thought it must be an infiltration caused by a dirty syringe. I was proud of the fact that in two years I had not caused a single infiltration; I took constant pains to be sure that the syringe was clean. In short, I was conscientious. The phlebitis brought me back once more to my wife, who had suffered from thrombosis during one of her pregnancies; and now three similar situations came to my recollection involving my wife, Irma, and the dead Mathilde. The identity of these situations had evidently enabled me to substitute the three figures for one another in the dream.

I have now completed the interpretation of the dream.[28] While I was carrying it out I had some difficulty in keeping at bay all the ideas which were bound to be provoked by a comparison between the content of the dream and the concealed thoughts lying behind it. And in the meantime the "meaning" of the dream was borne in upon me. I became aware of an intention which was carried into effect by the dream and which must have been my motive for dreaming it. The dream fulfilled certain wishes which were started in me by the events of the previous evening (the news given me by Otto and my writing out of the case history). The conclusion of the dream, that is to say, was that I was not responsible for the persistence of Irma's pains, but that Otto was. Otto had in fact annoyed me by his remarks about Irma's incomplete cure, and the dream gave me my revenge by throwing the reproach back on to him. The dream acquitted me of the responsibility for Irma's condition by showing that it was due to other factors—it produced a whole series of reasons. The dream represented a particular state of affairs as I should have wished it to be. *Thus its content was the fulfillment of a wish and its motive was a wish.*

---

27. This old lady makes frequent appearances in Freud's writings at this period. See below, and *The Psychopathology of Everyday Life* (1901*b*), chapter 8(*b* and *g*) and chapter 12(C*b*). Her death is reported in a letter to Fliess of July 8, 1901 (Freud, 1950*a*, Letter 145).

28. [*Footnote added* 1909:] Though it will be understood that I have not reported everything that occurred to me during the process of interpretation.

Thus much leapt to the eyes. But many of the details of the dream also became intelligible to me from the point of view of wish fulfillment. Not only did I revenge myself on Otto for being too hasty in taking sides against me by representing him as being too hasty in his medical treatment (in giving the injection); but I also revenged myself on him for giving me the bad liqueur which had an aroma of fusel oil. And in the dream I found an expression which united the two reproaches: the injection was of a preparation of propyl. This did not satisfy me and I pursued my revenge further by contrasting him with his more trustworthy competitor. I seemed to be saying: "I like *him* better than *you*." But Otto was not the only person to suffer from the vials of my wrath. I took revenge as well on my disobedient patient by exchanging her for one who was wiser and less recalcitrant. Nor did I allow Dr. M. to escape the consequences of his contradiction but showed him by means of a clear allusion that he was an ignoramus on the subject. ("*Dysentery will supervene, etc.*") Indeed I seemed to be appealing from him to someone else with greater knowledge (to my friend who had told me of trimethylamin) just as I had turned from Irma to her friend and from Otto to Leopold. "Take these people away! Give me three others of my choice instead! Then I shall be free of these undeserved reproaches!" The groundlessness of the reproaches was proved for me in the dream in the most elaborate fashion. *I* was not to blame for Irma's pains, since she herself was to blame for them by refusing to accept my solution. *I* was not concerned with Irma's pains, since they were of an organic nature and quite incurable by psychological treatment. Irma's pains could be satisfactorily explained by her widowhood (cf. the trimethylamin) which *I* had no means of altering. Irma's pains had been caused by Otto giving her an incautious injection of an unsuitable drug—a thing *I* should never have done. Irma's pains were the result of an injection with a dirty needle, like my old lady's phlebitis—whereas *I* never did any harm with my injections. I noticed, it is true, that these explanations of Irma's pains (which agreed in exculpating me) were not entirely consistent with one another, and indeed that they were mutually exclusive. The whole plea—for the dream was nothing else—reminded one vividly of the defence put forward by the man who was charged by one of his neighbors with having given him back a borrowed kettle in a damaged condition. The defendant asserted first, that he had given it back undamaged;

secondly, that the kettle had a hole in it when he borrowed it; and thirdly, that he had never borrowed a kettle from his neighbor at all. So much the better: if only a single one of these three lines of defense were to be accepted as valid, the man would have to be acquitted.[29]

Certain other themes played a part in the dream, which were not so obviously connected with my exculpation from Irma's illness: my daughter's illness and that of my patient who bore the same name, the injurious effect of cocaine, the disorder of my patient who was traveling in Egypt, my concern about my wife's health and about that of my brother and of Dr. M., my own physical ailments, my anxiety about my absent friend who suffered from suppurative rhinitis. But when I came to consider all of these, they could all be collected into a single group of ideas and labeled, as it were, "concern about my own and other people's health—professional conscientiousness." I called to mind the obscure disagreeable impression I had had when Otto brought me the news of Irma's condition. This group of thoughts that played a part in the dream enabled me retrospectively to put this transient impression into words. It was as though he had said to me: "You don't take your medical duties seriously enough. You're not conscientious; you don't carry out what you've undertaken." Thereupon, this group of thoughts seemed to have put itself at my disposal, so that I could produce evidence of how highly conscientious I was, of how deeply I was concerned about the health of my relations, my friends, and my patients. It was a noteworthy fact that this material also included some disagreeable memories, which supported my friend Otto's accusation rather than my own vindication. The material was, as one might say, impartial; but nevertheless there was an unmistakable connection between this more extensive group of thoughts which underlay the dream and the narrower subject of the dream which gave rise to the wish to be innocent of Irma's illness.

I will not pretend that I have completely uncovered the meaning of this dream or that its interpretation is without a gap. I could spend much more time over it, derive further information from it and discuss fresh problems raised by it. I myself know the points

---

29. This anecdote is discussed by Freud in relation to this passage in chapter 2, section 8, and chapter 7, section 2, of his book on jokes. (Freud, 1905c.)

from which further trains of thought could be followed. But considerations which arise in the case of every dream of my own restrain me from pursuing my interpretative work. If anyone should feel tempted to express a hasty condemnation of my reticence, I would advise him to make the experiment of being franker than I am. For the moment I am satisfied with the achievement of this one piece of fresh knowledge. If we adopt the method of interpreting dreams which I have indicated here, we shall find that dreams really have a meaning and are far from being the expression of a fragmentary activity of the brain, as the authorities have claimed. *When the work of interpretation has been completed, we perceive that a dream is the fulfillment of a wish.*[30]

Translated by James Strachey

---

30. In a letter to Fliess on June 12, 1900 (Freud, 1950a, Letter 137), Freud describes a later visit to Bellevue, the house where he had this dream. "Do you suppose," he writes, "that some day a marble tablet will be placed on the house, inscribed with these words?—*In This House, on July 24, 1895, the Secret of Dreams was Revealed to Dr. Sigm. Freud.* At the moment there seems little prospect of it."

4

From On Dreams

1

During the epoch which may be described as prescientific, men had no difficulty in finding an explanation of dreams. When they remembered a dream after waking up, they regarded it as either a favorable or a hostile manifestation by higher powers, demonic and divine. When modes of thought belonging to natural science began to flourish, all this ingenious mythology was transformed into psychology, and today only a small minority of educated people doubt that dreams are a product of the dreamer's own mind.

Since the rejection of the mythological hypothesis, however, dreams have stood in need of explanation. The conditions of their origin, their relation to waking mental life, their dependence upon stimuli which force their way upon perception during the state of sleep, the many peculiarities of their content which are repugnant to waking thought, the inconsistency between their ideational images and the affects attaching to them, and lastly their transitory character, the manner in which waking thought pushes them on one side as something alien to it, and mutilates or extinguishes them in memory—all of these and other problems besides have been awaiting clarification for many hundreds of years, and till now no satisfactory solution of them has been advanced. But what stands in the foreground of our interest is the question of the *significance* of dreams, a question which bears a double sense. It enquires in the first place as to the psychical significance of dreaming, as to the relation of dreams to other mental processes, and as to any biological function that they may have; in the second place it seeks to discover whether dreams can be interpreted, whether the content of individual dreams has a "meaning," such as we are accustomed to find in other psychical structures.

In the assessment of the significance of dreams three lines of thought can be distinguished. One of these, which echoes, as it were, the ancient overvaluation of dreams, is expressed in the writings of certain philosophers. They consider that the basis of dream-life is a peculiar state of mental activity, and even go so far as to acclaim that state as an elevation to a higher level. For instance, Schubert [1814] declares that dreams are a liberation of the spirit from the power of external nature, and a freeing of the soul from the bonds of the senses. Other thinkers, without going so far as this, insist nevertheless that dreams arise essentially from mental impulses and represent manifestations of mental forces which have been prevented from expanding freely during the daytime. (Cf. the "dream imagination" of Scherner [1861, 97f.] and Volkelt [1875, 28f.].) A large number of observers agree in attributing to dream-life a capacity for superior functioning in certain departments at least (e.g., in memory).

In sharp contrast to this, the majority of medical writers adopt a view according to which dreams scarcely reach the level of being psychical phenomena at all. On their theory, the sole instigators of dreams are the sensory and somatic stimuli which either impinge upon the sleeper from outside or become active accidentally in his internal organs. What is dreamt, they contend, has no more claim to sense and meaning than, for instance the sounds which would be produced if "the ten fingers of a man who knows nothing of music were wandering over the keys of a piano." [Strümpell, 1877, 84.] Dreams are described by Binz [1878, 35] as being no more than "somatic processes which are in every case useless and in many cases positively pathological." All the characteristics of dream-life would thus be explained as being due to the disconnected activity of separate organs or groups of cells in an otherwise sleeping brain, an activity forced upon them by physiological stimuli.

Popular opinion is but little affected by this scientific judgment, and is not concerned as to the sources of dreams; it seems to persist in the belief that nevertheless dreams have a meaning, which relates to the prediction of the future and which can be discovered by some process of interpretation of a content which is often confused and puzzling. The methods of interpretation employed consist in transforming the content of the dream as it is remembered, either by replacing it piecemeal in accordance with a fixed key, or by replacing the dream as a whole by another whole to which it stands in a symbolic relation. Serious-minded people smile at these efforts: *"Träume sind Schäume"*—"dreams are froth."

* * *

4

We shall be inclined to suppose that a transformation of some such kind has occurred even in confused dreams, though we cannot tell whether what has been transformed was an optative in their case too. There are, however, two passages in the specimen dream which I have reported, and with whose analysis we have made some headway, that give us reason to suspect something of the kind. The analysis showed that my wife had concerned herself with some other people at table, and that I had found this disagreeable; the dream contained precisely the opposite of this—the person who took the place of my wife was turning her whole attention to me. But a disagreeable experience can give rise to no more suitable wish than that its opposite might have occurred—which was what the dream represented as fulfilled. There was an exactly similar relation between the bitter thought revealed in the analysis that I had never had anything free of cost and the remark made by the woman in the dream—"You've always had such beautiful eyes." Some part of the opposition between the manifest and latent content of dreams is thus attributable to wish fulfillment.

But another achievement of the dream-work, tending as it does to produce incoherent dreams, is even more striking. If in any particular instance we compare the number of ideational elements or the space taken up in writing them down in the case of the dream and of the dream-thoughts to which the analysis leads us and of which traces are to be found in the dream itself, we shall be left in no doubt that the dream-work has carried out a work of compression or *condensation* on a large scale. It is impossible at first to form any judgment of the degree of this condensation; but the deeper we plunge into a dream-analysis the more impressive it seems. From every element in a dream's content associative threads branch out in two or more directions; every situation in a dream seems to be put together out of two or more impressions or experiences. For instance, I once had a dream of a sort of swimming pool, in which the bathers were scattering in all directions; at one point on the edge of the pool someone was standing and bending toward one of the people bathing, as though to help her out of the water. The situation was put together from a memory of an experience I had had at puberty and from two paintings, one of which I had seen shortly before the dream. One was a picture from Schwind's series illustrating the legend of Mélusine, which showed the water nymphs surprised in their pool (cf. the scattering bathers in the dream); the other was a picture of the Deluge by an Italian Master; while the little experience remembered from my puberty was of having seen the instructor at a swimming-school helping a lady out of the water who had stopped in until after the time set aside for men bathers.—In the case of the example which I chose for interpretation, an analysis of the situation led me to a small series of recollections each of which contributed something to the content of the dream. In the first place, there was the episode from the time of my engagement of which I have already spoken. The pressure upon my hand under the table, which was a part of that episode, provided the dream with the detail "under the table"—a detail which I had to add as an afterthought to my memory of the dream. In the episode itself there was of course no question of "turning to me"; the analysis showed that this element was the fulfillment of a wish by presenting the opposite of an actual event, and that it related to my wife's behavior at the table d'hôte. But behind this recent recollection there lay concealed an exactly similar and far more important scene from the time of our engagement, which estranged us for a whole day. The intimate laying of a hand on my knee belonged to a quite different context and was concerned with quite other people. This element in the dream was in turn the starting-point of two separate sets of memories—and so on.

The material in the dream-thoughts which is packed together for the purpose of constructing a dream-situation must of course in itself be adaptable for that purpose. There must be one or more *common elements* in all the components. The dream-work then proceeds just as Francis Galton did in constructing his family photographs. It superimposes, as it were, the different components upon one another. The common element in them then stands out clearly in the composite picture, while contradictory details more or less wipe one another out. This method of production also explains to some extent the varying degrees of characteristic vagueness shown by so many elements in the content of dreams. Basing itself on this discovery, dream-interpretation has laid down the following rule: in analyzing a dream, if an uncertainty can be resolved into an "either—or," we must replace it for purposes of interpretation by an "and," and take each of the apparent alternatives as an independent starting-point for a series of associations.

If a common element of this kind between the dream-thoughts is not present, the dream-work sets about *creating* one, so that it may be possible for the thoughts to be given a common representation in the dream. The most convenient way of bringing together two dream-thoughts which, to start with, have nothing in common, is to alter the verbal form of one of them, and thus bring it halfway to meet the other, which may be similarly clothed in a new form of words. A parallel process is involved in hammering out a rhyme, where a similar sound has to be sought for in the same way as a common element is in our present case. A large part of the dream-work consists in the creation of intermediate thoughts of this kind which are often highly ingenious, though they frequently appear far-fetched; these then form a link between the composite picture in the manifest content of the dream and the dream-thoughts, which are themselves diverse both in form and essence and have been determined by the exciting factors of the dream. The analysis of our sample dream affords us an instance of this kind in which a thought has been given a new form in order to bring it into contact with another which is essentially foreign to it. In carrying out the analysis I came upon the following thought: *"I should like to get something sometimes without paying for it."* But in that form the thought could not be employed in the dream-content. It was therefore given a fresh form: *"I should like to get some enjoyment without cost* [Kosten]."[1] Now the word *Kosten* in its second sense fits into the "table d'hôte" circle of ideas, and could thus be represented in the *spinach* which was served in the dream. When

---

1. The German word *"Kosten"* means both "cost" and "to taste."

a dish appears at our table and the children refuse it, their mother begins by trying persuasion, and urges them *"just to taste [kosten] a bit of it."* It may seem strange that the dream-work should make such free use of verbal ambiguity, but further experience will teach us that the occurrence is quite a common one.

The process of condensation further explains certain constituents of the content of dreams which are peculiar to them and are not found in waking ideation. What I have in mind are "collective" and "composite figures" and the strange "composite structures," which are creations not unlike the composite animals invented by the folk-imagination of the Orient. The latter, however, have already assumed stereotyped shapes in our thought, whereas in dreams fresh composite forms are being perpetually constructed in an inexhaustible variety. We are all of us familiar with such structures from our own dreams.

There are many sorts of ways in which figures of this kind can be put together. I may build up a figure by giving it the features of two people; or I may give it the *form* of one person but think of it in the dream as having the *name* of another person; or I may have a visual picture of one person, but put it in a situation which is appropriate to another. In all these cases the combination of different persons into a single representative in the content of the dream has a meaning; it is intended to indicate an "and" or "just as," or to compare the original persons with each other in some particular respect, which may even be specified in the dream itself. As a rule, however, this common element between the combined persons can only be discovered by analysis, and is only indicated in the contents of the dream by the formation of the collective figure.

The composite structures which occur in dreams in such immense numbers are put together in an equal variety of ways, and the same rules apply to their resolution. There is no need for me to quote any instances. Their strangeness disappears completely when once we have made up our minds not to class them with the objects of our waking perception, but to remember that they are products of dream-condensation and are emphasizing in an effectively abbreviated form some common characteristic of the objects which they are thus combining. Here again the common element has as a rule to be discovered by analysis. The content of the dream merely says as it were: "All these things have an element *x* in common." The dissection of these composite structures by means of analysis is often the shortest way to finding the meaning of a dream.—Thus, I dreamt on one occasion that I was sitting on a bench with one of my former university teachers, and that the bench, which was surrounded by other benches, was moving forward at a rapid pace. This was a combination of a lecture theater and a *trottoir roulant*.[2] I will not pursue this train of ideas further.—Another time I was sitting in a railway carriage and holding on my lap an object in the shape of a top hat [*Zylinderhut*, literally "cylinder-hat"], which however was made of transparent glass. The situation made me think at once of the proverb: *"Mit dem Hute in der Hand kommt man durchs ganze Land."*[3] The glass cylinder led me by a short *détour* to think of an incandescent gas-mantle; and I soon saw that I should like to make a discovery which would make me as rich and independent as my fellow countryman Dr. Auer von Welsbach was made by his, and that I should like to travel instead of stopping in Vienna. In the dream I was traveling with my discovery, the hat in the shape of a glass cylinder—a discovery which, it is true, was not as yet of any great practical use.—The dream-work is particularly fond of representing two *contrary* ideas by the same composite structure. Thus, for instance, a woman had a dream in which she saw herself carrying a tall spray of flowers, such as the angel is represented as holding in pictures of the Annunciation. (This stood for innocence; incidentally, her own name was Maria.) On the other hand, the spray was covered with large white[4] flowers like camellias. (This stood for the opposite of innocence; it was associated with *La dame aux camélias*.)

A good proportion of what we have learned about condensation in dreams may be summarized in this formula: each element in the content of a dream is "overdetermined" by material in the dream-thoughts; it is not derived from a *single* element in the dream-thoughts, but may be traced back to a whole number. These elements need not necessarily be closely related to each other in the

---

2. The *trottoir roulant* was a moving roadway installed at the Paris Exhibition of 1900.

3. If you go hat in hand, you can cross the whole land.

4. This should probably be "red." The flowers are so described in the much fuller account of the dream given in *The Interpretation of Dreams (Standard Ed., 5, 347).*

dream-thoughts themselves; they may belong to the most widely separated regions of the fabric of those thoughts. A dream-element is, in the strictest sense of the word, the "representative" of all this disparate material in the content of the dream. But analysis reveals yet another side of the complicated relation between the content of the dream and the dream-thoughts. Just as connections lead from each element of the dream to several dream-thoughts, so as a rule a single dream-thought is represented by more than one dream-element; the threads of association do not simply converge from the dream-thoughts to the dream-content, they cross and interweave with each other many times over in the course of their journey.

Condensation, together with the transformation of thoughts into situations ("dramatization"), is the most important and peculiar characteristic of the dream-work. So far, however, nothing has transpired as to any *motive* necessitating this compression of the material.

5

In the case of the complicated and confused dreams with which we are now concerned, condensation and dramatization alone are not enough to account for the whole of the impression that we gain of the dissimilarity between the content of the dream and the dream-thoughts. We have evidence of the operation of a third factor, and this evidence deserves careful sifting.

First and foremost, when by means of analysis we have arrived at a knowledge of the dream-thoughts, we observe that the manifest dream-content deals with quite different material from the latent thoughts. This, to be sure, is no more than an appearance, which evaporates under closer examination, for we find ultimately that the whole of the dream-content is derived from the dream-thoughts, and that almost all the dream-thoughts are represented in the dream-content. Nevertheless, something of the distinction still remains. What stands out boldly and clearly in the dream as its essential content must, after analysis, be satisfied with playing an extremely subordinate role among the dream-thoughts; and what, on the evidence of our feelings, can claim to be the most prominent among the dream-thoughts is either not present at all as ideational material in the content of the dream or is only remotely alluded to in some obscure region of it. We may put it in this way: *in the course of the dream-work the psychical intensity passes over from the thoughts and ideas to which it properly belongs on to others which in our judgment have no claim to any such emphasis.* No other process contributes so much to concealing the meaning of a dream and to making the connection between the dream-content and the dream-thoughts unrecognizable. In the course of this process, which I shall describe as "dream-displacement," the psychical intensity, significance or affective potentiality of the thoughts is, as we further find, transformed into sensory vividness. We assume as a matter of course that the most distinct element in the manifest content of a dream is the most important one; but in fact [owing to the displacement that has occurred] it is often an *indistinct* element which turns out to be the most direct derivative of the essential dream-thought.

What I have called dream-displacement might equally be described [in Nietzsche's phrase] as "a transvaluation of psychical values." I shall not have given an exhaustive estimate of this phenomenon, however, unless I add that this work of displacement of transvaluation is performed to a very varying degree in different dreams. There are dreams which come about almost without any displacement. These are the ones which make sense and are intelligible, such, for instance, as those which we have recognized as undisguised wishful dreams. On the other hand, there are dreams in which not a single piece of the dream-thoughts has retained its own psychical value, or in which everything that is essential in the dream-thoughts has been replaced by something trivial. And we can find a complete series of transitional cases between these two extremes. The more obscure and confused a dream appears to be, the greater the share in its construction which may be attributed to the factor of displacement.

Our specimen dream exhibits displacement to this extent at least, that its content seems to have a different *center* from its dream-thoughts. In the foreground of the dream-content a prominent place is taken by a situation in which a woman seems to be making advances to me; while in the dream-thoughts the chief emphasis is laid on a wish for once to enjoy unselfish love, love which "costs nothing"—an idea concealed behind the phrase about "beautiful eyes" and the far-fetched allusion to "spinach."

If we undo dream-displacement by means of analysis, we obtain what seems to be completely trustworthy information on two-much disputed problems concerning dreams: as to their instigators and as to their connection with waking life. There are dreams which immediately reveal their derivation from events of the day; there are others in which no trace of any such derivation is to be discovered. If we seek the help of analysis, we find that every dream without any possible exception goes back to an impression of the past few days, or, it is probably more correct to say, of the day immediately preceding the dream, of the "dream-day." The impression which plays the part of dream-instigator may be such an important one that we feel no surprise at being concerned with it in the daytime, and in that case we rightly speak of the dream as carrying on with the significant interests of our waking life. As a rule, however, if a connection is to be found in the content of the dream with any impression of the previous day, that impression is so trivial, insignificant and unmemorable, that it is only with difficulty that we ourselves can recall it. And in such cases the content of the dream itself, even if it is connected and intelligible, seems to be concerned with the most indifferent trivialities, which would be unworthy of our interest if we were awake. A good deal of the contempt in which dreams are held is due to the preference thus shown in their content for what is indifferent and trivial.

Analysis does away with the misleading appearance upon which this derogatory judgment is founded. If the content of a dream puts forward some indifferent impression as being its instigator, analysis invariably brings to light a significant experience, and one by which the dreamer has good reason to be stirred. This experience has been replaced by the indifferent one, with which it is connected by copious associative links. Where the content of the dream treats of insignificant and uninteresting ideational material, analysis uncovers the numerous associative paths connecting these trivialities with things that are of the highest psychical importance in the dreamer's estimation. *If what make their way into the content of dreams are impressions and material which are indifferent and trivial rather than justifiably stirring and interesting, that is only the effect of the process of displacement.* If we answer our questions about dream-instigators and the connection between dreaming and daily affairs on the basis of the new insight we have gained from replacing the manifest by the latent content of dreams, we arrive at these conclusions: *dreams are never concerned with things which we should not think it worth while to be concerned with during the day, and trivialities which do not affect us during the day are unable to pursue us in our sleep.*

What was the dream-instigator in the specimen that we have chosen for analysis? It was the definitely insignificant event of my friend giving me *a drive in a cab free of cost*. The situation in the dream at the table d'hôte contained an allusion to this insignificant precipitating cause, for in my conversation I had compared the taximeter cab with a table d'hôte. But I can also point to the important experience which was represented by this trivial one. A few days earlier I had paid out a considerable sum of money on behalf of a member of my family of whom I am fond. No wonder, said the dream-thoughts, if this person were to feel grateful to me: love of that sort would not be "free of cost." Love that is free of cost, however, stood in the forefront of the dream-thoughts. The fact that not long before I had had several *cab-drives* with the relative in question, made it possible for the cab-drive with my friend to remind me of my connections with this other person.

The indifferent impression which becomes a dream-instigator owing to associations of this kind is subject to a further condition which does not apply to the true source of the dream: it must always be a *recent* impression, derived from the dream-day.

I cannot leave the subject of dream-displacement without drawing attention to a remarkable process which occurs in the formation of dreams and in which condensation and displacement *combine* to produce the result. In considering condensation we have already seen the way in which two ideas in the dream-thoughts which have something in common, some point of contact, are replaced in the dream-content by a composite idea, in which a relatively distinct nucleus represents what they have in common, while indistinct subordinate details correspond to the respects in which they differ from each other. If displacement takes place in addition to condensation, what is constructed is not a composite idea but an "intermediate common entity," which stands in a relation to the two different elements similar to that in which the resultant in a parallelogram of forces stands to its components. For instance, in the content of one of my dreams there was a question of an injection with *propyl*. To begin with, the analysis only led me to an indifferent experience which had acted as dream-instigator, and in which a part was played by *amyl*. I was not yet able to justify the confusion between amyl and propyl. In the group of ideas behind this same dream, however, there was also a recollection of my first visit to Munich, where I had been struck by the *Propylaea*.[5] The details of the analysis made is plausible to suppose that it was the influence of this second group of ideas upon the first one that was responsible for the displacement from amyl to propyl. *Propyl* is as it were an intermediate idea between *amyl* and *Propylaea*, and found its way into the content of the dream as a kind of *compromise*, by means of simultaneous condensation and displacement.[6]

There is a still more urgent necessity in the case of the process of displacement than in that of condensation to discover the motive for these puzzling efforts on the part of the dream-work.

6

It is the process of displacement which is chiefly responsible for our being unable to discover or recognize the dream-thoughts in the dream-content, unless we understand the reason for their distortion. Nevertheless, the dream-thoughts are also submitted to another and milder sort of transformation, which leads to our discovering a new achievement on the part of the dream-work—one, however, which is easily intelligible. The dream-thoughts which we first come across as we proceed with our analysis often strike us by the unusual form in which they are expressed; they are not clothed in the prosaic language usually employed by our thoughts, but are on the contrary represented symbolically by means of similes and metaphors, in images resembling those of poetic speech. There is no difficulty in accounting for the constraint imposed upon the form in which the dream-thoughts are expressed. The manifest content of dreams consists for the most part in pictorial situations; and the dream-thoughts must accordingly be submitted in the first place to a treatment which will make them suitable for a representation of this kind. If we imagine ourselves faced by the problem of representing the arguments in a political leading article or the speeches of counsel before a court of law in a series of pictures, we shall easily understand the modifications which must necessarily

---

5. A ceremonial portico on the Athenian model.

6. The dream from which this detail is taken was the first one to be exhaustively analyzed by Freud. It is reported at length in *The Interpretation of Dreams*. (Cf. *Standard Ed.*, 4, 106ff., and, for this particular detail, 4, 294.)

be carried out by the dream-work owing to *considerations of representability in the content of the dream.*

The psychical material of the dream-thoughts habitually includes recollections of impressive experiences—not infrequently dating back to early childhood—which are thus themselves perceived as a rule as situations having a visual subject-matter. Wherever the possibility arises, this portion of the dream-thoughts exercises a determining influence upon the form taken by the content of the dream; it constitutes, as it were, a nucleus of crystallization, attracting the material of the dream-thoughts to itself and thus affecting their distribution. The situation in a dream is often nothing other than a modified repetition, complicated by interpolations, of an impressive experience of this kind; on the other hand, faithful and straight-forward reproductions of real scenes only rarely appear in dreams.

The content of dreams, however, does not consist entirely of situations, but also includes disconnected fragments of visual images, speeches, and even bits of unmodified thoughts. It may therefore perhaps be of interest to enumerate very briefly the modes of representation available to the dream-work for reproducing the dream-thoughts in the peculiar form of expression necessary in dreams.

The dream-thoughts which we arrive at by means of analysis reveal themselves as a psychical complex of the most intricate possible structure. Its portions stand in the most manifold logical relations to one another: they represent foreground and background, conditions, digressions and illustrations, chains of evidence, and counterarguments. Each train of thought is almost invariably accompanied by its contradictory counterpart. This material lacks none of the characteristics that are familiar to us from our waking thinking. If now all of this is to be turned into a dream, the psychical material will be submitted to a pressure which will condense it greatly, to an internal fragmentation and displacement which will, as it were, create new surfaces, and to a selective operation in favor of those portions of it which are the most appropriate for the construction of situations. If we take into account the genesis of the material, a process of this sort deserves to be described as a "regression." In the course of this transformation, however, the logical links which have hitherto held the psychical material together are lost. It is only, as it were, the substantive content of the dream-thoughts that the dream-work takes over and manipulates. The restoration of the connections which the dream-work has destroyed is a task which has to be performed by the work of analysis.

The modes of expression open to a dream may therefore be qualified as meagre by comparison with those of our intellectual speech; nevertheless a dream need not wholly abandon the possibility of reproducing the logical relations present in the dream-thoughts. On the contrary, it succeeds often enough in replacing them by formal characteristics to its own texture.

In the first place, dreams take into account the connection which undeniably exists between all the portions of the dream-thoughts by combining the whole material into a single situation. They reproduce *logical connection* by *approximation in time and space,* just as a painter will represent all the poets in a single group in a picture of Parnassus. It is true that they were never in fact assembled on a single mountaintop; but they certainly form a conceptual group. Dreams carry this method of reproduction down to details; and often when they show us two elements in the dream-content close together, this indicates that there is some specially intimate connection between what correspond to them among the dream-thoughts. Incidentally, it is to be observed that all dreams produced during a single night will be found on analysis to be derived from the same circle of thoughts.

A *causal relation* between two thoughts is either left unrepresented or is replaced by a *sequence* of two pieces of dream of different lengths. Here the representation is often reversed, the beginning of the dream standing for the consequence and its conclusion for the premise. An immediate *transformation* of one thing into another in a dream seems to represent the relation of *cause and effect.*

The alternative *"either—or"* is never expressed in dreams, both of the alternatives being inserted in the text of the dream as though they were equally valid. I have already mentioned that an "either—or" used in *recording* a dream is to be translated by "and."

Ideas which are contraries are by preference expressed in dreams by one and the same element.[7] "No" seems not to exist so far

---

7. [*Footnote added* 1911:] It deserves to be remarked that well-known philologists have asserted that the most ancient human languages tended in general to express contradictory opposites by the same word. (E.g., "strong-week," "inside-

as dreams are concerned. Opposition between two thoughts, the relation of *reversal,* may be represented in dreams in a most remarkable way. It may be represented by some *other* piece of the dream-content being turned into its opposite—as it were by an afterthought. We shall hear presently of a further method of expressing contradiction. The sensation of *inhibition of movement* which is so common in dreams also serves to express a contradiction between two impulses, a *conflict of will.*

One and one only of these logical relations—that of *similarity, consonance, the possession of common attributes*—is very highly favored by the mechanism of dream-formation. The dream-work makes use of such cases as a foundation for dream-condensation, by bringing together everything that shows an agreement of this kind into a new unity.

This short series of rough comments is of course inadequate to deal with the full extent of the formal means employed by dreams for the expression of logical relations in the dream-thoughts. Different dreams are more or less carefully constructed in this respect; they keep more or less closely to the text presented to them; they make more or less use of the expedients that are open to the dream-work. In the second case they appear obscure, confused, and disconnected. If, however, a dream strikes one as *obviously* absurd, if its content includes a piece of palpable nonsense, this is intentionally so; its apparent disregard of all the requirements of logic is expressing a piece of the intellectual content of the dream-thoughts. Absurdity in a dream signifies the presence in the dream-thoughts of *contradiction, ridicule, and derision.* Since this statement is in the most marked opposition to the view that dreams are the product of a dissociated and uncritical mental activity, I will emphasize it by means of an example.

One of my acquaintances, Herr M., had been attacked in an essay with an unjustifiable degree of violence, as we all thought— by no less a person than Goethe. Herr M. was naturally crushed by the attack. He complained of it bitterly to some company at table; his veneration for Goethe had not been affected, however, by this personal experience. I now tried to throw a little light on the chronological data, which seemed to me improbable. Goethe

---

outside." This has been described as "the antithetical meaning of primal words.") [Cf. Freud, 1910*e*.]

died in 1832. Since his attack on Herr M. must naturally have been made earlier than that, Herr M. must have been quite a young man at the time. It seemed to be a plausible notion that he was eighteen. I was not quite sure, however, what year we were actually in, so that my whole calculation melted into obscurity. Incidentally, the attack was contained in Goethe's well-known essay on "Nature."

The nonsensical character of this dream will be even more glaringly obvious, if I explain that Herr M. is a youngish businessman, who is far removed from any poetical and literary interests. I have no doubt, however, that when I have entered into the analysis of the dream I shall succeed in showing how much "method" there is in its nonsense.

The material of the dream was derived from three sources:

(1) Herr M., whom I had got to know among some *company at table,* asked me one day to examine his elder brother, who was showing signs of [general paralysis]. In the course of my conversation with the patient an awkward episode occurred, for he gave his brother away for no accountable reason by talking of his *youthful follies.* I had asked the patient the *year of his birth* (cf. the *year of* Goethe's *death* in the dream) and had made him carry out a number of calculations in order to test the weakness of his memory.

(2) A medical journal, which bore my name among others on its title page, had published a positively *"crushing"* criticism by a *youthful* reviewer of a book by my friend F. in Berlin. I took the editor to task over this; but, though he expressed his regret, he would not undertake to offer any redress. I therefore severed my connection with the journal, but in my letter of resignation expressed a hope that *our personal relations would not be affected by the event.* This was the true source of the dream. The unfavorable reception of my friend's work had made a profound impression on me. It contained, in my opinion, a fundamental biological discovery, which is only now—many years later—beginning to find favor with the experts.

(3) A woman patient of mine had given me an account a short time before of her brother's illness, and how he had broken out in a frenzy with cries of *"Nature! Nature!"* The doctors believed that his exclamation came from his having read *Goethe's* striking essay on that subject and that it showed he had been overworking at his studies. I had remarked that *it seemed to me more plausible* that his exclamation of the word *Nature* should be taken in the sexual

sense in which it is used by the less-educated people here. This idea of mine was at least not disproved by the fact that the unfortunate young man subsequently mutilated his own genitals. He was *eighteen* at the time of his outbreak.

Behind my own ego in the dream-content there lay concealed, in the first instance, my friend who had been so badly treated by the critic. *"I tried to throw a little light on the chronological data."* My friend's book dealt with the *chronological data* of life and among other things showed that the length of *Goethe's* life was a multiple of a number of days that has a significance in biology. But this ego was compared with a paralytic: *"I was not quite sure what year we were in."* Thus the dream made out that my friend was behaving like a paralytic, and in this respect it was a mass of absurdities. The dream-thoughts, however, were saying ironically: "Naturally, it's *he* [my friend F.] who is the crazy fool and it's *you* [the critics] who are the men of genius and know better. Surely it couldn't be the *reverse?*" There were plenty of examples of this *reversal* in the dream. For instance, Goethe attacked the young man, which is absurd, whereas it is still easy for quite a young man to attack the great Goethe.

I should like to lay it down that no dream is prompted by motives other than egoistic ones.[8] In fact, the ego in the present dream does not stand only for my friend but for myself as well. I was identifying myself with him, because the fate of his discovery seemed to foreshadow the reception of my own findings. If I were to bring forward my theory emphasizing the part played by sexuality in the etiology of psychoneurotic disorders (cf. the allusion to the eighteen-year-old patient's cry of "Nature! Nature!"), I should come across the same criticisms; and I was already preparing to meet them with the same derision.

If we pursue the dream-thoughts further, we shall keep on finding ridicule and derision as correlates of the absurdities of the manifest dream. It is well-known that it was the discovery of the split skull of a sheep on the Lido of Venice that gave Goethe the idea of the so-called vertebral theory of the skull. My friend boasts that, when he was a student, he released a storm which led to the

---

8. Freud has, however, qualified this statement in an additional footnote written in 1925, which will be found near the end of chapter 5 of *The Interpretation of Dreams* (*Standard Ed.*, **4**, 270).

resignation of an old professor who, though he had once been distinguished (among other things in connection precisely with the same branch of comparative anatomy), had become incapable of teaching owing to *senile dementia*. Thus, the agitation which my friend promoted served to combat the mischievous system according to which there is no *age limit* for academic workers in German universities—for *age is proverbially no defense against folly*.—In the hospital here I had the honor of serving for years under a chief who had long been a *fossil* and had for decades been notoriously *feebleminded*, but who was allowed to continue carrying on his responsible duties. At this point I thought of a descriptive term based upon the discovery on the Lido.[9] Some of my young contemporaries at the hospital concocted, in connection with this man, a version of what was then a popular song: *"Das hat kein Goethe g'schrieben, das hat kein Schiller g'dicht . . ."*[10]

7

We have not yet come to the end of our consideration of the dream-work. In addition to condensation, displacement, and pictorial arrangement of the psychical material, we are obliged to assign it yet another activity, though this is not to be found in operation in *every* dream. I shall not deal exhaustively with this part of the dream-work, and will therefore merely remark that the easiest way of forming an idea of its nature is to suppose—though the supposition probably does not meet the facts—that *it only comes into operation* AFTER *the dream-content has already been constructed.* Its function would then consist in arranging the constituents of the dream in such a way that they form an approximately connected whole, a dream-composition. In this way the dream is given a kind of façade (though this does not, it is true, hide its content at every point), and thus receives a first, preliminary interpretation, which is supported by interpolations and slight modifications. Incidentally, this revision of the dream-content is only possible if it is not too punctiliously carried out; nor does it present us with anything more than a glaring misunderstanding of the dream-thoughts. Be-

---

9. *Schafkopf*, literally "sheep's head," = "silly ass."
10. "This was written by no Goethe, this was composed by no Schiller."—This dream is also discussed at length in *The Interpretation of Dreams* (*Standard Ed.*, 5, 439, etc.).

fore we start upon the analysis of a dream we have to clear the ground of this attempt at an interpretation.

The motive for this part of the dream-work is particularly obvious. *Considerations of intelligibility* are what lead to this final revision of a dream; and this reveals the origin of the activity. It behaves toward the dream-content lying before it just as our normal psychical activity behaves in general toward any perceptual content that may be presented to it. It understands that content on the basis of certain anticipatory ideas, and arranges it, even at the moment of perceiving it, on the presupposition of its being intelligible; in so doing it runs a risk of falsifying it, and in fact, if it cannot bring it into line with anything familiar, is a prey to the strangest misunderstandings. As is well-known, we are incapable of seeing a series of unfamiliar signs or of hearing a succession of unknown words, without at once falsifying the perception from considerations of intelligibility, on the basis of something already known to us.

Dreams which have undergone a revision of this kind at the hands of a psychical activity completely analogous to waking thought may be described as "well-constructed." In the case of other dreams this activity has completely broken down; no attempt even has been made to arrange or interpret the material, and, since after we have woken up we feel ourselves identical with this last part of the dream-work, we make a judgment that the dream was "hopelessly confused." From the point of view of analysis, however, a dream that resembles a disordered heap of disconnected fragments is just as valuable as one that has been beautifully polished and provided with a surface. In the former case, indeed, we are saved the trouble of demolishing what has been superimposed upon the dream-content.

It would be a mistake, however, to suppose[11] that these dream-façades are nothing other than mistaken and somewhat arbitrary revisions of the dream-content by the conscious agency of our mental life. In the erection of a dream-façade use is not infrequently made of wishful fantasies which are present in the dream-thoughts in a preconstructed form, and are of the same character as the appropriately named "daydreams" familiar to us in waking life. The wishful fantasies revealed by analysis in night-dreams often

---

11. This paragraph was added in 1911.

turn out to be repetitions or modified versions of scenes from infancy; thus in some cases the façade of the dream directly reveals the dream's actual nucleus, distorted by an admixture of other material.

The dream-work exhibits no activities other than the four that have already been mentioned. If we keep to the definition of "dream-work" as the process of transforming the dream-thoughts into the dream-content, it follows that the dream-work is not creative, that it develops no fantasies of its own, that it makes no judgments and draws no conclusions; it has no functions whatever other than condensation and displacement of the material and its modification into pictorial form, to which must be added as a variable factor the final bit of interpretative revision. It is true that we find various things in the dream-content which we should be inclined to regard as a product of some other and higher intellectual function; but in every case analysis shows convincingly that *these intellectual operations have already been performed in the dream-thoughts and have only been* TAKEN OVER *by the dream-content.* A conclusion drawn in a dream is nothing other than the repetition of a conclusion in the dream-thoughts; if the conclusion is taken over into the dream unmodified, it will appear impeccable; if the dream-work has displaced it on to some other material, it will appear nonsensical. A calculation in the dream-content signifies nothing more than that there is a calculation in the dream-thoughts; but while the latter is always rational, a dream-calculation may produce the wildest results if its factors are condensed or if its mathematical operations are displaced or to other material. Not even the speeches that occur in the dream-content are original compositions; they turn out to be a hotchpotch of speeches made, heard, or read, which have been revived in the dream-thoughts of whose wording is exactly reproduced, while their origin is entirely disregarded and their meaning is violently changed.

It will perhaps be as well to support these last assertions by a few examples.

(I) Here is an innocent-sounding, well-constructed dream dreamt by a woman patient:

She dreamt she was going to the market with her cook, who was carrying the basket. After she had asked for something, the butcher said to her: "That's not obtainable any longer," and offered her something else, adding: "This is good too." She rejected it and went on to the woman who sells vegetables, who tried to get her to buy a peculiar vegetable that was tied up in bundles but was of a black color. She said: "I don't recognize that: I won't take it."

The remark *"That's not obtainable any longer"* originated from the treatment itself. A few days earlier I had explained to the patient in those very words that the earliest memories of childhood were *"not obtainable any longer* as such," but were replaced in analysis by "transferences" and dreams. So *I* was the butcher.

The second speech—*"I don't recognize that"*—occurred in an entirely different connection. On the previous day she had reproved her cook, who incidentally also appeared in the dream, with the words: *"Behave yourself properly! I don't recognize that!"* meaning, no doubt, that she did not understand such behavior and would not put up with it. As the result of a displacement, it was the more innocent part of this speech which made its way into the content of the dream; but in the dream-thoughts it was only the other part of the speech that played a part. For the dream-work had reduced to complete unintelligibility and extreme innocence an imaginary situation in which *I* was *behaving improperly* to the lady in a particular way. But this situation which the patient was expecting in her imagination was itself only a new edition of something she had once actually experienced.[12]

(II) Here is an apparently quite meaningless dream containing figures. *She was going to pay for something. Her daughter took three florins and sixty-five kreuzers from her (the mother's) purse. The dreamer said to her: "What are you doing? It only costs twenty-one kreuzers."*

The dreamer came from abroad and her daughter was at school here. She was in a position to carry on her treatment with me as long as her daughter remained in Vienna. The day before the dream the headmistress had suggested to her that she should leave her daughter at school for another year. In that case she could also have continued her treatment for a year. The figures in the dream become significant if we remember that "time is money." One year is equal to 365 days, or, expressed in money, 365 kreuzers or 3 florins 65 kreuzers. The 21 kreuzers corresponded to the three

---

12. This dream is reported in greater detail in *The Interpretation of Dreams* (*Standard Ed.*, 4, 183).

weeks which had still to run between the dream-day and the end of the school term and also to the end of the patient's treatment. It was clearly financial considerations which had induced the lady to refuse the headmistress's proposal, and which were responsible for the smallness of the sums mentioned in the dream.[13]

(III) A lady who, though she was still young, had been married for a number of years, received news that an acquaintance of hers, Fräulein Elise L., who was almost exactly her contemporary, had become engaged. This was the precipitating cause of the following dream:

She was at the theater with her husband. One side of the stalls was completely empty. Her husband told her that Elise L. and her fiancé had wanted to go too, but had only been able to get bad seats—three for one florin fifty kreuzers—and of course they could not take those. She thought it would not really have done any harm if they had.

What interests us here is the source of the figures in the material of the dream-thoughts and the transformations which they underwent. What was the origin of the 1 florin 50 kreuzers? It came from what was in fact an indifferent event of the previous day. Her sister-in-law had been given a present of 150 florins by her husband and had *been in a hurry* to get rid of them by buying a piece of jewelry. It is to be noticed that 150 florins is a *hundred* times as much as 1 florin 50 kreuzers. The only connection with the "three," which was the number of the theater tickets, was that her newly engaged friend was that number of months—three—her junior. The situation in the dream was a repetition of a small incident which her husband often teased her about. On one occasion she had been in a great hurry to buy tickets for a play in advance, and when she got to the theater she had found that one side of the stalls was almost completely empty. There had been *no need for her to be in such a hurry*. Finally, we must not overlook the *absurdity* in the dream of two people taking three tickets for a play.

Now for the dream-thoughts: "It was *absurd* to marry so early. There was *no need for me to be in such a hurry*. I see from Elise

---

13. For this dream see *The Interpretation of Dreams* (Standard Ed., 5, 414).— An Austrian florin was worth approximately 1s. 10d. or forty cents at the end of the nineteenth century.

L.'s example that I should have got a husband in the end. Indeed, I should have got one *a hundred times* better" (a treasure) "if I had only waited. My money" (or dowry) "could have bought *three* men just as good."[14]

8

Having been made acquainted with the dream-work by the foregoing discussion, we shall no doubt be inclined to pronounce it a quite peculiar psychical process, the like of which, so far as we are aware, does not exist elsewhere. It is as though we were carrying over on to the dream-work all the astonishment which used formerly to be aroused in us by its product, the dream. In fact, however, the dream-work is only the first to be discovered for a whole series of psychical processes, responsible for the generation of hysterical symptoms, of phobias, obsessions, and delusions. Condensation and, above all, displacement are invariable characteristics of these other processes as well. Modification into a pictorial form, on the other hand, remains a peculiarity of the dream-work. If this explanation places dreams in a single series alongside the structures produced by psychical illness, this makes it all the more important for us to discover the essential determining conditions of such processes as those of dream-formation. We shall probably be surprised to hear that neither the state of sleep nor illness is among these indispensable conditions. A whole number of the phenomena of the everyday life of healthy people—such as forgetting, slips of the tongue, bungled actions, and a particular class of errors—owe their origin to a psychical mechanism analogous to that of dreams and of the other members of the series.[15]

The heart of the problem lies in displacement, which is by far the most striking of the special achievements of the dream-work. If we enter deeply into the subject, we come to realize that the essential determining condition of displacement is a purely psychological one: something in the nature of a *motive*. One comes upon its track if one takes into consideration certain experiences which one cannot escape in analyzing dreams. In analyzing my specimen

---

14. This dream, which is mentioned again below, is discussed in *The Interpretation of Dreams (Standard Ed., 5, 415)* and at greater length in Freud's *Introductory Lectures* (1916–17), especially in Lectures 7 and 14.

15. See Freud's *Psychopathology of Everyday Life* (1901*b*).

dream I was earlier obliged to break off my report of the dream-thoughts, because, as I confessed, there were some among them which I should prefer to conceal from strangers and which I could not communicate to other people without doing serious mischief in important directions. I added that nothing would be gained if I were to choose another dream instead of that particular one with a view to reporting its analysis: I should come upon dream-thoughts which required to be kept secret in the case of *every* dream with an obscure or confused content. If, however, I were to continue the analysis on my own account, without any reference to other people (whom, indeed, an experience so personal as my dream cannot possibly have been intended to reach), I should eventually arrive at thoughts which would surprise me, whose presence in me I was unaware of, which were not only *alien* but also *disagreeable* to me, and which I should therefore feel inclined to dispute energetically, although the chain of thoughts running through the analysis insisted upon them remorselessly. There is only one way of accounting for this state of affairs, which is of quite universal occurrence; and that is to suppose that these thoughts really were present in my mind, and in possession of a certain amount of psychical intensity or energy, but that they were in a peculiar psychological situation, as a consequence of which they *could not become conscious* to me. (I describe this particular condition as one of "repression.") We cannot help concluding, then, that there is a causal connection between the obscurity of the dream-content and the state of repression (inadmissibility to consciousness) of certain of the dream-thoughts, and that the dream had to be obscure so as not to betray the proscribed dream-thoughts. Thus we are led to the concept of a "dream-distortion," which is the product of the dream-work and serves the purpose of dissimulation, that is, of disguise.

I will test this on the specimen dream which I chose for analysis, and enquire what the thought was which made its way into that dream in a distorted form, and which I should be inclined to repudiate if it were undistorted. I recall that my free cab-drive reminded me of my recent expensive drive with a member of my family, that the interpretation of the dream was "I wish I might for once experience love that cost me nothing," and that a short time before the dream I had been obliged to spend a considerable sum of money on this same person's account. Bearing this context in mind, I cannot escape the conclusion that *I regret having made that expenditure.* Not until I have recognized this impulse does my wish in the dream for the love which would call for *no* expenditure acquire a meaning. Yet I can honestly say that when I decided to spend this sum of money I did not hesitate for a moment. My regret at having to do so—the contrary current of feeling—did not become conscious to me. *Why* it did not, is another and a far-reaching question, the answer to which is known to me but belongs in another connection.

If the dream that I analyze is not my own, but someone else's, the conclusion will be the same, though the grounds for believing it will be different. If the dreamer is a healthy person, there is no other means open to me of obliging him to recognize the repressed ideas that have been discovered than by pointing out the context of the dream-thoughts; and I cannot help it if he refuses to recognize them. If, however, I am dealing with a neurotic patient, with a hysteric for instance, he will find the acceptance of the repressed thought forced upon him, owing to its connection with the symptoms of his illness, and owing to the improvement he experiences when he exchanges those symptoms for the repressed ideas. In the case, for instance, of the woman patient who had the dream I have just quoted about the three theater tickets which cost one florin fifty kreuzers, the analysis led to the inevitable conclusion that she had a low estimate of her husband (cf. her idea that she could have got one "a hundred times better"), that she regretted having married him, and that she would have liked to exchange him for another one. It is true that she asserted that she loved her husband, and that her emotional life knew nothing of any such low estimate of him, but all her symptoms led to the same conclusion as the dream. And after her repressed memories had been revived of a particular period during which she had consciously not loved her husband, her symptoms cleared up and her resistance against the interpretation of the dream disappeared.

9

Now that we have established the concept of repression and have brought dream-distortion into relation with repressed psychical material, we can express in general terms the principal finding to which we have been led by the analysis of dreams. In the case of dreams which are intelligible and have a meaning, we have found that they are undisguised wish fulfillments; that is, that in their case the dream-situation represents as fulfilled a wish which is known to consciousness, which is left over from daytime life, and which is deservedly of interest. Analysis has taught us something entirely analogous in the case of obscure and confused dreams: once again the dream-situation represents a wish as fulfilled—a wish which invariably arises from the dream-thoughts, but one which is represented in an unrecognizable form and can only be explained when it has been traced back in analysis. The wish in such cases is either itself a repressed one and alien to consciousness, or it is intimately connected with repressed thoughts and is based upon them. Thus the formula for such dreams is as follows: *they are disguised fulfillments of repressed wishes.* It is interesting in this connection to observe that the popular belief that dreams always foretell the future is confirmed. Actually the future which the dream shows us is not the one which *will* occur but the one which we should *like* to occur. The popular mind is behaving here as it usually does: what it wishes, it believes.

Dreams fall into three classes according to their attitude to wish fulfillment. The first class consists of those which represent an unrepressed wish undisguisedly; these are the dreams of an infantile type which become ever rarer in adults. Secondly there are the dreams which express a repressed wish disguisedly; these no doubt form the overwhelming majority of all our dreams, and require analysis before they can be understood. In the third place there are the dreams which represent a repressed wish, but do so with insufficient or no disguise. These last dreams are invariably accompanied by anxiety, which interrupts them. In their case anxiety takes the place of dream-distortion; and in dreams of the second class anxiety is only avoided owing to the dream-work. There is no great difficulty in proving that the ideational content which produces anxiety in us in dreams was once a wish but has since undergone repression.

There are also clear dreams with a distressing content, which, however, is not felt as distressing in the dream itself. For this reason they cannot be counted as anxiety-dreams; but they have always been taken as evidence of the fact that dreams are without meaning and have no psychical value. An analysis of a dream of this kind will show that we are dealing with well-disguised fulfillments of repressed wishes, that is to say with a dream of the second class;

it will also show how admirably the process of displacement is adapted for disguising wishes.

A girl had a dream of seeing her sister's only surviving child lying dead in the same surroundings in which a few years earlier she had in fact seen the dead body of her sister's *first* child. She felt no pain over this; but she naturally rejected the idea that this situation represented any wish of hers. Nor was there any need to suppose this. It had been beside the first child's coffin, however, that, years before, she had seen and spoken to the man she was in love with; if the second child died, she would no doubt meet the man again in her sister's house. She longed for such a meeting, but fought against the feeling. On the dream-day she had bought a ticket for a lecture which was to be given by this same man, to whom she was still devoted. Her dream was a simple dream of impatience of the kind that often occurs before journeys, visits to the theater, and similar enjoyments that lie ahead. But in order to disguise this longing from her, the situation was displaced onto an event of a kind most unsuitable for producing a feeling of enjoyment, though it had in fact done so in the past. It is to be observed that the emotional behavior in the dream was appropriate to the real content which lay in the background and not to what was pushed into the foreground. The dream-situation anticipated the meeting she had so long desired; it offered no basis for any painful feelings.[16]

10

Hitherto philosophers have had no occasion to concern themselves with a psychology of repression. We may therefore be permitted to make a first approach to this hitherto unknown topic by constructing a pictorial image of the course of events in dreamformation. It is true that the schematic picture we have arrived at—not only from the study of dreams—is a fairly complicated one; but we cannot manage with anything simpler. Our hypothesis is that in our mental apparatus there are two thought-constructing agencies, of which the second enjoys the privilege of having free access to consciousness for its products, whereas the activity of the first is in itself unconscious and can only reach consciousness by

---

16. This dream is reported in greater detail in *The Interpretation of Dreams* (*Standard Ed.*, **4**, 152ff.).

way of the second. On the frontier between the two agencies, where the first passes over to the second, there is a censorship, which only allows what is agreeable to it to pass through and holds back everything else. According to our definition, then, what is rejected by the censorship is in a state of repression. Under certain conditions, of which the state of sleep is one, the relation between the strength of the two agencies is modified in such a way that what is repressed can no longer be held back. In the state of sleep this probably occurs owing to a relaxation of the censorship; when this happens it becomes possible for what has hitherto been repressed to make a path for itself to consciousness. Since, however, the censorship is never completely eliminated but merely reduced, the repressed material must submit to certain alterations which mitigate its offensive features. What becomes conscious in such cases is a compromise between the intentions of one agency and the demands of the other. *Repression—relaxation of the censorship— the formation of a compromise,* this is the fundamental pattern for the generation not only of dreams but of many other psychopathological structures; and in the latter cases too we may observe that the formation of compromises is accompanied by processes of condensation and displacement and by the employment of superficial associations, which we have become familiar with in the dream-work.

We have no reason to disguise the fact that in the hypothesis which we have set up in order to explain the dream-work a part is played by what might be described as a "demonic" element. We have gathered an impression that the formation of obscure dreams occurs *as though* one person who was dependent upon a second person had to make a remark which was bound to be disagreeable in the ears of this second one; and it is on the basis of this simile that we have arrived at the concepts of dream-distortion and censorship, and have endeavored to translate our impression into a psychological theory which is no doubt crude but is at least lucid. Whatever it may be with which a further investigation of the subject may enable us to identify our first and second agencies, we may safely expect to find a confirmation of some correlate of our hypothesis that the second agency controls access to consciousness and can bar the first agency from such access.

When the state of sleep is over, the censorship quickly recovers its full strength; and it can now wipe out all that was won from it during the period of its weakness. This must be one part at least of the explanation of the forgetting of dreams, as is shown by an observation which has been confirmed on countless occasions. It not infrequently happens that during the narration of a dream or during its analysis a fragment of the dream-content which had seemed to be forgotten reemerges. This fragment which has been rescued from oblivion invariably affords us the best and most direct access to the meaning of the dream. And that, in all probability, must have been the only reason for its having been forgotten, that is, for its having been once more suppressed.

11

When once we have recognized that the content of a dream is the representation of a fulfilled wish and that its obscurity is due to alterations in repressed material made by the censorship, we shall no longer have any difficulty in discovering the *function* of dreams. It is commonly said that sleep is disturbed by dreams; strangely enough, we are led to a contrary view and must regard dreams as *the guardians of sleep*.

In the case of children's dreams there should be no difficulty in accepting this statement. The state of sleep or the psychical modification involved in sleep, whatever that may be, is brought about by a resolve to sleep which is either imposed upon the child or is reached on the basis of sensations of fatigue; and it is only made possible by the withholding of stimuli which might suggest to the psychical apparatus aims other than that of sleeping. The means by which *external* stimuli can be kept off are familiar to us; but what are the means available for controlling *internal* mental stimuli which set themselves against falling asleep? Let us observe a mother putting her child to sleep. The child gives vent to an unceasing stream of desires: he wants one more kiss, he wants to go on playing. His mother satisfies some of these desires, but uses her authority to postpone others of them to the next day. It is clear that any wishes or needs that may arise have an inhibiting effect upon falling asleep. We all know the amusing story told by Balduin Groller [a popular nineteenth-century Austrian novelist] of the bad little boy who woke up in the middle of the night and shouted across the night-nursery: "I want the rhino!" A better-behaved child, instead of shouting, would have *dreamt* that he was playing with the rhino. Since a dream that shows a wish as fulfilled is *believed* during sleep, it does away with the wish and makes sleep possible. It cannot be disputed that dream-images are believed in this way, for they are clothed in the psychical appearance of perceptions, and children have not yet acquired the later faculty of distinguishing hallucinations or fantasies from reality.

Adults have learned to make this distinction; they have also grasped the uselessness of wishing, and after lengthy practice know how to postpone their desires until they can find satisfaction by the long and roundabout path of altering the external world. In their case, accordingly, wish fulfillments along the short psychical path are rare in sleep too; it is even possible, indeed, that they never occur at all, and that anything that may seem to us to be constructed on the pattern of a child's dream in fact requires a far more complicated solution. On the other hand, in the case of adults—and this no doubt applies without exception to everyone in full possession of his senses—a differentiation has occurred in the psychical material, which was not present in children. A psychical agency has come into being, which, taught by experience of life, exercises a dominating and inhibiting influence upon mental impulses and maintains that influence with jealous severity, and which, owing to its relation to consciousness and to voluntary movement, is armed with the strongest instruments of psychical power. A portion of the impulses of childhood has been suppressed by this agency as being useless to life, and any thought-material derived from those impulses is in a state of repression.

Now while this agency, in which we recognize our normal ego, is concentrated on the wish to sleep, it appears to be compelled by the psychophysiological conditions of sleep to relax the energy with which it is accustomed to hold down the repressed material during the day. In itself, no doubt, this relaxation does no harm; however much the suppressed impulses of the childish mind may prance around, their access to consciousness is still difficult and their access to movement is barred, as the result of this same state of sleep. The danger of sleep being disturbed by them must, however, be guarded against. We must in any case suppose that even during deep sleep a certain amount of free attention is on duty as a guard against sensory stimuli, and that this guard may sometimes consider waking more advisable than a continuation of sleep. Otherwise there would be no explanation of how it is that we can be woken up at any moment by sensory stimuli of some particular *quality.* As the psysiologist Burdach (1838) insisted long ago, a mother, for instance, will be roused by the whimpering of her baby, or a miller if his mill comes to a stop, or most people if they are called softly by their own name. Now the attention which is thus on guard is also directed toward internal wishful stimuli arising from the repressed material, and combines with them to form the dream which, as a compromise, simultaneously satisfies both of the two agencies. The dream provides a kind of psychical consummation for the wish that has been suppressed (or formed with the help of repressed material) by representing it as fulfilled; but it also satisfies the other agency by allowing sleep to continue. In this respect our ego is ready to behave like a child; it gives credence to the dream-images, as though what it wanted to say was "Yes, yes! you're quite right, but let me go on sleeping!" The low estimate which we form of dreams when we are awake, and which we relate to their confused and apparently illogical character, is probably nothing other than the judgment passed by our sleeping ego upon the repressed impulses, a judgment based, with better right, upon the motor impotence of these disturbers of sleep. We are sometimes aware in our sleep of this contemptuous judgment. If the content of a dream goes too far in overstepping the censorship, we think: "After all, it's only a dream!"—and go on sleeping.

This view is not traversed by the fact that there are marginal cases in which the dream—as happens with anxiety-dreams—can no longer perform its function of preventing an interruption of sleep, but assumes instead the other function of promptly bringing sleep to an end. In doing so it is merely behaving like a conscientious night watchman, who first carries out his duty by suppressing disturbances so that the townsmen may not be woken up, but afterwards continues to do his duty by himself waking the townsmen up, if the causes of the disturbance seem to him serious and of a kind that he cannot cope with alone.

The function of the dream as a guardian of sleep becomes particularly evident when an external stimulus impinges upon the senses of a sleeper. It is generally recognized that sensory stimuli arising during sleep influence the content of dreams; this can be proved experimentally and is among the few certain (but, incidentally, greatly overvalued) findings of medical investigation into dreams. But this finding involves a puzzle which has hitherto proved insoluble. For the sensory stimulus which the experimenter causes to impinge upon the sleeper is not correctly recognized in the dream; it is subjected to one of an indefinite number of possible interpretations, the choice being apparently left to an arbitrary psychical determination. But there is, of course, no such thing as arbitrary determination in the mind. There are several ways in which a sleeper may react to an external sensory stimulus. He may wake up or he may succeed in continuing his sleep in spite of it. In the latter case he may make use of a dream in order to get rid of the external stimulus, and here again there is more than one method open to him. For instance, he may get rid of the stimulus by dreaming that he is in a situation which is absolutely incompatible with the stimulus. Such was the line taken by a sleeper who was subject to disturbance by a painful abscess on the perineum. He dreamt that he was riding on a horse, making use of the poultice that was intended to mitigate his pain as a saddle, and in this way he avoided being disturbed.[17] Or, as happens more frequently, the external stimulus is given an interpretation which brings it into the context of a repressed wish which is at the moment awaiting fulfillment; in this way the external stimulus is robbed of its reality and is treated as though it were a portion of the psychical material. Thus someone dreamt that he had written a comedy with a particular plot; it was produced in a theater, the first act was over, and there were thunders of applause; the clapping was terrific. . . . The dreamer must have succeeded in prolonging his sleep till after the interference had ceased; for when he woke up he no longer heard the noise, but rightly concluded that someone must have been beating a carpet or mattress. Every dream which occurs immediately before the sleeper is woken by a loud noise has made an attempt at explaining away the arousing stimulus by providing another explanation of it and has thus sought to prolong sleep, even if only for a moment.

12[18]

No one who accepts the view that the censorship is the chief reason for dream-distortion will be surprised to learn from the results of dream-interpretation that most of the dreams of adults are traced

---

17. This dream is reported in full in *The Interpretation of Dreams* (1900a) (*Standard Ed.*, 4, 229).

18. The whole of this section was added in 1911.

back by analysis to *erotic wishes*. This assertion is not aimed at dreams with an *undisguised* sexual content, which are no doubt familiar to all dreamers from their own experience and are as a rule the only ones to be described as "sexual dreams." Even dreams of this latter kind offer enough surprises in their choice of the people whom they make into sexual objects, in their disregard of all the limitations which the dreamer imposes in his waking life upon his sexual desires, and by their many strange details, hinting at what are commonly known as "perversions." A great many other dreams, however, which show no sign of being erotic in their manifest content, are revealed by the work of interpretation in analysis as sexual wish fulfillments; and, on the other hand, analysis proves that a great many of the thoughts left over from the activity of waking life as "residues of the previous day" only find their way to representation in dreams through the assistance of repressed erotic wishes.

There is no theoretical necessity why this should be so; but to explain the fact it may be pointed out that no other group of instincts has been submitted to such far-reaching suppression by the demands of cultural education, while at the same time the sexual instincts are also the ones which, in most people, find it easiest to escape from the control of the highest mental agencies. Since we have become acquainted with infantile sexuality, which is often so unobtrusive in its manifestations and is always overlooked and misunderstood, we are justified in saying that almost every civilized man retains the infantile forms of sexual life in some respect or other. We can thus understand how it is that repressed infantile sexual wishes provide the most frequent and strongest motive-forces for the construction of dreams.[19]

There is only one method by which a dream which expresses erotic wishes can succeed in appearing innocently nonsexual in its manifest content. The material of the sexual ideas must not be represented as such, but must be replaced in the content of the dream by hints, allusions, and similar forms of indirect representation. But, unlike other forms of indirect representation, that which is employed in dreams must not be immediately intelligible. The modes of representation which fulfill these conditions are usually described as "symbols" of the things which they represent. Particu-

---

19. See my *Three Essays on the Theory of Sexuality* (1905d).

lar interest has been directed to them since it has been noticed that dreamers speaking the same language make use of the same symbols, and that in some cases, indeed, the use of the same symbols extends beyond the use of the same language. Since dreamers themselves are unaware of the meaning of the symbols they use, it is difficult at first sight to discover the source of the connection between the symbols and what they replace and represent. The fact itself, however, is beyond doubt, and it is important for the technique of dream-interpretation. For, with the help of a knowledge of dream-symbolism, it is possible to understand the meaning of separate elements of the content of a dream or separate pieces of a dream or in some cases even whole dreams, without having to ask the dreamer for his associations.[20] Here we are approaching the popular ideal of translating dreams and on the other hand are returning to the technique of interpretation used by the ancients, to whom dream-interpretation was identical with interpretation by means of symbols.

Although the study of dream-symbols is far from being complete, we are in a position to lay down with certainty a number of general statements and a quantity of special information on the subject. There are some symbols which bear a single meaning almost universally: thus the emperor and empress (or the king and queen) stand for the parents, rooms represent women,[21] and their entrances and exits the openings of the body. The majority of dream-symbols serve to represent persons, parts of the body and activities invested with erotic interest; in particular, the genitals are represented by a number of often very surprising symbols, and the greatest variety of objects are employed to denote them symbolically. Sharp weapons, long and stiff objects, such as tree trunks and sticks, stand for the male genital; while cupboards, boxes, carriages, or ovens may represent the uterus. In such cases as these the *tertium comparationis,* the common element in these substitutions, is immediately intelligible; but there are other symbols in which it is not so easy to grasp the connection. Symbols such as a staircase or going upstairs to represent sexual intercourse, a tie or cravat for the male organ, or wood for the female one, provoke

---

20. See, however, the qualification three paragraphs lower down.
21. Cf. *Frauenzimmer* [literally "women's apartment," commonly used in German as a slightly derogatory word for "woman"].

our unbelief until we can arrive at an understanding of the symbolic relation underlying them by some other means. Moreover a whole number of dream-symbols are bisexual and can relate to the male or femal genitals according to the context.

Some symbols are universally disseminated and can be met with in all dreamers belonging to a single linguistic or cultural group; there are others which occur only within the most restricted and individual limits, symbols constructed by an individual out of his own ideational material. Of the former class we can distinguish some whose claim to represent sexual ideas is immediately justified by linguistic usage (such, for instance, as those derived from agriculture, e.g., "fertilization" or "seed") and others whose relation to sexual ideas appears to reach back into the very earliest ages and to the most obscure depths of our conceptual functioning. The power of constructing symbols has not been exhausted in our own days in the case of either of the two sorts of symbols which I have distinguished at the beginning of this paragraph. Newly discovered objects (such as airships) are, as we may observe, at once adopted as universally available sexual symbols.

It would, incidentally, be a mistake to expect that if we had a still-profounder knowledge of dream-symbolism (of the "language of dreams") we could do without asking the dreamer for his associations to the dream and go back entirely to the technique of dream-interpretation of antiquity. Quite apart from individual symbols and oscillations in the use of universal ones, one can never tell whether any particular element in the content of a dream is to be interpreted symbolically or in its proper sense, and one can be certain that the *whole* content of a dream is not to be interpreted symbolically. A knowledge of dream-symbolism will never do more than enable us to translate certain constituents of the dream-content, and will not relieve us of the necessity for applying the technical rules which I gave earlier. It will, however, afford the most valuable assistance to interpretation precisely at points at which the dreamer's associations are insufficient or fail altogether.

Dream-symbolism is also indispensable to an understanding of what are known as "typical" dreams, which are common to everyone, and of "recurrent" dreams in individuals.

If the account I have given in this short discussion of the symbolic mode of expression in dreams appears incomplete, I can justify my neglect by drawing attention to one of the most important pieces of knowledge that we possess on this subject. Dream-symbolism extends far beyond dreams: it is not peculiar to dreams, but exercises a similar dominating influence on representation in fairy tales, myths, and legends, in jokes and in folklore. It enables us to trace the intimate connections between dreams and these latter productions. We must not suppose that dream-symbolism is a creation of the dream-work; it is in all probability a characteristic of the unconscious thinking which provides the dream-work with the material for condensation, displacement, and dramatization.[22]

13

I lay no claim to having thrown light in these pages upon *all* the problems of dreams, nor to having dealt in a convincing way with those that I *have* discussed. Anyone who is interested in the whole extent of the literature of dreams may be referred to a work by Sante de Sanctis (*I sogni,* 1899); and anyone who wishes to hear more detailed arguments in favor of the view of dreams which I myself have put forward should turn to my volume *The Interpretation of Dreams,* 1900.[23] It only remains for me now to indicate the direction in which my exposition of the subject of the dream-work calls for pursuit.

I have laid it down as the task of dream-interpretation to replace the dream by the latent dream-thoughts, that is, to unravel what the dream-work has woven. In so doing I have raised a number of new psychological problems dealing with the mechanism of this dream-work itself, as well as with the nature and conditions of what is described as repression; on the other hand I have asserted the existence of the dream-thoughts—a copious store of psychical structures of the highest order, which is characterized by all the signs of normal intellectual functioning, but is nevertheless withdrawn from consciousness till it emerges in distorted form in the dream-content. I cannot but assume that thoughts of this kind

---

22. Further information on dream-symbolism may be found in the works of early writers on dream-interpretation, e.g., Artemidorus of Daldis and Scherner (1861), and also in my own *Interpretation of Dreams* (1900a) [chapter 6, section E], in the mythological studies of the psychoanalytic school, as well as in some of W. Stekel's writings (e.g., 1911). [See further Lecture 10 (on "Symbolism in Dreams") in Freud's *Introductory Lectures* (1916–17).]

23. Cf. also the eleven lectures on dreams which constitute part 2 of Freud's *Introductory Lectures* (1916–17).

are present in everyone, since almost everyone, including the most normal people, is capable of dreaming. The unconscious material of the dream-thoughts and its relation to consciousness and to repression raise further questions of significance to psychology, the answers to which must no doubt be postponed until analysis has clarified the origin of other psychopathological structures, such as hysterical symptoms and obsessional ideas.

Translated by James Strachey

5

Infantile Sexuality

Neglect of the Infantile Factor

One feature of the popular view of the sexual instinct is that it is absent in childhood and only awakens in the period of life described as puberty. This, however, is not merely a simple error but one that has had grave consequences, for it is mainly to this idea that we owe our present ignorance of the fundamental conditions of sexual life. A thorough study of the sexual manifestations of childhood would probably reveal the essential characters of the sexual instinct and would show us the course of its development and the way in which it is put together from various sources.

It is noticeable that writers who concern themselves with explaining the characteristics and reactions of the adult have devoted much more attention to the primeval period which is comprised in the life of the individual's ancestors—have, that is, ascribed much more influence to heredity—than to the other primeval period, which falls within the lifetime of the individual himself—that is, to childhood. One would surely have supposed that the influence of this latter period would be easier to understand and could claim to be considered before that of heredity.[1] It is true that in the literature of the subject one occasionally comes across remarks upon precocious sexual activity in small children—upon erections, masturbation, and even activities resembling coitus. But these are always quoted only as exceptional events, as oddities or as horrifying instances of precocious depravity. So far as I know, not a single author has clearly recognized the regular existence of a sex-

---

1. [*Footnote added* 1915:] Nor is it possible to estimate correctly the part played by heredity until the part played by childhood has been assessed.

ual instinct in childhood; and in the writings that have become so numerous on the development of children, the chapter on "Sexual Development" is as a rule omitted.[2]

Infantile Amnesia

The reason for this strange neglect is to be sought, I think, partly in considerations of propriety, which the authors obey as a result of their own upbringing, and partly in a psychological phenomenon which has itself hitherto eluded explanation. What I have in mind is the peculiar amnesia which, in the case of most people, though by no means all, hides the earliest beginnings of their childhood up to their sixth or eighth year. Hitherto it has not occurred to us to feel any astonishment at the fact of this amnesia, though we might have had good grounds for doing so. For we learn from other people that during these years, of which at a later date we retain nothing in our memory but a few unintelligible and fragmen-

---

2. The assertion made in the text has since struck me myself as being so bold that I have undertaken the task of testing its validity by looking through the literature once more. The outcome of this is that I have allowed my statement to stand unaltered. The scientific examination of both the physical and mental phenomena of sexuality in childhood is still in its earliest beginnings. One writer, Bell (1902, 327), remarks: "I know of no scientist who has given a careful analysis of the emotion as it is seen in the adolescent." Somatic sexual manifestations from the period before puberty have only attracted attention in connection with phenomena of degeneracy and as indications of degeneracy. In none of the accounts which I have read of the psychology of this period of life is a chapter to be found on the erotic life of children; and this applies to the well-known works of Preyer [1882], Baldwin (1898), Pérez (1886), Strümpell (1899), Groos (1904), Heller (1904), Sully (1895), and others. We can obtain the clearest impression of the state of things in this field today from the periodical *Die Kinderfehler* from 1896 onwards. Nevertheless the conviction is borne in upon us that the existence of love in childhood stands in no need of discovery. Pérez (1886, 272ff) argues in favor of its existence. Groos (1899, 326) mentions as a generally recognized fact that "some children are already accessible to sexual impulses at a very early age and feel an urge to have contact with the opposite sex." The earliest instance of the appearance of "sex-love" recorded by Bell (1902, 330) concerns a child in the middle of his third year. On this point compare further Havelock Ellis (1913, Appendix B).

[*Added* 1910:] This judgment upon the literature of infantile sexuality need no longer be maintained since the appearance of Stanley Hall's exhaustive work (1904). No such modification is necessitated by Moll's recent book (1909). See, on the other hand, Bleuler (1908). [*Added* 1915:] Since this was written, a book by Hug-Hellmuth (1913) has taken the neglected sexual factor fully into account.

tary recollections, we reacted in a lively manner to impressions, that we were capable of expressing pain and joy in a human fashion, that we gave evidence of love, jealousy, and other passionate feelings by which we were strongly moved at the time, and even that we gave utterance to remarks which were regarded by adults as good evidence of our possessing insight and the beginnings of a capacity for judgment. And of all this we, when we are grown up, have no knowledge of our own! Why should our memory lag so far behind the other activities of our minds? We have, on the contrary, good reason to believe that there is no period at which the capacity for receiving and reproducing impressions is greater than precisely during the years of childhood.[3]

On the other hand we must assume, or we can convince ourselves by a psychological examination of other people, that the very same impressions that we have forgotten have none the less left the deepest traces on our minds and have had a determining effect upon the whole of our later development. There can, therefore, be no question of any real abolition of the impressions of childhood, but rather of an amnesia similar to that which neurotics exhibit for later events, and of which the essence consists in a simple withholding of these impressions from consciousness, viz., in their repression. But what are the forces which bring about this repression of the impressions of childhood? Whoever could solve this riddle would, I think, have explained *hysterical* amnesia as well.

Meanwhile we must not fail to observe that the existence of infantile amnesia provides a new point of comparison between the mental stages of children and psychoneurotics. We have already come across another such point in the formula to which we were led, to the effect that the sexuality of psychoneurotics has remained at, or been carried back to, an infantile stage. Can it be, after all, that infantile amnesia, too, is to be brought into relation with the sexual impulses of childhood?

Moreover, the connection between infantile and hysterical amnesia is more than a mere play upon words. Hysterical amnesia, which occurs at the bidding of repression, is only explicable by the fact that the subject is already in possession of a store of memory-

---

3. I have attempted to solve one of the problems connected with the earliest memories of childhood in a paper on "Screen Memories" (1899a). [*Added* 1924:] See also chapter 4 of my *Psychopathology of Everyday Life* (1901b).

traces which have been withdrawn from conscious disposal, and which are now, by an associative link, attracting to themselves the material which the forces of repression are engaged in repelling from consciousness.[4] It may be said that without infantile amnesia there would be no hysterical amnesia.

I believe, then, that infantile amnesia, which turns everyone's childhood into something like a prehistoric epoch and conceals from him the beginnings of his own sexual life, is responsible for the fact that in general no importance is attached to childhood in the development of sexual life. The gaps in our knowledge which have arisen in this way cannot be bridged by a single observer. As long ago as in the year 1896[5] I insisted on the significance of the years of childhood in the origin of certain important phenomena connected with sexual life, and since then I have never ceased to emphasize the part played in sexuality by the infantile factor.

The Period of Sexual Latency
in Childhood and Its Interruptions

The remarkably frequent reports of what are described as irregular and exceptional sexual impulses in childhood, as well as the uncovering in neurotics of what have hitherto been unconscious memories of childhood, allow us to sketch out the sexual occurrences of that period in some such way as this.[6]

There seems no doubt that germs of sexual impulses are already present in the newborn child and that these continue to develop for a time, but are then overtaken by a progressive process of suppression; this in turn is itself interrupted by periodical advances

---

4. [*Footnote added* 1915:] The mechanism of repression cannot be understood unless account is taken of *both* of these two concurrent processes. They may be compared with the manner in which tourists are conducted to the top of the Great Pyramid of Giza by being pushed from one direction, and pulled from the other. [Cf. Freud's paper on "Repression" (1915*d*).]

5. E.g., in the last paragraph of section 1 of his paper on the etiology of hysteria (1896*c*).

6. We are able to make use of the second of these two sources of material since we are justified in expecting that the early years of children who are later to become neurotic are not likely in this respect to differ *essentially* from those of children who are to grow up into normal adults, [*added* 1915:] but only in the intensity and clarity of the phenomena involved.

in sexual development or may be held up by individual peculiarities. Nothing is known for certain concerning the regularity and periodicity of this oscillating course of development. It seems, however, that the sexual life of children usually emerges in a form accessible to observation round about the third or fourth year of life.[7]

Sexual Inhibitions

It is during this period of total or only partial latency that are built up the mental forces which are later to impede the course of the sexual instinct and, like dams, restrict its flow—disgust, feelings of shame, and the claims of aesthetic and moral ideals. One gets an impression from civilized children that the construction of these dams is a product of education, and no doubt education has much

---

7. There is a possible anatomical analogy to what I believe to be the course of development of the infantile sexual function in Bayer's discovery (1902) that the internal sexual organ is (i.e., the uterus) are as a rule larger in newborn children than in older ones. It is not certain, however, what view we should take of this involution that occurs after birth (which has been shown by Halban to apply also to other portions of the genital apparatus). According to Halban (1904) the process of involution comes to an end after a few weeks of extrauterine life. [*Added* 1920:] Those authorities who regard the interstitial portion of the sex gland as the organ that determines sex have on their side been led by anatomical researches to speak of infantile sexuality and a period of sexual latency. I quote a passage from Lipschütz's book (1919, 168), which I earlier mentioned: "We shall be doing more justice to the facts if we say that the maturation of the sexual characters which is accomplished at puberty is only due to a great acceleration which occurs at that time of processes which began much earlier—in my view as early as during intrauterine life." "What has hitherto been described in a summary way as puberty is probably only a second major phase of puberty which sets in about the middle of the second decade of life. . . . Childhood, from birth until the beginning of this second major phase, might be described as 'the intermediate phase of puberty'" (ibid., 170). Attention was drawn to this coincidence between anatomical findings and psychological observation in a review [of Lipschütz's book] by Ferenczi (1920). The agreement is marred only by the fact that the "first peak" in the development of the sexual organs occurs during the early intrauterine period, whereas the early efflorescence of infantile sexual life must be ascribed to the third and fourth years of life. There is, of course, no need to expect that anatomical growth and psychical development must be exactly simultaneous. The researches in question were made on the sex glands of human beings. Since a period of latency in the psychological sense does not occur in animals, it would be very interesting to know whether the anatomical findings which have led these writers to assume the occurrence of two peaks in sexual development are also demonstrable in the higher animals.

to do with it. But in reality this development is organically determined and fixed by heredity, and it can occasionally occur without any help at all from education. Education will not be trespassing beyond its appropriate domain if it limits itself to following the lines which have already been laid down organically and to impressing them somewhat more clearly and deeply.

Reaction-Formation and Sublimation

What is it that goes to the making of these constructions which are so important for the growth of a civilized and normal individual? They probably emerge at the cost of the infantile sexual impulses themselves. Thus the activity of those impulses does not cease even during this period of latency, though their energy is diverted, wholly or in great part, from their sexual use and directed to other ends. Historians of civilization appear to be at one in assuming that powerful components are acquired for every kind of cultural achievement by this diversion of sexual instinctual forces from sexual aims and their direction to new ones—a process which deserves the name of "sublimation." To this we would add, accordingly, that the same process plays a part in the development of the individual and we would place its beginning in the period of sexual latency of childhood.[8]

It is possible further to form some idea of the mechanism of this process of sublimation. On the one hand, it would seem, the sexual impulses cannot be utilized during these years of childhood, since the reproductive functions have been deferred—a fact which constitutes the main feature of the period of latency. On the other hand, these impulses would seem in themselves to be perverse—that is, to arise from erotogenic zones and to derive their activity from instincts which, in view of the direction of the subject's development, can only arouse unpleasurable feelings. They consequently evoke opposing mental forces (reacting impulses) which, in order to suppress this unpleasure effectively, build up the mental dams that I have already mentioned—disgust, shame, and morality.[9]

---

8. Once again, it is from Fliess that I have borrowed the term *period of sexual latency.*

9. [*Footnote added* 1915:] In the case which I am here discussing, the sublimation of sexual instinctual forces takes place along the path of reaction-formation. But in general it is possible to distinguish the concepts of sublimation and reaction-

Interruptions of the Latency Period

We must not deceive ourselves as to the hypothetical nature and insufficient clarity of our knowledge concerning the processes of the infantile period of latency or deferment; but we shall be on firmer ground in pointing out that such an application of infantile sexuality represents an educational ideal from which individual development usually diverges at some point and often to a considerable degree. From time to time a fragmentary manifestation of sexuality which has evaded sublimation may break through; or some sexual activity may persist through the whole duration of the latency period until the sexual instinct emerges with greater intensity at puberty. In so far as educators pay any attention at all to infantile sexuality, they behave exactly as though they shared our views as to the construction of the moral defensive forces at the cost of sexuality, and as though they knew that sexual activity makes a child ineducable: for they stigmatize every sexual manifestation by children as a "vice," without being able to do much against it. We, on the other hand, have every reason for turning our attention to these phenomena which are so much dreaded by education, for we may expect them to help us to discover the original configuration of the sexual instincts.

The Manifestations
of Infantile Sexuality

Thumb Sucking

For reasons which will appear later, I shall take thumb sucking (or sensual sucking) as a sample of the sexual manifestations of childhood. (An excellent study of this subject has been made by the Hungarian pediatrician, Lindner, 1879.)[10]

---

formation from each other as two different processes. Sublimation can also take place by other and simpler mechanisms. [Further theoretical discussions of sublimation will be found in section 3 of Freud's paper on narcissism (1914c) and at several points in The Ego and the Id (1923b, chapters 3, 4, and 5).]

10. There seems to be no nursery word in English equivalent to the German *lutschen* and *ludeln,* used by Freud alongside *wonnesaugen* (sensual sucking). Conrad in *Struwwelpeter* was a *Lutscher;* but, as will be seen from the context, "suck-a-thumbs" and "thumb-sucking" have in fact too narrow a connotation for the present purpose.

Thumb sucking appears already in early infancy and may continue into maturity, or even persist all through life. It consists in the rhythmic repetition of a sucking contact by the mouth (or lips). There is no question of the purpose of this procedure being the taking of nourishment. A portion of the lip itself, the tongue, or any other part of the skin within reach—even the big toe—may be taken as the object upon which this sucking is carried out. In this connection a grasping-instinct may appear and may manifest itself as a simultaneous rhythmic tugging at the lobes of the ears or a catching hold of some part of another person (as a rule the ear) for the same purpose. Sensual sucking involves a complete absorption of the attention and leads either to sleep or even to a motor reaction in the nature of an orgasm.[11] It is not infrequently combined with rubbing some sensitive part of the body such as the breast or the external genitalia. Many children proceed by this path from sucking to masturbation.

Lindner himself[12] clearly recognized the sexual nature of this activity and emphasized it without qualification. In the nursery, sucking is often classed along with the other kinds of sexual "naughtiness" of children. This view has been most energetically repudiated by numbers of pediatricians and nerve-specialists, though this is no doubt partly due to a confusion between "sexual" and "genital." Their objection raises a difficult question and one which cannot be evaded: what is the general characteristic which enables us to recognize the sexual manifestations of children? The concatenation of phenomena into which we have been given an

---

11. Thus we find at this early stage, what holds good all through life, that sexual satisfaction is the best soporific. Most cases of nervous insomnia can be traced back to lack of sexual satisfaction. It is well-known that unscrupulous nurses put crying children to sleep by stroking their genitals.

12. This paragraph was added in 1915. In its place the following paragraph appears in the editions of 1905 and 1910 only: "No observer has felt any doubt as to the sexual nature of this activity. Nevertheless, the best theories formed by adults in regard to this example of the sexual behavior of children leave us in the lurch. Consider Moll's [1898] analysis of the sexual instinct into an instinct of detumescence and an instinct of contrectation. The first of these factors cannot be concerned in our present instance, and the second one can only be recognized with difficulty, since, according to Moll, it emerges later than the instinct of detumescence and is directed toward other people."—In 1910 the following footnote was attached to the first sentence of this canceled paragraph: "With the exception of Moll (1909)."

insight by psycho analytic investigation justifies us, in my opinion, in regarding thumb sucking as a sexual manifestation and in choosing it for our study of the essential features of infantile sexual activity.[13]

Autoerotism

We are in duty bound to make a thorough examination of this example. It must be insisted that the most striking feature of this sexual activity is that the instinct is not directed toward other people, but obtains satisfaction from the subject's own body. It is "autoerotic," to call it by a happily chosen term introduced by Havelock Ellis (1910).[14]

Furthermore, it is clear that the behavior of a child who indulges in thumb sucking is determined by a search for some pleasure which has already been experienced and is now remembered. In the simplest case he proceeds to find this satisfaction by sucking rhythmically at some part of the skin or mucous membrane. It is also easy to guess the occasions on which the child had his first experiences of the pleasure which he is now striving to renew. It was the child's first and most vital activity, his sucking at his mother's breast, or at substitutes for it, that must have familiarized him with this pleasure. The child's lips, in our view, behave like an erotogenic zone, and no doubt stimulation by the warm flow

---

13. [*Footnote added* 1920:] In 1919, a Dr. Galant published, under the title of "Das Lutscherli," the confession of a grown-up girl who had never given up this infantile sexual activity and who represents the satisfaction to be gained from sucking as something completely analogous to sexual satisfaction, particularly when this is obtained from a lover's kiss: "Not every kiss, is equal to a '*Lutscherli*'—no, no, not by any means! It is impossible to describe what a lovely feeling goes through your whole body when you suck; you are right away from this world. You are absolutely satisfied, and happy beyond desire. It is a wonderful feeling; you long for nothing but peace—uninterrupted peace. It is just unspeakably lovely: you feel no pain and no sorrow, and ah! you are carried into another world."

14. [*Footnote added* 1920:] Havelock Ellis, it is true, uses the word *autoerotic* in a somewhat different sense, to describe an excitation which is not provoked from outside but arises internally. What psychoanalysis regards as the essential point is not the genesis of the excitation, but the question of its relation to an object.—[In all editions before 1920 this footnote read as follows: "Havelock Ellis, however, has spoilt the meaning of the term he invented by including the whole of hysteria and all the manifestation of masturbation among the phenomena of autoerotism."]

of milk is the cause of the pleasurable sensation. The satisfaction of the erotogenic zone is associated, in the first instance, with the satisfaction of the need for nourishment. To begin with, sexual activity attaches itself to functions serving the purpose of self-preservation and does not become independent of them until later.[15] No one who has seen a baby sinking back satiated from the breast and falling asleep with flushed cheeks and a blissful smile can escape the reflection that this picture persists as a prototype of the expression of sexual satisfaction in later life. The need for repeating the sexual satisfaction now becomes detached from the need for taking nourishment—a separation which becomes inevitable when the teeth appear and food is no longer taken in only by sucking, but is also chewed up. The child does not make use of an extraneous body for his sucking, but prefers a part of his own skin because it is more convenient, because it makes him independent of the external world, which he is not yet able to control, and because it that way he provides himself, as it were, with a second erotogenic zone, though one of an inferior kind. The inferiority of this second region is among the reasons why at a later date he seeks the corresponding part—the lips—of another person. ("It's a pity I can't kiss myself," he seems to be saying.)

It is not every child who sucks in this way. It may be assumed that those children do so in whom there is a constitutional intensification of the erotogenic significance of the labial region. If that significance persists, these same children when they are grown up will become epicures in kissing, will be inclined to perverse kissing, or, if males, will have a powerful motive for drinking and smoking. If, however, repression ensues, they will feel disgust at food and will produce hysterical vomiting. The repression extends to the nutritional instinct owing to the dual purpose served by the labial zone. Many[16] of my women patients who suffer from disturbances of eating, *globus hystericus,* constriction of the throat and vomiting, have indulged energetically in sucking during their childhood.

---

15. This sentence was added in 1915. Cf. section 2 of Freud's paper on narcissism (1914c).]

[In the first edition only this reads "all."]

16. This clause was added in 1915; and in the earlier editions the word *three* in the last sentence is replaced by *two.*

Our study of thumb sucking or sensual sucking has already given us the three essential characteristics of an infantile sexual manifestation. At its origin it attaches itself to one of the vital somatic functions; it has as yet no sexual object, and is thus autoerotic; and its sexual aim is dominated by an erotogenic zone. It is to be anticipated that these characteristics will be found to apply equally to most of the other activities of the infantile sexual instincts.

The Sexual Aim of Infantile Sexuality
Characteristics of Erotogenic Zones

The example of thumb sucking shows us still more about what constitutes an erotogenic zone. It is part of the skin or mucous membrane in which stimuli of a certain sort evoke a feeling of pleasure possessing a particular quality. There can be no doubt that the stimuli which produce the pleasure are governed by special conditions, though we do not know what those are. A rhythmic character must play a part among them and the analogy of tickling is forced upon our notice. It seems less certain whether the character of the pleasurable feeling evoked by the stimulus should be described as a "specific" one—a "specific" quality in which the sexual factor would precisely lie. Psychology is still so much in the dark in questions of pleasure and unpleasure that the most cautious assumption is the one most to be recommended. We may later come upon reasons which seem to support the idea that the pleasurable feeling does in fact possess a specific quality.

The character of erotogenicity can be attached to some parts of the body in a particularly marked way. There are predestined erotogenic zones, as is shown by the example of sucking. The same example, however, also shows us that any other part of the skin or mucous membrane can take over the functions of an erotogenic zone, and must therefore have some aptitude in that direction. Thus the quality of the stimulus has more to do with producing the pleasurable feeling than has the nature of the part of the body concerned. A child who is indulging in sensual sucking searches about his body and chooses some part of it to suck—a part which is afterwards preferred to him from force of habit; if he happens to hit upon one of the predestined regions (such as the nipples or genitals) no doubt it retains the preference. A precisely analogous tendency to displacement is also found in the symptomatology of hysteria. In that neurosis repression affects most of all the actual genital zones and these transmit their susceptibility to stimulation to other erotogenic zones (normally neglected in adult life), which then behave exactly like genitals. But besides this, precisely as in the case of sucking, any other part of the body can acquire the same susceptibility to simulation as is possessed by the genitals and can become an erotogenic zone. Erotogenic and hysterogenic zones show the same characteristics.[17]

The Infantile Sexual Aim

The sexual aim of the infantile instinct consists in obtaining satisfaction by means of an appropriate stimulation of the erotogenic zone which has been selected in one way or another. This satisfaction must have been previously experienced in order to have left behind a need for its repetition; and we may expect that Nature will have made safe provisions so that this experience of satisfaction shall not be left to chance.[18] We have already learned what the contrivance is that fulfills this purpose in the case of the labial zone: it is the simultaneous connection which links this part of the body with the taking in of food. We shall come across other, similar contrivances as sources of sexuality. The state of being in need of a repetition of the satisfaction reveals itself in two ways: by a peculiar feeling of tension, possessing, rather, the character of unpleasure, and by a sensation of itching or stimulation which is centrally conditioned and projected on the peripheral erotogenic zone. We can therefore formulate a sexual aim in another way: it consists in replacing the projected sensation of stimulation in the erotogenic zone by an external stimulus which removes that sensation by producing a feeling of satisfaction. This external stimulus

---

17. [*Footnote added* 1915:] After further reflection and after taking other observations into account, I have been led to ascribe the qualify of erotogenicity to all parts of the body and to all the internal organs. Cf. also in this connection what is said below on narcissism. [In the 1910 edition only, the following footnote appeared at this point: "The biological problems relating to the hypothesis of erotogenic zones have been discussed by Alfred Adler (1907)."]

18. [*Footnote added* 1920:] In biological discussions it is scarcely possible to avoid a teleological way of thinking, even though one is aware that in any particular instance one is not secure against error.

will usually consist in some kind of manipulation that is analogous to the sucking.[19]

The fact that the need can be evoked peripherally, by a real modification of the erotogenic zone, is in complete harmony with our physiological knowledge. This strikes us as somewhat strange only because, in order to remove one stimulus, it seems necessary to adduce a second one at the same spot.

Masturbatory Sexual Manifestations[20]

It must come as a great relief to find that, when once we have understood the nature of the instinct arising from a single one of the erotogenic zones, we shall have very little more to learn of the sexual activity of children. The clearest distinctions as between one zone and another concern the nature of the contrivance necessary for satisfying the instinct; in the case of the labial zone it consisted of sucking, and this has to be replaced by other muscular actions according to the position and nature of the other zones.

Activity of the Anal Zone

Like the labial zone, the anal zone is well suited by its position to act as a medium through which sexuality may attach itself to other somatic functions. It is to be presumed that the erotogenic significance of this part of the body is very great from the first. We learn with some astonishment from psychoanalysis of the transmutations normally undergone by the sexual excitations arising from this

---

19. This account of the way in which a particular sexual desire becomes established on the basis of an "experience of satisfaction"is only a special application of Freud's general theory of the mechanism of wishes, as explained in section C of chapter 7 of *The Interpretation of Dreams* (1900*a*, Standard Ed., 5, 565f.). This theory had already been sketched out by him in his posthumously published "Project for a Scientific Psychology" (Freud, 1950*a*, appendix, part 1, section 16). In both these passages the example chosen as an illustration is in fact that of an infant at the breast. The whole topic links up with Freud's views on "reality-testing," as discussed, for instance, in his paper on "Negation" (1925*h*).

20. Cf. the very copious literature on the subject of masturbation, which for the most part, however, is at sea upon the main issues., e.g., Rohleder (1899). [*Added* 1915:] See also the report of the discussion on the subject in the Vienna Psycho-Analytical Society (*Diskussionen,* 1912)—[and especially Freud's own contributions to it (1912*f*)].

zone and of the frequency with which it retains a considerable amount of susceptibility to genital stimulation throughout life.[21] The intestinal disturbances which are so common in childhood see to it that the zone shall not lack intense excitations. Intestinal catarrhs at the tenderest age make children "nervy," as people say, and in cases of later neurotic illness they have a determining influence on the symptoms in which the neurosis is expressed, and they put at its disposal the whole range of intestinal disturbances. If we bear in mind the erotogenic significance of the outlet of the intestinal canal, which persists, at all events in a modified form, we shall not be inclined to scoff at the influence of hemorrhoids, to which old-fashioned medicine used to attach so much importance in explaining neurotic conditions.

Children who are making use of the susceptibility to erotogenic stimulation of the anal zone betray themselves by holding back their stool till its accumulation brings about violet muscular contractions and, as it passes through the anus, is able to produce powerful stimulation of the mucous membrane. In so doing it must no doubt cause not only painful but also highly pleasurable sensations. One of the clearest signs of subsequent eccentricity or nervousness is to be seen when a baby obstinately refuses to empty his bowels when he is put on the pot—that is, when his nurse wants him to—and holds back that function till he himself chooses to exercise it. He is naturally not concerned with dirtying the bed, he is only anxious not to miss the subsidiary pleasure attached to defecating. Educators are once more right when they describe children who keep the process back as "naughty."

The contents of the bowels,[22] which act as a stimulating mass upon a sexually sensitive portion of mucous membrane, behave like forerunners of another organ, which is destined to come into action after the phase of childhood. But they have other important meanings for the infant. They are clearly treated as a part of the infant's own body and represent his first "gift": by producing them he can express his active compliance with his environment and, by

21. [*Footnote added* 1910:] Cf. my papers on "Character and Anal Erotism" (1980b) [*added* 1920:] and "On Transformations of Instinct as Exemplified in Anal Erotism" (1917c).

22. This paragraph was added in 1915. Its contents were expanded in one of the papers (1917c) mentioned in the last footnote.

withholding them, his disobedience. From being a "gift" they later come to acquire the meaning of "baby"—for babies, according to one of the sexual theories of children [see below, p. 103], are acquired by eating and are born through the bowels.

The retention of the fecal mass, which is thus carried out intentionally by the child to begin with, in order to serve, as it were, as a masturbatory stimulus upon the anal zone or to be employed in his relation to the people looking after him, is also one of the roots of the constipation which is so common among neuropaths. Further, the whole significance of the anal zone is reflected in the fact that few neurotics are to be found without their special scatological practices, ceremonies, and so on, which they carefully keep secret.[23]

Actual masturbatory stimulation of the anal zone by means of the finger, provoked by a centrally determined or peripherally maintained sensation of itching, is by no means rare among older children.

Activity of the Genital Zones

Among the erotogenic zones that form part of the child's body there is one which certainly does not play the opening part, and which cannot be the vehicle of the oldest sexual impulses, but which is destined to great things in the future. In both male and female children it is brought into connection with micturition (in the glans and clitoris) and in the former is enclosed in a pouch of mucous membrane, so that there can be no lack of stimulation of it by secretions which may give an early start to sexual excitation.

---

23. [*Footnote added* 1920:] Lou Andreas-Salomé (1916), in a paper which has given us a very much deeper understanding of the significance of anal erotism, has shown how the history of the first prohibition which a child comes across—the prohibition against getting pleasure from anal activity and its products—has a decisive effect on his whole development. This must be the first occasion on which the infant has a glimpse of an environment hostile to his instinctual impulses, on which he learns to separate his own entity from this alien one and on which he carries out the first "repression" of his possibilities for pleasure. From that time on, what is "anal" remains the symbol of everything that is to be repudiated and excluded from life. The clear-cut distinction between anal and genital processes which is later insisted upon is contradicted by the close anatomical and functional analogies and relations which hold between them. The genital apparatus remains the neighbor of the cloaca, and actually [to quote Lou Andreas-Salomé] "in the case of women is only taken from it on lease."

The sexual activities of this erotogenic zone, which forms part of the sexual organs proper, are the beginning of what is later to become "normal" sexual life. The anatomical situation of this region, the secretions in which it is bathed, the washing and rubbing to which it is subjected in the course of a child's toilet, as well as accidental stimulation (such as the movement of intestinal worms in the case of girls), make it inevitable that the pleasurable feeling which this part of the body is capable of producing should be noticed by children even during their earliest infancy, and should give rise to a need for its repetition. If we consider this whole range of contrivances and bear in mind that both making a mess and measures for keeping clean are bound to operate in much the same way, it is scarcely possible to avoid the conclusion that the foundations for the future primacy over sexual activity exercised by this erotogenic zone are established by early infantile masturbation, which scarcely a single individual escapes.[24] The action which disposes of the stimulus and brings about satisfaction consists in a rubbing movement with the hand or in the application of pressure (no doubt on the lines of a pre-existing reflex) either from the hand or by bringing the thighs together. This last method is by far the more common in the case of girls. The preference for the hand which is shown by boys is already evidence of the important contribution which the instinct for mastery is destined to make a masculine sexual activity.[25]

It will be in the interests of clarity[26] if I say at once that three phases of infantile masturbation are to be distinguished. The first

---

24. In the editions of 1905 and 1910 the last part of this sentence read: "it is difficult to overlook Nature's purpose of establishing the future primacy over sexual activity exercised by this erotogenic zone by means of early infantile masturbation, which scarcely a single individual escapes." The teleological nature of this argument in favor of the universality of infantile masturbation was sharply criticized by Rudolf Reitler in the course of the discussions on that topic in the Vienna Psycho-Analytical Society in 1912 (*Diskussionen*, 1912, 92f.). In his own contribution to the discussion (ibid., 134; Freud, 1912*f*), Freud agreed that phrasing he had used was unfortunate, and undertook to alter it in later reprints. The present version of the sentence was accordingly substituted in 1915.

25. [*Footnote added* 1915:] Unusual techniques in carrying out masturbation in later years seem to point to the influence of a prohibition against masturbation which has been overcome.

26. This paragraph was added in 1915. In the edition of that year there were also added the title of the next paragraph and the parenthesis "as a rule before the fourth year" in its second sentence. Moreover, in the first sentence of the same paragraph the words "after a short time" were substituted for the words "at the

of these belongs to early infancy, and the second to the brief efflorescence of sexual activity about the fourth year of life; only the third phase corresponds to pubertal masturbation, which is often the only kind taken into account.

Second Phase of Infantile Masturbation

The masturbation of early infancy seems to disappear after a short time; but it may persist uninterruptedly until puberty, and this would constitute the first great deviation from the course of development laid down for civilized men. At some point of childhood after early infancy, as a rule before the fourth year, the sexual instinct belonging to the genital zone usually revives and persists again for a time until it is once more suppressed, or it may continue without interruption. This second phase of infantile sexual activity may assume a variety of different forms which can only be determined by a precise analysis of individual cases. But all its details leave behind the deepest (unconscious) impressions in the subject's memory, determine the development of his character, if he is to remain healthy, and the symptomatology of his neurosis, if he is to fall ill after puberty.[27] In the latter case we find that this sexual period has been forgotten and that the conscious memories that bear witness to it have been displaced. (I have already mentioned that I am also inclined to relate normal infantile amnesia to this infantile sexual activity.) Psychoanalytic investigation enables us to make what has been forgotten conscious and thus do away with a compulsion that arises from the unconscious psychical material.

---

onset of the latency period" which had appeared in 1905 and 1910. Finally, in those first two editions, the *following* paragraph began with the words "During the years of childhood (it has not yet been possible to generalize as to the chronology) the sexual excitation of early infancy returns . . ." The motive for all these changes made in 1915 was evidently to distinguish more sharply between the second and first phases of infantile sexual activity and to assign a more precise date—"about the fourth year"—to the second phase.

27. [*Footnote added* 1915:] The problem of why the sense of guilt of neurotics is, as Bleuler [1913] recently recognized, regularly attached to the memory of some masturbatory activity, usually at puberty, still awaits an exhaustive analytic explanation. [*Added* 1920:] The most general and most important factor concerned must no doubt be that masturbation represents the executive agency of the whole of infantile sexuality and is, therefore, able to take over the sense of guilt attaching to it.

Return of Early Infantile Masturbation

During the years of childhood with which I am now dealing, the sexual excitation of early infancy returns, either as a centrally determined tickling stimulus which seeks satisfaction in masturbation, or as a process in the nature of a nocturnal emission which, like the nocturnal emissions of adult years, achieves satisfaction without the help of any action by the subject. The latter case is the more frequent with girls and in the second half of childhood; its determinants are not entirely intelligible and often, though not invariably, it seems to be conditioned by a period of earlier *active* masturbation. The symptoms of these sexual manifestations are scanty; they are mostly displayed on behalf of the still-undeveloped sexual apparatus by the *urinary* apparatus, which thus acts, as it were, as the former's trustee. Most of the so-called bladder disorders of this period are sexual disturbances; nocturnal enuresis, unless it represents an epileptic fit, corresponds to a nocturnal emission.

The reappearance of sexual activity is determined by internal causes and external contingencies, both of which can be guessed in cases of neurotic illness from the form taken by their symptoms and can be discovered with certainty by psychoanalytic investigation. I shall have to speak presently of the internal causes; great and lasting importance attaches at this period to the accidental *external* contingencies. In the foreground we find the effects of seduction, which treats a child as a sexual object prematurely and teaches him, in highly emotional circumstances, how to obtain satisfaction from his genital zones, a satisfaction which he is then usually obliged to repeat again and again by masturbation. An influence of this kind may originate either from adults or from other children. I cannot admit that in my paper on "The Aetiology of Hysteria" (1896c) I exaggerated the frequency or importance of that influence, though I did not then know that persons who remain normal may have had the same experiences in their childhood, and though I consequently overrated the importance of seduction in comparison with the factors of sexual constitution and development.[28] Obviously seduction is not required in order to

28. Havelock Ellis [1913, Appendix B] has published a number of autobiographical narratives written by people who remained predominantly normal in later life and describing the first sexual impulses of their childhood and the occasions which

arouse a child's sexual life; that can also come about spontaneously from internal causes.

Polymorphously Perverse Disposition

It is an instructive fact that under the influence of seduction children can become polymorphously perverse, and can be led into all possible kinds of sexual irregularities. This shows that an aptitude for them is innately present in their disposition. There is consequently little resistance toward carrying them out, since the mental dams against sexual excesses—shame, disgust, and morality—have either not yet been constructed at all or are only in course of construction, according to the age of the child. In this respect children behave in the same kind of way as an average uncultivated woman in whom the same polymorphously perverse disposition persists. Under ordinary conditions she may remain normal sexually, but if she is led on by a clever seducer she will find every sort of perversion to her taste, and will retain them as part of her own sexual activities. Prostitutes exploit the same polymorphous, that is, infantile, disposition for the purposes of their profession; and, considering the immense number of women who are prostitutes or who must be supposed to have an aptitude for prostitution without becoming engaged in it, it becomes impossible not to recognize that this same disposition to perversions of every kind is a general and fundamental human characteristic.

Component Instincts

Moreover, the effects of seduction do not help to reveal the early history of the sexual instinct; they rather confuse our view of it by presenting children prematurely with a sexual object for which the infantile sexual instinct at first shows no need. It must, however, be admitted that infantile sexual life, in spite of the preponderating dominance of erotogenic zones, exhibits components which from

---

gave rise to them. These reports naturally suffer from the fact that they omit the prehistoric period of the writers' sexual lives, which is veiled by infantile amnesia and which can only be filled in by psychoanalysis in the case of an individual who has developed a neurosis. In more than one respect, nevertheless, the statements are valuable, and similar narratives were what led me to make the modification in my etiological hypotheses which I have mentioned in the text.

the very first involve other people as sexual objects. Such are the instincts of scopophilia, exhibitionism, and cruelty, which appear in a sense independently of erotogenic zones; these instincts do not enter into intimate relations which genital[29] life until later, but are already to be observed in childhood as independent impulses, distinct in the first instance from erotogenic sexual activity. Small children are essentially without shame, and at some periods of their earliest years show an unmistakable satisfaction in exposing their bodies, with especial emphasis on the sexual parts. The counterpart of this supposedly perverse inclination, curiosity to see other people's genitals, probably does not become manifest until somewhat later in childhood, when the obstacle set up by a sense of shame has already reached a certain degree of development.[30] Under the influence of seduction the scopophilic perversion can attain great importance in the sexual life of a child. But my researches into the early years of normal people, as well as of neurotic patients, force me to the conclusion that scopophilia can also appear in children as a spontaneous manifestation. Small children whose attention has once been drawn—as a rule by masturbation—to their own genitals usually take the further step without help from outside and develop a lively interest in the genitals of their playmates. Since opportunities for satisfying curiosity of this kind usually occur only in the course of satisfying the two kinds of need for excretion, children of this kind turn into *voyeurs,* eager spectators of the processes of micturition and defecation. When repression of these inclinations sets in, the desire to see other people's genitals (whether of their own or the opposite sex) persists as a tormenting compulsion, which in some cases of neurosis later affords the strongest motive force for the formation of symptoms.

The cruel component of the sexual instinct develops in childhood even more independently of the sexual activities that are attached to erotogenic zones. Cruelty in general comes easily to the childish nature, since the obstacle that brings the instinct for mastery to

---

29. "Sexual" in 1905 and 1910.

30. In the first (1905) edition this sentence read: "The counterpart . . . does not join in until later in childhood, when. . . ." In 1910 the word *probably* was inserted; in 1915 "join in" was replaced by "become manifest"; and in 1920 "somewhat" was inserted before "later."—The subject of exhibitionism in young children had been discussed at some length by Freud in his *Interpretation of Dreams*, chapter 5, section D(*a*) (Standard Ed., 4, 224f.).

a halt at another person's pain—namely, a capacity for pity—is developed relatively late. The fundamental psychological analysis of this instinct has, as we know, not yet been satisfactorily achieved. It may be assumed that the impulse of cruelty arises from the instinct for mastery and appears at a period of sexual life at which the genitals have not yet taken over their later role. It then dominates a phase of sexual life which we shall later describe as a pregenital organization.[31] Children who distinguish themselves by special cruelty toward animals and playmates usually give rise to a just suspicion of an intense and precocious sexual activity arising from erotogenic zones; and, though all the sexual instincts may display simultaneous precocity, *erotogenic* sexual activity seems, nevertheless, to be the primary one. The absence of the barrier of pity brings with it a danger that the connection between the cruel and the erotogenic instincts, thus established in childhood, may prove unbreakable in later life. Ever since Jean-Jacques Rousseau's *Confessions,* it has been well-known to all educationalists that the painful stimulation of the skin of the buttocks is one of the erotogenic roots of the *passive* instinct of cruelty (masochism). The conclusion has rightly been drawn by them that corporal punishment, which is usually applied to this part of the body, should not be inflicted upon any children whose libido is liable to be forced into collateral channels by the later demands of cultural education.[32]

---

31. The last two sentences were given their present form in 1915. In 1905 and 1910 they read as follows: "It may be assumed that the impulses of cruelty arise from sources which are in fact independent of sexuality, but may become united with it at an early stage owing to an anastomosis [cross-connection] near their points of origin. Observation teaches us, however, that sexual development and the development of the instinct of scopophilia and cruelty are subject to mutual influences which limit this presumed independence of the two sets of instincts."

32. [*Footnote added* 1910:] When the account which I have given above of infantile sexuality was first published in 1905, it was founded for the most part on the results of psychoanalytic research upon adults. At that time it was impossible to make full use of direct observation on children: only isolated hints and some valuable pieces of confirmation came from that source. Since then it has become possible to gain direct insight into infantile psychosexuality by the analysis of some cases of neurotic illness during the early years of childhood. It is gratifying to be able to report that direct observation has fully confirmed the conclusions arrived at by psychoanalysis—which is incidentally good evidence of the trustworthiness of that method of research. In addition to this, the "Analysis of a Phobia in a Five-Year-Old Boy" (1909*b*) has taught us much that is new for which we have not been prepared by psychoanalysis: for instance, the fact that sexual symbolism—the

The Sexual Researches of Childhood[33]

The Instinct for Knowledge

At about the same time as the sexual life of children reaches its first peak, between the ages of three and five, they also begin to show signs of the activity which may be ascribed to the instinct for knowledge or research. This instinct cannot be counted among the elementary instinctual components, nor can it be classed as exclusively belonging to sexuality. Its activity corresponds on the one hand to a sublimated manner of obtaining mastery, while on the other hand it makes use of the energy of scopophilia. Its relations to sexual life, however, are of particular importance, since we have learned from psychoanalysis that the instinct for knowledge in children is attracted unexpectedly early and intensively to sexual problems and is in fact possibly first aroused by them.

The Riddle of the Sphinx

It is not by theoretical interests but by practical ones that activities of research are set going in children. The threat to the bases of a child's existence offered by the discovery or the suspicion of the arrival of a new baby and the fear that he may, as a result of it, cease to be cared for and loved, make him thoughtful and clear-sighted. And this history of the instinct's origin is in line with the fact that the first problem with which it deals is not the question

---

representation of what is sexual by nonsexual objects and relations—extends back into the first years of possession of the power of speech. I was further made aware of a defect in the account I have given in the text, which, in the interests of lucidity, describes the conceptual distinction between the two phases of autoerotism and object-love as though it were also a separation in time. But the analyses that I have just mentioned, as well as the findings of Bell quoted on p. 81, *n.* 2, above, show that children between the ages of three and five are capable of very clear object-choice, accompanied by strong affects.—[In 1910 only, this footnote continued as follows: "Another addition to our knowledge of infantile sexual life which has not yet been mentioned in the text relates to the sexual researches of children, to the theories to which children are led by them (cf. my paper on the subject, 1908c), to the important bearing of these theories upon later neuroses, to the outcome of these infantile researches and to their relation to the development of children's intellectual powers."

33. The whole of this section on the sexual researches of children first appeared in 1915.

of the distinction between the sexes but the riddle of where babies come from.[34] (This, in a distorted form which can easily be rectified, is the same riddle that was propounded by the Theban Sphinx.) On the contrary, the existence of two sexes does not to begin with arouse any difficulties or doubts in children. It is self-evident to a male child that genital like his own is to be attributed to everyone he knows, and he cannot make its absence tally with his picture of these other people.

Castration Complex and Penis Envy

This conviction is energetically maintained by boys, is obstinately defended against the contradictions which soon result from observation, and is only abandoned after severe internal struggles (the castration complex). The substitutes for this penis which they feel is missing in women play a great part in determining the form taken by many perversions.[35]

The assumption that all human beings have the same (male) form of genital is the first of the many remarkable and momentous sexual theories of children. It is of little use to a child that the science of biology justifies his prejudice and has been obliged to recognize the female clitoris as a true substitute for the penis.

Little girls do not resort to denial of this kind when they see that boys's genitals are formed differently from their own. They are ready to recognize them immediately and are overcome by envy for the penis—an envy culminating in the wish, which is so important in its consequences, to be boys themselves.

Theories of Birth

Many people can remember clearly what an intense interest they took during the prepubertal period in the question of where babies come from. The anatomical answers to the question were at the

---

34. In a later work, Freud (1925*j*) corrected this statement, saying that it is not true of girls, and not always true of boys.

35. [*Footnote added* 1920:] We are justified in speaking of a castration complex in women as well. Both male and female children form a theory that women no less than men originally had a penis, but that they have lost it by castration. The conviction which is finally reached by males that women have no penis often leads them to an enduringly low opinion of the other sex.

very various: babies come out of the breast, or are cut out of the body, or the navel opens to let them through.[36] Outside analysis, there are very seldom memories of any similar researches having been carried out in the *early* years of childhood. These earlier researches fell a victim to repression long since, but all their findings were of a uniform nature: people get babies by eating some particular thing (as they do in fairy tales) and babies are born through the bowel like a discharge of feces. These infantile theories remind us of conditions that exist in the animal kingdom—and especially of the cloaca in types of animals lower than mammals.

Sadistic View of Sexual Intercourse

If children at this early age witness sexual intercourse between adults—for which an opportunity is provided by the conviction of grown-up people that small children cannot understand anything sexual—they inevitably regard the sexual act as a sort of ill-treatment or act of subjugation: they view it, that is, in a sadistic sense. Psychoanalysis also shows us that an impression of this kind in early childhood contributes a great deal toward a predisposition to a subsequent sadistic displacement of the sexual aim. Furthermore, children are much concerned with the problem of what sexual intercourse—or, as they put it, being married—consists in: and they usually seek a solution of the mystery in some common activity concerned with the function of micturition or defecation.

Typical Failure of Infantile Sexual Researches

We can say in general of the sexual theories of children that they are reflections of their own sexual constitution, and that in spite of their grotesque errors the theories show more understanding of sexual processes than one would have given their creators credit for. Children also perceive the alterations that take place in their mother owing to pregnancy and are able to interpret them correctly. The fable of the stork is often told to an audience that receives it with deep, though mostly silent, mistrust. There are, however, two elements that remain undiscovered by the sexual

---

36. [*Footnote added* 1924:] In these later years of childhood there is a great wealth of sexual theories, of which only a few examples are given in the text.

researches of children: the fertilizing role of semen and the existence of the female sexual orifice—the same elements, incidentally, in which the infantile organization is itself undeveloped. It therefore follows that the efforts of the childish investigator are habitually fruitless, and end in a renunciation which not infrequently leaves behind it a permanent injury to the instinct for knowledge. The sexual researches of these early years of childhood are always carried out in solitude. They constitute a first step toward taking an independent attitude in the world, and imply a high degree of alienation of the child from the people in his environment who formerly enjoyed his complete confidence.

The Phases of Development of the Sexual Organization[37]

The characteristics of infantile sexual life which we have hitherto emphasized are the facts that it is essentially autoerotic (i.e., that it finds its object in the infant's own body) and that its individual component instincts are upon the whole disconnected and independent of one another in their search for pleasure. The final outcome of sexual development lies in what is known as the normal sexual life of the adult, in which the pursuit of pleasure comes under the sway of the reproductive function and in which the component instincts, under the primacy of a single erotogenic zone, form a firm organization directed toward a sexual aim attached to some extraneous sexual object.

Pregenital Organizations

The study, with the help of psychoanalysis, of the inhibitions and disturbances of this process of development enables us to recognize abortive beginnings and preliminary stages of a firm organization of the component instincts such as this—preliminary stages which themselves constitute a sexual régime of a sort. These phases of

---

37. The whole of this section, too, first appeared in 1915. The concept of a "pregenital organization" of sexual life seems to have been first introduced by Freud in his paper on "The Predisposition to Obsessional Neurosis" (1913*i*), which, however, deals only with the sadistic-anal organization. The oral organization was apparently recognized as such for the first time in the present passage.

sexual organization are normally passed through smoothly, without giving more than a hint of their existence. It is only in pathological cases that they become active and recognizable to superficial observation.

We shall give the name of "pregenital" to organizations of sexual life in which the genital zones have not yet taken over their predominant part. We have hitherto identified two such organizations, which almost seem as though they were harking back to early animal forms of life.

The first of these is the oral or, as it might be called, cannibalistic pregenital sexual organization. Here sexual activity has not yet been separated from the ingestion of food; nor are opposite currents within the activity differentiated. The *object* of both activities is the same; the sexual *aim* consists in the incorporation of the object—the prototype of a process which, in the form of identification, is later to play such an important psychological part. A relic of this constructed phase of organization, which is forced upon our notice by pathology, may be seen in thumb sucking, in which the sexual activity, detached from the nutritive activity, has substituted for the extraneous object one situated in the subject's own body.[38]

A second pregenital phase is that of the sadistic-anal organization. Here the opposition between two currents, which runs through all sexual life, is already developed: they cannot yet, however, be described as "masculine" and "feminine," but only as "active" and "passive." The *activity* is put into operation by the instinct for mastery through the agency of the somatic musculature; the organ which, more than any other, represents the *passive* sexual aim is the erotogenic mucous membrane of the anus. Both of these currents have objects, which, however, are not identical. Alongside these, other component instincts operate in an autoerotic manner. In this phase, therefore, sexual polarity and an extraneous object are already observable. But organization and subordination to the reproductive function are still absent.[39]

---

38. [*Footnote added* 1920:] For remnants of this phase in adult neurotics, cf. Abraham (1916). [*Added* 1924:] In another, later work (1924) the same writer has divided both this oral phase, and also the later sadistic-anal one, into two subdivisions, which are characterized by differing attitudes toward the object.

39. [*Footnote added* 1924:] Abraham, in the paper last quoted (1924), points out that the anus is developed from the embryonic blastopore—a fact which seems like a biological prototype of psychosexual development.

Ambivalence

This form of sexual organization can persist throughout life and can permanently attract a large portion of sexual activity to itself. The predominance in it of sadism and the cloacal part played by the anal zone give it a quite peculiarly archaic coloring. It is further characterized by the fact that in it the opposing pairs of instincts are developed to an approximately equal extent, a state of affairs described by Bleuler's happily chosen term *ambivalence*.

The assumption of the existence of pregenital organizations of sexual life is based on the analysis of the neuroses, and without a knowledge of them can scarcely be appreciated. Further analytic investigation may be expected to provide us with far more information on the structure and development of the normal sexual function.

In order to complete our picture of infantile sexual life, we must also suppose that the choice of an object, such as we have shown to be characteristic of the pubertal phase of development, has already frequently or habitually been effected during the years of childhood: that is to say, the whole of the sexual currents have become directed toward a single person in relation to whom they seek to achieve their aims. This then is the closest approximation possible in childhood to the final form taken by sexual life after puberty. The only difference lies in the fact that in childhood the combination of the component instincts and their subordination under the primacy of the genitals have been effected only very incompletely or not at all. Thus the establishment of that primacy in the service of reproduction is the last phase through which the organization of sexuality passes.[40]

Diphasic Choice of Object

It may be regarded as typical of the choice of an object that the process is diphasic, that is, that it occurs in two waves. The first

---

40. [*Footnote added* 1924:] At a later date (1923), I myself modified this account by inserting a third phase in the development of childhood, subsequent to the two pregenital organizations. This phase, which already deserves to be described as genital, presents a sexual object and some degree of convergence of the sexual impulses upon that object; but it is differentiated from the final organization of sexual maturity in one essential respect. For it knows only one kind of genital: the

of these begins between the ages of two[41] and five, and it brought to a halt or to a retreat by the latency period; it is characterized by the infantile nature of the sexual aims. The second wave sets in with puberty and determines the final outcome of sexual life.

Although the diphasic nature of object-choice comes down in essentials to no more than the operation of the latency period, it is of the highest importance in regard to disturbances of that final outcome. The resultants of infantile object-choice are carried over into the later period. They either persist as such or are revived at the actual time of puberty. But as a consequence of the repression which has developed between the two phases they prove unutilizable. Their sexual aims have become mitigated and they now represent what may be described as the "affectionate current" of sexual life. Only psychoanalytic investigation can show that behind this affection, admiration and respect there lie concealed the old sexual longings of the infantile component instincts which have now become unserviceable. The object-choice of the pubertal period is obliged to dispense with the objects of childhood and to start afresh as a "sensual current." Should these two currents fail to converge, the result is often that one of the ideals of sexual life, the focusing of all desires upon a single object, will be unattainable.

The Sources of Infantile Sexuality

Our efforts to trace the origins of the sexual instinct have shown us so far that sexual excitation arises (*a*) as a reproduction of a satisfaction experienced in connection with other organic processes, (*b*) through appropriate peripheral stimulation of erotogenic zones and (*c*) as an expression of certain "instincts" (such as the scopophilic instinct and the instinct of cruelty) of which the origin is not yet completely intelligible. Psychoanalytic investigation, reaching back into childhood from a later time, and contemporary observation of children combine to indicate to us still other regularly active sources of sexual excitation. The direct observation of children has the disadvantage of working upon data which are

---

male one. For that reason I have named it the "phallic" stage of organization. (Freud, 1923*e*). According to Abraham [1924], it has a biological prototype in the embryo's undifferentiated genital disposition, which is the same for both sexes.

41. In 1915 this figure was "three"; it was altered to "two" in 1920.

easily misunderstandable; psychoanalysis is made difficult by the fact that it can only reach its data, as well as its conclusions, after long detours. But by cooperation the two methods can attain a satisfactory degree of certainty in their findings.

We have already discovered in examining the erotogenic zones that these regions of the skin merely show a special intensification of a kind of susceptibility to stimulus which is possessed in a certain degree by the whole cutaneous surface. We shall therefore not be surprised to find that very definite erotogenic effects are to be ascribed to certain kinds of general stimulation of the skin. Among these we may especially mention thermal stimuli, whose importance may help us to understand the therapeutic effects of warm baths.

Mechanical Excitations

At this point we must also mention the production of sexual excitation by rhythmic mechanical agitation of the body. Stimuli of this kind operate in three different ways: on the sensory apparatus of the vestibular nerves, on the skin, and on the deeper parts (e.g., the muscles and articular structures). The existence of these pleasurable sensations—and it is worth emphazing the fact that in this connection the concepts of "sexual excitation" and "satisfaction" can to a great extent be used without distinction, a circumstance which we must later endeavor to explain—the existence, then, of these pleasurable sensations, caused by forms of mechanical agitation of the body, is confirmed by the fact that children are so fond of games of passive movement, such as swinging and being thrown up into the air, and insist on such games being incessantly repeated.[42] It is well-known that rocking is habitually used to induce sleep in restless children. The shaking produced by driving in carriages and later by railway-travel exercises such a fascinating effect upon older children that every boy, at any rate, has at one time or other in his life wanted to be an engine driver or a coachman. It is a puzzling fact that boys take such an extraordinarily intense

---

42. Some people can remember that in swinging they felt the impact of moving air upon their genitals as an immediate sexual pleasure. [A specific instance of this is quoted in a footnote to a passage in *The Interpretation of Dreams* (1900a, near the end of chapter 5) in which this whole topic is discussed (Standard Ed., 4, 272).]

interest in things connected with railways, and, at the age at which the production of fantasies is most active (shortly before puberty), use those things as the nucleus of a symbolism that is peculiarly sexual. A compulsive link of this kind between railway-travel and sexuality is clearly derived from the pleasurable character of the sensations of movement. In the event of repression, which turns so many childish preferences into their opposite, these same individuals, when they are adolescents or adults, will react to rocking or swinging with a feeling of nausea, will be terribly exhausted by a railway journey, or will be subject to attacks of anxiety on the journey and will protect themselves against a repetition of the painful experience by a dread of railway travel.

Here again we must mention the fact, which is not yet understood, that the combination of fright and mechanical agitation produces the severe, hysteriform, traumatic neurosis. It may at least be assumed that these influences, which, when they are of small intensity, become sources of sexual excitation, lead to a profound disorder in the sexual mechanism or chemistry[43] if they operate with exaggerated force.

Muscular Activity

We are all familiar with the fact that children feel a need for a large amount of active muscular exercise and derive extraordinary pleasure from satisfying it. Whether this pleasure has any connection with sexuality, whether it itself comprises sexual satisfaction or whether it can become the occasion of sexual excitation—all of this is open to critical questioning, which may indeed also be directed against the view maintained in the previous paragraphs that the pleasure derived from sensations of *passive* movement is of a sexual nature or may produce sexual excitation. It is, however, a fact that a number of people report that they experienced the first signs of excitement in their genitals while they were romping or wrestling with playmates—a situation in which, apart from general muscular exertion, there is a large amount of contact with the skin of the opponent. An inclination to physical struggles with some one particular person, just as in later years an inclination to *verbal*

---

43. The last two words were added in 1924.

disputes,[44] is a convincing sign that object-choice has fallen on him. One of the roots of the sadistic instinct would seem to lie in the encouragement of sexual excitation by muscular activity. In many people the infantile connection between romping and sexual excitation is among the determinants of the direction subsequently taken by their sexual instinct.[45]

Affective Processes

The further sources of sexual excitation in children are open to less doubt. It is easy to establish, whether by contemporary observation or by subsequent research, that all comparatively intense affective processes, including even terrifying ones, trench upon sexuality—a fact which may incidentally help to explain the pathogenic effect of emotions of that kind. In schoolchildren dread of going in for an examination or tension over a difficult piece of work can be important not only in affecting the child's relations at school but also in bringing about an irruption of sexual manifestations. For quite often in such circumstances a stimulus may be felt which urges the child to touch his genitals, or something may take place akin to a nocturnal emission with all its bewildering consequences. The behavior of children at school, which confronts a teacher with plenty of puzzles, deserves in general to be brought into relation with their budding sexuality. The sexually exciting effect of many emotions which are in themselves unpleasurable, such as feelings of apprehension, fright, or horror, persists in a great number of people throughout their adult life. There is no doubt that this is the explanation of why so many people seek opportunities for sensations of this kind, subject to the proviso that the seriousness of the unpleasurable feeling is damped down by certain qualifying facts, such as its occurring in an imaginary world, in a book, or in a play.

---

44. "Was sich liebt, das neckt sich." [Lovers' quarrels are proverbial.]

45. [*Footnote added* 1910:] The analysis of cases of neurotic abasia and agoraphobia removes all doubt as to the sexual nature of pleasure in movement. Modern education, as we know, makes great use of games in order to divert young people from sexual activity. It would be more correct to say that in these young people it replaces sexual enjoyment by pleasure in movement—and forces sexual activity back to one of its autoerotic components.

If we assume that a similar erotogenic effect attaches even to intensely painful feelings, especially when the pain is toned down or kept at a distance by some accompanying condition, we should here have one of human roots of the masochistic-sadistic instinct, into whose numerous complexities we are very gradually gaining some insight.[46]

Intellectual Work

Finally, it is an unmistakable fact that concentration of the attention upon an intellectual task and intellectual strain in general produce a concomitant sexual excitation in many young people as well as adults. This is no doubt the only justifiable basis for what is in other respects the questionable practice of ascribing nervous disorders to intellectual "overwork."[47]

If we now cast our eyes over the tentative suggestions which I have made as to the sources of infantile sexual excitation, though I have not described them completely nor enumerated them fully, the following conclusions emerge with more or less certainty. It seems that the fullest provisions are made for setting in motion the process of sexual excitation—a process the nature of which has, it must be confessed, become highly obscure to us. The setting in motion of this process is first and foremost provided for in a more or less direct fashion by the excitations of the sensory surfaces—the skin and the sense organs—and, most directly of all, by the operation of stimuli on certain areas known as erotogenic zones. The decisive element in these sources of sexual excitation is no doubt the *quality* of the stimuli, though the factor of intensity, in the case of pain, is not a matter of complete indifference. But apart from these sources there are present in the organism contrivances which bring it about that in the case of a great number of internal processes sexual excitation arises as a concomitant effect, as soon as the intensity of those processes passes beyond certain quantitative lim-

46. [*Footnote added* 1924:] I am here referring to what is known as "erotogenic" masochism.

47. Some earlier remarks by Freud on this subject will be found in the middle of his first paper on "Sexuality in the Aetiology of the Neuroses" (1898*a*), and some later ones in a footnote to section 3 of "Analysis Terminable and Interminable" (1937*c*).

its. What we have called the component instincts of sexuality are either derived directly from these internal sources or are composed of elements both from those sources and from the erotogenic zones. It may well be that nothing of considerable importance can occur in the organism without contributing some component to the excitation of the sexual instinct.

It does not seem to me possible at present to state these general conclusions with any greater clarity or certainty. For this I think two factors are responsible: first, the novelty of the whole method of approach to the subject, and secondly, the fact that the whole nature of sexual excitation is completely unknown to us. Nevertheless I am tempted to make two observations which promise to open out wide future prospects:

Varieties of Sexual Constitution

(a) Just as we had seen previously, that it was possible to derive a multiplicity of innate sexual constitutions from variety in the development of the erotogenic zones, so we can now make a similar attempt by including the *indirect* sources of sexual excitation. It may be assumed that, although contributions are made from these sources in the case of everyone, they are not in all cases of equal strength, and that further help toward the differentiation of sexual constitutions may be found in the varying development of the individual sources of sexual excitation.[48]

Pathways of Mutual Influence

(b) If we now drop the figurative expression that we have so long adopted in speaking of the "sources" of sexual excitation, we are led to the suspicion that all the connecting pathways that lead from other functions to sexuality must also be traversable in the reverse direction. If, for instance, the common possession of the labial zone

---

48. [*Footnote added* 1920:] An inevitable consequence of these considerations is that we must regard each individual as possessing an oral erotism, an anal erotism, a urethral erotism, etc., and that the existence of mental complexes corresponding to these implies no judgment of abnormality or neurosis. The differences separating the normal from the abnormal can lie only in the relative strength of the individual components of the sexual instinct and in the use to which they are put in the course of development.

by the two functions is the reason why sexual satisfaction arises during the taking of nourishment, then the same factor also enables us to understand why there should be disorders of nutrition if the erotogenic functions of the common zone are disturbed. Or again, if we know that concentration of attention may give rise to sexual excitation, it seems plausible to assume that by making use of the same path, but in a contrary direction, the condition of sexual excitation may influence the possibility of directing the attention. A good portion of the symptomatology of the neuroses, which I have traced to disturbances of the sexual processes, is expressed in disturbances of other, nonsexual, somatic functions; and this circumstance, which has hitherto been unintelligible, becomes less puzzling if it is only the counterpart of the influences which bring about the production of sexual excitation.

The same pathways, however, along which sexual disturbances trench upon the other somatic functions must also perform another important function in normal health. They must serve as paths for the attraction of sexual instinctual forces to aims that are other than sexual, that is to say, for the sublimation of sexuality. But we must end with a confession that very little is as yet known with certainty of these pathways though they certainly exist and can probably be traversed in both directions.

Translated by James Strachey

6

Freud's Psycho-Analytic Procedure

The particular psychotherapeutic procedure which Freud practices and describes as "psychoanalysis" is an outgrowth of what was known as the "cathartic" method and was discussed by him in collaboration with Josef Breuer in their *Studies on Hysteria* (1895). This cathartic therapy was a discovery of Breuer's, and was first used by him some ten years earlier in the successful treatment of a hysterical woman patient, in the course of which he obtained an insight into the pathogenesis of her symptoms. As the result of a personal suggestion from Breuer, Freud revived this procedure and tested it on a considerable number of patients.

The cathartic method of treatment presupposed that the patient could be hypnotized, and was based on the widening of consciousness that occurs under hypnosis. Its aim was the removal of the pathological symptoms, and it achieved this by inducing the patient to return to the psychical state in which the symptom had appeared for the first time. When this was done, there emerged in the hypnotized patient's mind memories, thoughts, and impulses which had previously dropped out of his consciousness; and, as soon as he had related these to the physician, to the accompaniment of intense expressions of emotion, the symptom was overcome and its return prevented. This experience, which could be regularly repeated, was taken by the authors in their joint paper to signify that the symptom takes the place of suppressed processes which have not reached consciousness, that is, that it represents a transformation ("conversion") of these processes. They explained the therapeutic effectiveness of their treatment as due to the discharge of what had previously been, as it were, "strangulated" affect attaching to the suppressed mental acts ("abreaction"). But in practice the simple schematic outline of the therapeutic operation was almost always complicated by the circumstance that it was not a *single* ("traumatic") impression, but in most cases a *series* of impressions—not easily scanned—which had participated in the creation of the symptom.

The main characteristic of the cathartic method, in contrast to all other methods used in psychotherapy, consists in the fact that its therapeutic efficacy does not lie in a prohibitive suggestion by the physician. The expectation is rather that the symptoms will disappear automatically as soon as the operation, based on certain hypotheses concerning the psychical mechanism, succeeds in diverting the course of mental processes from their previous channel, which found an outlet in the formation of the symptom.

The changes which Freud introduced in Breuer's cathartic method of treatment were at first changes in technique; these, however, led to new findings and have finally necessitated a different though not contradictory conception of the therapeutic process.

The cathartic method had already renounced suggestion; Freud went a step further and gave up hypnosis as well. At the present time he treats his patients as follows. Without exerting any other kind of influence, he invites them to lie down in a comfortable attitude on a sofa, while he himself sits on a chair behind them outside their field of vision. He does not even ask them to close their eyes,[1] and avoids touching them in any way, as well as any other procedure which might be reminiscent of hypnosis. The session thus proceeds like a conversation between two people equally awake, but one of whom is spared every muscular exertion and every distracting sensory impression which might divert his attention from his own mental activity.

Since, as we all know, it depends upon the choice of the patient whether he can be hypnotized or not, no matter what the skill of the physician may be, and since a large number of neurotic patients cannot be hypnotized by any means whatever, it followed that with the abandonment of hypnosis the applicability of the treatment

---

1. In his account of his procedure given in *The Interpretation of Dreams* (1900*a*, chapter 2; Standard Ed., 4, 101) Freud still recommended that the subject should keep his eyes closed.

was assured to an unlimited number of patients. On the other hand, the widening of consciousness, which had supplied the physician with precisely the psychical material of memories and images by the help of which the transformation of the symptoms and the liberation of the affects was accomplished, was now missing. Unless a substitute could be produced for this missing element, any therapeutic effect was out of the question.

Freud found such a substitute—and a completely satisfactory one—in the "associations" of his patients; that is, in the involuntary thoughts (most frequently regarded as disturbing elements and therefore ordinarily pushed aside) which so often break across the continuity of a consecutive narrative.

In order to secure these ideas and associations he asks the patient to "let himself go" in what he says, "as you would do in a conversation in which you were rambling on quite disconnectedly and at random." Before he asks them for a detailed account of their case history he insists that they must include in it whatever comes into their heads, even if they think it unimportant or irrelevant to nonsensical; he lays special stress on their not omitting any thought or idea from their story because to relate it would be embarrassing or distressing to them. In the course of collecting this material of otherwise neglected ideas Freud made the observations which became the determining factor of his entire theory. Gaps appear in the patient's memory even while he narrates his case: actual occurrences are forgotten, the chronological order is confused, or causal connections are broken, with unintelligible results. No neurotic case history is without amnesia of some kind or other. If the patient is urged to fill these gaps in his memory by an increased application of attention, it is noticed that all the ideas which occur to him are pushed back by every possible critical expedient, until at last he feels positive discomfort when the memory really returns. From this experience Freud concludes that the amnesias are the result of a process which he calls *repression* and the motive for which he finds in feelings of unpleasure. The psychical forces which have brought about this repression can also be detected, according to him, in the *resistance* which operates against the recovery of the lost memories.

The factor of resistance has become one of the cornerstones of his theory. The ideas which are normally pushed aside on every sort of excuse—such as those mentioned above—are regarded by him as derivatives of the repressed psychical phenomena (thoughts and impulses), distorted owing to the resistance against their reproduction.

The greater the resistance, the greater is the distortion. The value of these unintentional thoughts for the purposes of the therapeutic technique lies in this relation of theirs to the repressed psychical material. If one possess a procedure which makes it possible to arrive at the repressed material from the associations, at the distorted material from the distortions, then what was formerly unconscious in mental life can be made accessible to consciousness even without hypnosis.

Freud has developed on this basis an art of interpretation which takes on the task of, as it were, extracting the pure metal of the repressed thoughts from the ore of the unintentional ideas. This work of interpretation is applied not only to the patient's ideas but also to his dreams, which open up the most direct approach to a knowledge of the unconscious, to his unintentional as well as to his purposeless actions (symptomatic acts) and to the blunders he makes in everyday life (slips of the tongue, bungled actions, and so on). The details of this technique of interpretation or translation have not yet been published by Freud. According to indications he has given, they comprise a number of rules, reached empirically, of how the unconscious material may be reconstructed from the associations, directions on how to know what it means when the patient's ideas cease to flow, and experiences of the most important typical resistances that arise in the course of such treatments. A bulky volume called *The Interpretation of Dreams,* published by Freud in 1900, may be regarded as the forerunner of an initiation into his technique.

From these remarks on the technique of the psychoanalytic method the conclusion might be drawn that its inventor has given himself needless trouble and has made a mistake in abandoning the less-complicated hypnotic mode of procedure. However, in the first place, the technique of psychoanalysis is much easier in practice, when once one has learned it, than any description of it would indicate; and, secondly, there is no other way which leads to the desired goal, so that the hard road is still the shortest one to travel. The objection to hypnosis is that it conceals the resistance and for that reason has obstructed the physician's insight into the play of psychical forces. Hypnosis does not do away with the resistance but only evades it and therefore yields only incomplete information and transitory therapeutic success.

The task which the psychoanalytic method seeks to perform may be formulated in different ways, which are, however, in their essence equivalent. It may, for instance, be stated thus: the task of the treatment is to remove the amnesias. When all gaps in memory have been filled in, all the enigmatic products of mental life elucidated, the continuance and even a renewal of the morbid condition are made impossible. Or the formula may be expressed in this fashion: all repressions must be undone. The mental condition is then the same as one in which all amnesias have been removed. Another formulation reaches further: the task consists in making the unconscious accessible to consciousness, which is done by overcoming the resistances. But it must be remembered that an ideal condition such as this is not present even in the normal, and further that it is only rarely possible to carry the treatment to a point approaching it. Just as health and sickness are not different from each other in essence but are only separated by a quantitative line of demarcation which can be determined in practice, so the aim of the treatment will never be anything else but the *practical* recovery of the patient, the restoration of his ability to lead an active life and of his capacity for enjoyment. In a treatment which is incomplete or in which success is not perfect, one may at any rate achieve a considerable improvement in the general mental condition, while the symptoms (though now of smaller importance to the patient) may continue to exist without stamping him as a sick man.

The therapeutic procedure remains the same, apart from insignificant modifications, for all the various clinical pictures that may be presented in hysteria, and all forms of obsessional neurosis. This does not imply, however, that it can have an unlimited application. The nature of the psychoanalytic method involves indications and contraindications with respect to the person to be treated as well as with respect to the clinical picture. Chronic cases of psychoneuroses without any very violent or dangerous symptoms are the most favorable ones for psychoanalysis: thus in the first place every species of obsessional neurosis, obsessive thinking and acting, and cases of hysteria in which phobias and abulias play the most important part; further, all somatic expressions of hysteria whenever they do not, as in anorexia, require the physician to attend promptly to the speedy removal of symptoms. In acute cases of hysteria it will be necessary to wait for a calmer stage; in all cases where nervous exhaustion dominates the clinical picture a treatment which in itself demands effort, brings only slow improvement and for a time cannot take the persistence of the symptoms into account, will have to be avoided.

Various qualifications are required of anyone who is to be beneficially affected by psychoanalysis. To begin with, he must be capable of a psychically normal condition; during periods of confusion or melancholic depression nothing can be accomplished even in cases of hysteria. Furthermore, a certain measure of natural intelligence and ethical development are to be required of him; if the physician has to deal with a worthless character, he soon loses the interest which makes it possible for him to enter profoundly into the patient's mental life. Deep-rooted malformations of character, traits of an actually degenerate constitution, show themselves during treatment as sources of a resistance that can scarcely be overcome. In this respect the constitution of the patient sets a general limit to the curative effect of psychotherapy. If the patient's age is in the neighborhood of the fifties the conditions for psychoanalysis become unfavorable. The mass of psychical material is then no longer manageable; the time required for recovery is too long; and the ability to undo psychical processes begins to grow weaker.

In spite of all these limitations, the number of persons suitable for psychoanalytic treatment is extraordinarily large and the extension which has come to our therapeutic powers from this method is, according to Freud, very considerable. Freud requires long periods, six months to three years, for an effective treatment; yet he informs us that up to the present, owing to various circumstances which can easily be guessed, he has for the most part been in a position to try his treatment only on very severe cases: patients have come to him after many years of illness, completely incapacitated for life, and, after being disappointed by all kinds of treatments, have had recourse as a last resort to a method which is novel and has been greeted with many doubts. In cases of less-severe illness the duration of the treatment might well be much shorter, and very great advantage in the direction of future prevention might be achieved.

Translated by J. Bernays

7

The "Uncanny"

1

It is only rarely that a psychoanalyst feels impelled to investigate the subject of aesthetics, even when aesthetics is understood to mean not merely the theory of beauty but the theory of the qualities of feeling. He works in other strata of mental life and has little to do with the subdued emotional impulses which, inhibited in their aims and dependent on a host of concurrent factors, usually furnish the material for the study of aesthetics. But it does occasionally happen that he has to interest himself in some particular province of that subject; and this province usually proves to be a rather remote one, and one which has been neglected in the specialist literature of aesthetics.

The subject of the "uncanny"[1] is a province of this kind. It is undoubtedly related to what is frightening—to what arouses dread and horror; equally certainly, too, the word is not always used in a clearly definable sense, so that it tends to coincide with what excites fear in general. Yet we may expect that a special core of feeling is present which justifies the use of a special conceptual term. One is curious to know what this common core is which allows us to distinguish as "uncanny" certain things which lie within the field of what is frightening.

As good as nothing is to be found upon this subject in comprehensive treatises on aesthetics, which in general prefer to concern themselves with what is beautiful, attractive, and sublime—that is,

---

1. The German word, translated throughout this paper by the English "uncanny," is *unheimlich,* literally "unhomely." The English term is not, of course, an exact equivalent of the German one.'

with feelings of a positive nature—and with the circumstances and the objects that call them forth, rather than with the opposite feelings of repulsion and distress. I know of only one attempt in medico-psychological literature, a fertile but not exhaustive paper by Jentsch (1906). But I must confess that I have not made a very thorough examination of the literature, especially the foreign literature, relating to this present modest contribution of mine, for reasons which, as may easily be guessed, lie in the times in which we live;[2] so that my paper is presented to the reader without any claim to priority.

In his study of the "uncanny" Jentsch quite rightly lays stress on the obstacle presented by the fact that people vary so very greatly in their sensitivity to this quality of feeling. The writer of the present contribution, indeed, must himself plead guilty to a special obtuseness in the matter, where extreme delicacy of perception would be more in place. It is long since he has experienced or heard of anything which has given him an uncanny impression, and he must start by translating himself into that state of feeling, by awakening in himself the possibility of experiencing it. Still, such difficulties make themselves powerfully felt in many other branches of aesthetics; we need not on that account despair of finding instances in which the quality in question will be unhesitatingly recognized by most people.

Two courses are open to us at the outset. Either we can find out what meaning has come to be attached to the word *uncanny* in the course of its history; or we can collect all those properties of persons, things, sense-impressions, experiences, and situations which arouse in us the feeling of uncanniness, and then infer the unknown nature of the uncanny from what all these examples have in common. I will say at once that both courses lead to the same result: the uncanny is that class of the frightening which leads back to what is known of old and long familiar. How this is possible, in what circumstances the familiar can become uncanny and frightening, I shall show in what follows. Let me also add that my investigation was actually begun by collecting a number of individual cases, and was only later confirmed by an examination of linguistic usage. In this discussion, however, I shall follow the reverse course.

---

2. An allusion to the First World War only just concluded.

* * *

The German word *unheimlich* is obviously the opposite of *heimlich* ["homely"], *heimisch* [native]—the opposite of what is familiar; and we are tempted to conclude that what is "uncanny" is frightening precisely because it is *not* known and familiar. Naturally not everything that is new and unfamiliar is frightening, however; the relation is not capable of inversion. We can only say that what is novel can easily become frightening and uncanny; some new things are frightening but not by any means all. Something has to be added to what is novel and unfamiliar in order to make it uncanny.

On the whole, Jentsch did not get beyond this relation of the uncanny to the novel and unfamiliar. He ascribes the essential factor in the production of the feeling of uncanniness to intellectual uncertainty; so that the uncanny would always, as it were, be something one does not know one's way about in. The better orientated in his environment a person is, the less readily will he get the impression of something uncanny in regard to the objects and events in it.

It is not difficult to see that this definition is incomplete, and we will therefore try to proceed beyond the equation "uncanny" = "unfamiliar." We will first turn to other languages. But the dictionaries that we consult tell us nothing new, perhaps only because we ourselves speak a language that is foreign. Indeed, we get an impression that many languages are without a word for this particular shade of what is frightening.

I should like to express my indebtedness to Dr. Theodor Reik for the following excerpts:—

LATIN: (K. E. Georges, *Deutschlateinisches Wöterbuch*, 1898). An uncanny place: *locus suspectus;* at an uncanny time of night: *intempesta nocte.*

GREEK: (Rosts's and Schenkl's Lexikons). *Xenos* (i.e., strange, foreign).

ENGLISH: (from the dictionaries of Lucas, Bellows, Flügel, and Muret-Sanders). Uncomfortable, uneasy, gloomy, dismal, uncanny, ghastly; (of a house) haunted; (of a man) a repulsive fellow.

FRENCH: (Saches-Villatte). *Inquiétant, sinistre, lugubre, mal à son aise.*

SPANISH: (Tollhausen, 1889). *Sospechoso, de mal agüero, lúgubre, siniestro.*

The Italian and Portuguese languages seem to content themselves with words which we should describe as circumlocutions. In Arabic and Hebrew "uncanny" means the same as "demonic," "gruesome."

Let us therefore return to the German language. In Daniel Sanders's *Wörterbuch der Deutschen Sprache* (1860, **1**, 729), the following entry, which I here reproduce in full, is to be found under the world *heimlich*. I have laid stress on one or two passages by italicizing them.[3]

Heimlich, adj., subst. *Heimlichkeit* (p. *Heimlichkeiten*): I. Also *heimelich, heimelig,* belonging to the house, not strange, familiar, tame, intimate, friendly, etc.

(a) (Obsolete) belonging to the house or the family, or regarded as so belonging (cf. Latin *familiaris,* familiar): *Die Heimlichen,* the members of the household; *Der heimliche Rat* (Gen. 41:45; 2 Sam. 23:23; 1 Chron. 12:25; Wisd. 8:4), now more usually *Geheimer Rat* [Privy Councillor].

(b) Of animals: tame, companionable to man. As opposed to wild, e.g., "Animals which are neither wild nor *heimlich,*" etc. "Wild animals . . . that are trained to be *heimlich* and accustomed to men." "If these young creatures are brought up from early days among men they become quite *heimlich,* friendly" etc.—So also: "It (the lamb) is so *heimlich* and eats out of my hand." "Nevertheless, the stork is a beautiful, *heimlich* bird."

(c) Intimate, friendly comfortable; the enjoyment of quiet content, etc., arousing a sense of agreeable restfulness and security as in one within the four walls of his house.[4] "Is it still *heimlich* to you in your country where strangers are felling your woods?" "She did not feel too *heimlich* with him." "Along a high, *heimlich,* shady path . . . , beside a purling, gushing, and babbling woodland brook." "To destroy the *Heimlichkeit* of the home." "I could not readily find another spot so intimate and *heimlich* as this." "We

---

3. In the translation which follows in the text above, a few details, mainly giving the sources of the quotations, have been omitted. For purposes of reference, we reprint in an Appendix the entire extract from Sanders's Dictionary exactly as it is given in German in Freud's original paper except that a few minor misprints have been put right.

4. It may be remarked that the English *canny,* in addition to its more usual meaning of "shrewd," can mean "pleasant," "cosy."

pictured it so comfortable, so nice, so cosy and *heimlich*." "In quiet *Heimlichkeit,* surrounded by close walls." "A careful housewife, who knows how to make a pleasing *Heimlichkeit (Häuslichkeit* [domesticity]) out of the smallest means." "The man who till recently had been so strange to him now seemed to him all the more *heimlich*." "The protestant landowners do not feel . . . *heimlich* among their catholic inferiors." "When it grows *heimlich* and still, and the evening quiet alone watches over your cell." "Quiet, lovely and *heimlich,* no place more fitted for their rest." "He did not feel at all *heimlich* about it."—Also, [in compounds] "The place was so peaceful, so lonely, so shadily-*heimlich*." "The in-and out-flowing waves of the current, dreamy and lullaby-*heimlich*." Cf. in especial *Unheimlich* [see below]. Among Swabian Swiss authors in especial, often as a trisyllable: "How *heimelich* it seemed to Ivo again of an evening, when he was at home." "It was so *heimelig* in the house." "The warm room and the *heimelig* afternoon." "When a man feels in his heart that he is so small and the Lord so great—that is what is truly *heimelig*." "Little by little they grew at ease and *heimelig* among themselves." "Friendly *Heimeligkeit*." "I shall be nowhere more *heimelich* than I am here." "That which comes from afar . . . assuredly does not live quite *heimelig (heimat-lich* [at home], *freundnachbarlich* [in a neighborly way]) among the people." "The cottage where he had once sat so often among his own people, so *heimelig,* so happy." "The sentinel's horn sounds so *heimelig* from the tower, and his voice invites so hospitably." "You go to sleep there so soft and warm, so wonderfully *heim'lig*."—*This form of the word deserves to become general in order to protect this perfectly good sense of the word from becoming obsolete through an easy confusion with* II [see below]. *Cf:* "'*The Zecks* [a family name] *are all "heimlich".'* (in sense II) "'*Heimlich"? . . . What do you understand by "heimlich"?' 'Well, . . . they are like a buried spring or a dried-up pond. One cannot walk over it without always having the feeling that water might come up there again.' 'Oh, we call it "unheimlich", you call it "heimlich." Well, what makes you think that there is something secret and untrustworthy about this family?'"* (Gutzkow).

(d) Especially in Silesia: gay, cheerful; also of the weather.

II. Concealed, kept from sight, so that others do not get to know of or about it, withheld from others. To do something *heimlich,* i.e., behind someone's back; to steal away *heimlich; heimlich* meetings and appointments; to look on with *heimlich* pleasure at someone's discomfiture; to sign or weep *heimlich;* to behave *heimlich,* as though there was something to conceal; *heimlich* love affair, love, sin; *heimlich* places (which good manners oblige us to conceal) (1 Sam. 5:6). "The *heimlich* chamber" (privy) (2 Kings 10:27.). Also "the *heimlich* chair." "To throw into pits or *Heimlichkeiten.*"—"Led the steeds *heimlich* before Laomedon."—"As secretive, *heimlich,* deceitful and malicious towards cruel masters ... as frank, open, sympathetic and helpful towards a friend in misfortune." "You have still to learn what is *heimlich* holiest to me." "The *heimlich* art" (magic). "Where public ventilation has to stop, there *heimlich* machinations begin." "Freedom is the whispered watchword of *heimlich* conspirators and the loud battle-cry of professed revolutionaries." "A holy, *heimlich* effect." "I have roots that are most *heimlich.* I am grown in the deep earth." "My *heimlich* pranks." "If he is not given it openly and scrupulously he may seize it *heimlich* and unscrupulously." "He had achromatic telescopes constructed *heimlich* and secretly." "Henceforth I desire that there should be nothing *heimlich* any longer between us."—To discover, disclose, betray someone's *Heimlichkeiten;* "to concoct *Heimlichkeiten* behind my back." "In my time we studied *Heimlichkeit.*" "The hand of understanding can alone undo the powerless spell of the *Heimlichkeit* (of hidden gold)." "Say, where is the place of concealment ... in what place of hidden *Heimlichkeit?*" "Bees, who make the lock of *Heimlichkeiten*" (i.e., sealing wax). Learned in strange *Heimlichkeiten* (magic arts).

For compounds see above, Ic. Note especially the negative "*un-*": eerie, weird, arousing gruesome fear: "Seeming quite *unheimlich* and ghostly to him." "The *unheimlich,* fearful hours of night." "I had already long since felt an *unheimlich,* even gruesome feeling." "Now I am beginning to have an *unheimlich* feeling." ... "Feels an *Unheimlich* horror." "*Unheimlich* and motionless like a stone image." "The *unheimlich* mist called hill-fog." "These pale youths are *unheimlich* and are brewing heaven knows what mischief." "'*Unheimlich*' *is the name for everything that ought to have remained ... secret and hidden but has come to light*" (Schelling).—"To veil the divine, to surround it with a certain *Unheimlichkeit.*"—*Unheimlich* is not often used as opposite to meaning II (above).

* * *

What interests us most in this long extract is to find that among its different shades of meaning the word *heimlich* exhibits one which is identical with its opposite, *unheimlich*. What is *heimlich* thus comes to be *unheimlich*. (Cf. the quotation from Gutzkow: "We call it '*unheimlich*'; you call it '*heimlich*.'") In general we are reminded that the word *heimlich* is not unambiguous, but belongs to two sets of ideas, which, without being contradictory, are yet very different: on the one hand it means what is familiar and agreeable, and on the other, what is concealed and kept out of sight.[5] *Unheimlich* is customarily used, we are told, as the contrary only of the first signification of *heimlich,* and not of the second. Sanders tells us nothing concerning a possible genetic connection between these two meanings of *heimlich*. On the other hand, we notice that Schelling says something which throws quite a new light on the concept of the *Unheimlich,* for which we were certainly not prepared. According to him, everything is *unheimlich* that ought to have remained secret and hidden but has come to light.

Some of the doubts that have thus arisen are removed if we consult Grimm's dictionary. (1877, **4,** part 2, 873ff.)

We read:

Heimlich; adj. and adv. *vernaculus, occultus;* MHG, heimelîch, heimlîch.

(P. 874.) In a slightly different sense: "I feel *heimlich* well, free from fear." . . .

[3] *(b) Heimlich* is also used of a place free from ghostly influences . . . familiar, friendly, intimate.

(P. 875: β) Familiar, amicable, unreserved.

4. *From the idea of "homelike," "belonging to the house," the further idea is developed of something withdrawn from the eyes of strangers, something concealed, secret; and this idea is expanded in many ways* . . .

(P. 876.) "On the left bank of the lake there lies a meadow *heimlich* in the wood." (Schiller, *Wilhelm Tell,* I. 4.) . . . Poetic license, rarely so used in modern speech . . . *Heimlich* is used in conjunction with a verb expressing the act of concealing: "In the

---

5. According to the Oxford English Dictionary, a similar ambiguity attaches to the English "canny," which may mean not only "cosy" but also "endowed with occult or magical powers."

secret of his tabernacle he shall hide me *heimlich*." (Ps. 27:5.) . . .
Heimlich parts of the human body, *pudenda* . . . "the men that died
not were smitten on their *heimlich* parts." (1 Samuel 5:12.) . . .

(c) Officials who give important advice which has to be kept
secret in matters of state are called *heimlich* councillors; the adjec-
tive, according to modern usage, has been replaced by *geheim* [se-
cret] . . . "Pharaoh called Joseph's name 'him to whom secrets are
revealed'" (*heimlich* councillor). (Gen. 41:45.)

(P. 878.) 6. *Heimlich,* as used of knowledge—mystic, allegorical: a *heimlich* meaning, *mysticus, divinus, occultus, figuratus.*

(P. 878.) *Heimlich* in a different sense, as withdrawn from
knowledge, unconscious. . . . *Heimlich* also has the meaning of that
which is obscure, inaccessible to knowledge. . . . "Do you not see?
They do not trust us; they fear the *heimlich* face of the Duke of
Friedland." (Schiller, *Wallensteins Lager,* scene 2.)

9. *The notion of something hidden and dangerous, which is expressed in the last paragraph, is still further developed, so that
"heimlich" comes to have the meaning usually ascribed to "unheimlich."* Thus: "At time I feel like a man who walks in the night
and believes in ghosts; every corner is *heimlich* and full of terrors
for him." (Klinger, *Theater,* 3.298).

Thus *heimlich* is a word the meaning of which develops in the
direction of ambivalence, until it finally coincides with its opposite,
unheimlich. Unheimlich is in some way or other a subspecies of
heimlich. Let us bear this discovery in mind, though we cannot
yet rightly understand it, alongside of Schelling's[6] definition of the
Unheimlich. If we go on to examine individual instances of uncanniness, these hints will become intelligible to us.

2

When we proceed to review the things, persons, impressions,
events, and situations which are able to arouse in us a feeling of
the uncanny in a particularly forcible and definite form, the first
requirement is obviously to select a suitable example to start on.
Jentsch has taken as a very good instance "doubts whether an
apparently animate being is really alive; or conversely, whether a

---

6. In the original version of the paper (1919) only, the name "Schleiermacher"
was printed here, evidently in error.

lifeless object might not be in fact animate"; and he refers in this connection to the impression made by waxwork figures, ingeniously constructed dolls, and automata. To these he adds the uncanny effect of epileptic fits, and of manifestations of insanity, because these excite in the spectator the impression of automatic, mechanical processes at work behind the ordinary appearance of mental activity. Without entirely accepting this author's view, we will take it as a starting-point for our own investigation because in what follows he reminds us of a writer who has succeeded in producing uncanny effects better than anyone else.

Jentsch writes: "In telling a story, one of the most successful devices for easily creating uncanny effects is to leave the reader in uncertainty whether a particular figure in the story is a human being or an automaton, and to do it in such a way that his attention is not focused directly upon his uncertainty, so that he may not be led to go into the matter and clear it up immediately. That, as we have said, would quickly dissipate the peculiar emotional effect of the thing. E. T. A. Hoffmann has repeatedly employed this psychological artifice with success in his fantastic narratives."

This observation, undoubtedly a correct one, refers primarily to the story of "The Sand-Man" in Hoffmann's *Nachtstücken*,[7] which contains the original of Olympia, the doll that appears in the first act of Offenbach's opera, *Tales of Hoffmann*. But I cannot think—and I hope most readers of the story will agree with me—that the theme of the doll Olympia, who is to all appearances a living being, is by any means the only, or indeed the most important, element that must be held responsible for the quite unparalleled atmosphere of uncanniness evoked by the story. Nor is this atmosphere heightened by the fact that the author himself treats the episode of Olympia with a faint touch of satire and uses it to poke fun at the young man's idealization of his mistress. The main theme of the story is, on the contrary, something different, something which gives it its name, and which is always reintroduced at critical moments: it is the theme of the "Sand-Man" who tears our children's eyes.

---

7. Hoffmann's *Sämtliche Werke*, Grisebach Edition, 3. [A translation of "The Sand-Man" is included in *Eight Tales of Hoffmann*, translated by J. M. Cohen, London, Pan Books, 1952.]

This fantastic tale opens with the childhood recollections of the student Nathaniel. In spite of his present happiness, he cannot banish the memories associated with the mysterious and terrifying death of his beloved father. On certain evenings his mother used to send the children to bed early, warning them that "the Sand-Man was coming"; and, sure enough, Nathaniel would not fail to hear the heavy tread of a visitor, with whom his father would then be occupied for the evening. When questioned about the Sand-Man, his mother, it is true, denied that such a person existed except as a figure of speech; but his nurse could give him more definite information: "He's a wicked man who comes when children won't go to bed, and throws handfuls of sand in their eyes so that they jump out of their heads all bleeding. Then he puts the eyes in a sack and carries them off to the half-moon to feed his children. They sit up there in their nest, and their beaks are hooked like owls' beaks, and they use them to peck up naughty boys' and girls' eyes with."

Although little Nathaniel was sensible and old enough not to credit the figure of the Sand-Man with such gruesome attributes, yet the dread of him became fixed in his heart. He determined to find out what the Sand-Man looked like; and one evening, when the Sand-Man was expected again, he hid in his father's study. He recognized the visitor as the lawyer Coppelius, a repulsive person whom the children were frightened of when he occasionally came to a meal; and he now identified this Coppelius with the dreaded Sand-Man. As regards the rest of the scene, Hoffmann already leaves us in doubt whether what we are witnessing is the first delirium of the panic-stricken boy, or a succession of events which are to be regarded in the story as being real. His father and the guest are at work at a brazier with glowing flames. The little eavesdropper hears Coppelius call out: "Eyes here! Eyes here!" and betrays himself by screaming aloud. Coppelius seizes him and is on the point of dropping bits of red-hot coal from the fire into his eyes, and then of throwing them into the brazier, but his father begs him off and saves his eyes. After this the boy falls into a deep swoon; and a long illness brings his experience to an end. Those who decide in favor of the rationalistic interpretation of the Sand-Man will not fail to recognize in the child's fantasy the persisting influence of his nurse's story. The bits of sand that are to be thrown into the child's eyes turn into bits of red-hot coal from the flames;

and in both cases they are intended to make his eyes jump out. In the course of another visit of the Sand-Man's, a year later, his father is killed in his study by an explosion. The lawyer Coppelius disappears from the place without leaving a trace behind.

Nathaniel, now a student, believes that he has recognized this phantom of horror from his childhood in an itinerant optician, an Italian called Giuseppe Coppola, who at his university town, offers him weatherglasses for sale. When Nathaniel refuses, the man goes on: "Not weatherglasses? not weatherglasses? also got fine eyes, fine eyes!" The student's terror is allayed when he finds that the proffered eyes are only harmless spectacles, and he buys a pocket spyglass from Coppola. With its aid he looks across into Professor Spalanzani's house opposite and there spies Spalanzani's beautiful, but strangely silent and motionless daughter, Olympia. He soon falls in love with her so violently that, because of her, he quite forgets the clever and sensible girl to whom he is betrothed. But Olympia is an automaton whose clockwork has been made by Spalanzani, and whose eyes have been put in by Coppola, the Sand-man. The student surprises the two Masters quarreling over their handiwork. The optician carries off the wooden eyeless doll; and the mechanician, Spalanzani, picks up Olympia's bleeding eyes from the ground and throws them at Nathaniel's breast, saying that Coppola had stolen them from the student. Nathaniel succumbs to a fresh attack of madness, and in his delirium his recollection of his father's death is mingled with this new experience. "Hurry up! hurry up! ring of fire!" he cries. "Spin about, ring of fire—Hurrah! Hurry up, wooden doll! lovely wooden doll, spin about—." He then falls upon the professor, Olympia's "father," and tries to strangle him.

Rallying from a long and serious illness, Nathaniel seems at last to have recovered. He intends to marry his betrothed, with whom he has become reconciled. One day he and she are walking through the city marketplace, over which the high tower of the Town Hall throws its huge shadow. On the girl's suggestion, they climb the tower, leaving her brother, who is walking with them, down below. From the top, Clara's attention is drawn to a curious object moving along the street. Nathaniel looks at this thing through Coppola's spyglass, which he finds in his pocket, and falls into a new attack of madness. Shouting, "Spin about, wooden doll!" he tries to throw the girl into the gulf below. Her brother, brought to her side by her cries, rescues her and hastens down with her to safety. On the tower above, the madman rushes round, shrieking, "Ring of fire, spin about!"—and we know the origin of the words. Among the people who begin to gather below there comes forward the figure of the lawyer Coppelius, who has suddenly returned. We may suppose that it was his approach, seen through the spyglass, which threw Nathaniel into his fit of madness. As the onlookers prepare to go up and overpower the madman, Coppelius laughs and says: "Wait a bit; he'll come down of himself." Nathaniel suddenly stands still, catches sight of Coppelius, and with a wild shriek "Yes! 'Fine eyes—fine eyes'!" flings himself over the parapet. While he lies on the paving-stones with a shattered skull the Sand-Man vanishes in the throng.

This short summary leaves no doubt, I think, that the feeling of something uncanny is directly attached to the figure of the Sand-Man, that is, to the idea of being robbed of one's eyes, and that Jentsch's point of an intellectual uncertainty has nothing to do with the effect. Uncertainty whether an object is living or inanimate, which admittedly applied to the doll Olympia, is quite irrelevant in connection with this other, more striking instance of uncanniness. It is true that the writer creates a kind of uncertainty in us in the beginning by not letting us know, no doubt purposely, whether he is taking us into the real world or into a purely fantastic one of his own creation. He has, of course, a right to do either; and if he chooses to stage his action in a world peopled with spirits, demons, and ghosts, as Shakespeare does in *Hamlet,* in *Macbeth* and, in a different sense, in *The Tempest* and *A Midsummer-Night's Dream,* we must bow to his decision and treat his setting as though it were real for as long as we put ourselves into his hands. But this uncertainty disappears in the course of Hoffmann's story, and we perceive that he intends to make us, too, look through the demon optician's spectacles or spyglass—perhaps, indeed, that the author in his very own person once peered through such an instrument. For the conclusion of the story makes it quite clear that Coppola the optician really *is* the lawyer Coppelius[8] and also, therefore, the Sand-Man.

---

8. Frau Dr. Rank has pointed out the association of the name with *coppella* = crucible, connecting it with the chemical operations that caused the father's death; and also with *coppo* = eye socket. [Except in the first (1919) edition this footnote

There is no question therefore, of any intellectual uncertainty here: we know now that we are not supposed to be looking on at the products of a madman's imagination, behind which we, with the superiority of rational minds, are able to detect the sober truth; and yet this knowledge does not lessen the impression of uncanniness in the least degree. The theory of intellectual uncertainty is thus incapable of explaining that impression.

We know from psychoanalytic experience, however, that the fear of damaging or losing one's eyes is a terrible one in children. Many adults retain their apprehensiveness in this respect, and no physical injury is so much dreaded by them as an injury to the eye. We are accustomed to say, too, that we will treasure a thing as the apple of our eye. A study of dreams, fantasies, and myths has taught us that anxiety about one's eyes, the fear of going blind, is often enough a substitute for the dread of being castrated. The self-blinding of the mythical criminal, Oedipus, was simply a mitigated form of the punishment of castration—the only punishment that was adequate for him by the *lex talionis*. We may try on rationalistic grounds to deny that fears about the eye are derived from the fear of castration, and may argue that it is very natural that so precious an organ as the eye should be guarded by a proportionate dread. Indeed, we might go further and say that the fear of castration itself contains no other significance and no deeper secret than a justifiable dread of this rational kind. But this view does not account adequately for the substitutive relation between the eye and the male organ which is seen to exist in dreams and myths and fantasies; nor can it dispel the impression that the threat of being castrated in especial excites a peculiarly violent and obscure emotion, and that this emotion is what first gives the idea of losing other organs its intense coloring. All further doubts are removed when we learn the details of their "castration complex" from the analysis of neurotic patients, and realize its immense importance in their mental life.

Moreover, I would not recommend any opponent of the psychoanalytic view to select this particular story of the Sand-Man with which to support his argument that anxiety about the eyes has nothing to do with the castration complex. For why does Hoff-

was attached, it seems erroneously, to the first occurrence of the name Coppelius on this page.]

mann bring the anxiety about eyes into such intimate connection with the father's death? And why does the Sand-Man always appear as a disturber of love? He separates the unfortunate Nathaniel from his betrothed and from her brother, his best friend; he destroys the second object of his love, Olympia, the lovely doll; and he drives him into suicide at the moment when he has won back his Clara and is about to be happily united to her. Elements in the story like these, and many others, seem arbitrary and meaningless so long as we deny all connection between fears about the eye and castration; but they become intelligible as soon as we replace the Sand-Man by the dreaded father at whose hands castration is expected.[9]

We shall venture, therefore, to refer the uncanny effect of the Sand-Man to the anxiety belonging to the castration complex of

---

9. In fact, Hoffmann's imaginative treatment of his material has not made such wild confusion of its elements that we cannot reconstruct their original arrangement. In the story of Nathaniel's childhood, the figures of his father and Coppelius represent the two opposites into which the father-imago is split by his ambivalence; whereas the one threatens to blind him—that is, to castrate him—the other, the "good" father, intercedes for his sight. The part of the complex which is most strongly repressed, the death wish against the "bad" father, finds expression in the death of the "good" father, and Coppelius is made answerable for it. This pair of fathers is represented later, in his student days, by Professor Spalanzani and Coppola the optician. The professor is in himself a member of the father-series, and Coppola is recognized as identical with Coppelius the lawyer. Just as they used before to work together over the secret brazier, so now they have jointly created the doll Olympia; the Professor is even called the father of Olympia. This double occurrence of activity in common betrays them as divisions of the father-imago: both the mechanician and the optician were the father of Nathaniel (and of Olympia as well). In the frightening scene in childhood, Coppelius, after sparing Nathaniel's eyes, had screwed off his arms and legs as an experiment; that is, he had worked on him as a mechanician would on a doll. This singular feature, which seems quite outside the picture of the Sand-Man, introduces a new castration equivalent; but it also points to the inner identity of Coppelius with his later counterpart, Spalanzani the mechanician, and prepares us for the interpretation of Olympia. This automatic doll can be nothing else than a materialization of Nathaniel's feminine attitude toward his father in his infancy. Her fathers, Spalanzani and Coppola, are, after all, nothing but new editions, reincarnations of Nathaniel's pair of fathers. Spalanzani's otherwise incomprehensible statement that the optician has stolen Nathaniel's eyes (see above, [p. 130]), so as to set them in the doll, now becomes significant as supplying evidence of the identity of Olympia and Nathaniel. Olympia is, as it were, a dissociated complex of Nathaniel's which confronts him as a person, and Nathaniel's enslavement to this complex is expressed in his senseless obsessive love for Olympia. We may with justice call love of this kind narcissistic, and we can

childhood. But having reached the idea that we can make an infantile factor such as this responsible for feelings of uncanniness, we are encouraged to see whether we can apply it to other instances of the uncanny. We find in the story of the Sand-Man the other theme on which Jentsch lays stress, of a doll which appears to be alive. Jentsch believes that a particularly favorable condition for awakening uncanny feelings is created when there is intellectual uncertainty whether an object is alive or not, and when an inanimate object becomes too much like an animate one. Now, dolls are of course rather closely connected with childhood life. We remember that in their early games children do not distinguish at all sharply between living and inanimate objects, and that they are especially fond of treating their dolls like live people. In fact, I have occasionally heard a woman patient declare that even at the age of eight she had still been convinced that her dolls would be certain to come to life if she were to look at them in a particular, extremely concentrated, way. So that here, too, it is not difficult to discover a factor from childhood. But, curiously enough, while the Sand-Man story deals with the arousing of an early childhood fear, the idea of a "living doll" excites no fear at all; children have no fear of their dolls coming to life, they may even desire it. The source of uncanny feelings would not, therefore, be an infantile fear in this case, but rather an infantile wish or even merely an infantile belief. There seems to be a contradiction here; but perhaps it is only a complication, which may be helpful to us later on.

Hoffmann is the unrivaled master of the uncanny in literature. His novel, *Die Elixire des Teufels* [The Devil's Elixir], contains a whole mass of themes to which one is tempted to ascribe the uncanny effect of the narrative;[10] but it is too obscure and intricate a story

---

understand why someone who has fallen victim to it should relinquish the real, external object of his love. The psychological truth of the situation in which the young man, fixated upon his father by his castration complex, becomes incapable of loving a woman, is amply proved by numerous analyses of patients whose story, though less fantastic, is hardly less tragic than that of the student Nathaniel.

Hoffmann was the child of an unhappy marriage. When he was three years old, his father left his small family, and was never united to them again. According to Grisebach, in his biographical introduction to Hoffmann's works, the writer's relation to his father was always a most sensitive subject with him.

10. Under the rubric "Varia" in one of the issues of the *Internationale Zeitschrift für Psychoanalyse* for 1919 (5, 308), the year in which the present paper was first published, there appears over the initials "S.F." a short note which it is not

for us to venture upon a summary of it. Toward the end of the book the reader is told the facts, hitherto concealed from him, from which the action springs; with the result, not that he is at last enlightened, but that he falls into a state of complete bewilderment. The author has piled up too much material of the same kind. In consequence one's grasp of the story as a whole suffers, though not the impression it makes. We must content ourselves with selecting those themes of uncanniness which are most prominent, and with seeing whether they too an fairly be traced back to infantile sources. These themes are all concerned with the phenomenon of the "double," which appears in every shape and in every degree of development. Thus we have characters who are to be considered identical because they look alike. This relation is accentuated by mental processes leaping from one of these characters to another— by what we should call telepathy—, so that the one possesses knowledge, feelings, and experience in common with the other. Or it is marked by the fact that the subject identifies himself with someone else, so that he is in doubt as to which his self is, or substitutes the extraneous self for his own. In other words, there is a doubling, dividing, and interchanging of the self. And finally there is the constant recurrence of the same thing[11]—the repetition of the same features or character-traits or vicissitudes, of the same crimes, or even the same names through several consecutive generations.

The theme of the "double" has been very thoroughly treated by Otto Rank (1914). He has gone into the connections which the

---

unreasonable to attribute to Freud. Its insertion here, though strictly speaking irrelevant, may perhaps be excused. The note is headed: "E. T. A. Hoffmann on the Function of Consciousness" and it proceeds: "In *Die Elixire des Teufels* (part 2, p. 210, in Hesse's edition)—a novel rich in masterly descriptions of pathological mental states—Schönfeld comforts the hero, whose consciousness is temporarily disturbed, with the following words: 'And what do you get out of it? I mean out of the particular mental function which we call consciousness, and which is nothing but the confounded activity of a damned toll-collector—excise-man—deputy-chief customs officer, who has set up his infamous bureau in our top story and who exclaims, whenever any goods try to get out: "Hi! hi! exports are prohibited . . . they must stay here . . . here, in this country. . . .""'

11. This phase seems to be an echo from Nietzsche (e.g., from the last part of *Also Sprach Zarathustra*). In chapter 3 of *Beyond the Pleasure Principle* (1920g), *Standard Ed.*, 18, 22, Freud puts a similar phrase "the perpetual recurrence of the same thing" into inverted commas.

"double" has with reflections in mirrors, with shadows, with guardian spirits, with the belief in the soul and with the fear of death; but he also lets in a flood of light on the surprising evolution of the idea. For the "double" was originally an insurance against the destruction of the ego, an "energetic denial of the power of death," as Rank says; and probably the "immortal" soul was the first "double" of the body. This invention of doubling as a preservation against extinction has its counterpart in the language of dreams, which is fond of representing castration by a doubling or multiplication of a genital symbol.[12] The same desire led the Ancient Egyptians to develop the art of making images of the dead in lasting materials. Such ideas, however, have sprung from the soil of unbounded self-love, from the primary narcissism which dominates the mind of the child and of primitive man. But when this stage has been surmounted, the "double" reverses its aspect. From having been an assurance of immortality, it becomes the uncanny harbinger of death.

The idea of the "double" does not necessarily disappear with the passing of primary narcissism, for it can receive fresh meaning from the later stages of the ego's development. A special agency is slowly formed there, which is able to stand over against the rest of the ego, which has the function of observing and critizing the self and of exercising a censorship within the mind, and which we become aware of as our "conscience." In the pathological case of delusions of being watched, this mental agency becomes isolated, dissociated from the ego, and discernible to the physician's eye. The fact that an agency of this kind exists, which is able to treat the rest of the ego like an object—the fact, that is, that man is capable of self-observation—renders it possible to invest the old idea of a "double" with a new meaning and to ascribe a number of things to it—above all, those things which seem to self-criticism to belong to the old surmounted narcissism of earliest times.[13]

But it is not this latter material, offensive as it is to the criticism of the ego, which may be incorporated in the idea of a double.

---

12. Cf. *The Interpretation of Dreams*, Standard Ed., 5, 357.

13. I believe that when poets complain that two souls dwell in the human breast, and when popular psychologists talk of the splitting of people's egos, what they are thinking of is this division (in the sphere of ego-psychology) between the critical agency and the rest of the ego, and not the antithesis discovered by psychoanalysis between the ego and what is unconscious and repressed. It is true that the distinction

There are also all the unfulfilled but possible futures to which we still like to cling in fantasy, all the strivings of the ego which adverse external circumstances have crushed, and all our suppressed acts of volition which nourish in us the illusion of Free Will.[14] [Cf. Freud, 1901b, chapter 12 (B).]

But after having thus considered the *manifest* motivation of the figure of a "double," we have to admit that none of this helps us to understand the extraordinarily strong feeling of something uncanny that pervades the conception; and our knowledge of pathological mental processes enables us to add that nothing in this more superficial material could account for the urge toward defense which has caused the ego to project that material outward as something foreign to itself. When all is said and done, the quality of uncanniness can only come from the fact of the "double" being a creation dating back to a very early mental stage, long since surmounted—a stage, incidentally, at which it wore a more friendly aspect. The "double" has become a thing of terror, just as, after the collapse of their religion, the gods turned into demons.[15]

The other forms of ego-disturbance exploited by Hoffmann can easily be estimated along the same lines as the theme of the "double." They are a harking-back to particular phases in the evolution of the self-regarding feeling, a regression to a time when the ego had not yet marked itself off sharply from the external world and from other people. I believe that these factors are partly responsible for the impression of uncanniness, although it is not easy to isolate and determine exactly their share of it.

The factor of the repetition of the same thing will perhaps not appeal to everyone as a source of uncanny feeling. From what I have observed, this phenomenon does undoubtedly, subject to cer-

---

between these two antitheses is to some extent effaced by the circumstance that foremost among the things that are rejected by the criticism of the ego are derivatives of the repressed.—[Freud had already discussed this critical agency at length in section 3 of his paper on narcissism (1914c), and it was soon to be further expanded into the "ego-ideal" and "super-ego" in chapter 11 of his *Group Psychology* (1921c) and chapter 3 of *The Ego and the Id* (1923b) respectively.]

14. In Ewer's *Der Student von Prag*, which serves as the starting-point of Rank's study on the "double," the hero has promised his beloved not to kill his antagonist in a duel. But on his way to the dueling-ground he meets his "double," who has already killed his rival.

15. Heine, *Die Götter im Exil.*

tain conditions and combined with certain circumstances, arouse an uncanny feeling, which, furthermore, recalls the sense of helplessness experienced in some dream-states. As I was walking, one hot summer afternoon, through the deserted streets of a provincial town in Italy which was unknown to me, I found myself in a quarter of whose character I could not long remain in doubt. Nothing but painted women were to be seen at the windows of the small houses, and I hastened to leave the narrow street at the next turning. But after having wandered about for a time without enquiring my way, I suddenly found myself back in the same street, where my presence was now beginning to excite attention. I hurried away once more, only to arrive by another detour at the same place yet a third time. Now, however, a feeling overcame me which I can only describe as uncanny, and I was glad enough to find myself back at the piazza I had left a short while before, without any further voyages of discovery. Other situations which have in common with my adventure an unintended recurrence of the same situation, but which differ radically from it in other respects, also result in the same feeling of helplessness and of uncanniness. So, for instance, when, caught in a mist perhaps, one has lost one's way in a mountain forest, every attempt to find the marked or familiar path may bring one back again and again to one and the same spot, which one can identify by some particular landmark. Or one may wander about in a dark, strange room, looking for the door of the electric switch, and collide time after time with the same piece of furniture—though it is true that Mark Twain succeeded by wild exaggeration in turning this latter situation into something irresistibly comic.[16]

If we take another class of things, it is easy to see that there, too, it is only this factor of involuntary repetition which surrounds what would otherwise be innocent enough with an uncanny atmosphere, and forces upon us the idea of something fateful and inescapable when otherwise we should have spoken only of "chance." For instance, we naturally attach no importance to the event when we hand in an overcoat and get a cloakroom ticket with the number, let us say, sixty-two; or when we find that our cabin on a ship bears that number. But the impression is altered if two such events, each in itself indifferent, happen close together—if we come across

16. Mark Twain, *A Tramp Abroad*, London, 1880, 1, 107.

the number sixty-two several times in a single day, or if we begin to notice that everything which has a number—addresses, hotel rooms, compartments in railway trains—invariably has the same one, or at all events one which contains the same figures. We do feel this to be uncanny. And unless a man is utterly hardened and proof against the lure of superstition, he will be tempted to ascribe a secret meaning to this obstinate recurrence of a number; he will take it, perhaps, as an indication of the span of life allotted to him.[17] Or suppose one in engaged in reading the works of the famous physiologist, Hering, and within the space of a few days receives two letters from two different countries, each from a person called Hering, though one has never before had any dealings with anyone of that name. Not long ago an ingenious scientist (Kammerer, 1919) attempted to reduce coincidences of this kind to certain laws and so deprive them of their uncanny effect. I will not venture to decide whether he has succeeded or not.

How exactly we can trace back to infantile psychology the uncanny effect of such similar recurrences is a question I can only lightly touch on in these pages; and I must refer the reader instead to another work,[18] already completed, in which this has been gone into in detail, but in a different connection. For it is possible to recognize the dominance in the unconscious mind of a "compulsion to repeat" proceeding from the instinctual impulses and probably inherent in the very nature of the instincts—a compulsion powerful enough to overrule the pleasure principle, lending to certain aspects of the mind their demonic character, and still very clearly expressed in the impulses of small children; a compulsion, too, which is responsible for a part of the course taken by the analyses of neurotic patients. All these considerations prepare us for the discovery that whatever reminds us of this inner "compulsion to repeat" is perceived as uncanny.

Now, however, it is time to turn from these aspects of the matter, which are in any case difficult to judge, and look for some undeni-

---

17. Freud had himself reached the age of sixty-two a year earlier, in 1918.

18. This was published a year later as *Beyond the Pleasure Principle* (1920g). The various manifestations of the "compulsion to repeat" enumerated here are enlarged upon in chapters 2 and 3 of that work. The "compulsion to repeat" had already been described by Freud as a clinical phenomenon, in a technical paper published five years earlier (1914g).

able instances of the uncanny, in the hope that an analysis of them will decide whether our hypothesis is a valid one.

In the story of "The Ring of Polycrates,"[19] The King of Egypt turns away in horror from his host, Polycrates, because he sees that his friend's every wish is at once fulfilled, his every care promptly removed by kindly fate. His host has become "uncanny" to him. His own explanation, that the too fortunate man has to fear the envy of the gods seems obscure to us; its meaning is veiled in mythological language. We will therefore turn to another example in a less-grandiose setting. In the case history of an obsessional neurotic,[20] I have described how the patient once stayed in a hydropathic establishment and benefited greatly by it. He had the good sense, however, to attribute his improvement not to the therapeutic properties of the water, but to the situation of his room, which immediately adjoined that of a very accommodating nurse. So on his second visit to the establishment he asked for the same room, but was told that it was already occupied by an old gentleman, whereupon he gave vent to his annoyance in the words: "I wish he may be struck dead for it." A fortnight later the old gentleman really did have a stroke. My patient thought this an "uncanny" experience. The impression of uncanniness would have been stronger still if less time had elapsed between his words and the untoward event, or if he had been able to report innumerable similar coincidences. As a matter of fact, he had no difficulty in producing coincidences of this sort; but then not only he but every obsessional neurotic I have observed has been able to relate analogous experiences. They are never surprised at their invariably running up against someone they have just been thinking of, perhaps for the first time for a long while. If they say one day, "I haven't had any news of so-and-so for a long time," they will be sure to get a letter from him the next morning, and an accident or a death will rarely take place without having passed through their mind a little while before. They are in the habit of referring to this state of affairs in the most modest manner, saying that they have "presentiments" which "usually" come true.

---

19. Schiller's poem based on Herodotus.
20. "Notes upon a Case of Obsessional Neurosis" (1909d) [Standard Ed., 10, 234].

One of the most uncanny and widespread forms of superstition is the dread of the evil eye, which has been exhaustively studied by the Hamburg oculist Seligmann (1910–11). There never seems to have been any doubt about the source of this dread. Whoever possesses something that is at once valuable and fragile is afraid of other people's envy, insofar as he projects on to them the envy he would have felt in their place. A feeling like this betrays itself by a look[21] even though it is not put into words; and when a man is prominent owing to noticeable, and particularly owing to unattractive, attributes, other people are ready to believe that his envy is rising to a more than usual degree of intensity and that this intensity will convert it into effective action. What is feared is thus a secret intention of doing harm, and certain signs are taken to mean that that intention has the necessary power at its command.

These last examples of the uncanny are to be referred to the principle which I have called "omnipotence of thoughts," taking the name from an expression used by one of my patients.[22] And now we find ourselves on familiar ground. Our analysis of instances of the uncanny has led us back to the old, animistic conception of the universe. This was characterized by the idea that the world was peopled with the spirits of human beings; by the subject's narcissistic overvaluation of his own mental processes; by the belief in the omnipotence of thoughts and the technique of magic based on that belief; by the attribution to various outside persons and things of carefully graded magical powers, or *mana*; as well as by all the other creations with the help of which man, in the unrestricted narcissism of that stage of development, strove to fend off the manifest prohibitions of reality. It seems as if each one of us has been through a phase of individual development corresponding to this animistic stage in primitive men, that none of us has passed through it without preserving certain residues and traces of it which are still capable of manifesting themselves, and that everything which now strikes us as "uncanny" fulfils the condition of touching those residues of animistic mental activity within us and bringing them to expression.[23]

---

21. "The evil eye" in German is *der böse Blick*, literally "the evil look."

22. The obsessional patient referred to just above—the "Rat Man" (1909*d*), *Standard Ed.*, 10, 233f.

23. Cf. my book *Totem and Taboo* (1912–13), essay 3, "Animism, magic, and the Omnipotence of Thoughts," where the following footnote will be found: "We appear to attribute an 'uncanny' quality to impressions that seek to confirm the

At this point I will put forward two considerations which, I think, contain the gist of this short study. In the first place, if psychoanalytic theory is correct in maintaining that every affect belonging to an emotional impulse, whatever its kind, is transformed, if it is repressed, into anxiety, then among instances of frightening things there must be one class in which the frightening element can be shown to be something repressed which *recurs*. This class of frightening things would then constitute the uncanny; and it must be a matter of indifference whether what is uncanny was itself originally frightening or whether it carried some *other* affect. In the second place, if this is indeed the secret nature of the uncanny, we can understand why linguistic usage has extended *das Heimliche* into its opposite, *das Unheimliche*; for this uncanny is in reality nothing new or alien, but something which is familiar and old-established in the mind and which has become alienated from it only through the process of repression. This reference to the factor of repression enables us, furthermore, to understand Schelling's definition of the uncanny as something which ought to have remained hidden but has come to light.

It only remains for us to test our new hypothesis on one or two more examples of the uncanny.

Many people experience the feeling in the highest degree in relation to death and dead bodies, to the return of the dead, and to spirits and ghosts. As we have seen some languages in use today can only render the German expression "an *unheimlich* house" by "a *haunted* house." We might indeed have begun our investigation with this example, perhaps the most striking of all, of something uncanny, but we refrained from doing so because the uncanny in it is too much intermixed with what is purely gruesome and is in part overlaid by it. There is scarcely any other matter, however, upon which our thoughts and feelings have changed so little since the very earliest times, and in which discarded forms have been so completely preserved under a thin disguise, as our relation to death. Two things account for our conservatism: the strength of our original emotional reaction to death and the insufficiency of our scientific knowledge about it. Biology has not yet been able to decide

---

omnipotence of thoughts and the animistic mode of thinking in general, after we have reached a stage at which, in our *judgment*, we have abandoned such beliefs." [*Standard Ed.*, **13**, 86.]

whether death is the inevitable fate of every living being or whether it is only a regular but yet perhaps avoidable event in life.[24] It is true that the statement "All men are mortal" is paraded in textbooks of logic as an example of a general proposition; but no human being really grasps it, and our unconscious has as little use now as it ever had for the idea of its own mortality.[25] Religions continue to dispute the importance of the undeniable fact of individual death and to postulate a life after death; civil governments still believe that they cannot maintain moral order among the living if they do not uphold the prospect of a better life hereafter as a recompense for mundane existence. In our great cities, placards announce lectures that undertake to tell us how to get into touch with the souls of the departed; and it cannot be denied that not a few of the most able and penetrating minds among our men of science have come to the conclusion, especially toward the close of their own lives, that a contact of this kind is not impossible. Since almost all of us still think as savages do on this topic, it is no matter for surprise that the primitive fear of the dead is still strong within us and always ready to come to the surface on any provocation. Most likely our fear still implies the old belief that the dead man becomes the enemy of his survivor and seeks to carry him off to share his new life with him. Considering our unchanged attitude toward death, we might rather enquire what has become of the repression, which is the necessary condition of a primitive feeling recurring in the shape of something uncanny. But repression is there, too. All supposedly educated people have ceased to believe officially that the dead can become visible as spirits, and have made any such appearances dependent on improbable and remote conditions; their emotional attitude toward their dead, moreover, once a highly ambiguous and ambivalent one, has been toned down in the higher strata of the mind into an unambiguous feeling of piety.[26]

We have now only a few remarks to add—for animism, magic and sorcery, the omnipotence of thoughts, man's attitude to death,

24. This problem figures prominently in *Beyond the Pleasure Principle* (1920g), on which Freud was engaged while writing the present paper. See *Standard Ed.*, 18, 44ff.

25. Freud had discussed the individual's attitude to death at greater length in the second part of his paper "Thoughts for the Times on War and Death" (1915b).

26. Cf. *Totem and Taboo* [*Standard Ed.*, 13, 66].

involuntary repetition, and the castration complex comprise practically all the factors which turn something frightening into something uncanny.

We can also speak of a living person as uncanny, and we do so when we ascribe evil intentions to him. But that is not all; in addition to this we must feel that his intentions to harm us are going to be carried out with the help of special powers. A good instance of this is the *Gettatore*,[27] that uncanny figure of Romanic superstition which Schaeffer, with intuitive poetic feeling and profound psychoanalytic understanding, has transformed into a sympathetic character in his *Josef Montfort*. But the question of these secret powers brings us back again to the realm of animism. It was the pious Gretchen's intuition that Mephistopheles possessed secret powers of this kind that made him so uncanny to her.

> Sie fühlt dass ich ganz sicher ein Genie,
> Vielleicht sogar der Teufel bin.[28]

The uncanny effect of epilepsy and of madness has the same origin. The layman sees in them the working of forces hitherto unsuspected in his fellowmen, but at the same time he is dimly aware of them in remote corners of his own being. The Middle Ages quite consistently ascribed all such maladies to the influence of demons, and in this their psychology was almost correct. Indeed, I should not be surprised to hear that psychoanalysis, which is concerned with laying bare these hidden forces, has itself become uncanny to many people for that very reason. In one case, after I had succeeded—though none too rapidly—in effecting a cure in a girl who had been an invalid for many years, I myself heard this view expressed by the patient's mother long after her recovery.

Dismembered limbs, a severed head, a hand cut off at the wrist, as in a fairy tale of Hauff's,[29] feet which dance by themselves, as in the book by Schaeffer which I mentioned above—all of them

---

27. Literally "thrower" (of bad luck), or "one who casts" (the evil eye). —Schaeffer's novel was published in 1918.

28. She feels that surely I'm a genius now,—
   Perhaps the very Devil indeed!
   Goethe, *Faust*, part 1 (scene 16),
   (Bayard Taylor's translation).

29. *Die Geshichte von der abgehauenen Hand* (The story of the severed hand).

have something peculiarly uncanny about them, especially when, as in the last instance, they prove capable of independent activity in addition. As we already know, this kind of uncanniness springs from its proximity to the castration complex. To some people the idea of being buried alive by mistake is the most uncanny thing of all. And yet psychoanalysis has taught us that this terrifying fantasy is only a transformation of another fantasy which had originally nothing terrifying about it at all, but was qualified by a certain lasciviousness—of fantasy, I mean, of intrauterine existence.[30]

There is one more point of general application which I should like to add, though, strictly speaking, it has been included in what has already been said about animism and modes of working of the mental apparatus that have been surmounted; for I think it deserves special emphasis. This is that an uncanny effect is often and easily produced when the distinction between imagination and reality is effaced, as when something that we have hitherto regarded as imaginary appears before us in reality, or when a symbol takes over the full functions of the thing it symbolizes, and so on. It is this factor which contributes not a little to the uncanny effect attaching to magical practices. The infantile element in this, which also dominates the minds of neurotics is the overaccentuation of psychical reality in comparison with material reality—a feature closely allied to the belief in the omnipotence of thoughts. In the middle of the isolation of wartime a number of the English *Strand Magazine* fell into my hands; and, among other somewhat redundant matter, I read a story about a young married couple who move into a furnished house in which there is a curiously shaped table with carvings of crocodiles on it. Toward evening an intolerable and very specific smell begins to pervade the house; they stumble over something in the dark; they seem to see a vague form gliding over the stairs—in short, we are given to understand that the presence of the table causes ghostly crocodiles to haunt the place, or that the wooden monsters come to life in the dark, or something of the sort. It was a naive enough story, but the uncanny feeling it produced was quite remarkable.

To conclude this collection of examples, which is certainly not complete, I will relate an instance taken from psychoanalytic ex-

---

30. See section 8 of Freud's analysis of the "Wolf Man" (1918*b*).

perience; if it does not rest upon mere coincidence, it furnishes a beautiful confirmation of our theory of the uncanny. It often happens that neurotic men declare that they feel there is something uncanny about the female genital organs. This *unheimlich* place, however, is the entrance to the former *Heim* [home] of all human beings, to the place where each one of us lived once upon a time and in the beginning. There is a joking saying that "Love is homesickness"; and whenever a man dreams of a place or a country and says to himself, while he is still dreaming: "this place is familiar to me, I've been here before," we may interpret the place as being his mother's genitals or her body.[31] In this case too, then, the *unheimlich* is what was once *heimisch*, familiar; the prefix *un* [un-] is the token of repression.[32]

3

In the course of this discussion the reader will have felt certain doubts arising in his mind; and he must now have an opportunity of collecting them and bringing them forward.

It may be true that the uncanny [*unheimlich*] is something which is secretly familiar [*heimlich-heimisch*], which has undergone repression and then returned from it, and that everything that is uncanny fulfils this condition. But the selection of material on this basis does not enable us to solve the problem of the uncanny. For our proposition is clearly not convertible. Not everything that fulfils this condition—not everything that recalls repressed desires and surmounted modes of thinking belonging to the prehistory of the individual and of the race—is on that account uncanny.

Nor shall we conceal the fact that for almost every example adduced in support of our hypothesis one may be found which rebuts it. The story of the severed hand in Hauff's fairy tale certainly has an uncanny effect, and we have traced that effect back to the castration complex; but most readers will probably agree with me in judging that no trace of uncanniness is provoked by Herodotus's story of the treasure of Rhampsinitus, in which the master thief, whom the princess tries to hold fast by the hand, leaves his brother's severed hand behind with her instead. Again, the prompt fulfillment of the wishes of Polycrates undoubtedly

---

31. Cf. *The Interpretation of Dreams* (1900*a*), *Standard Ed.*, 5, 399.
32. See Freud's paper on "Negation" (1925*h*).

affects us in the same uncanny way as it did the king of Egypt; yet our own fairy stories are crammed with instantaneous wish fulfillments which produce no uncanny effect whatever. In the story of "The Three Wishes," the woman is tempted by the savory smell of a sausage to wish that she might have one too, and in an instant it lies on a plate before her. In his annoyance at her hastiness her husband wishes it may hang on her nose. And there it is, dangling from her nose. All this is very striking but not in the least uncanny. Fairy tales quite frankly adopt the animistic standpoint of the omnipotence of thoughts and wishes, and yet I cannot think of any genuine fairy story which has anything uncanny about it. We have heard that it is in the highest degree uncanny when an inanimate object—a picture or a doll—comes to life; nevertheless in Hans Andersen's stories the household utensils, furniture, and tin soldiers are alive, yet nothing could well be more remote from the uncanny. And we should hardly call it uncanny when Pygmalion's beautiful statue comes to life.

Apparent death and the reanimation of the dead have been represented as most uncanny themes. But things of this sort too are very common in fairy stories. Who would be so bold as to call it uncanny, for instance, when Snow White opens her eyes once more? And the resuscitation of the dead in accounts of miracles, as in the New Testament, elicits feelings quite unrelated to the uncanny. Then, too, the theme that achieves such an indubitably uncanny effect, the unintended recurrence of the same thing, serves other and quite different purposes in another class of cases. We have already come across one example in which it is employed to call up a feeling of the comic; and we could multiply instances of this kind. Or again, it works as a means of emphasis, and so on. And once more: what is the origin of the uncanny effect of silence, darkness, and solitude? Do not these factors point to the part played by danger in the genesis of what is uncanny, notwithstanding that in children these same factors are the most frequent determinants of the expression of fear [rather than of the uncanny]? And are we after all justified in entirely ignoring intellectual uncertainty as a factor, seeing that we have admitted its importance in relation to death?

It is evident therefore, that we must be prepared to admit that there are other elements besides those which we have so far laid down as determining the production of uncanny feelings. We might say that these preliminary results have satisfied *psychoanalytic* interest in the problem of the uncanny, and that what remains probably calls for an *aesthetic* enquiry. But that would be to open the door to doubts about what exactly is the value of our general contention that the uncanny proceeds from something familiar which has been repressed.

We have noticed one point which may help us to resolve these uncertainties: nearly all the instances that contradict our hypothesis are taken from the realm of fiction, of imaginative writing. This suggests that we should differentiate between the uncanny that we acutally experience and the uncanny that we merely picture or read about.

What is *experienced* as uncanny is much more simply conditioned but comprises far fewer instances. We shall find, I think, that it fits in perfectly with our attempt at a solution, and can be traced back without exception to something familiar that has been repressed. But here, too, we must make a certain important and psychologically significant differentiation in our material, which is best illustrated by turning to suitable examples.

Let us take the uncanny associated with the omnipotence of thoughts, with the prompt fulfillment of wishes, with secret injurious powers and with the return of the dead. The condition under which the feeling of uncanniness arises here is unmistakable. We— or our primitive forefathers—once believed that these possibilities were realities, and were convinced that they actually happened. Nowadays we no longer believe in them, we have *surmounted* these modes of thought; but we do not feel quite sure of our new beliefs, and the old ones still exist within us ready to seize upon any confirmation. As soon as something *actually happens* in our lives which seems to confirm the old, discarded beliefs we get a feeling of the uncanny; it is as though we were making a judgment something like this: "So, after all, it is *true* that one can kill a person by the mere wish!" or, "So the dead *do* live on and appear on the scene of their former activities!" and so on. Conversely, anyone who has completely and finally rid himself of animistic beliefs will be insensible to this type of the uncanny. The most remarkable coincidences of wish and fulfillment, the most mysterious repetition of similar experiences in a particular place or on a particular date, the most deceptive sights and suspicious noises—none of these things will disconcert him or raise the kind of fear which can be described as "a fear of something uncanny." The whole thing is purely an affair of "reality-testing," a question of the material reality of the phenomena.[33]

The state of affairs is different when the uncanny proceeds from repressed infantile complexes, from the castration complex, womb-fantasies, etc.; but experiences which arouse this kind of uncanny feeling are not of very frequent occurrence in real life. The uncanny which proceeds from actual experience belongs for the most part to the first group [the group dealt with in the previous paragraph]. Nevertheless the distinction between the two is theoretically very important. Where the uncanny comes from infantile complexes the question of material reality does not arise; its place is taken by psychical reality. What is involved is an actual repression of some content of thought and a return of this repressed content, not a cessation of *belief in the reality* of such a content. We might say that in the one case what had been repressed is a particular ideational content, and in the other the belief in its (material) reality. But this last phrase no doubt extends the term *repression* beyond its legitimate meaning. It would be more correct to take into account a psychological distinction which can be detected here, and to say that the animistic beliefs of civilized people are in a state of having been (to a greater or lesser extent) *surmounted* [rather than repressed]. Our conclusion could then be stated thus: an uncanny

---

33. Since the uncanny effect of a "double" also belongs to this same group it is interesting to observe that the effect is of meeting one's own image unbidden and unexpected. Ernst Mach has related two such observations in his *Analyse der Empfindungen* (1900, 3). On the first occasion he was not a little startled when he realized that the face before him was his own. The second time he formed a very unfavorable opinion about the supposed stranger who entered the omnibus, and thought, "What a shabby-looking schoolmaster that man is who is getting in!"—I can report a similar adventure. I was sitting alone in my *wagon-lit* compartment when a more than usually violent jolt of the train swung back the door of the adjoining washing-cabinet, and an elderly gentleman in a dressing gown and a traveling cap came in. I assumed that in leaving the washing-cabinet, which lay between the two compartments, he had taken the wrong direction and come into my compartment by mistake. Jumping up with the intention of putting him right, I at once realized to my dismay that the intruder was nothing but my reflection in the looking glass on the open door. I can still recollect that I thoroughly disliked his appearance. Instead, therefore, of being *frightened* by our "doubles," both Mach and I simply failed to recognize them as such. Is it not possible, though, that our dislike of them was a vestigial trace of the archaic reaction which feels the "double" to be something uncanny?

experience occurs either when infantile complexes which have been repressed are once more revived by some impression, or when primitive beliefs which have been surmounted seem once more to be confirmed. Finally, we must not let our predilection for smooth solutions and lucid exposition blind us to the fact that these two classes of uncanny experience are not always sharply distinguishable. When we consider that primitive beliefs are most intimately connected with infantile complexes, and are, in fact, based on them, we shall not be greatly astonished to find that the distinction is often a hazy one.

The uncanny as it is depicted in *literature*, in stories and imaginative productions merits in truth a separate discussion. Above all, it is a much more fertile province than the uncanny in real life, for it contains the whole of the latter and something more besides, something that cannot be found in real life. The contrast between what has been repressed and what has been surmounted cannot be transposed on to the uncanny in fiction without profound modification; for the realm of fantasy depends for its effect on the fact that its content is not submitted to reality-testing. The somewhat paradoxical result is that *in the first place a great deal that is not uncanny in fiction would be so if it happened in real life; and in the second place that there are many more means of creating uncanny effects in fiction than there are in real life.*

The imaginative writer has this license among many others, that he can select his world of representation so that it either coincides with the realities we are familiar with or departs from them in what particulars he pleases. We accept his ruling in every case. In fairy tales, for instance, the world of reality is left behind from the very start, and the animistic system of beliefs is frankly adopted. Wish fulfillments, secret powers, omnipotence of thoughts, animation of inanimate objects, all the elements so common in fairy stories, can exert no uncanny influence here; for, as we have learned, that feeling cannot arise unless there is a conflict of judgment as to whether things which have been "surmounted" and are regarded as incredible may not, after all, be possible; and this problem is eliminated from the outset by the postulates of the world of fairy tales. Thus we see that fairy stories, which have furnished us with most of the contradictions to our hypothesis of the uncanny, confirm the first part of our proposition—that in the realm of fiction many things are not uncanny which would be so if they happened in real life. In the case of these stories there are other contributory factors, which we shall briefly touch upon later.

The creative writer can also choose a setting which though less imaginary than the world of fairy tales, does yet differ from the real world by admitting superior spiritual beings such as demonic spirits or ghosts of the dead. So long as they remain within their setting of poetic reality, such figures lose any uncanniness which they might possess. The souls in Dante's *Inferno,* or the supernatural apparitions in Shakespeare's *Hamlet, Macbeth,* or *Julius Caesar,* may be gloomy and terrible enough, but they are not more really uncanny than Homer's jovial world of gods. We adapt our judgment to the imaginary reality imposed on us by the writer, and regard souls, spirits, and ghosts as though their existence had the same validity as our own has in material reality. In this case too we avoid all trace of the uncanny.

The situation is altered as soon as the writer pretends to move in the world of common reality. In this case he accepts as well all the conditions operating to produce uncanny feelings in real life; and everything that would have an uncanny effect in reality has it in his story. But in this case he can even increase his effect and multiply it far beyond what could happen in reality, by bringing about events which never or very rarely happen in fact. In doing this he is in a sense betraying us to the superstitiousness which we have ostensibly surmounted; he deceives us by promising to give us the sober truth, and then after all overstepping it. We react to his inventions as we would have reacted to real experiences; by the time we have seen through his trick it is already too late and the author has achieved his object. But it must be added that his success is not unalloyed. We retain a feeling of dissatisfaction, a kind of grudge against the attempted deceit. I have noticed this particularly after reading Schnitzler's *Die Weissagung* [The prophecy] and similar stories which flirt with the supernatural. However, the writer has one more means which he can use in order to avoid our recalcitrance and at the same time to improve his chances of success. He can keep us in the dark for a long time about the precise nature of the presuppositions on which the world he writes about is based, or he can cunningly and ingeniously avoid any definite information on the point to the last. Speaking generally, however, we find a confirmation of the second part of our proposition—that fiction presents more opportunities for creating uncanny feelings than are possible in real life.

Strictly speaking, all these complications relate only to that class of the uncanny which proceeds from forms of thought that have been surmounted. The class which proceeds from repressed complexes is more resistant and remains as powerful in fiction as in real experience, subject to one exception [see p. 252]. The uncanny belonging to the first class—that proceeding from forms of thought that have been surmounted—retains its character not only in experience but in fiction as well, so long as the setting is one of material reality; but where it is given an arbitrary and artificial setting in fiction, it is apt to lose that character.

We have clearly not exhausted the possibilities of poetic license and the privileges enjoyed by story writers in evoking or in excluding an uncanny feeling. In the main we adopt an unvarying passive attitude toward real experience and are subject to the influence of our physical environment. But the storyteller has a *peculiarly* directive power over us; by means of the moods he can put us into, he is able to guide the current of our emotions, to dam it up in one direction and make it flow in another, and he often obtains a great variety of effects from the same material. All this is nothing new, and has doubtless long since been fully taken into account by students of aesthetics. We have drifted into this field of research half involuntarily, through the temptation to explain certain instances which contradicted our theory of the causes of the uncanny. Accordingly we will now return to the examination of a few of those instances.

We have already asked [p. 246] why it is that the severed hand in the story of the treasure of Rhampsinitus has no uncanny effect in the way that the severed hand has in Hauff's story. The question seems to have gained in importance now that we have recognized that the class of the uncanny which proceeds from repressed complexes is the more resistant of the two. The answer is easy. In the Herodotus story our thoughts are concentrated much more on the superior cunning of the master thief than on the feelings of the princess. The princess may very well have had an uncanny feeling, indeed she very probably fell into a swoon; but *we* have no such sensations, for we put ourselves in the thief's place, not in hers. In Nestroy's farce, *Der Zerrissene* [The torn man], another means is used to avoid any impression of the uncanny in the scene in which the fleeing man, convinced that he is a murderer, lifts up one trap-door after another and each time sees what he takes to be the ghost of his victim rising up out of it. He calls out in despair, "But I've only killed *one* man. Why this ghastly multiplication?" We know what went before this scene and do not share his error, so what must be uncanny to him has an irresistibly comic effect on us. Even a "real" ghost, as in Oscar Wilde's *Canterville Ghost,* loses all power of at least arousing *gruesome* feelings in us as soon as the author begins to amuse himself by being ironical about it and allows liberties to be taken with it. Thus we see how independent emotional effects can be of the actual subject matter in the world of fiction. In fairy stories feelings of fear—including therefore un-canny feelings—are ruled out altogether. We understand this, and that is why we ignore any opportunities we find in them for de-veloping such feelings.

Concerning the factors of silence, solitude, and darkness, we can only say that they are actually elements in the production of the infantile anxiety from which the majority of human beings have never become quite free. This problem has been discussed from a psychoanalytic point of view elsewhere.[34]

Translated by Alix Strachey

---

34. See the discussion of children's fear of the dark in section 5 of the third of Freud's *Three Essays* (1905*d*), *Standard Ed.*, 7, 224*n.*

8

Psychopathology
of Everyday Life

Remembering in adults, as is well known, makes use of a variety of psychical material. Some people remember in visual images; their memories have a visual character. Other people can scarcely reproduce in their memory even the scantiest [visual] outlines of what they have experienced. Following Charcot's proposal, such people are called *auditifs* and *moteurs* in contrast to the *visuels*. In dreams these distinctions disappear: we all dream predominantly in visual images. But this development[1] is similarly reversed in the case of childhood memories; they are plastically visual even in people whose later function of memory has to do without any visual element. Visual memory accordingly preserves the type of infantile memory. In my own case the earliest childhood memories are the only ones of a visual character: they are regular scenes worked out in plastic form, comparable only to representations on the stage. In these scenes of childhood, whether in fact they prove to be true or falsified, what one sees invariably includes oneself as a child, with a child's shape and clothes. This circumstance must cause surprise: in their recollections of later experiences adult *visuels* no longer see themselves.[2] Furthermore it contradicts all that we have learnt to supposed that in his experiences a child's attention is directed to himself instead of exclusively to impressions from outside. One is thus forced by various considerations to suspect that in the so-called earliest childhood memories we possess not the genuine memory-trace but a later revision of it,

---

1. I.e., the development of the distinctions proposed by Charcot.
2. This statement is based on a number of enquires I have made.

a revision which may have been subject to the influences of a variety of later psychical forces. Thus the "childhood memories" of individuals come in general to acquire the significance of "screen memories" and in doing so offer a remarkable analogy with the childhood memories that a nation preserves in its store of legends and myths.[3]

Anyone who has investigated a number of people psychologically by the method of psychoanalysis will in the course of his work have collected numerous examples of every kind of screen memory. However, the reporting of these examples is made extraordinarily difficult owing to the nature of the relations, which I have just discussed, between childhood memories and later life. In order to show that a childhood memory is to be regarded as a screen memory, it would often be necessary to present the complete life history of the person in question. Only rarely is it possible to lift a single screen memory out of its context in order to give an account of it, as in the following good example.

A man of twenty-four has preserved the following picture from his fifth year. He is sitting in the garden of a summer villa, on a small chair beside his aunt, who is trying to teach him the letters of the alphabet. He is in difficulties over the difference between *m* and *n* and he asks his aunt to tell him how to know one from the other. His aunt points out to him that the *m* has a whole piece more than the *n*—the third stroke. There appeared to be no reason for challenging the trustworthiness of this childhood memory; it had, however, only acquired its meaning at a later date, when it showed itself suited to represent symbolically another of the boys curiosities. For just as at that time he wanted to know the difference between *m* and *n,* so later he was anxious to find out the difference between boys and girls, and would have been very willing for this particular aunt to be the one to teach him. He also discovered then that the difference was a similar one—that a boy, too, has a whole piece more than a girl; and at the time when he acquired this piece of knowledge he called up the recollection of the parallel curiosity of his childhood.

---

3. This analogy between the childhood memories of an individual and the myths and legends of a nation relating to its prehistoric past is developed by Freud in chapter 2 of his essay on Leonardo da Vinci (1920*c*), *Standard Ed.,* 11, 84–4.

Here is another example, from the later years of childhood.[4] A man who is severely inhibited in his erotic life, and who is now over forty, is the eldest of nine children. At the time that the youngest of his brothers and sisters was born he was fifteen, yet he maintains firmly and obstinately that he had never noticed any of his mother's pregnancies. Under pressure from my skepticism a memory presented itself to him: once at the age of eleven or twelve he had seen his mother hurriedly *unfasten* her skirt in front of the mirror. He now added of his own accord that she had come in from the street and had been overcome by unexpected labor pains. The unfastening [*Aufbinden*] of the skirt was a screen memory for the confinement [*Entbindung*]. We shall come across the use of "verbal bridges" of this kind in further cases.[5]

I should like now to give a single example of the way in which a childhood memory, which previously appeared to have no meaning, can acquire one as a result of being worked over by analysis. When I began in my forty-third year to direct my interest to what was left of my memory of my own childhood there came to my mind a scene which had for a long while back (from the remotest past, as it seemed to me) come into consciousness from time to time, and which I had good evidence for assigning to a date before the end of my third year.[6] I saw myself standing in front of a

---

4. This paragraph was added in 1920.

5. See below. In Freud's interleaved copy of the 1904 edition (cf. editor's introduction, p. xiii) the following notes on screen memories are to be found. "Dr. B—— showed very neatly one Wednesday [i.e., at a meeting of the 'Vienna psychoanalytical Society' (cf Jones, 1955, 9)] that fairy tales can be made use of as screen memories in the same kind of way that empty shells are used as a home by the hermit crab. These fairy tales then become favorites, without the reason being known."— "From a dream of P.'s it appears that ice is in fact a symbol of antithesis for an erection: i.e., something that becomes hard in the cold instead of—like a penis— in heat (in excitation). The two antithetical concepts of sexuality and death are frequently linked through the idea that death makes things stiff. One of the Henris' informants instanced a piece of ice as a screen memory for his grandmother's death. See my paper on "Screen Memories" [1899a, where the paper by V. and C. Henri (1897) is more fully discussed]."

6. The important part played by this screen memory is Freud's self-analysis, and the progressive stages in its elucidation, can be followed in two letters which he wrote to Fliess on October 3–4 and October 15, 1897 (Freud, 1950a, letters 70 and 71). At that date Freud was, in fact, in his forty-*second* year. The nurse who figures prominently in the story is also referred to in *The Interpretation of Dreams* (1900a), *Standard Ed.*, 4, 247–48.

cupboard [*Kasten*] demanding something and screaming, while my half brother, my senior by twenty years, held it open. Then suddenly my mother, looking beautiful and slim, walked into the room, as if she had come in from the street. These were the words in which I described the scene, of which I had a plastic picture, but I did not know what more I could make of it. Whether my brother wanted to open or shut the cupboard—in my first translation of the picture I called it a "wardrobe" [*Schrank*]—why I was crying, and what the arrival of my mother had to do with it—all this was obscure to me. The explanation I was tempted to give myself was that what was in question was a memory of being teased by my elder brother and of my mother putting a stop to it. Such misunderstandings of a childhood scene which is preserved in the memory are by no means rare: a situation is recalled, but it is not clear what its central point is, and one does not know on which of its elements the psychical accent is to be placed. Analytic effort led me to take a quite unexpected view of the picture. I had missed my mother, and had come to suspect that she was shut up in this wardrobe or cupboard; and it was for that reason that I was demanding that my brother should open the cupboard. When he did what I asked and I had made certain that my mother was not in the cupboard, I began to scream. This is the moment that my memory has held fast; and I was followed by once by the appearance of my mother, which allayed my anxiety or longing. But how did the child get the idea of looking for his absent mother in the cupboard? Dreams which I had at the same time [as the analysis of this memory] contained obscure allusions to a nurse of whom I had other recollections, such as, for example, that she used to insist on my dutifully handing over to her the small coins I received as presents—a detail which can itself claim to have the value of a screen memory for later experiences.[7] I accordingly resolved that this time I would make the problem of interpretation easier for myself and would ask my mother, who was by then grown old, about the nurse. I leaned a variety of details, among them that this clever but dishonest person had carried out considerable thefts in the house during my mother's confinement and had been taken to court on a charge preferred by my half brother. This information

---

7. More details about this will be found in the two letters to Fliess referred to in the last footnote.

threw a flood of light on the childhood scene, and so enabled me to understand it. The sudden disappearance of the nurse had not been a matter of indifference to me: the reason why I had turned in particular to this brother, and had asked him where she was, was probably because I had noticed that he played a part in her disappearance; and he had answered in the elusive and punning fashion that was[8] characteristic of him: "She's 'boxed up' [*eingekastelt*]." At the time I understood this answer in a child's way [i.e., literally], but I stopped asking any more questions as there was nothing more to learn. When my mother left me a short while later, I suspected that my naughty brother had done the same thing to her that he had done to the nurse and I forced him to open the cupboard [*Kasten*] for me. I now understand, too, why in the translation of this visual childhood scene my mother's slimness was emphasized: it must have struck me as having just been restored to her. I am two and a half years older than the sister who was born at that time, and when I was three years old my half brother and I ceased living in the same place.[9]

Translated by Alan Tyson

---

8. In the editions of 1907, 1910, and 1912: "that is even today."

9. [*Footnote added* 1924:] Anyone who is interested in the mental life of these years of childhood will find it easy to guess the deeper determinant of the demand made on the big brother. The child of not yet three had understood that the little sister who had recently arrived had grown inside his mother. He was very far from approving of this addition to the family, and was full of mistrust and anxiety that his mother's inside might conceal still more children. The wardrobe or cupboard was a symbol for him of his mother's inside. So he insisted on looking into this cupboard, and turned for this to his big brother, who (as is clear from other material) had taken his father's place as the child's rival. Besides the well-founded suspicion that this brother had had the lost nurse "boxed up," there was a further suspicion against him—namely, that he had in some way introduced the recently born baby into his mother's inside. The affect of disappointment when the cupboard was found to be empty derived, therefore, from the superficial motivation for the child's demand. As regards the *deeper* trend of thought, the affect was in the wrong place. On the other hand his great satisfaction over his mother's slimness on her return can only be fully understood in the light of this deeper layer.—[Freud returned repeatedly to the subject of childhood memories. In his study of Leonardo da Vinci (1910c) and his paper on a memory of Geothe's (1917b) he applied his clinical observations to historical characters.

9

A Disturbance of
Memory on the Acropolis

An Open Letter to Romain Rolland on the Occasion
of His Seventieth Birthday

My dear Friend,

I have been urgently pressed to make some written contribution to the celebration of your seventieth birthday and I have made long efforts to find something that might in any way be worthy of you and might give expression to my admiration for your love of the truth, for your courage in your beliefs and for your affection and goodwill towards humanity; or, again, something that might bear witness to my gratitude to you as a writer who has afforded me so many moments of exaltation and pleasure. But it was in vain. I am ten years older than you and my powers of production are at an end. All that I can find to offer you is the gift of an impoverished creature, who has "seen better days."

You know that the aim of my scientific work was to throw light upon unusual, abnormal, or pathological manifestations of the mind—that is to say, to trace them back to the psychical forces operating behind them and to indicate the mechanisms at work. I began by attempting this upon myself and then went on to apply it to other people and finally, by a bold extension, to the human race as a whole. During the last few years, a phenomenon of this sort, which I myself had experienced a generation ago, in 1904, and which I had never understood, has kept on recurring to my mind.[1] I did not at first see why; but at last I determined to analyze the incident—and I now present you with the results of that enquiry. In the process, I shall have, of course, to ask you to give more attention to some events in my private life than they would otherwise deserve.

Every year, at that time, toward the end of August or the beginning of September, I used to set out with my younger brother on a holiday trip, which would last for some weeks and would take us to Rome or to some other region of Italy or to some part of the Mediterranean seaboard. My brother is ten years younger than I am, so he is the same age as you—a coincidence which has only now occurred to me. In that particular year my brother told me that his business affairs would not allow him to be away for long: a week would be the most that he could manage and we should have to shorten our trip. So we decided to travel by way of Trieste to the island of Corfu and there spend a few days of our holiday. At Trieste he called upon a business acquaintance who lived there, and I went with him. Our host enquired in a friendly way about our plans, and, hearing that it was our intention to go to Corfu, advised us strongly against it: "What makes you think of going there at this time of year? It would be too hot for you to do anything. You had far better go to Athens instead. The Lloyd boat sails this afternoon; it will give you three days there to see the town and will pick you up on its return voyage. That would be more agreeable and more worthwhile."

As we walked away from this visit, we were both in remarkably depressed spirits. We discussed the plan that had been proposed, agreed that it was quite impracticable, and saw nothing but difficulties in the way of carrying it out; we assumed, moreover, that we should not be allowed to land in Greece without passports. We spent the hours that elapsed before the Lloyd offices opened in wandering about the town in a discontented and irresolute frame of mind. But when the time came, we went up to the counter and

---

1. Freud had made a short allusion to the episode some ten years earlier, in chapter 5 of *The Future of an Illusion* (1927c), *Standard Ed.,* 21, 25, but had not put forward the explanation.

booked our passages for Athens as though it were a matter of course, without bothering in the least about the supposed difficulties and indeed without having discussed with one another the reasons for our decision. Such behavior, it must be confessed, was most strange. Later on we recognized that we had accepted the suggestion that we should go to Athens instead of Corfu instantly and most readily. But, if so, why had we spent the interval before the offices opened in such a gloomy state and foreseen nothing but obstacles and difficulties?

When, finally, on the afternoon after our arrival, I stood on the Acropolis and cast my eyes around upon the landscape, a surprising thought suddenly entered my mind: "So all this really *does* exist, just as we learned at school!" To describe the situation more accurately, the person who gave expression to the remark was divided, far more sharply than was usually noticeable, from another person who took cognizance of the remark; and both were astonished, though not by the same thing. The first behaved as though he were obliged, under the impact of an unequivocal observation, to believe in something the reality of which had hitherto seemed doubtful. If I may make a slight exaggeration, it was as if someone, walking beside Loch Ness, suddenly caught sight of the form of the famous Monster stranded upon the shore and found himself driven to the admission: "So it really *does* exist—the sea serpent we've never believed in!" The second person, on the other hand, was justifiably astonished, because he had been unaware that the real existence of Athens, the Acropolis, and the landscape around it had ever been objects of doubt. What he had been expecting was rather some expression of delight or admiration.

Now it would be easy to argue that this strange thought that occurred to me on the Acropolis only serves to emphasize the fact that seeing something with one's own eyes is after all quite a different thing from hearing or reading about it. But it would remain a very strange way of clothing an uninteresting commonplace. Or it would be possible to maintain that it was true that when I was a schoolboy I had *thought* I was convinced of the historical reality of the city of Athens and its history, but that the occurrence of this idea on the Acropolis had precisely shown that in my unconsciousness I had *not* believed in it, and that I was only now acquiring a conviction that "reached down to the unconscious." An explanation of this sort sounds very profound, but it is easier to assert than to prove; moreover, it is very much open to attack upon theoretical grounds. No. I believe that the two phenomena, the depression at Trieste and the idea on the Acropolis, were intimately connected. And the first of these is more easily intelligible and may help us toward an explanation of the second.

The experience at Trieste was, it will be noticed, also no more than an expression of incredulity: "We're going to see Athens? Out of the question!—it will be far too difficult!" The accompanying depression corresponded to a regret that it *was* out of the question: it would have been so lovely. And now we know where we are. It is one of those cases of "too good to be true"[2] that we come across so often. It is an example of the incredulity that arises so often when we are surprised by a piece of good news, when we hear we have won a prize, for instance, or drawn a winner, or when a girl learns that the man whom she has secretly loved has asked her parents for leave to pay his addresses to her.

When we have established the existence of a phenomenon, the next question is of course as to its cause. Incredulity of this kind is obviously an attempt to repudiate a piece of reality; but there is something strange about it. We should not be in the least astonished if an attempt of this kind were aimed at a piece of reality that threatened to bring unpleasure: the mechanism of our mind is, so to speak, planned to work along just such lines. But why should such incredulity arise in something which, on the contrary, promises to bring a high degree of pleasure? Truly paradoxical behavior! But I recollect that on a previous occasion I dealt with the similar case of the people who, as I put it, are "wrecked by success."[3] As a rule people fall ill as a result of frustration, of the nonfulfillment of some vital necessity or desire. But with these people the opposite is the case; they fall ill, or even go entirely to pieces, because an overwhelmingly powerful wish of theirs has been fulfilled. But the contrast between the two situations is not so great as it seems at first. What happens in the paradoxical case is merely that the place of the external frustration is taken by an internal one. The sufferer does not permit himself happiness: the internal frustration commands him to cling to the external one. But why? Because—so

---

2. In English in the original.
3. Section 2 of "Some Character-Types Met with in Psycho-Analytic Work" (1916*d*).

runs the answer in a number of cases—one cannot expect Fate to grant one anything so good. In fact, another instance of "too good to be true," the expression of a pessimism of which a large portion seems to find a home in many of us. In another set of cases, just as in those who are wrecked by success, we find a sense of guilt or inferiority, which can be translated: "I'm not worthy of such happiness, I don't deserve it." But these two motives are essentially the same, for one is only a projection of the other. For, as has long been known, the Fate which we expect to treat us so badly is a materialization of our conscience, of the severe super-ego within us, itself a residue to the punitive agency of our childhood.[4]

This, I think, explains our behavior in Trieste. We could not believe that we were to be given the joy of seeing Athens. The fact that the piece of reality that we were trying to repudiate was to begin with only a *possibility* determined the character of our immediate reactions. But when we were standing on the Acropolis the possibility had become an actuality, and the same disbelief found a different but far clearer expression. In an undistorted form this should have been: "I could really not have imagined it possible that I should ever be granted the sight of Athens with my own eyes—as is now indubitably the case!" When I recall the passionate desire to travel and see the world by which I was dominated at school and later, and how long it was before that desire began to find its fulfillment, I am not surprised at its aftereffect on the Acropolis; I was then forty-eight years old. I did not ask my younger brother whether he felt anything of the same sort. A certain amount of reserve surrounded the whole episode; and it was this which had already interfered with our exchanging thoughts at Trieste.

If I have rightly guessed the meaning of the thought that came to me on the Acropolis and if it did in fact express my joyful astonishment at finding myself at that spot, the further question now arises why this meaning should have been subjected in the thought itself to such a distorted and distorting disguise.

The essential subject matter of the thought, to be sure, was retained even in the distortion—that is, incredulity: "By the evidence of my senses I am now standing on the Acropolis, but I cannot believe it." This incredulity, however, this doubt of a piece of real-

---

4. Cf. chapter 3 of *The Future of an Illusion* (1927c), Standard Ed., **21**, 17f.

ity, was doubly displaced in its actual expression: first, it was shifted back into the past, and secondly it was transposed from my relation to the Acropolis on to the very existence of the Acropolis. And so something occurred which was equivalent to an assertion that at some time in the past I had doubted the real existence of the Acropolis—which, however, my memory rejected as being incorrect and, indeed, impossible.

The two distortions involve two independent problems. We can attempt to penetrate deeper into the process of transformation. Without for the moment particularizing as to how I have arrived at the idea, I will start from the presumption that the original factor must have been a sense of some feeling of the unbelievable and the unreal in the situation at the moment. The situation included myself, the Acropolis, and my perception of it. I could not account for this doubt; I obviously could not attach the doubt to my sensory impressions of the Acropolis. But I remembered that in the past I had had a doubt about something which had to do with this precise locality, and I thus found the means for shifting the doubt into the past. In the process, however, the subject matter of the doubt was changed. I did not simply recollect that in my early years I had doubted whether I myself would ever see the Acropolis, but I asserted that at that time I had disbelieved in the reality of the Acropolis itself. It is precisely this effect of the displacement that leads me to think that the actual situation on the Acropolis contained an element of doubt of reality. I have certainly not yet succeeded in making the process clear; so I will conclude by saying briefly that the whole psychical situation, which seems so confused and is so difficult to describe, can be satisfactorily cleared up by assuming that at the time I had (or might have had) a momentary feeling: *"What I see here is not real."* Such a feeling is known as a "feeling of derealization" [*Entfremdungsgefühl*].[5] I made an attempt to ward that feeling off, and I succeeded, at the cost of making a false pronouncement about the past.

These derealizations are remarkable phenomena which are still little understood. They are spoken of as "sensations," but they

---

5. The word has been rendered variously into English. Henderson and Gillespie *Text-book of Psychiatry* (Fifth Edition, 1940), 102, use the term *derealization*, and make the same distinction as Freud between it and *depersonalization* (Freud's *Depersonalization*).

are obviously complicated processes, attached to particular mental contents and bound up with decisions made about those contents. They arise very frequently in certain mental diseases, but they are not unknown among normal people, just as hallucinations occasionally occur in the healthy. Nevertheless they are certainly failures in functioning and, like dreams, which, in spite of their regular occurrence in healthy people, serve us all models of psychological disorder, they are abnormal structures. These phenomena are to be observed in two forms: the subject feels either that a piece of reality or that a piece of his own self is strange to him. In the latter case we speak of "depersonalizations"; derealizations and depersonalizations are intimately connected. There is another set of phenomena which may be regarded as their positive counterparts—what are known as *fausse reconnaissance, déjà vu, déjà raceonté*, etc.,[6] illusions in which we seek to accept something as belonging to our ego, just as in the derealizations we are anxious to keep something out of us. A naïvely mystical and unpsychological attempt at explaining the phenomena of *déjà vu* endeavors to find evidence in it of a former existence of our mental self. Depersonalization leads us on to the extraordinary condition of *double conscience*,[7] which is more correctly described as "split personality." But all of this is so obscure and has been so little mastered scientifically that I must refrain from talking about it anymore to you.

It will be enough for my purposes if I return to two general characteristics of the phenomena of derealization. The first is that they all serve the purpose of defense; they aim at keeping something away from the ego, at disavowing it. Now, new elements, which may give occasion for defensive measures, approach the ego from two directions—from the real external world and from the internal world of thoughts and impulses that emerge in the ego. It is possible that this alternative coincides with the choice between derealizations proper and depersonalizations. There are an extraordinarily large number of methods (or mechanisms, as we say) used by our ego in the discharge of its defensive functions. An investigation is at this moment being carried on close at hand which is

---

6. Freud discussed these phenomena twice at some length: in chapter 6 (D) of *The Psychopathology of Everyday Life* (1901*b*), *Standard Ed.*, 6, 265ff., and in a paper on *"Fausse Reconnaissance"* (1914*a*).

7. The French term: *dual consciousness*.

devoted to the study of these methods of defense: my daughter, the child analyst, is writing a book upon them.[8] The most primitive and thoroughgoing of these methods, "repression," was the starting-point of the whole of our deeper understanding of psychopathology. Between repression and what may be termed the normal method of fending off what is distressing or unbearable, by means of recognizing it, considering it, making a judgment upon it, and taking appropriate action about it, there lie a whole series of more or less clearly pathological methods of behavior on the part of the ego. May I stop for a moment to remind you of a marginal case of this kind of defense? You remember the famous lament of the Spanish Moors *"Ay de mi Alhama"* [Alas for my Alhama], which tells how King Boabdil[9] received the news of the fall of his city of Alhama. He feels that this loss means the end of his rule. But he will not "let it be true," he determines to treat the news as *non arrive*.[10] The verse runs:

> *Cartas le fueron venidas*
> *que Alhama era ganada:*
> *las cartas echo en el fuego,*
> *y al mensajero matara.*[11]

It is easy to guess that a further determinant of this behavior of the king was his need to combat a feeling of powerlessness. By burning the letters and having the messenger killed he was still trying to show his absolute power.

The second general characteristic of the derealizations—their dependence upon the past, upon the ego's store of memories and upon earlier distressing experiences which have since perhaps fallen victim to repression—is not accepted without dispute. But precisely my own experience on the Acropolis, which actually culminated

---

8. Anna Freud, *The Ego and the Mechanisms of Defence* (1936).

9. The last Moorish king of Granada at the end of the fifteenth century. Alhama, some twenty miles distant, was the key fortress to the capital.

10. Freud used the same phrase to describe the defensive process in section 1 of his first paper on "The Neuro-Psychoses of Defence" (1894a), *Standard Ed.*, 3, 48, and again in chapter 6 of *Inhibitions, Symptoms, and Anxiety* (1926d), ibid, 20, 120.

11. Letters had reached him telling that Alhama was taken. He threw the letters in the fire and killed the messenger.

in a disturbance of memory and a falsification of the past, helps us to demonstrate this connection. It is not true that in my school-days I ever doubted the real existence of Athens. I only doubted whether I should ever see Athens. It seemed to me beyond the realms of possibility that I should travel so far—that I should "go such a long way." This was linked up with the limitations and poverty of our conditions of life in my youth. My longing to travel was no doubt also the expression of a wish to escape from that pressure, like the force which drives so many adolescent children to run away from home. I had long seen clearly that a great part of the pleasure of travel lies in the fulfillment of these early wishes—that it is rooted, that is, in dissatisfaction with home and family. When first one catches sight of the sea, crosses the ocean, and experiences as realities cities and lands which for so long had been distant, unattainable things of desire—one feels oneself like a hero who has performed deeds of improbable greatness. I might that day on the Acropolis have said to my brother: "Do you still remember how, when we were young, we used day after day to walk along the same streets on our way to school, and how every Sunday we used to go to the Prater or on some excursion we knew so well? And now, here we are in Athens, and standing on the Acropolis! We really *have* gone a long way!" So too, if I may compare such a small event with a greater one, Napoleon, during his coronation as emperor in Notre Dame,[12] turned to one of his brothers—it must no doubt have been the eldest one, Joseph—and remarked: "What would *Monsieur notre Père* have said to this, if he could have been here today?"

But here we come upon the solution of the little problem of why it was that already at Trieste we interfered with our enjoyment of the voyage to Athens. It must be that a sense of guilt was attached to the satisfaction in having gone such a long way: there was something about it that was wrong, that from earliest times had been forbidden. It was something to do with a child's criticism of his father, with the undervaluation which took the place of the over-valuation of earlier childhood. It seems as though the essence of success was to have got further than one's father, and as though to excel one's father was still something forbidden.

---

12. The story is usually told of his assumption of the Iron Crown of Lombardy in Milan.

As an addition to this generally valid motive there was a special factor present in our particular case. The very theme of Athens and the Acropolis in itself contained evidence of the son's superiority. Our father had been in business, he had had no secondary education, and Athens could not have meant much to him. Thus what interfered with our enjoyment of the journey to Athens was a feeling of *filial piety*. And now you will no longer wonder that the recollection of this incident on the Acropolis should have troubled me so often since I myself have grown old and stand in need of forbearance and can travel no more.

I am ever sincerely yours,

January 1936 SIGM. FREUD

Translated by James Strachey

10

Dreams and Telepathy

A t the present time, when such great interest is felt in what are called "occult" phenomena, very definite anticipations will doubtless be aroused by the announcement of a paper with this title. I will therefore hasten to explain that there is no ground for any such anticipations. You will learn nothing from this paper of mine about the enigma of telepathy; indeed, you will not even gather whether I believe in the existence of "telepathy" or not. On this occasion I have set myself the very modest task of examining the relation of the telepathic occurrences in question, whatever their origin may be, to dreams, or more exactly, to our theory of dreams. You will know that the connection between dreams and telepathy is commonly held to be a very intimate one; I shall put forward the view that the two have little to do with each other, and that if the existence of telepathic dreams were to be established there would be no need to alter our conception of dreams in any way.

The material on which the present communication is based is very slight. In the first place, I must express my regret that I could make no use of my own dreams, as I did when I wrote my *Interpretation of Dreams* (1900a). But I have never had a "telepathic" dream. Not that I have been without dreams of the kind that convey an impression that a certain definite event is happening at some distant place, leaving it to the dreamer to decide whether the event is happening at that moment or will do so at some later time. In waking life, too, I have often become aware of presentiments of distant events. But these hints, foretellings and premonitions have none of them "come true," as we say; there proved to be no external reality corresponding to them, and they had therefore to be regarded as purely subjective anticipations.

For example, I once dreamt during the war that one of my sons then serving at the front had been killed. This was not directly stated in the dream, but was expressed in an unmistakable manner, by means of the well-known death-symbolism of which an account was first given by Stekel [1911*a*]. (We must not omit to fulfill the duty, often felt to be inconvenient, of making literary acknowledgements.) I saw the young soldier standing on a landing stage, between land and water, as it were; he looked to me very pale. I spoke to him but he did not answer. There were other unmistakable indications. He was not wearing military uniform, but a skiing costume that he had worn when a serious skiing accident had happened to him several years before the war. He stood on something like a footstool with a cupboard in front of him; a situation always closely associated in my mind with the idea of "falling," through a memory of my own childhood. As a child of little more than two years old I had myself climbed on a footstool like this to get something off the top of a cupboard—probably something good to eat—and I fell down and gave myself an injury, of which I can even now show the scar. My son, however, whom the dream pronounced to be dead, came home from the war unscathed.[1]

Only a short time ago, I had another dream bearing ill tidings; it was, I think, just before I decided to put together these few remarks. This time there was not much attempt at disguise. I saw my two nieces who live in England. They were dressed in black and said to me, "We buried her on Thursday." I knew the reference was to the death of their mother, now eighty-seven years of age, the widow of my eldest brother.

A time of disagreeable anticipation followed; there would of course be nothing surprising in such an old lady suddenly passing away, yet it would be very unpleasant for the dream to coincide exactly with the occurrence. The next letter from England, however, dissipated this fear. For the benefit of those who are concerned for the wish-fulfillment theory of dreams I may interpolate

---

1. This dream is fully discussed in a passage added in 1919 to *The Interpretation of Dreams* (1900*a*, Standard Ed., 5, 558 ff.) It may be remarked that the object described above as "something like a footstool" is referred to in *The Interpretation of Dreams* as a "basket."

a reassurance by saying that there was no difficulty in detecting by analysis the unconscious motives that might be presumed to exist in these death-dreams just as in others.

I hope you will not object that what I have just related is value-less because negative experiences prove as little here as they do in less occult matters. I am well aware of that and have not adduced these instances with any intention whatever of proving anything or of surreptitiously influencing you in any particular direction. My sole purpose was to explain the paucity of my material.

Another fact certainly seems to me of more significance, namely, that during some twenty-seven years of work as an analyst I have never been in a position to observe a truly telepathic dream in any of my patients. And yet those patients made up a fair collection of severely neuropathic and "highly sensitive" natures. Many of them have related to me most remarkable incidents in their earlier life on which they based a belief in mysterious occult influences. Events such as accidents or illnesses of near relatives, in particular the death of a parent, have often enough happened during the treat-ment and interrupted it; but not on one single occasion did these occurrences, eminently suitable as they were in character, afford me the opportunity of registering a single telepathic dream, al-though treatment extended over several months or even years. Any-one who cares to may look for an explanation of this fact, which still further restricts the material at my disposal. In any case it will be seen that such an explanation would not affect the subject of this paper.

Nor does it embarrass me to be asked why I have made no use of the abundant store of telepathic dreams that have appeared in the literature of the subject. I should not have had far to seek, since the publications of the English as well as of the American Society for Psychical Research are accessible to me as a member of both societies. In none of these communications is any attempt ever made to subject such dreams to analytic investigation, which would be our first interest in such cases.[2] Moreover, you will soon perceive that for the purposes of this paper one single dream will serve well enough:

---

2. In two publications by W. Stekel, the author mentioned above (*Der telepath-ische Traum,* no date, and *Die Sprache des Traumes,* Second Edition, 1922), there are at least attempts to apply the analytic technique to alleged telepathic dreams. The author expresses his belief in the reality of telepathy.

My material thus consists simply and solely of two communications which have reached me from correspondents in Germany. The writers are not personally known to me, but they give their names and addresses: I have not the least ground for presuming any intention to mislead on their part.

1

With the first of the two[3] I had already been in correspondence; he had been good enough to send me, as many of my readers do, observations of everyday occurrences and the like. He is obviously an educated and highly intelligent man; this time he expressly places his material at my disposal if I care to turn it "to literary account."

His letter runs as follows:

"I consider the following dream of sufficient interest for me to hand it on to you as material for your researches.

"I must first state the following facts. My daughter, who is married and lives in Berlin, was expecting her first confinement in the middle of December of this year. I intended to go to Berlin about that time with my (second) wife, my daughter's stepmother. During the night of November 16–17 I dreamt with a vividness and clearness I have never before experienced, that *my wife had given birth to twins. I saw the two healthy infants quite plainly with their chubby faces lying in their cot side by side. I did not observe their sex; one with fair hair had distinctly my features and something of my wife's, the other with chestnut brown hair clearly resembled her with a look of me. I said to my wife, who has red-gold hair, 'Probably "your" child's chestnut hair will also go red later on.' My wife gave them the breast. In the dream she had also made some jam in a washbasin and the two children crawled about on all fours in the basin and licked up the contents.*

"So much for the dream. Four or five times I had halfwoken from it, asked myself if it were true that we had twins, but did not come to the conclusion with any certainty that it was only a dream. The dream lasted till I woke, and after that it was some little time before I felt quite clear about the true state of affairs. At breakfast I told my wife the dream, which much amused her. She said, 'Surely

---

3. This example will be found described more briefly in Lecture XXX of Freud's *New Introductory Lectures* (1933a).

Ilse (my daughter) won't have twins?' I answered, 'I should hardly think so, as twins are not the usual thing either in my family or in G's' (her husband). On November 18, at ten o'clock in the morning, I received a telegram from my son-in-law, handed in the afternoon before, telling me of the birth of twins, a boy and a girl. The birth thus took place at the time when I was dreaming that my wife had twins. The confinement occurred four weeks earlier than any of us had expected on the basis of my daughter and son-in-law's calculations.

"But there is a further circumstance: the next night [i.e., also before receipt of the telegram] I dreamt *that my deceased wife, my daughter's own mother, had undertaken the care of forty-eight-new-born infants. When the first dozen were being brought in, I protested.* At that point the dream ended.

"My late wife was very fond of children. She often talked about it, saying she would like a whole troop round her, the more the better, and that she would do very well if she had charge of a Kindergarten and would be quite happy so. The noise children make was music to her. From time to time she would invite in a whole troop of children from the streets and regale them with chocolate and cakes in the courtyard of our villa. My daughter must have thought at once of her mother after her confinement, especially because of the surprise of its coming on prematurely, the arrival of twins, and their difference in sex. She knew her mother would have greeted the event with the liveliest joy and sympathy. 'Only think what mother would say, if she were with me now!' This thought must undoubtedly have gone through her mind. And then I dream of my dead wife, of whom I very seldom dream, and had neither spoken of nor thought of after the first dream.

"Do you think that the coincidence between dream and event was accidental in both cases? My daughter is much attached to me and was most certainly thinking of me during her labor, particularly because we had often exchanged letters about her mode of living during her pregnancy and I had constantly given her advice."

It is easy to guess what my answer to this letter was. I was sorry to find that my correspondent's interest in analysis had been so completely killed by his interest in telepathy. I therefore avoided his direct question, and, remarking that the dream contained a good deal besides its connection with the birth of the twins, I asked him to give me any information or ideas that occurred to him which could give me a clue to the meaning of the dream.

Thereupon I received the following second letter which, it must be admitted, did not give me quite all I wanted:

"I have not been able to answer your kind letter of the 24th until today. I shall be only too pleased to tell you 'without omission or reserve' all the associations that occur to me. Unfortunately there is not much; more would come out in talking.

"Well then—my wife and I do not wish for any more children. We almost never have sexual intercourse; at any rate at the time of the dream there was certainly no 'danger.' My daughter's confinement, which was expected about the middle of December, was naturally a frequent subject of conversation between us. My daughter had been examined and X-rayed in the summer, and the doctor making the examination was certain that the child would be a boy. My wife said at the time, 'I should laugh if it was a girl after all.' At the time she also remarked that it would be better if it were an H. rather than a G. (my son-in-law's family name); my daughter is handsomer and has a better figure than my son-in-law, although he has been a naval officer. I have made some study of the question of heredity and am in the habit of looking at babies to see whom they resemble. One more thing. We have a small dog which sits with us at table in the evening to have his food and licks the plates and dishes. All this material appears in the dream.

"I am fond of small children and have often said that I should like to have the bringing up of a child once more, now that I should have so much more understanding, interest, and time to devote to it; but with my wife I should not wish it, as she does not possess the necessary qualities for rearing a child judiciously. The dream makes me a present of two children—I did not observe their sex. I see them even at this moment lying in the bed and I recognize the features, the one more 'me,' the other more my wife, but each with minor traits from the other side. My wife has red-gold hair, but the one child had chestnut (reddish) brown hair. I said, 'Oh well, it will go red, too, later on.' Both the children crawl round a large washbasin in which my wife has been stirring jam and lick its bottom and sides (dream). The origin of this detail is easily explicable, just as is the dream as a whole. The dream would not be difficult to understand or interpret if it had not coincided with the unexpectedly early arrival of my grandchildren (three weeks too soon), a coincidence of time almost to the hour. (I cannot exactly say when the dream began; my grandchildren were born at nine P.M. and a quarter past; I went to bed at about eleven and had my dream during the course of the night.) Our knowledge too that the child would be a boy adds to the difficulty, though possibly the doubt whether this had been fully established might account for the appearance of twins in the dream. All the same, there remains the coincidence of the dream with the unexpected and premature appearance of my daughter's twins.

"It is not the first time that distant events have become known to me before I received the actual news. To give one instance among many. In October I had a visit from my three brothers. We had not all been together for thirty years, except for quite a short time, once at my father's funeral and once at my mother's. Both deaths were expected, and I had had no "presentiments" in either case. But about twenty-five years ago my youngest brother died quite suddenly and unexpectedly when he was ten. As the postman handed me the postcard with the news of his death, before I had glanced at it, the thought came to me at once, 'It is to say that your brother is dead.' He was the only one left at home, a strong healthy lad, while we four elder brothers were already fully fledged and had left our parents' house. At the time of my brothers' visit the talk by chance came round to this experience of mine, and, as if at the word of command, all three brothers came out with the declaration that exactly the same thing had happened to them. Whether it happened in exactly the same manner I cannot say; at all events each one said that he had felt perfectly certain of the death just before the quite unexpected news had arrived. We are all from the mother's side of a sensitive disposition, though tall, strong men, but not one of us is in the least inclined towards spiritualism or occultism; on the contrary, we disclaim adherence to either. My brothers are all three University men, two are schoolmasters, one a surveyor, all rather pedants than visionaries.—That is all I can tell you in regard to the dream. If you can turn it to literary account, I am delighted to place it at your disposal."

I am afraid that you may behave like the writer of these two letters. You, too, will be primarily interested in the question whether this dream can really be regarded as a telepathic notification of the unexpected birth of the twin children, and you will not be disposed to submit this dream to analysis like any other. I foresee that it will always be so when psychoanalysis and occultism encounter each other. The former has, so to speak, all our mental instincts against it; the latter is met halfway by powerful and mysterious sympathies. I am not, however, going to take up the position that I am nothing but a psychoanalyst, that the problems of occultism do not concern me: you would rightly judge that to be only an evasion of a problem. On the contrary, I may say that it would be a great satisfaction to me if I could convince myself and others on unimpeachable evidence of the existence of telepathic processes, but I also consider that the information provided about this dream is altogether inadequate to justify any such pronouncement. You will observe that it does not once occur to this intelligent man, deeply interested as he is in the problem of his dream, to tell us when he had last seen his daughter or what news he had lately had from her. He writes in the first letter that the birth was a month too soon; in the second, however, the month has become three weeks only, and in neither are we told whether the birth was really premature, or whether as so often happens, those concerned were out in their reckoning. But we should have to consider these and other details of the occurrence if we are to weigh the probability of the dreamer having made unconscious estimates and guesses. I felt too that it would be of no use even if I succeeded in getting answers to such questions. In the course of arriving at the information new doubts would constantly rise, which could only be set at rest if one had the man in front of one and could revive all the relevant memories which he had perhaps dismissed as unessential. He is certainly right in what he says at the beginning of his second letter that more would come out in talking.

Consider another and similar case, in which the disturbing interest of occultism has no part. You must often have been in a position to compare the anamnesis and the information about the illness given during the first session by any neurotic with what you have gained from him after some months of psychoanalysis. Apart from inevitable abbreviations, how many essentials were left out or suppressed, how many connections were displaced—in fact, how much that was incorrect or untrue was told you on that first occasion! You will not call me hypercritical if I refuse in the circumstances to make any pronouncement whether the dream in question is a telepathic event or a particularly subtle achievement on the part of the dreamer's unconscious or whether it is simply to be taken as a striking coincidence. Our curiosity must be satisfied with the hope of some later occasion on which it may be possible to make a detailed oral examination of the dreamer. But you cannot say that this outcome of our investigation has disappointed you, for I prepared for it; I said you would hear nothing which would throw any light on the problem of telepathy.

If we now pass on to the analytic treatment of this dream, we are obliged once more to express dissatisfaction. The thoughts that the dreamer associates with the manifest content of the dream are again insufficient; they do not enable us to make any analysis of the dream. For instance, the dream goes into great detail over the likeness of the children to the parents, discusses the color of their hair and the probable change of color at a later age, and as an explanation as these elaborate details we only have the dry piece of information from the dreamer that he has always been interested in questions of likeness and heredity. We are accustomed to expect rather more material than this! But at *one* point the dream does admit of an analytic interpretation, and precisely at this point analysis, which has otherwise no connection with occultism, comes to the aid of telepathy in a remarkable way. It is only on account of this single point that I am asking for your attention to this dream at all.

Correctly speaking, this dream has no right whatever to be called "telepathic." It did not inform the dreamer of anything which (outside his normal knowledge) was taking place elsewhere. What the dream did relate was something quite different from the event reported in the telegram received on the second day after the night of the dream. The dream and the actual occurrence diverge at a particularly important point, but they agree, apart from the coincidence of time, in another very interesting element. In the dream the dreamer's *wife* had twins. The occurrence, however, was that his *daughter* had given birth to twins in her distant home. The dreamer did not overlook this difference; he did not seem to know any way of getting over it and, as according to his own account he had no leaning towards the occult, he only asked quite tentatively whether the coincidence between dream and occurrence on the point of the twin birth could be more than an accident. The psychoanalytic interpretation of dreams, however, does away with this difference between the dream and the event, and gives both the same content. If we consult the associative material to this dream, it shows, in spite of its sparseness, that an intimate bond of feeling existed between the father and daughter, a bond of feeling which is so usual and so natural that we ought to cease to be ashamed of it, one that in daily life merely finds expression as a tender interest and is only pushed to its logical conclusion in dreams. The father knew that his daughter clung to him, he was convinced that she often thought of him during her labor. In his heart I think he grudged her to his son-in-law, to whom in one letter he makes a few disparaging references. On the occasion of her confinement (whether expected or communicated by telepathy) the unconscious wish became active in the repressed part of his mind: "she ought to be my (second) wife instead"; it was this wish that had distorted the dream-thoughts and was the cause of the difference between the manifest content of the dream and the event. We are entitled to replace the second wife in the dream by the daughter. If we possessed more associations to the dream, we could undoubtedly verify and deepen this interpretation.

And now I have reached the point I wish to put before you. We have endeavored to maintain the strictest impartiality and have allowed two conceptions of the dream to rank as equally probable and equally unproved. According to the first the dream is a reaction to a telepathic message: "your daughter has just brought twins into the world." According to the second an unconscious process of thought underlies the dream, which may be reproduced somewhat as follows: "Today is the day the confinement should take place if the young couple in Berlin are really out in their reckoning by a month, as I suspect. And if my (first) wife were still alive, she certainly would not be content with one grandchild. To please her there would have to be at least twins!" If this second view is right, no new problems arise. It is simply a dream like any other. The (preconscious) dream-thoughts as outlined above are reinforced by the (unconscious) wish that no other than the daughter should be the dreamer's second wife, and thus the manifest dream as described to us arises.

If you prefer to assume that a telepathic message about the daughter's confinement reached the sleeper, further questions arise of the relation of a message such as this to a dream and of its influence on the formation of dreams. The answer is not far to seek and is quite unambiguous. A telepathic message will be treated as a portion of the material that goes to the formation of a dream, like any other external or internal stimulus, like a disturbing noise in the street or an insistent organic sensation in the sleeper's own body. In our example it is evident how the message, with the help of a lurking repressed wish, became remodeled into a wish-fulfillment; it is unfortunately less easy to show that it combined with other material that had become active at the same time and was blended into a dream. Telepathic messages—if we are justified in recognizing their existence—can thus make no alteration in the process of forming a dream; telepathy has nothing to do with the nature of dreams. And in order to avoid the impression that I am trying to conceal a vague notion behind abstract and fine-sounding words, I am willing to repeat: the essential nature of dreams consists in the peculiar process of "dream-work" which, with the help of an unconscious wish, carries the preconscious thoughts (day's residues) over into the manifest content of the dream. The problem of telepathy concerns dreams as little as does the problem of anxiety.[4]

I am hoping that you will grant this, but that you will raise the objection that there are, nevertheless, other telepathic dreams in which there is no difference between the event and the dream, and in which there is nothing else to be found but an undistorted reproduction of the event. I have no knowledge of such dreams from my own experience, but I know they have often been reported. If we assume that we have such an undisguised and unadulterated telepathic dream to deal with, another question arises. Ought we to call a telepathic experience a "dream" at all? You will certainly do so as long as you keep to popular usage, in which everything that takes place in mental life during sleep is called a dream. You, too, perhaps say, "I tossed about in my dream," and still less are you conscious of anything incorrect when you say, "I shed tears in my dream" or "I felt apprehensive in my dream." But you will no doubt notice that in all these cases you are using "dream" and "sleep" and "state of being asleep" interchangeably, as if there were no distinction between them. I think it would be in the interests of scientific accuracy to keep "dream" and "state of sleep" more distinctly separate. Why should we provide a counterpart to the confusion evoked by Maeder who, by refusing to

---

4. See *The Interpretation of Dreams*, Chapter VII (D), *Standard Ed.*, 5, 582.

distinguish between the dream-work and the latent dream-thoughts, has discovered a new function for dreams?[5] Supposing, then, that we are brought face to face with a pure telepathic "dream," let us rather call it instead a telepathic experience in a state of sleep. A dream without condensation, distortion, dramatization, above all, without wish-fulfillment, surely does not deserve the name. You will remind me that, if so, there are *other* mental products in sleep to which the right to be called "dreams" would have to be refused. Actual experiences of the day are sometimes simply repeated in sleep; reproductions of traumatic scenes in "dreams" have led us only lately to revise the theory of dreams. There are dreams which are to be distinguished from the usual type by certain special qualities, which are, properly speaking, nothing but night fantasies, not having undergone additions or alterations of any kind and being in all other ways similar to the familiar daydreams. It would be awkward, no doubt, to exclude these structures from the domain of "dreams."[6] But still they all come from within, are products of our mental life, whereas the very conception of the purely "telepathic dream" lies in its being a perception of something external, in relation to which the mind remains passive and receptive.[7]

2

The second case which I shall bring before your notice in fact follows along other lines. This is not a telepathic dream, but a dream that has recurred from childhood onwards, in a person who has had many telepathic experiences. Her letter, which I reproduce here, contains some remarkable things, about which we cannot form any judgment. A part of it is of interest in connection with the problem of the relation of telepathy to dreams.

(1) " . . . My doctor, Herr Dr. N., advises me to give you an account of a dream that has pursued me for some thirty or thirty-two years. I am following his advice, and perhaps the dream may possess

---

5. The supposed "prospective" function of dreams is fully discussed in two footnotes added in 1914 and 1925 to *The Interpretation of Dreams* (*Standard Ed.*, 5, 506–7 and 579–80).

6. Cf. *The Interpretation of Dreams, Standard Ed.*, 4, 331.

7. A general discussion of the definition of dreams will be found in the fifth of Freud's *Introductory Lectures* (1916–17).

interest for you in some scientific respect. Since, in your opinion, such dreams are to be traced to an experience of a sexual nature in the first years of my childhood, I relate some reminiscences of childhood. They are experiences whose impression on me still persists and which were of so marked a character as to have determined my religion for me.

"May I beg of you to send me word in what way you explain this dream and whether it is not possible to banish it from my life, for it haunts me like a ghost, and the circumstances that always accompany it—I always fall out of bed, and have inflicted on myself not inconsiderable injuries—make it particularly disagreeable and distressing."

(2) "I am thirty-seven years old, very strong and in good physical health, but in childhood I had, besides measles and scarlet fever, an attack of nephritis. Furthermore, in my fifth year I had a very severe inflammation of the eyes, which left double vision. The images are at an angle to each other and their outline is blurred, as the scars from the ulcers affect clearness of vision. In the specialist's opinion there is nothing more to be done to the eyes and no chance of improvement. The left side of my face is drawn up from having screwed up my left eye to see better. By dint of practice and determination I can do the finest needlework; and similarly, when a six-year-old child, I broke myself of squinting by practicing in front of a looking glass, so that now there is no external sign of the defect in vision.

"From my very earliest years I was always solitary. I kept apart from other children, and had visions (clairvoyance and clairaudience). I was not able to distinguish these from reality, and in consequence often found myself in conflict with other people in embarrassing positions, with the result that I have become a very reserved and shy person. Since as a quite small child I already knew far more than I could have learnt, I simply did not understand children of my own age. I am myself the eldest of a family of twelve.

"From six to ten years old I attended the parish school and up to sixteen the high school of the Ursuline Nuns in B——. At ten I had taken in as much French in four weeks, in eight lessons, as other children learn in two years. I had only to say it over. It was just as if I had already learnt it and only forgotten it. I have never had any need to learn French, in contradistinction to English, which gave me no trouble, certainly, but which was not known to me beforehand. The same thing happened to me with Latin as with French and I have never properly learnt it, only knowing it from Church Latin, which is, however, quite familiar to me. If I read a French book today, then I immediately begin thinking in French, whereas this never happens to me with English, although I have more command of English. My parents are peasant people who for generations have never spoken any languages except German and Polish.

"*Visions.*—Sometimes reality vanishes for some moments and I see something quite different. In my house, for example, I often see an old married couple and a child; and the house is then differently furnished. In the sanatorium a friend once came into my room at about four in the morning; I was awake, had the lamp burning, and was sitting at my table reading, as I suffer much from sleeplessness. This apparition of her always means a trying time for me—as it did on this occasion.

"In 1914 my brother was on active service; I was not with my parents in B——, but in C——. It was ten A.M. on August 22 when I heard my brother's voice calling, 'Mother! Mother!' It came again ten minutes later, but I saw nothing. On August 24 I came home, found my mother greatly depressed, and in answer to my questions she said that she had had a message from the boy on August 22. She had been in the garden in the morning, when she had heard him call 'Mother! Mother!' I comforted her and said nothing about myself. Three weeks later there came a card from my brother, written on August 22 between nine and ten in the morning; shortly after that he died.

"On September 27, 1921, while in the sanatorium, I received a message of some kind. There were violent knockings two or three times repeated on the bed of the patient who shared my room. We were both awake; I asked if she had knocked; she had not even heard anything. Eight weeks later I heard that one of my friends had died in the night of September 26–27.

"Now something which is regarded as a hallucination—a matter of opinion! I have a friend who married a widower with five children; I got to know the husband only through my friend. Nearly every time that I have been to see her, I have seen a lady going in and out of the house. It was natural to suppose that this was the husband's first wife. I asked at some convenient opportunity for a portrait of her, but could not identify the apparition with the photograph. Seven years later I saw a picture with the features of the lady, belonging to one of the children. It was the first wife after all. In the picture she looked in much better health: she had just been through a feeding-up treatment and that alters the appearance of a consumptive patient.—These are only a few examples out of many.

"*The [recurrent] dream.*—*I saw a tongue of land surrounded by water. The waves were being driven forward and then back by the breakers. On this piece of land stood a palm tree, bent somewhat towards the water. A woman had her arm wound round the stem of the palm and was bending low towards the water, where a man was trying to reach the shore. At last she lay down on the ground, held tightly to the palm tree with her left hand and stretched out her right hand as far as she could towards the man in the water, but without reaching him.* At that point I would fall out of bed and wake. I was about fifteen or sixteen years old when I realized that this woman was myself, and from that time I not only experienced all the woman's apprehensions on behalf of the man but sometimes stood there as a third person looking on at the scene without taking part in it. I dreamed this dream too in separate scenes. As an interest in men awoke in me (at eighteen to twenty years old), I tried to see the man's face; but this was never possible. The foam hid everything but his neck and the back of his head. I have twice been engaged to be married, but judging by his head and build he was neither of the two men I was engaged to.— Once, when I was lying in the sanatorium under the influence of paraldehyde, I saw the man's face, which I now always see in this dream. It was that of the doctor under whose care I was. I liked him as a doctor, but I was not drawn to him in any other way.

"*Memories. Six to nine months old.*—I was in a perambulator. On my right were two horses; one, a brown, was looking at me very intently and expressively. This was my most vivid experience; I had the feeling that it was a human being.

"*One year old.*—Father and I in the town park, where a park keeper was putting a little bird in my hand. Its eyes looked back into mine. I felt 'That is a creature like yourself.'

"*Animals being slaughtered.*—When I heard the pigs squealing I always called for help and cried out 'You are killing a person' (four years old). I always refused to eat meat. Pork always makes me vomit. It was not till the war that I came to eat meat, and only unwillingly; now I am learning to do without it again.

"*Five years old.*—My mother was confined and I heard her cry out. I had the feeling, 'There is a human being or an animal in greatest distress,' just as I had over the pig killing.

"I was quite indifferent as a child to sexual matters; at ten years old I had as yet no conception of offences against chastity. Menstruation came on at the age of twelve. The woman first awakened in me at six-and-twenty, after I had given life to a child; up to that time (six months) I constantly had violent vomiting after intercourse. This also came on whenever I was at all oppressed in mood.

"I have extraordinarily keen powers of observation, and quite exceptionally sharp hearing, also a very keen sense of smell. With my eyes bandaged I can pick out by smell people I know from among a number of others.

"I do not regard my abnormal powers of sight and hearing as pathological, but ascribe them to finer perceptions and greater quickness of thought; but I have only spoken of it to my pastor and to Dr.—— (very unwittingly to the latter, as I was afraid he would tell me that what I regarded as *plus*-qualities were *minus*-qualities, and also because from being misunderstood in childhood I am very reserved and shy)."

The dream which the writer of the letter asks us to interpret is not hard to understand. It is a dream of rescuing from water, a typical birth-dream.[8] The language of symbolism, as you are aware, knows no grammar; it is an extreme case of a language of infinitives, and even the active and passive are represented by one and the same image. If in a dream a woman pulls (or tries to pull) a man out of the water, that may mean that she wants to be his mother (takes him for her son as Pharaoh's daughter did with Moses). Or it may mean that she wants him to make her into a mother: she wants to have a son by him, who, as a likeness of him, can be his equivalent. The tree trunk to which the woman was clinging is easily recognized as a phallic symbol, even though it is not standing straight up, but inclined towards the surface of the water—in the dream the word is "bent." The onrush and recoil of the breakers brought to the mind of another dreamer who was relating a similar dream,

---

8. See *The Interpretation of Dreams* (1900*a*), *Standard Ed.*,5, 403.

a comparison with the intermittent pains of labor; and when, knowing that she had not yet borne a child, I asked her how she knew of this characteristic of labor, she said that she imagined labor as a kind of colic—a quite unimpeachable description physiologically. She gave the association *The Waves of the Sea and of Love*.[9] How our present dreamer at so early an age can have arrived at the finer details of symbolism—tongue of land, palm tree—I am naturally unable to say. We must not, moreover, overlook the fact that, when people assert that they have for years been pursued by the same dream, it often turns out that the manifest content is not quite the same. Only the kernel of the dream has recurred each time; the details of the content are changed or additions are made to them.[10]

At the end of this dream, which is clearly charged with anxiety, the dreamer falls out of bed. This is a fresh representation of childbirth. Analytic investigation of the fear of heights, of the dread of an impulse to throw oneself out of the window, has doubtless led you all to the same conclusion.

Who then is the man, by whom the dreamer wishes to have a child, or of whose likeness she would like to be the mother? She often tried to see his face, but the dream never allowed her to; the man had to remain incognito. We know from countless analyses what this concealment means, and the conclusion we should base on analogy is verified by another statement of the dreamer's. Under the influence of paraldehyde she once recognized the face of the man in the dream as that of the hospital physician who was treating her, and who meant nothing more to her conscious emotional life. The original thus never divulged its identity, but this impression of it in "transference" establishes the conclusion that earlier it must always have been her father. Ferenczi [1917] is perfectly right in pointing out that these "dreams of the unsuspecting" are valuable sources of information, as confirming the conjectures of analysis. Our dreamer was the eldest of twelve children; how often must she have suffered the pangs of jealousy and disappointment when it was not she but her mother who obtained from her father the child she longed for!

---

9. *Des Meeres und der Liebe Wellen*, the title of a play about Hero and Leander by Grillparzer.

10. This point is discussed at some length in Freud's analysis of the case of "Dora" (1905e), *Standard Ed.*, 7, 92–93.

Our dreamer quite correctly supposed that her first memories of childhood would be of value in the interpretation of her early and recurrent dream. In the first scene, before she was one year old, as she was sitting in her perambulator she saw two horses beside her, one looking at her. This she described as her most vivid experience; she had the feeling that it was a human being. This was a feeling which we can understand only if we assume that the two horses represented, in this case as so often, a married couple, father and mother. It was, as it were, a flash of infantile totemism. If we could, we should ask the writer whether the *brown* horse who looked at her so humanly could not be recognized by its coloring as her father. The second recollection was associatively connected with the first through the same "understanding" gaze. Taking the little bird in her hand, however, reminds the analyst, who has prejudices of his own, of a feature in the dream in which the woman's hand was in contact with another phallic symbol.

The next two memories belong together; they make still slighter demands on the interpreter. The mother crying out during her confinement reminded the daughter directly of the pigs squealing when they were being killed and put her into the same frenzy of pity. But we may also conjecture that this was a violent reaction against an angry death-wish directed at the mother.

With these indications of tenderness for her father, of contact with his genitals, and of death-wishes against her mother, the outline of the female Oedipus complex is sketched in. Her long retention of her ignorance of sexual matters, and her frigidity at a later period bear out these suppositions. The writer of the letter became potentially—and at times no doubt actually—a hysterical neurotic. The forces of life have, for her own happiness, carried her along with them. They have awakened in her the sexual feelings of a woman and brought her the joys of motherhood, and the capacity to work. But a portion of her libido still clings to its points of fixation in childhood; she still dreams the dream that throws her out of bed and punishes her for her incestuous object-choice by "not inconsiderable injuries."

And now an explanation, given in writing by a doctor who was a stranger to her, was expected to effect what all the most important experiences of her later life had failed to do! Probably a regular analysis continued for a considerable time would have succeeded in this. As things were, I was obliged to content myself with writing to her that I was convinced she was suffering from the aftereffects of a strong emotional tie binding her to her father and from a corresponding identification with her mother, but that I did not myself expect that this explanation would help her. Spontaneous cures of neurosis usually leave scars behind, and these become painful again from time to time. We are very proud of our art if we achieve a cure through psychoanalysis, yet here too we cannot always prevent the formation of a painful scar as an outcome.

The little series of reminiscences must engage our attention for a while longer. I have stated elsewhere that such scenes of childhood are "screen memories"[11] selected at a later period, put together, and not infrequently falsified in the process. This subsequent remodeling serves a purpose that is sometimes easy to guess. In our case one can almost hear the writer's ego glorifying or soothing itself by means of this series of recollections. "I was from infancy a particularly noble and compassionate creature. I learnt quite early that animals have souls as we have, and could not endure cruelty to animals. The sins of the flesh were far from me and I preserved my chastity till late in life." With declarations such as these she was loudly contradicting the inferences that we have to make about her early childhood on the basis of our analytical experience, namely, that she had an abundance of premature sexual impulses and violent feelings of hatred for her mother and her younger brothers and sisters. (Besides the genital significance I have just assigned to it, the little bird may also be a symbol of a child, like all small animals; her recollection thus accentuated very insistently the fact that this small creature had the same right to exist as she herself.) Hence the short series of recollections furnishes a very nice example of a mental structure with a twofold aspect. Viewed superficially, we may find in it the expression of an abstract idea, here, as usually, with an ethical reference. In Silberer's nomenclature the structure has an *anagogic* content. On deeper investigation it reveals itself as a chain of phenomena belonging to the region of the repressed life of the instincts—it displays its *psychoanalytic* content. As you know, Silberer, who was among the first to issue a warning to us not to lose sight of the nobler side of the human soul, has put forward the view that all or nearly all dreams

---

11. See Freud's paper on "Screen Memories" (1899a), and chapter 4 of his *Psychopathology of Everyday Life* (1901b).

permit such a twofold interpretation, a purer, anagogic one beside the ignoble, psychoanalytic one. This is, however, unfortunately not so. On the contrary, an overinterpretation of this kind is rarely possible. To my knowledge no valid example of such a dream-analysis with a double meaning has been published up to the present time. But observations of this kind can often be made upon the series of associations that our patients produce during analytic treatment. On the one hand the successive ideas are linked by a line of association which is plain to the eye, while on the other hand you become aware of an underlying theme which is kept secret but which at the same time plays a part in all these areas. The contrast between the two themes that dominate the same series of ideas is not always one between the lofty anagogic and the low psychoanalytic, but one rather between offensive and respectable or indifferent ideas—a fact that easily explains why such a chain of associations with a twofold determination arises. In our present example it is of course not accidental that the anagogic and the psychoanalytic interpretations stood in such a sharp contrast to each other; both related to the same material, and the later trend was no other than that of the reaction formations which had been erected against the disowned instinctual impulses.[12]

But why do we look for a psychoanalytic interpretation at all instead of contenting ourselves with the more accessible anagogic one? The answer to this is linked up with many other problems—with the existence in general of neurosis and the explanations it inevitably demands—with the fact that virtue does not reward a man with as much joy and strength in life as one would expect, as though it brought with it too much of its origin (our dreamer, too, had not been well rewarded for her virtue), and with other things which I need not discuss before this audience.

So far, however, we have completely neglected the question of telepathy, the other point of interest for us in this case; it is time to return to it. In a sense we have here an easier task than in the case of Herr H.[13] With a person who so easily and so early in life lost touch with reality and replaced it by the world of fantasy, the

---

12. Cf. the passage added in 1919 to *The Interpretation of Dreams, Standard Ed.*, 5, 523 f.

13. All the German editions read "Herr G.," which is an evident slip. The mistake was pointed out in Devereux (1953).

temptation is irresistible to connect her telepathic experiences and "visions" with her neurosis and to derive them from it, although here too we should not allow ourselves to be deceived as to the cogency of our own arguments. We shall merely be replacing what is unknown and unintelligible by possibilities that are least comprehensible.

On August 22, 1914, at ten o'clock in the morning, our correspondent experienced a telepathic impression that her brother, who was at the time on active service, was calling, "Mother! Mother!"; the phenomenon was purely acoustic, it was repeated shortly after, but nothing was seen. Two days later she saw her mother and found her much depressed because the boy had announced himself to her with a repeated call of "Mother! Mother!" She immediately remembered the same telepathic message, which she had experienced at the same time, and as a matter of fact some weeks later it was established that the young soldier had died on that day at the hour in question.

It cannot be proved, but also cannot be disproved, that instead of this, what happened was the following. Her mother told her one day that her son had sent a telepathic message; whereupon a conviction at once arose in her mind that she had had the same experience at the same time. Such illusions of memory arise in the mind with a compelling force which they draw from real sources; but they turn psychical reality into material reality. The strength of the illusion lies in its being an excellent way of expressing the sister's proneness to identify herself with her mother. "You are anxious about the boy, but I am really his mother, and his cry was meant for me; *I* had this telepathic message." The sister would naturally firmly reject our attempt at explanation and would hold to her belief in the authenticity of her experience. But she could not do otherwise. She would be bound to believe in the reality of the pathological effect so long as the reality of its unconscious premises were unknown to her. Every such delusion derives its strength and its unassailable character from having a source in unconscious psychical reality. I note in passing that it is not incumbent on us here to explain the mother's experience or to investigate its authenticity.

The dead brother, however, was not only our correspondent's imaginary child; he also represented a rival whom she had regarded with hatred from the time of his birth. By far the greater number of all telepathic intimations relate to death or the possibility of death; when patients under analysis keep telling us of the frequency and infallibility of their gloomy forebodings, we can with equal regularity show them that they are fostering particularly strong death-wishes in their unconscious against their nearest relations and have long been thus suppressing them. The patient whose history I related in 1909[14] was an example to the point; he was called a "carrion crow" by his relations. But when this kindly and highly intelligent man—who has since himself perished in the war—began to make progress towards recovery, he himself gave me considerable assistance in clearing up his own psychological conjuring tricks. In the same way, the account given in our first correspondent's letter, of how he and his three brothers had received the news of their youngest brother's death as a thing they had long been inwardly aware of, appears to need no other explanation. The elder brothers would all have been equally convinced of the superfluousness of the youngest arrival.

Here is another of our dreamer's "visions" which will probably become more intelligible in the light of analytic knowledge. Women friends obviously had a great significance in her emotional life. Only recently the death of one of them was conveyed to her by a knocking at night on the bed of a roommate in the sanatorium. Another friend had many years before married a widower with several (five) children. On the occasion of her visits to their house she regularly saw the apparition of a lady, who she could not help supposing was the husband's first wife; this did not at first permit of confirmation, and only became a matter of certainty with her seven years later, on the discovery of a fresh photograph of the dead woman. This achievement in the way of a vision on the part of our correspondent had the same intimate dependence on the family complexes familiar to us as had her presentiment of her brother's death. By identifying herself with her friend she could in the person of the latter find the fulfillment of her own wishes; for every eldest daughter of a numerous family builds up in her unconscious the fantasy of becoming her father's second wife by the death of her mother. If the mother is ill or dies, the eldest daughter takes her place as a matter of course in relation to her younger brothers and sisters, and may even take over some part

14. "Notes upon a Case of Obsessional Neurosis" [*Standard Ed.*, 10, 235].

of the functions of the wife in respect to the father. The unconscious wish fills in the other part.

I am now almost at the end of what I wish to say. I might, however, add the observation that the instances of telepathic messages or productions which have been discussed here are clearly connected with emotions belonging to the sphere of the Oedipus complex. This may sound startling; I do not intend to give it out as a great discovery, however. I would rather revert to the result we arrived at through investigating the dream I considered first. Telepathy has no relation to the essential nature of dreams; it cannot deepen in any way what we already understand of them through analysis. On the other hand, psychoanalysis may do something to advance the study of telepathy, insofar as, by the help of its interpretations, many of the puzzling characteristics of telepathic phenomena may be rendered more intelligible to us; or other, still doubtful, phenomena may for the first time definitely be ascertained to be of a telepathic nature.

There remains one element of the apparently intimate connection between telepathy and dreams which is not affected by any of these considerations: namely, the incontestable fact that sleep creates favorable conditions for telepathy. Sleep is not, it is true, indispensable to the occurrence of telepathic processes—whether they originate in messages or in unconscious activity. If you are not already aware of this, you will learn it from the instance given by our second correspondent, of the young man's message which came between nine and ten in the morning. We must add, however, that no one has a right to take exception to telepathic occurrences if the event and the intimation (or message) do not exactly coincide in astronomical time. It is perfectly conceivable that a telepathic message might arrive contemporaneously with the event and yet only penetrate to consciousness the following night during sleep (or even in waking life only after a while, during some pause in the activity of the mind). We are, as you know, of opinion that dream formation itself does not necessarily wait for the onset of sleep before it begins.[15] Often the latent dream-thoughts may have been being got ready during the whole day, till at night they find the contact with the unconscious wish that shapes them into a

---

15. See *The Interpretation of Dreams*, Standard Ed., 5, 575–76.

dream. But if the phenomenon of telepathy is only an activity of the unconscious mind, then, of course, no fresh problem lies before us. The laws of unconscious mental life may then be taken for granted as applying to telepathy.

Have I given you the impression that I am secretly inclined to support the reality of telepathy in the occult sense? If so, I should very much regret that it is so difficult to avoid giving such an impression. For in reality I have been anxious to be strictly impartial. I have every reason to be so, since I have no opinion on the matter and know nothing about it.

Translated by C. J. M. Hubback

11

Delusions and Dreams in Jensen's *Gradiva*

1

A group of men who regarded it as a settled fact that the essential riddles of dreaming have been solved by the efforts of the author of the present work[1] found their curiosity aroused one day by the question of the class of dreams that have never been dreamt at all—dreams created by imaginative writers and ascribed to invented characters in the course of a story. The notion of submitting this class of dreams to an investigation might seem a waste of energy and a strange thing to undertake; but from one point of view it could be considered justifiable. It is far from being generally believed that dreams have a meaning and can be interpreted. Science and the majority of educated people smile if they are set the task of interpreting a dream. Only the common people, who cling to superstitions and who on this point are carrying on the convictions of antiquity, continue to insist that dreams can be interpreted. The author of *The Interpretation of Dreams* has ventured, in the face of the reproaches of strict science, to become a partisan of antiquity and superstition. He is, it is true, far from believing that dreams foretell the future, for the unveiling of which men have vainly striven from time immemorial by every forbidden means. But even he has not been able entirely to reject the relation of dreams to the future. For the dream, when the laborious work of translating it had been accomplished, revealed itself to him as a wish of the dreamer's represented as fulfilled; and who could deny that wishes are predominantly turned toward the future?

---

1. See Freud, *The Interpretation of Dreams* (1990a).

I have just said that dreams are fulfilled wishes. Anyone who is not afraid of making his way through an abstruse book, and who does not insist on a complicated problem being represented to him as easy and simple in order to save him trouble and at the cost of honesty and truth, may find the detailed proof of this thesis in the work I have mentioned. Meanwhile, he may set on one side the objections which will undoubtedly occur to him against equating dreams and wish fulfillments.

But we have gone a long way ahead. It is not a question yet of establishing whether the meaning of a dream can always be rendered by a fulfilled wish, or whether it may not just as often stand for an anxious expectation, an intention, a reflection, and so on. On the contrary, the question that first arises is whether dreams have a meaning at all, whether they ought to be assessed as mental events. Science answers no: it explains dreaming as a purely physiological process, behind which, accordingly, there is no need to look for sense, meaning, or purpose. Somatic stimuli, so it says, play upon the mental instrument during sleep and thus bring to consciousness now one idea and now another, robbed of all mental content: dreams are comparable only to twitchings, not to expressive movements, of the mind.

Now in this dispute as to the estimation in which dreams should be held, imaginative writers seem to be on the same side as the ancients, as the superstitious public and as the author of *The Interpretation of Dreams*. For when an author makes the characters constructed by his imagination dream, he follows the everyday experience that people's thoughts and feelings are continued in sleep and he aims at nothing else than to depict his heroes' states of mind by their dreams. But creative writers are valuable allies and their evidence is to be prized highly, for they are apt to know a whole host of things between heaven and earth of which our philosophy has not yet let us dream. In their knowledge of the mind they are far in advance of us everyday people, for they draw upon sources which we have not yet opened up for science. If only this support given by writers in favor of dreams having a meaning were less ambiguous! A strictly critical eye might object that writers take their stand neither for nor against particular dreams having a psychical meaning; they are content to show how the sleeping mind twitches under the excitations which have remained active in it as offshoots of waking life.

But even this sobering thought does not damp our interest in the fashion in which writers make use of dreams. Even if this enquiry should teach us nothing new about the nature of dreams, it may perhaps enable us from this angle to gain some small insight into the nature of creative writing. Real dreams were already regarded as unrestrained and unregulated structures—and now we are confronted by unfettered imitations of these dreams! There is far less freedom and arbitrariness in mental life, however, than we are inclined to assume—there may even be none at all. What we call chance in the world outside can, as is well-known, be resolved into laws. So, too, what we call arbitrariness in the mind rests upon laws, which we are only now beginning dimly to suspect. Let us, then, see what we find!

There are two methods that we might adopt for this enquiry. One would be to enter deeply into a particular case, into the dream-creations of one author in one of his works. The other would be to bring together and contrast all the examples that could be found of the use of dreams in the works of different authors. The second method would seem to be far the more effective and perhaps the only justifiable one, for it frees us at once from the difficulties involved in adopting the artificial concept of "writers" as a class. On investigation this class falls apart into individual writers of the most various worth—among them some whom we are accustomed to honor as the deepest observers of the human mind. In spite of this, however, these pages will be devoted to an enquiry of the first sort. It happened that in the group of men among whom the notion first arose there was one[2] who recalled that in the work of fiction that had last caught his fancy there were several dreams which had, as it were, looked at him with familiar faces and invited him to attempt to apply to them the method of *The Interpretation of Dreams*. He confessed that the subject matter of the little work and the scene in which it was laid may no doubt have played the chief part in creating his enjoyment. For the story was set in the frame of Pompeii and dealt with a young archaeologist who had surrendered his interest in life in exchange for an interest in the remains of classical antiquity and who was now brought back to real life by a roundabout path which was strange but perfectly logical. During the treatment of this genuinely poetic material the

---

2. This was Jung.

reader had been stirred by all kinds of thoughts akin to it and in harmony with it. The work was a short tale by Wilhelm Jensen— *Gradiva*—which its author himself described as a "Pompeian fantasy."

And now I ought properly to ask all my readers to put aside this little essay and instead to spend some time in acquainting themselves with *Gradiva* (which first appeared in the bookshops in 1903), so that what I refer to in the following pages may be familiar to them. But for the benefit of those who have already read *Gradiva* I will recall the substance of the story in a brief summary; and I shall count upon their memory to restore to it all the charm of which this treatment will deprive it.

A young archaeologist, Norbert Hanold, had discovered in a museum of antiquities in Rome a relief which had so immensely attracted him that he was greatly pleased at obtaining an excellent plaster cast of it which he could hang in his study in a German university town and gaze at with interest. The sculpture represented a fully grown girl stepping along, with her flowing dress a little pulled up so as to reveal her sandaled feet. One foot rested squarely on the ground; the other, lifted from the ground in the act of following after, touched it only with the tips of the toes, while the sole and heel rose almost perpendicularly. It was probably the unusual and peculiarly charming gait thus presented that attracted the sculptor's notice and that still, after so many centuries, riveted the eyes of its archaeological admirer.

The interest taken by the hero of the story in this relief is the basic psychological fact in the narrative. It was not immediately explicable. "Dr. Norbert Hanold, Lecturer in Archaeology, did not in fact find in the relief anything calling for special notice from the point of view of his branch of science." (3.)[3] "He could not explain to himself what there was in it that had provoked his attention. He only knew that he had been attracted by something and that the effect had continued unchanged ever since." But his imagination was occupied with the sculpture without ceasing. He found something "of today" about it, as though the artist had had a glimpse in the street and captured it "from the life." He gave the

---

3. Plain numbers in brackets in the present translation are page references to Jensen, *Gradiva,* 1903.

girl thus pictured as she stepped along the name of "Gradiva"—
"the girl who steps along."[4] He made up a story that she was no
doubt the daughter of an aristocratic family, perhaps "of a patrician aedile,[5] who carried out his office in the service of Ceres,"
and that she was on her way to the goddess's temple. Then he
found it hard to fit her quiet, calm nature into the busy life of a
capital city. He convinced himself, rather, that she must be transported to Pompeii, and that somewhere there she was stepping
across the curious stepping-stones which have been dug up and
which made it possible to cross dry-foot from one side of the street
to the other in rainy weather, though allowing carriage-wheels to
pass between them as well. Her features struck him as having a
Greek look and he had no doubt that she was of Hellenic origin.
Little by little he brought the whole of his archaeological learning
into the service of these and other fantasies relating to the original
who had been the model for the relief.

But now he found himself confronted by an ostensibly scientific
problem which called for a solution. It was a question of his arriving at a critical judgment as to "whether Gradiva's gait as she
stepped along had been reproduced by the sculptor in a lifelike
manner." He found that he himself was not capable of imitating
it, and in his quest for the "reality" of this gait he was led "to
make observations of his own from the life in order to clear the
matter up." (9.) This, however, forced him into a course of behavior that was quite foreign to him. "Hitherto, the female sex had
been to him no more than the concept of something made of marble
or bronze, and he had never paid the slightest attention to its contemporary representatives." Social duties had always seemed to
him an unavoidable nuisance; he saw and heard young ladies
whom he came across in society so little that when he next met
them he would pass them by without a sign; and this, of course,
made no favorable impression on them. Now, however, the scientific task which he had taken on compelled him, in dry, but more
especially in wet, weather, to look eagerly in the street at women's
and girls' feet as they came into view—an activity which brought
him some angry, and some encouraging, glances from those who
came under his observation; "but he was aware of neither the one

---

4. The derivation of the name is further explained below.
5. A magistrate in charge of public buildings.

nor the other." (10.) As an outcome of these careful studies he was forced to the conclusion that Gradiva's gait was not discoverable in reality; and this filled him with regret and vexation.

Soon afterwards he had a terrifying dream, in which he found himself in ancient Pompeii on the day of the eruption of Vesuvius and witnessed the city's destruction. "As he was standing at the edge of the forum beside the Temple of Jupiter, he suddenly saw Gradiva at no great distance from him. Till then he had had no thought of her presence, but now it occurred to him all at once and as though it was something natural that, since she was a Pompeian, she was living in her native town, and, *without his having suspected it, living as his contemporary.*" (12.) Fear of the fate that lay before her provoked him to utter a warning cry, whereupon the figure, as she calmly stepped along, turned her face toward him. But she then proceeded on her way untroubled, till she reached the portico of the temple;[6] there she took her seat on one of the steps and slowly laid her head down on it, while her face grew paler and paler, as though it were turning into marble. When he hurried after he, he found her stretched out on the broad step with a peaceful expression, like someone asleep, till the rain of ashes buried her form.

When he awoke, the confused shouts of the inhabitants of Pompeii calling for help still seemed to echo in his ears, and the dull muttering of the breakers in the agitated sea. But even after his returning reflection recognized the sounds as the awakening signs of noisy life in a great city, he retained his belief for a long time in the reality of what he had dreamt. When at length he had freed himself of the notion that he himself had been present at the destruction of Pompeii almost two thousand years earlier, he was nevertheless left with what seemed a true conviction that Gradiva had lived in Pompeii and been buried there with the others in the year 79 A.D. The dream had as its result that now for the first time in his fantasies about Gradiva he mourned for her as someone who was lost.

While he was leaning out of the window, absorbed in these thoughts, his attention was caught by a canary warbling its song from a cage in the open window of the house opposite. Suddenly something passed with a start through the mind of the young man,

---

6. The Temple of Apollo.

who seems not yet to have fully woken from his dream. He thought he saw in the street a form like his Gradiva, and thought he even recognized her characteristic gait. Without thinking, he hurried into the street so as to catch up with her; and it was only the laughter and jeers of the passersby at his early-morning attire that quickly drove him back into his house. When he was in his room again, the singing of the canary in its cage once more caught his attention and suggested a comparison with himself. He too, so it seemed to him, was like someone sitting in a cage, though it was easier for him to escape from it. As though as a further aftermath of his dream, and perhaps, too, under the influence of the mild air of spring, a resolve took shape in him to make a springtime journey to Italy. A scientific excuse for it soon presented itself, even though "the impulse to make this journey had arisen from a feeling he could not name." (24.)

Let us pause for a moment at this journey, planned for such remarkably uncogent reasons, and take a closer look at our hero's personality and behavior. He still appears to us as incomprehensible and foolish; we have no idea how his peculiar folly will be linked to human feeling and so arouse our sympathy. It is an author's privilege to be allowed to leave us in such uncertainty. The charm of his language and the ingenuity of his ideas offer us a provisional reward for the reliance we place in him and for the still-unearned sympathy which we are ready to feel for his hero. Of this hero we are further told that he was preordained by family tradition to become an archaeologist, that in his later isolation and independence he was wholly absorbed in his studies and had turned completely away from life and its pleasures. Marble and bronze alone were truly alive for him; they alone expressed the purpose and value of human life. But nature, perhaps with benevolent intent, had infused into his blood a corrective of an entirely unscientific sort—an extremely lively imagination, which could show itself not only in his dreams but often in his waking life as well. This division between imagination and intellect destined him to become an artist or a neurotic; he was one of those whose kingdom is not of this world. Thus it was that it could come about that his interest was attached to a relief representing a girl stepping along in a peculiar fashion, that he wove his fantasies around her, imagined a name and origin for her, placed the figure he had created in the setting of the Pompeii that was buried more than eighteen hundred years before, and finally, after a strange anxiety-dream, magnified his fantasy of the existence and death of this girl named Gradiva into a delusion, which gained an influence over his actions. Such products of the imagination would seem to us astonishing and inexplicable if we met them in someone in real life. Since our hero, Norbert Hanold, is a fictitious person, we may perhaps put a timid question to his author, and ask whether his imagination was determined by forces other than its own arbitrary choice.

We had left our hero at the moment when he was apparently being led by the song of a canary to decide on a journey to Italy, the purpose of which was evidently not clear to him. We learn further that he had no fixed plan or goal for his journey. An inner restlessness and dissatisfaction drove him from Rome to Naples and from thence further still. He found himself among the swarm of honeymooners and was forced to notice the loving couples of "Edwins" and "Angelinas,"[7] but was quite unable to understand their goings-on. He came to the conclusion that of all the follies of mankind "getting married takes first place, as the greatest and most incomprehensible, and the senseless honeymoon trips to Italy are, in a way, the crowning touch of this idiocy." (27.) Having been disturbed in his sleep by the proximity of a loving couple in Rome, he hurriedly fled to Naples, only to find other "Edwins" and "Angelinas" there. Having gathered from their conversation that the majority of these pairs of birds had no intention of nesting among the ruins of Pompeii, but were flying toward Capri, he determined to do what they did not, and only a few days after his departure found himself "contrary to his expectation and intentions" in Pompeii.

But without finding there the repose he was in search of. The part which had so far been played by the honeymoon couples, who had troubled his spirits and harassed his thoughts, was now taken over by the houseflies, which he was inclined to regard as the incarnation of all that is absolutely evil and unnecessary. The two sorts of tormenting spirits melted into a unity: some of the pairs of flies

---

7. "August" and "Grete" in the original. The names recur frequently in the course of the story and it has seemed best to replace them by those conventionally applied to English honeymoon couples of the late Victorian age.

reminded him of the honeymooners, and he suspected that they too were addressing each other in their language as "dearest Edwin" and "darling Angelina." Eventually, he could not but realize that "his dissatisfaction was not caused only by his surroundings but that its source was in part derived from within himself." (42.) He felt that "he was discontented because he lacked something, though it was not clear to him what."

Next morning he passed through the *Ingresso* into Pompeii, and, after getting rid of the guide, strolled aimlessly through the town, without, strangely enough, remembering that only a short time before he had been present in his dream at its burial. When later on, at the "hot and holy"[8] midday hour, which the ancients regarded as the hour of ghosts, the other visitors had taken flight and the heaps of ruins lay before him desolate and bathed in sunlight, he found that he was able to carry himself back into the life that had been buried—but not by the help of science. "What it taught was a lifeless, archaeological way of looking at things, and what came from its mouth was a dead, philological language. These were of no help to an understanding through the spirit, the feelings, the heart—put it as you please. Whoever had a longing for that must stand here alone, the only living creature, in the hot silence of midday, among the relics of the past, and look, but not with bodily eyes, and listen, but not with physical ears. And then . . . the dead wakened and Pompeii began to live once more." (55.)

While he was thus animating the past with his imagination, he suddenly saw the unmistakable Gradiva of his relief come out of a house and step trippingly over the lava steppingstones to the other side of the street, just as he had seen her do in his dream the other night, when she had lain down as though to sleep, on the steps of the Temple of Apollo. "And together with his memory something else came into his consciousness for the first time: without being aware himself of the impulse within him, he had come to Italy and had traveled on to Pompeii, without stopping in Rome or Naples, in order to see whether he could find any traces of her. And "traces" literally; for with her peculiar gait she must have left behind an imprint of her toes in the ashes distinct from all the rest." (58.)

---

8. *Gradiva,* 51.

At this point the tension in which the author has hitherto held us grows for a moment into a painful sense of bewilderment. It is not only our hero who has evidently lost his balance; we too have lost our bearings in the face of the apparition of Gradiva, who was first a marble figure and then an imaginary one. Is she a hallucination of our hero, led astray by his delusions? Is she a "real" ghost? or a living person? Not that we need believe in ghosts when we draw up this list. The author, who has called his story a "fantasy," has found no occasion so far for informing us whether he intends to leave us in our world, decried for being prosaic and governed by the laws of science, or whether he wishes to transport us into another and imaginary world, in which spirits and ghosts are given reality. As we know from the examples of *Hamlet* and *Macbeth,* we are prepared to follow him there without hesitation. If so, the imaginative archaeologist's delusion would have to be measured by another standard. Indeed, when we consider how improbable it must be that a real person could exist who bore an exact resemblance to the antique sculpture, our list of alternatives shrinks to two: a hallucination or a midday ghost. A small detail in the account soon cancels the first possibility. A large lizard was lying motionless, stretched out in the sunshine, but fled at the approach of Gradiva's foot and darted away across the lava paving-stones. So it was no hallucination, but something outside our dreamer's mind. But could the reality of a *rediviva* startle a lizard?

Gradiva disappeared in front of the House of Meleager. We shall not be surprised to hear that Norbert Hanold pursued his delusion that Pompeii had come to life around him at the midday hour of ghosts and supposed that Gradiva too had come to life again and had entered the house in which she had lived before the fatal August day in A.D. 79. Ingenious speculations upon the personality of its owner (after whom the house was probably named), and upon Gradiva's relationship to him, shot through his head, and proved that his science was now completely in the service of his imagination. He entered the house, and suddenly found the apparition once more, sitting on some low steps between two yellow columns. "There was something white stretched out across her knees; he could not clearly discern what it was; it seemed to be a sheet of papyrus . . ." On the basis of his latest theories of her origin he addressed her in Greek, and waited with trepidation to learn whether, in her phantom presence she possessed the power of speech. Since she made no reply, he addressed her instead in Latin. Then, with a smile on her lips: "If you want to speak to me," she said, "you must do it in German."

What a humiliation for us readers! So the author has been making fun of us, and, with the help, as it were, of a reflection of the Pompeian sunshine, has inveigled *us* into a delusion on a small scale, so that we may be forced to pass a milder judgment on the poor wretch on whom the midday sun was really shining. Now, however, that we have been cured of our brief confusion, we know that Gradiva was a German girl of flesh and blood—a solution which we were inclined to reject as the most improbable one. And now, with a quiet sense of superiority, we may wait to learn what the relation was between the girl and her marble image, and how our young archaeologist arrived at the fantasies which pointed toward her real personality.

But our hero was not torn from his delusion as quickly as we have been, for, as the author tells us, "though his belief made him happy, he had to take the acceptance of quite a considerable number of mysteries into the bargain." (140.) Moreover, this delusion probably had internal roots in him of which we know nothing and which do not exist in ourselves. In his case, no doubt, energetic treatment would seem necessary before he could be brought back to reality. Meanwhile all he could do was to fit his delusion into the wonderful experience he had just had. Gradiva, who had perished with the rest in the destruction of Pompeii, could be nothing other than a midday ghost who had returned to life for a brief ghostly hour. But what was it that, after hearing her reply delivered in German, he exclaimed, "I knew your voice sounded like that"? Not only we, but the girl herself was bound to ask the question, and Hanold had to admit that he had never heard it, though he had expected to in his dream, when he called to her as she lay down to sleep on the temple steps. He begged her to do the same thing again as she had then; but now she rose, gave him a strange look, and in a few paces disappeared between the columns of the court. A pretty butterfly had shortly before fluttered round her for a while; and he interpreted it as a messenger from Hades reminding the dead girl that she must return, since the midday hour of ghosts was at an end. Hanold still had time to call after the girl as she vanished: "Will you return here tomorrow at the midday hour?" To us, however, who can now venture upon more sober interpretations, it looks as though the young lady had seen something improper in the remark addressed to her by Hanold and had left him with a sense of having been insulted; for after all she could have known nothing of his dream. May not her sensibility have detected the erotic nature of his request, whose motive in Hanold's eyes lay in its relation to his dream?

After Gradiva's disappearance our hero had a careful look at all the guests congregated for their midday meal at the Hotel Diomède and went on to do the same at the Hotel Suisse, and he was then able to feel assured that in neither of the only two hotels known to him in Pompeii was there anyone bearing the remotest resemblance to Gradiva. He would of course have rejected as nonsensical the idea that he might actually meet Gradiva in one of the two inns. And presently the wine pressed from the hot soil of Vesuvius helped to intensify the whirl of feeling in which he spent the day.

For the following day one thing only was fixed: that Hanold must once more be in the House of Meleager at midday; and, in expectation of that moment, he made his way into Pompeii by an irregular route—over the ancient city wall. A sprig of asphodel, hung about with its white bell-shaped blossoms, seemed to him significant enough, as the flower of the underworld, for him to pluck it and carry it with him. But as he waited, the whole science of archaeology seemed to him the most pointless and indifferent thing in the world, for another interest had taken possession of him: the problem of "what could be the nature of the bodily apparition of a being like Gradiva, who was at once dead and, even though only at the midday hour, alive." (80.) He was fearful, too, that he might not meet her that day, for perhaps her return could be permitted only at long intervals; and when he perceived her once again between the columns, he thought her apparition was only a trick of his imagination, and in his pain exclaimed: "Oh! if only you still existed and lived!" This time, however, he had evidently been too critical, for the apparition possessed a voice, which asked him if he was meaning to bring her the white flower, and engaged him, disconcerted once again, in a long conversation.

To his readers, however, to whom Gradiva has already grown of interest as a living person, the author explains that the displeased and repelling look which she had given him the day before had yielded to an expression of searching interest and curiosity. And indeed she now proceeded to question him, asked for an explanation of his remark on the previous day and enquired when it was that he had stood beside her as she lay down to sleep. In this way she learned of his dream, in which she had perished along with her native city, and then of the marble relief and the posture of the foot which had so much attracted the archaeologist. And now she showed herself ready to demonstrate her gait, and this proved that the only divergence from the original portrait of Gradiva was that her sandals were replaced by light sand-colored shoes of fine leather—which she explained as being an adaptation to the present day. She was evidently entering into his delusion, the whole compass of which she elicited from him, without ever contradicting it. Only once did she seem to be distracted from the part she was playing, by an emotion of her own; and this was when, with his thoughts on the relief, he declared that he had recognized her at the first glance. Since at this stage of their conversation she still knew nothing about the relief, it was natural for her to misunderstand Hanold's words; but she quickly recovered herself, and it is only to us that some of her remarks sound as though they had a double sense, as though besides their meaning in the context of the delusion they also meant something real and present-day—for instance, when she regretted that he had not succeeded in confirming the Gradiva gait in his experiments in the streets: "What a pity! perhaps you would not have had to make the long journey here!" (89.) She also learned that he had given her portrait on the relief the name of "Gradiva," and told her real name, "Zoe." "The name suits you beautifully, but it sounds to me like a bitter mockery, for Zoe means life." "One must bow to the inevitable," was her reply, "and I have long grown used to being dead." Promising to be at the same place again at the midday hour next day, she bade him farewell after once more asking him for the sprig of asphodel: "to those who are more fortunate people give roses in the spring; but to me it is right that you should give the flower of forgetfulness." No doubt melancholy suited some one who had been so long dead and had returned to life again for a few short hours.

We are beginning to understand now, and to feel some hope. If the young lady in whose form Gradiva had come to life again accepted

Hanold's delusion so fully, she was probably doing so in order to set him free from it. There was no other way of doing so; to contradict it would have put an end to any such possibility. Even the serious treatment of a real case of illness of the kind could proceed in no other way than to begin by taking up the same ground as the delusional structure and then investigating it as completely as possible. If Zoe was the right person for the job, we shall soon learn, no doubt, how to cure a delusion like our hero's. We should also be glad to know how such delusions arise. It would be a strange coincidence—but, nevertheless, not without an example or parallel—if the treatment of the delusion were to coincide with its investigation and if the explanation of its origin were to be revealed precisely while it was being dissected. We may suspect, of course, that, if so, our case of illness might end up as a "commonplace" love-story. But the healing power of love against a delusion is not to be despised—and was not our hero's infatuation for his Gradiva sculpture a complete instance of being in love, though of being in love with something past and lifeless?

After Gradiva's disappearance, there was only a distant sound, like the laughing call of a bird flying over the ruined city. The young man, now by himself, picked up a white object that had been left behind by Gradiva: not a sheet of papyrus, but a sketchbook with pencil drawings of various scenes in Pompeii. We should be inclined to regard her having forgotten the book there as a pledge of her return, for it is our belief that no one forgets anything without some secret reason or hidden motive.

The remainder of the day brought Hanold all manner of strange discoveries and confirmations, which he failed to synthesize into a whole. He perceived today in the wall of the portico where Gradiva had vanished a narrow gap, which was wide enough, however, to allow someone unusually slim to pass through it. He recognized that Zoe-Gradiva need not have sunk into the earth here—an idea which now seemed to him so unreasonable that he felt ashamed of having once believed in it; she might well have used the gap as a way of reaching her grave. A slight shadow seemed to him to melt away at the end of the Street of the Tombs in front of what is known as the Villa of Diomedes.

In the same whirl of feeling as on the previous day, and deep in the same problems, he now strolled round the environs of Pompeii.

What, he wondered, might be the bodily nature of Zoe-Gradiva? Would one feel anything if one touched her hand? A strange urge drove him to a determination to put this experiment to the test. Yet an equally strong reluctance held him back even from the very idea.

On a sun-bathed slope he met an elderly gentleman who, from his accoutrements, must be a zoologist or botanist and who seemed to be engaged in a hunt. This individual turned toward him and said: "Are you interested in *faraglionensis* as well? I should hardly have suspected it, but it seems to be quite probable that it occurs not only on the Faraglioni Islands off Capri, but has established itself on the mainland too. The method prescribed by our colleague Eimer[9] is a really good one; I have made use of it many times already with excellent results. Please keep quite still . . ." (96.) Here the speaker broke off and placed a snare made of a long blade of grass in front of a crack in the rocks out of which the small iridescent blue head of a lizard was peering. Hanold left the lizard-hunter with a critical feeling that it was scarcely credible what foolish and strange purposes could lead people to make the long journey to Pompeii—without, needless to say, including in his criticism himself and his intention of searching in the ashes of Pompeii for Gradiva's footprints. Moreover, the gentleman's face seemed familiar, as though he had had a glimpse of it in one of the two hotels; his manner of address, too, had been as though he were speaking to an acquaintance.

In the course of his further walk, he arrived by a side road at a house which he had not yet discovered and which turned out to be a third hotel, the "Albergo del Sole."[10] The landlord, with nothing else to do, took the opportunity of showing off his house and the excavated treasures it contained to their best advantage. He asserted that he had been present when the pair of young lovers had been found in the neighborhood of the Forum, who, in the knowledge of the inevitable doom, had awaited death closely embraced in each other's arms. Hanold had heard of this before, and had shrugged his shoulders over it as a fabulous tale invented by some imaginative storyteller; but today the landlord's words aroused his belief and this was increased when a metal clasp was produced, covered with a green patina, which was said to have

---

9. A well-known zoologist of the second half of the nineteenth century.
10. The "Hotel of the Sun."

been retrieved from the ashes beside the girl's remains. He purchased this clasp without any further critical doubts, and when, as he left the *albergo,* he saw in an open window a nodding sprig of asphodel covered with white blossoms, the sight of the funeral flowers came over him as a confirmation of the genuineness of his new possession.

But with the clasp a new delusion took possession of him, or rather the old one had a small piece added to it—no very good augury, it would seem, for the treatment that had been begun. A pair of young lovers in an embrace had been dug out not far from the Forum, and it was in that very neighborhood, by the Temple of Apollo, that in his dream he had seen Gradiva lie down to sleep [p. 12f.]. Was it not possible that in fact she had gone further along from the Forum and had met someone and that they had then died together? A tormenting feeling, which we might perhaps liken to jealousy, arose out of this suspicion. He appeased it by reflecting on the uncertainty of the construction, and brought himself to his senses far enough to be able to take his evening meal at the Hotel Diomède. There his attention was drawn by two newly arrived visitors, a He and a She, whom he was obliged to regard as a brother and sister on account of a certain resemblance between them—in spite of the difference in the color of their hair. They were the first people he had met on his journey who made a sympathetic impression on him. A red Sorrento rose worn by the girl aroused some kind of memory in him, but he could not think what. At last he went to bed and had a dream. It was a remarkably senseless affair, but was obviously hashed up from his day's experiences. "Somewhere in the sun Gradiva was sitting, making a snare out of a blade of grass to catch a lizard in, and said: 'Please keep quite still. Our lady colleague is right; the method is a really good one and she has made use of it with excellent results.'" He fended off this dream while he was still asleep, with the critical thought that it was utter madness, and he succeeded in freeing himself from it with the help of an invisible bird which uttered a short laughing call and carried off the lizard in its beak.

In spite of all this turmoil, he woke up in a rather clearer and steadier frame of mind. A branch of a rose tree bearing flowers of the sort he had seen the day before on the young lady's breast reminded him that during the night someone had said that people give roses in the spring. Without thinking, he picked a few of the roses, and there must have been something connected with them that had a relaxing effect on his mind. He felt relieved of his unsociable feelings, and went by the usual way to Pompeii, burdened with the roses, the metal clasp, and the sketch book, and occupied with a number of problems concerning Gradiva. The old delusion had begun to show cracks: he was beginning to wonder whether she might be in Pompeii, not at the midday hour only, but at other times as well. The stress had shifted, however, to the latest addition, and the jealousy attaching to it tormented him in all sorts of disguises. He could almost have wished that the apparition might remain visible to his eyes alone, and elude the perception of others: then, in spite of everything, he could look on her as his own exclusive property. While he was strolling about, waiting for the midday hour, he had an unexpected encounter. In the *Casa del Fauno* he came upon two figures in a corner in which they must have thought themselves out of sight, for they were embraced in each other's arms and their lips were pressed together. He was astonished to recognize in them the sympathetic couple from the previous evening. But their behavior now did not seem to fit a brother and sister: their embrace and their kiss seemed to him to last too long. So after all they were a pair of lovers, presumably a young honeymoon couple—yet another Edwin and Angelina. Curiously enough, however, this time the sight of them caused him only satisfaction; and with a sense of awe, as though he had interrupted some secret act of devotion, he withdrew unobserved. An attitude of respectfulness, which he had long been without, had returned to him.

When he reached the House of Meleager, he was once more overcome by such a violent dread of finding Gradiva in someone else's company that when she appeared the only words he found to greet her with were: "Are you alone?" It was with difficulty that he allowed her to bring him to realize that he had picked the roses for her. He confessed his latest delusion to her—that she was the girl who had been found in the forum in a lover's embrace and who had owned the green clasp. She enquired, not without a touch of mockery, whether he had found the thing in the sun perhaps: the sun (and she used the [Italian] word "sole") produced all kinds of things like that. He admitted that he was feeling dizzy in his head, and she suggested as a cure that he should share her small picnic meal with her. She offered him half of a roll wrapped up in tissue paper and ate the other half herself with an obviously good appetite. At the same time her perfect teeth flashed between her lips and made a slight crunching sound as they bit through the crust. "I feel as though we had shared a meal like this once before, two thousand years ago," she said; "can't you remember?" (118.) He could think of no reply, but the improvement in his head brought about by the food, and the many indications she gave of her actual presence, were not without their effect on him. Reason began to rise in him and to throw doubt on the whole delusion of Gradiva's being no more than a midday ghost—though no doubt it might be argued on the other hand that she herself had just said that she had shared a meal with him two thousand years ago. As a means of settling the conflict an experiment suggested itself: and this he carried our craftily and with regained courage. Her left hand, with its delicate fingers, was resting on her knees, and one of the house flies whose impertinence and uselessness had so much roused his indignation alighted on it. Suddenly Hanold's hand was raised in the air and descended with a vigorous slap on the fly and Gradiva's hand.

This bold experiment had two results: first, a joyful conviction that he had without any doubt touched a real, living, warm human hand, but afterwards a reproof that made him jump up in a fright from his seat on the steps. For, from Gradiva's lips, when she had recovered from her astonishment, there rang out these words: "There's no doubt you're out of your mind, Norbert Hanold!" As everyone knows, the best method of waking a sleeper or a sleep-walker is to call him by his own name. But unluckily there was no chance of observing the effects produced on Norbert Hanold by Gradiva's calling him by his name (which he had told no one in Pompeii). For at this critical moment the sympathetic pair of lovers from the *Casa del Fauno* appeared, and the young lady exclaimed in a tone of joyful surprise: "Zoe! Are you here too? And on your honeymoon like us? You never wrote me a word about it!" In face of this new evidence of Gradiva's living reality, Hanold took flight.

Nor was Zoe-Gradiva very agreeably surprised by this unexpected visit, which interrupted her in what was apparently an important task. But she quickly pulled herself together and made a fluent reply to the question, in which she explained the situation to her friend—and even more to us—and which enabled her to get rid of the young couple. She congratulated them; but she was not on her honeymoon. "The young man who's just gone off is laboring, like you, under a remarkable aberration. He seems to think there's a fly buzzing in his head. Well, I expect everyone has some sort of insect there. It's my duty to know something about entomology, so I can help a little in cases like that. My father and I are staying at the Sole. Something got into *his* head too, and the brilliant idea occurred to him besides of bringing me here with him on condition that I amused myself on my own at Pompeii and made no demands of any kind on him. I told myself I should dig out something interesting here even by myself. Of course I hadn't counted on making the find that I have—I mean my luck in meeting you, Gisa." (124.) But now, she added, she must hurry off, so as to be company for her father at his lunch in the "Sun." And she departed, after having introduced herself to us as the daughter of the zoologist and lizard-catcher and after having, by all kinds of ambiguous remarks, admitted her therapeutic intention and other secret designs as well.

The direction she took, however, was not toward the Hotel of the Sun, where her father was waiting for her. But it seemed to her too as though a shadowy form was seeking its grave near the Villa of Diomedes, and was vanishing beneath one of the monuments. And for that reason she directed her steps toward the Street of the Tombs, with her foot lifted almost perpendicularly at each step. It was to this same place that Hanold had fled in his shame and confusion. He wandered ceaselessly up and down in the portico of the garden, engaged in the task of disposing of the remains of his problem by an intellectual effort. One thing had become undeniably clear to him: that he had been totally without sense or reason in believing that he had been associating with a young Pompeian woman who had come to life again in a more or less physical shape. It could not be disputed that this clear insight into his delusion was an essential step forward on his road back to a sound understanding. But, on the other hand, this living woman, with whom other people communicated as though she were as physically real as themselves, was Gradiva, and she knew his name; and his scarcely awakened reason was not strong enough to solve this riddle. He was hardly calm enough emotionally, either, to show himself capable of facing so hard a task, for he would have preferred to have been buried along with the rest two thousand years before in the Villa of Diomedes, so as to be quite certain of not meeting Zoe-Gradiva again.

Nevertheless, a violent desire to see her again struggled against what was left of the inclination to flight still lingering in him.

As he turned one of the four corners of the colonnade, he suddenly recoiled. On a broken fragment of masonry was sitting one of the girls who had perished here in the Villa of Diomedes. This, however, was a last attempt, quickly rejected, at taking flight into the realm of delusion. No, it was Gradiva, who had evidently come to give him the final portion of her treatment. She quite correctly interpreted his first instinctive movement as an attempt to leave the building, and showed him that it was impossible for him to run away, for a terrific downpour of rain had begun outside. She was ruthless, and began her examination by asking him what he had been trying to do with the fly on her hand. He had not the courage to make use of a particular pronoun,[11] but he did have the courage for something more important—for asking her the decisive question:

"As someone said, I was rather confused in my head, and I must apologize for treating the hand . . . I can't understand how I could be so senseless . . . but I can't understand either how its owner could point out my . . . my unreasonableness to me by my own name." (134.)

"So your understanding has not got as far as that, Norbert Hanold. But I can't say I'm surprised at it, you've accustomed me to it so long. I needn't have come to Pompeii to discover it again, and you could have confirmed it a good hundred miles nearer home.

"A hundred miles nearer," she explained, as he still failed to understand, "diagonally across the street from where you live—in the house at the corner. There's a cage in my window with a canary in it!"

These last words, as he heard them, affected him like a distant memory: that must have been the same bird whose song had given him the idea of his journey to Italy.

"My father lives in that house: the professor of zoology, Richard Bertgang."

---

11. The pronoun of the second person singular. The point of some of what follows is necessarily lost in English. In all his remarks to Gradiva hitherto, Hanold had used the second person singular, partly, no doubt, because that would be the classical usage. Now, however, that he was beginning to realize that he was talking to a modern German girl, he felt that the second person singular was far too familiar

So, since she was his neighbor, she knew him by sight and by name. We feel a sense of disillusionment: the solution falls flat and seems unworthy of our expectations.

Norbert Hanold showed that he had not yet regained his independence of thought when he replied: "So you[12] . . . you are Fräulein Zoe Bertgang? But she looked quite different . . ."

Fräulein Bertgang's answer shows us that all the same there had been other relations between the two of them besides their simply being neighbors. She could argue in favor of the familiar *du*, which he had used naturally to the midday ghost but had drawn back from in speaking to the live girl, but on behalf of which she claimed ancient rights: "If you find this formal mode of address more suitable, I can use it too. But I find the other comes to my lips more naturally. I don't know if I looked different in the early days when we used to run about together in a friendly way or sometimes, by way of a change, used to bump and thump each other. But if you[13] had even once looked at me attentively in recent years, it might have dawned on you that I've looked like this for quite a time."

So there had been a childhood friendship between them—perhaps a childhood love—which justified the *du*. This solution, it may be, falls just as flat as the one we first suspected. We are brought to a much deeper level, however, when we realize that this childhood relationship unexpectedly explains a number of details in what had happened in their contemporary contact. Consider, for instance, the slapping of Zoe-Gradiva's hand. Norbert Hanold found a most convincing reason for it in the necessity for reaching an experimental answer to the problem of the apparition's physical reality. But was it not at the same time remarkably like a revival of the impulse for the "bumping and thumping" whose dominance in their childhood was shown by Zoe's words? And think, again, of how Gradiva asked the archaeologist whether it did not seem to him that they had shared a meal like this two thousand years before. This

---

and affectionate. Gradiva, on the other hand, has used the second person singular throughout in speaking to him.

12. *Sie,* the German pronoun of the third person plural, which is always used in formal speech instead of the *du* of the second person singular.

13. From this point to the middle of her next speech, when, as will be seen, she finally rebels, Zoe makes a valiant attempt to use the formal *Sie.*

unintelligible question suddenly seems to have a sense, if we once more replace the historical past by the personal one—childhood—, of which the girl still had lively memories but which the young man appeared to have forgotten. And now the discovery dawns upon us that the young archaeologist's fantasies about his Gradiva may have been an echo of his forgotten childhood memories. If so, they were not capricious products of his imagination, but determined, without his knowing it, by the store of childhood impressions which he had forgotten, but which were still at work in him. It should be possible for us to show the origin of the fantasies in detail, even though we can only guess at them. He imagined, for instance, that Gradiva must be of *Greek* origin and that she was the daughter of a respected personage—a priest of Ceres, perhaps. This seems to fit in pretty well with his knowing that she bore the Greek name of Zoe and that she belonged to the family of a professor of zoology. But if Hanold's fantasies were transformed memories, we may expect to find an indication of the source of those fantasies in the information given us by Zoe Bertgang. Let us listen to what she has to say. She has told us of their intimate friendship in their childhood, and we shall now hear of the further course taken by this childhood relationship.

"At that time, as a matter of fact, up to about the age when, I don't know why, people begin to call us *Backfish*,[14] I had got accustomed to being remarkably dependent on you and believed I could never in the world find a more agreeable friend. I had no mother or sister or brother, my father found a slowworm in spirits considerably more interesting than me; and everyone (and I include girls) must have *something* to occupy their thoughts and whatever goes along with them. That was what you were then. But when archaeology took hold of you I discovered—you must forgive me, but really your polite innovation sounds to me *too* ridiculous and, besides, it doesn't fit in with what I want to express—as I was saying, it turned out that you'd[15] become an unbearable person who (at any rate so far as I was concerned) no longer had any eyes in his head or tongue in his mouth, or any memory, where my

14. Literally "fish for frying." The common German slang term equivalent to "flapper" or "teenager."
15. From this point onwards she finally reverts to *du*.

memory had stuck, of our friendship when we were children. No doubt that was why I looked different from before. For when from time to time I met you in society—it happened once as recently as last winter—you didn't see me, still less did I hear you say a word. Not that there was any distinction for me in that, for you treated everyone else alike. I was thin air for you, and you—with your tuft of fair hair that I'd rumpled for you often enough in the past—you were as dull, as dried-up, and as tongue-tied as a stuffed cockatoo, and at the same time as grandiose as an—*archaeopteryx*—yes, that's right, that's what they call the antediluvian bird-monstrosity they've dug up. Only there was one thing I hadn't suspected: that there was an equally grandiose fantasy lodged in your head of looking on me too, here in Pompeii, as something that had been dug up and come to life again. And when all at once there you were standing in front of me quite unexpectedly, it took me quite a lot of trouble at first to make out what an incredible cobweb your imagination had spun in your brain. After that, it amused me and quite pleased me in spite of its lunacy. For, as I told you, I hadn't suspected it of you."

Thus she tells us plainly enough what with the years had become of their childhood friendship. In her it grew until she was thoroughly in love, for a girl must have something to which she can give her heart. Fräulein Zoe, the embodiment of cleverness and clarity, makes her own mind quite transparent to us. While it is in any case the general rule for a normally constituted girl to turn her affection toward her father in the first instance, Zoe, who had no one in her family but her father, was especially ready to do so. But her father had nothing left over for her; all his interest was engrossed by the objects of his science. So she was obliged to cast her eyes around upon other people, and became especially attached to her young playmate. When he too ceased to have any eyes for her, her love was not shaken by it but rather increased, for he had become like her father, was, like him, absorbed by science and held apart by it from life and from Zoe. Thus it was made possible for her to remain faithful in her unfaithfulness—to find her father once more in her loved one, to include both of them with the same emotion, or, as we may say, to identify both of them in her feeling. What is our justification for this piece of psychological analysis, which might well seem arbitrary? The author has presented us with it in a single, but highly characteristic, detail. When Zoe described the transformation in her former playmate which had so greatly disturbed her, she abused him by comparing him to an archaeopteryx, the birdlike monstrosity which belongs to the archaeology of zoology. In that way she found a single concrete expression of the identity of the two figures. Her complaint applies with the same word to the man she loved and to her father. The archaeopteryx is, we might say, a compromise idea or an intermediate idea[16] in which her thought about the folly of the man she loved coincided with the analogous thought about her father.

With the young man, things had taken a different turn. Archaeology took hold of him and left him with an interest only in women of marble and bronze. His childhood friendship, instead of being strengthened into a passion, was dissolved, and his memories of it passed into such profound forgetfulness that he did not recognize or notice his early playmate when he met her in society. It is true that when we look further we may doubt whether "forgetfulness" is the correct psychological description of the fate of these memories in our young archaeologist. There is a kind of forgetting which is distinguished by the difficulty with which the memory is awakened even by a powerful external summons, as though some internal resistance were struggling against its revival. A forgetting of this kind has been given the name of *repression* in psychopathology; and the case which our author has put before us seems to be an example of this repression. Now we do not know in general whether the forgetting of an impression is linked with the dissolution of its memory-trace in the mind; but we can assert quite definitely of "repression" that it does not coincide with the dissolution or extinction of the memory. What is repressed cannot, it is true, as a rule make its way into memory without more ado; but it retains a capacity for effective action, and, under the influence of some external event, it may one day bring about psychical consequences which can be regarded as products of a modification of the forgotten memory and as derivatives of it and which remain unintelligible unless we take this view of them. We have already

---

16. Ideas of this kind play an important part in dreams and, indeed, wherever the primary psychical process is dominant. See *The Interpretation of Dreams* (1900a) *Standard Ed.*, 5, 596. Some good examples are given in chapter 4 of *On Dreams* (1901a), ibid., 648ff.

seemed to recognize in Norbert Hanold's fantasies about Gradiva derivatives of his repressed memories of his childhood friendship with Zoe Bertgang. A return like this of what has been repressed is to be expected with particular regularity when a person's erotic feelings are attached to the repressed impressions—when his erotic life has been attacked by repression. In such cases the old Latin saying holds true, though it may have been coined first to apply to expulsion by external influences and not to internal conflicts: "Naturam expelles furca, tamen usque recurret."[17] But it does not tell us everything. It only informs us of the *fact* of the return of the piece of nature that has been repressed; it does not describe the highly remarkable *manner* of that return, which is accomplished by what seems like a piece of malicious treachery. It is precisely what was chosen as the instrument of repression—like the *furca* of the Latin saying—that becomes the vehicle for the return: in and behind the repressing force, what is repressed proves itself victor in the end. This fact, which has been so little noticed and deserves so much consideration, is illustrated—more impressively than it could be by many examples—in a well-known etching by Félicien Rops; and it is illustrated in the typical case of repression in the life of saints and penitents. An ascetic monk has fled, no doubt from the temptations of the world, to the image of the crucified Saviour. And now the cross sinks down like a shadow, and in its place, radiant, there rises instead the image of a voluptuous, naked woman, in the same crucified attitude. Other artists with less psychological insight have, in similar representations of temptation, shown Sin, insolent and triumphant, in some position alongside of the Saviour on the cross. Only Rops has placed Sin in the very place of the Saviour on the cross. He seems to have known that, when what has been repressed returns, it emerges from the repressing force itself.

It is worthwhile pausing in order to convince oneself from pathological cases how sensitive a human mind becomes in states of repression to any approach by what has been repressed, and how even trivial similarities suffice for the repressed to emerge behind the repressing force and take effect by means of it. I once had under

---

17. "You may drive out Nature with a pitchfork, but she will always return." This is actually a line of Horace (*Epistles*, I, 10, 24). It is misquoted in the German editions.

medical treatment a young man—he was still almost a boy—who, after he had first unwillingly become acquainted with the processes of sex, had taken flight from every sexual desire that arose in him. For that purpose he made use of various methods of repression: he intensified his zeal in learning, exaggerated his dependence on his mother, and in general assumed a childish character. I will not here enter into the manner in which his repressed sexuality broke through once more precisely in his relation to his mother; but I will describe a rarer and stranger instance of how another of his bulwarks collapsed on an occasion which could scarcely be regarded as sufficient. Mathematics enjoys the greatest reputation as a diversion from sexuality. This had been the very advice to which Jean-Jacques Rousseau was obliged to listen from a lady who was dissatisfied with him: "Lascia le donne e studia la matematica!"[18] So too our fugitive threw himself with special eagerness into the mathematics and geometry which he was taught at school, till suddenly one day his powers of comprehension were paralyzed in the face of some apparently innocent problems. It was possible to establish two of these problems: "Two bodies come together, one with a speed of . . . etc." and "On a cylinder, the diameter of whose surface is *m*, describe a cone . . . etc." Other people would certainly not have regarded these as very striking allusions to sexual events; but he felt that he had been betrayed by mathematics as well, and took flight from it too.

If Norbert Hanold were someone in real life who had in this way banished love and his childhood friendship with the help of archaeology, it would have been logical and according to rule that what revived in him the forgotten memory of the girl he had loved in his childhood should be precisely an antique sculpture. It would have been his well-deserved fate to fall in love with the marble portrait of Gradiva, behind which, owing to an unexplained similarity, the living Zoe whom he had neglected made her influence felt.

Fräulein Zoe seems herself to have shared our view of the young archaeologist's delusion, for the satisfaction she expressed at the end of her "frank, detailed, and instructive speech of castigation" could scarcely have been based on anything but a recognition that

18. Give up women and study mathematics!

from the very first his interest in Gradiva had related to herself. It was *this* which she had not expected of him, but which, in spite of all its delusional disguise, she saw for what it was. The psychical treatment she had carried out, however, had now accomplished its beneficent effect on him. He felt free, for his delusion had now been replaced by the thing of which it could only have been a distorted and inadequate copy. Nor did he any longer hesitate to remember her and to recognize her as the kid, cheerful clever play-mate who in essentials was not in any way changed. But he found something else very strange—

"You mean," said the girl, "the fact of someone having to die so as to come alive; but no doubt that must be so for archaeologists." (141.) Evidently she had not forgiven him yet for the round-about path by way of archaeology which he had followed from their childhood friendship to the new relation that was forming.

"No, I mean your name . . . Because 'Bertgang' means the same as 'Gradiva' and describes someone 'who steps along brilliantly.'" (142.)[19]

We ourselves were unprepared for this. Our hero was beginning to cast off his humility and to play an active part. Evidently he was completely cured of his delusion and had risen above it; and he proved this by himself tearing the last threads of the cobweb of his delusion. This, too, is just how patients behave when one has loosened the compulsion of their delusional thoughts by revealing the repressed material lying behind them. Once they have understood, they themselves bring forward the solutions of the final and most important riddles of their strange condition in a number of ideas that suddenly occur to them. We had already guessed that the Greek origin of the imaginary Gradiva was an obscure result of the Greek name "Zoe"; but we had not ventured to approach the name "Gradiva" itself, and had let it pass as the untrammeled creation of Norbert Hanold's imagination. But, lo and behold! that very name now turns out to have been a derivative—indeed a translation—of the repressed surname of the girl he had loved in the childhood which he was supposed to have forgotten.

---

19. The German root *bert* or *brecht* is akin to the English "bright"; similarly *gang* is akin to "go" (in Scotland "gang").

The tracing back of the delusion and its resolution were now complete. What the author now adds is no doubt designed to serve as a harmonious end to his story. We cannot but feel reassured about the future when we hear that the young man, who had earlier been obliged to play the pitiable part of a person in urgent need of treatment, advanced still further on the road to recovery and succeeded in arousing in her some of the feelings under which he himself had suffered before. Thus it was that he made her jealous by mentioning the sympathetic young lady who had previously interrupted their tête-à-tête in the House of Meleager, and by confessing that she had been the first woman for whom he had felt a very great liking. Whereupon Zoe prepared to take a chilly leave of him, remarking that everything had now returned to reason—she herself not least; he could look up Gisa Hartleben (or whatever she was now called) again and give her some scientific assistance over the purpose of her visit to Pompeii; she herself, however, must go back to the Albergo del Sole where her father was expecting her for lunch; perhaps they would meet again some time at a party in Germany or in the moon. But once more he was able to make the troublesome fly an excuse for taking possession first of her cheek and then of her lips, and to set in motion the aggressiveness which is a man's inevitable duty in lovemaking. Once only a shadow seemed to fall on their happiness, when Zoe declared that now she really must go back to her father or he will starve at the Sole. "Your father? . . . what will happen? . . ." (147). But the clever girl was able swiftly to quiet his concern. "Probably nothing will happen. I'm not an indispensable part of his zoological collection. If I had been, perhaps I shouldn't have been so foolish as to give my heart to you." In the exceptional event, however, of her father taking a different view from hers, there was a safe expedient. Hanold need only cross to Capri, catch a *Lacerta faraglionensis* there (he could practice the technique on her little finger), set the creature free over here, catch it again before the zoologist's eyes, and let him choose between a *faraglionensis* on the mainland and his daughter. The scheme, it is easy to see, was one in which the mockery was tinged with bitterness; it was a warning, as it were, to her fiancé not to keep too closely to the model on which she had chosen him. Here again Norbert Hanold reassures us, by showing by all sorts of apparently small signs the great transformation that had taken place in him. He proposed that he and his Zoe should come for their honeymoon to Italy and Pompeii, just as though he had never been indignant with the honeymooning Edwins and Angelinas. He had completely lost from his memory all his feelings against those happy pairs, who had so unnecessarily traveled more than a hundred miles from their German home. The author is certainly right in bringing forward a loss of memory like this as the most trustworthy sign of a change of attitude. Zoe's reply to the plan for the scene of their honeymoon suggested by "her childhood friend who had also in a sense been dug out of the ruins again" (150) was that she did not feel quite alive enough yet to make a geographical decision of that sort.

The delusion had now been conquered by a beautiful reality; but before the two lovers left Pompeii it was still to be honored once again. When they reached the Herculanean Gate, where, at the entrance to the Via Consolare, the street is crossed by some ancient stepping-stones, Norbert Hanold paused and asked the girl to go ahead of him. She understood him "and, pulling up her dress a little with her left hand, Zoe Bertgang, Gradiva *rediviva,* walked past, held in his eyes, which seemed to gaze as though in a dream; so, with her quietly tripping gait, she stepped through the sunlight over the stepping-stones to the other side of the street." With the triumph of love, what was beautiful and precious in the delusion found recognition as well.

In his last simile, however,—of the "childhood friend who had been dug out of the ruins"—the author has presented us with the key to the symbolism of which the hero's delusion made use in disguising his repressed memory. There is, in fact, no better analogy for repression, by which something in the mind is at once made inaccessible and preserved, than burial of the sort to which Pompeii fell a victim and from which it could emerge once more through the work of spades. Thus it was that the young archaeologist was obliged in his fantasy to transport to Pompeii the original of the relief which reminded him of the object of his youthful love. The author was well justified, indeed, in lingering over the valuable similarity which his delicate sense had perceived between a particular mental process in the individual and an isolated historical event in the history of mankind.[20]

---

20. Freud himself adopted the fate of Pompeii as a simile for repression in more than one later passage. See, for instance, the "Rat Man," case history (1909*d*), written not long after the present work, *Standard Ed.*, **10**, 176–77.

2

But after all, what we really intended to do originally was only to investigate two or three dreams that are to be found here and there in *Gradiva* with the help of certain analytic methods. How has it come about, then, that we have been led into dissecting the whole story and examining the mental processes in the two chief characters? This has not in fact been an unnecessary piece of work; it was an essential preliminary. It is equally the case that when we try to understand the real dreams of a real person we have to concern ourselves intensively with his character and his career, and we must get to know not only his experiences shortly before the dream but also those dating far back into the past. It is even my view that we are still not free to turn to our proper task, but that we must linger a little more over the story itself and carry out some further preliminary work.

My readers will no doubt have been puzzled to notice that so far I have treated Norbert Hanold and Zoe Bertgang, in all their mental manifestations and activities, as though they were real people and not the author's creations, as though the author's mind were an absolutely transparent medium and not a refractive or obscuring one. And my procedure must seem all the more puzzling since the author has expressly renounced the portrayal of reality by calling his story a "phantasy." We have found, however, that all his descriptions are so faithfully copied from reality that we should not object if *Gradiva* were described not as a fantasy but as a psychiatric study. Only at two points has the author availed himself of the license open to him of laying down premisses which do not seem to have their roots in the laws of reality. The first time is where he makes the young archaeologist come upon what is undoubtedly an ancient relief but which so closely resembles a person living long afterwards, not only in the peculiarity of the posture of the foot as it steps along but in every detail of facial structure and bodily attitude, that the young man is able to take the physical appearance of that person to be the sculpture come to life. And the second time is where he makes the young man meet the living woman precisely in Pompeii; for the dead woman had been placed there only by his imagination, and the journey to Pompeii had in fact carried him away from the living woman, whom he had just seen in the street of the town in which he lived. This second provision of the author's, however, involves no violent departure from actual possibility; it merely makes use of chance, which unquestionably plays a part in many human histories; and furthermore he uses it to good purpose, for this chance reflects the fatal truth that has laid it down that flight is precisely an instrument that delivers one over to what one is fleeing from. The first premiss seems to lean more toward fantasy and to spring entirely from the author's arbitrary decision—the premiss on which all that follows depends, the far-reaching resemblance between the sculpture and the live girl, which a more sober choice might have restricted to the single feature of the posture of the foot as it steps along. We might be tempted here to allow the play of our own fantasy to forge a link with reality. The name of "Bertgang" might point to the fact that the women of that family had already been distinguished in ancient days by the peculiarity of their graceful gait; and we might suppose that the Germanic Bertgangs were descended from a Roman family one member of which was the woman who had led the artist to perpetuate the peculiarity of her gait in the sculpture. Since, however, the different variations of the human form are not independent of one another, and since in fact even among ourselves the ancient types reappear again and again (as we can see in art collections), it would not be totally impossible that a modern Bertgang might reproduce the shape of her ancient ancestress in all the other features of her bodily structure as well. But it would no doubt be wiser, instead of such speculations, to enquire from the author himself what were the sources from which this part of his creation was derived; we should then have a good prospect of showing once again how what was ostensibly an arbitrary decision rested in fact upon law. But since access to the sources in the author's mind is not open to us, we will leave him with an undiminished right to construct a development that is wholly true to life upon an improbable premiss—a right of which Shakespeare, for instance, availed himself in *King Lear*.[21]

Apart from this, it must be repeated, the author has presented us with a perfectly correct psychiatric study, on which we may measure our understanding of the workings of the mind—a case

---

21. Some further comment on the "improbable premiss" to *King Lear* will be found at the end of Freud's paper on "The Theme of the Three Caskets" (1913*f*), *Standard Ed.*, **12**, 301.

history and the history of a cure which might have been designed to emphasize certain fundamental theories of medical psychology. It is strange enough that the author should have done this. But how if, on being questioned, he were completely to deny any such purpose? It is so easy to draw analogies and to read meanings into things. Is it not rather we who have slipped into this charming poetic story a secret meaning very far from its author's intentions? Possibly. We shall come back to the question later. For the moment, however, we have tried to save ourselves from making any such tendentious interpretation by giving the story almost entirely in the author's own words. Anyone who compares our reproduction with the actual text of *Gradiva* will have to concede us that much.

Perhaps, too, in most people's eyes we are doing our author a poor service in declaring his work to be a psychiatric study. An author, we hear them say, should keep out of the way of any contact with psychiatry and should leave the description of pathological metal states to the doctors. The truth is that no truly creative writer has ever obeyed this injunction. The description of the human mind is indeed the domain which is most his own; he has from time immemorial been the precursor of science, and so too of scientific psychology. But the frontier between states of mind described as normal and pathological is in part a conventional one and in part so fluctuating that each of us probably crosses it many times in the course of a day. On the other hand, psychiatry would be doing wrong if it tried to restrict itself permanently to the study of the severe and gloomy illnesses that arise from gross injuries to the delicate apparatus of the mind. Deviations from health which are slighter and capable of correction, and which today we can trace back no further than to disturbances in the interplay of mental forces, arouse its interest no less. Indeed, only through the medium of these can it understand either normal states or the phenomena of severe illness. Thus the creative writer cannot evade the psychiatrist nor the psychiatrist the creative writer, and the poetic treatment of a psychiatric theme can turn out to be correct without any sacrifice of its beauty.[22]

And it is really correct—this imaginative picture of the history of a case and its treatment. Now that we have finished telling the

---

22. Another discussion by Freud of the use of psychopathological material by creative writers will be found in a posthumously published essay, "Psychopathic

story and satisfied our own suspense, we can get a better view of it, and we shall now reproduce it with the technical terminology of our science, and in doing so we shall not feel disconcerted at the necessity for repeating what we have said before.

Norbert Hanold's condition is often spoken of by the author as a "delusion," and we have no reason to reject that designation. We can state two chief characteristics of a "delusion," which do not, it is true, describe it exhaustively, but which distinguish it recognizably from other disorders. In the first place it is one of the group of pathological states which do not produce a direct effect upon the body but are manifested only by mental indications. And secondly it is characterized by the fact that in it "fantasies" have gained the upper hand—that is, have obtained belief and have acquired an influence on action. If we recall Hanold's journey to Pompeii in order to look for Gradiva's peculiarly formed footprints in the ashes, we shall have a fine example of an action under the dominance of a delusion. A psychiatrist would perhaps place Norbert Hanold's delusion in the great group of "paranoia" and possibly describe it as "fetishistic erotomania," because the most striking thing about it was his being in love with the piece of sculpture and because in the psychiatrist's view, with its tendency to coarsen everything, the young archaeologist's interest in feet and the postures of feet would be bound to suggest "fetishism." Nevertheless all such systems of nomenclature and classification of the different kinds of delusion according to their subject matter have something precarious and barren about them.[23]

Furthermore, since our hero was a person capable of developing a delusion on the basis of such a strange preference, a strict psychiatrist would at once stamp him as a *dégénéré* and would investigate the heredity which had remorselessly driven him to this fate. But here the author does not follow the psychiatrist, and with good reason. He wishes to bring the hero closer to us so as to make "empathy" easier; the diagnosis of *"dégénéré"*, whether it is right or wrong, at once puts the young archaeologist at a distance from

---

Characters on the Stage" (1942*a*), probably written a year or two before the present work.

23. In point of fact, the case of N. H. would have to be described as a *hysterical* delusion, not a paranoic one. The indications of paranoia are absent from it.

us, for we readers are the normal people and the standard of humanity. Nor is the author greatly concerned with the hereditary and constitutional preconditions of the state, but on the other hand he plunges deep into the personal mental makeup which can give rise to such a delusion.

In one important respect Norbert Hanold behaved quite differently from an ordinary human being. He took no interest in living women; the science of which he was the servant had taken that interest away from him and displaced it on to women of marble or bronze. This is not to be regarded as a trivial peculiarity; on the contrary, it was the basic precondition of the events to be described. For one day it came about that one particular sculpture of that kind laid claim to the whole of the interest which is ordinarily directed only to a living woman, and with that his delusion was there. We then see unrolled before our eyes the manner in which his delusion is cured through a happy turn of events, and his interest displaced back from the marble to a living woman. The author does not let us follow the influences which led our hero to turn away from women; he only informs us that his attitude was not explained by his innate disposition, which, on the contrary, included some amount of imaginative (and, we might add, erotic) needs. And, as we learn later in the story, he did not avoid other children in his childhood: he had a friendship at that age with a little girl, was her inseparable companion, shared his little meals with her, used to thump her too, and let her rumple his hair. It is in attachments such as this, in combinations like this of affection and aggressiveness, that the immature erotism of childhood finds its expression; its consequences only emerge later, but then they are irresistible, and during childhood itself it is as a rule recognized as erotism only by doctors and creative writers. Our own writer shows us clearly that he too is of the same opinion; for he makes his hero suddenly develop a lively interest in women's feet and their way of placing them. This interest was bound to bring him a bad reputation both among scientists and among the women of the town he lived in, a reputation of being a foot-fetishist; but *we* cannot avoid tracing the interest back to the memory of his childhood playmate. For there can be no doubt that even in her childhood the girl showed the same peculiarity of a graceful gait, with her toes almost perpendicularly raised as she stepped along; and it was because it represented that same gait that an ancient marble

relief acquired such great importance for Norbert Hanold. Incidentally we may add that in his derivation of the remarkable phenomenon of fetishism the author is in complete agreement with science.
Ever since Binet [1888] we have in fact tried to trace fetishism back
to erotic impressions in childhood.[24]

The state of permanently turning away from women produces a
personal susceptibility, or, as we are accustomed to say, a "disposition" to the formation of a delusion. The development of the mental disorder sets in at the moment when a chance impression
arouses the childhood experiences which have been forgotten and
which have traces, at least, of an erotic coloring. "Arouses," however, is certainly not the right description, if we take into account
what follows. We must repeat the author's accurate account in
correct psychological technical terms. When Norbert Hanold saw
the relief, he did not remember that he had already seen a similar
posture of the foot in his childhood friend; he remembered nothing
at all, but all the effects brought about by the relief originated from
this link that was made with the impression of his childhood. Thus
the childhood impression was stirred up, it became active, so that it
began to produce effects, but it did not come into consciousness—it
remained "unconscious," to use a term which has today become
unavoidable in psychopathology. We are anxious that this unconscious shall not be involved in any of the disputes of philosophers
and natural philosophers, which have often no more than an ety-
mological importance. For the time being we possess no better
name for psychical processes which behave actively but nevertheless do not reach the consciousness of the person concerned, and
that is all we mean by our "unconsciousness." When some thinkers
try to dispute the existence of an unconscious of this kind, on the
ground that it is nonsensical, we can only suppose that they have
never had to do with the corresponding mental phenomena, that
they are under the spell of the regular experience that everything
mental that becomes active and intense becomes at the same time
conscious as well, and that they have still to learn (what our author

24. Binet's views on fetishism were described in Freud's *Three Essays on the
Theory of Sexuality* (1905d), to which however he added a footnote in 1920 casting
doubts on their adequacy. A number of references to other discussions of fetishism
in Freud's own writings are given in another footnote to the same passage (*Standard
Ed.*, 7, 154–55).

knows very well) that there are most certainly mental processes which, in spite of being intense and producing effects, nonetheless remain apart from consciousness.

We said a little earlier that Norbert Hanold's memories of his childhood relations with Zoe were in a state of "repression"; and here we have called them "unconscious" memories. So we must now pay a little attention to the relation between these two technical terms, which, indeed, appear to coincide in their meaning. It is not difficult to make the matter plain. *Unconscious* is the wider concept; *repressed* is the narrower one. Everything that is repressed is unconscious; but we cannot assert that everything unconscious is repressed. If when Hanold saw the relief he had remembered his Zoe's gait, what had earlier been an unconscious memory of his would have become simultaneously active and conscious, and this would have shown that it had not earlier been repressed. *Unconscious* is a purely descriptive term, one that is indefinite in some respects and, as we might say, static. *Repressed* is a dynamic expression, which takes account of the interplay of mental forces; it implies that there is a force present which is seeking to bring about all kinds of psychical effects, including that of becoming conscious, but that there is also an opposing force which is able to obstruct some of these psychical effects, once more including that of becoming conscious. The mark of something repressed is precisely that in spite of its intensity it is unable to enter consciousness. In Hanold's case, therefore, from the moment of the appearance of the relief onwards, we are concerned with something unconscious that is repressed, or, more briefly, with something repressed.

Norbert Hanold's memories of his childhood relations with the girl with the graceful gait were repressed; but this is not yet the correct view of the psychological situation. We remain on the surface so long as we are dealing only with memories and ideas. What is alone of value in mental life is rather the feelings. No mental forces are significant unless they possess the characteristic of arousing feelings. Ideas are only repressed because they are associated with the release of feelings which ought not to occur. It would be more correct to say that repression acts upon feelings, but we can only be aware of these in their association with ideas.[25] So that it

---

25. Some of this would need to be expressed differently in order to fit in with Freud's later and more elaborate discussions of repression, which are to be found, for instance, in sections 3 and 4 of his paper on "The Unconscious" (1915*e*).

was Norbert Hanold's erotic feelings that were repressed; and since his erotism knew and had known no other object than Zoe Bertgang in his childhood, his memories of her were forgotten. The ancient relief aroused the slumbering erotism in him, and made his childhood memories active. On account of a resistance to erotism that was present in him, these memories could only become operative as unconscious ones. What now took place in him was a struggle between the power of erotism and that of the forces that were repressing it; the manifestation of this struggle was a delusion.

Our author has omitted to give the reasons which led to the repression of the erotic life of his hero; for of course Hanold's concern with science was only the instrument which the repression employed. A doctor would have to dig deeper here, but perhaps without hitting upon the reason in this case. But, as we have insisted with admiration, the author has not failed to show us how the arousing of the repressed erotism came precisely from the field of the instruments that served to bring about the repression. It was right that an antique, the marble sculpture of a woman, should have been what tore our archaeologist away from his retreat from love and warned him to pay off the debt to life with which we are burdened from our birth.

The first manifestations of the process that had been set going in Hanold by the relief were fantasies, which played round the figure represented in it. The figure seemed to him to have something "of today" about her, in the best sense of the words, and it was as though the artist had captured her "from the life" stepping along the street. He gave the girl in the ancient relief the name of "Gradiva," which he constructed on the model of an epithet of the war-god striding into battle—"Mars Gradivus." He endowed her personality with more and more characteristics. She may have been the daughter of a respected personage, of a patrician, perhaps, who was connected with the temple-service of a deity. He thought he could trace a Greek origin in her features; and finally he felt compelled to remove her from the busy life of a capital and to transport her to the more peaceful Pompeii, and there he made her step across the lava stepping-stones which made it possible to cross from one side of the street to the other. [P. 11.] These products of his fantasy seem arbitrary enough, but at the same time innocently unsuspicious. And, indeed, even when for the first time they gave rise to an incitement to action—when the archaeologist, obsessed by the problem of whether this posture of the feet corresponded to reality, began to make observations from life in order to examine the feet of contemporary women and girls—even this action was screened by conscious scientific motives, as though all his interest in the sculpture of Gradiva had sprung from the soil of his professional concern with archaeology. [P. 12.] The women and girls in the street, whom he chose as the subjects of his investigation, must, of course, have taken another, crudely erotic view of his behavior, and we cannot but think them right. We ourselves can be in no doubt that Hanold was as much in ignorance of the motives of his researches as he was of the origin of his fantasies about Gradiva. These, as we learned later, were echoes of his memories of his youthful love, derivatives of those memories, transformations and distortions of them, after they had failed to make their way into his consciousness in an unmodified form. The ostensibly aesthetic judgment that the sculpture had something "of today" about it took the place of his knowledge that a gait of that kind belonged to a girl whom he knew and who stepped across the street *at the present time*. Behind the impression of the sculpture being "from the life" and the fantasy of its subject being Greek lay his memory of the name Zoe, which means "life" in Greek. "Gradiva," as we learn from our hero himself at the end of the story, after he has been cured of his delusion, is a good translation of the surname "Bertgang" which means something like "someone who steps along brilliantly or splendidly." [P. 37.] The details about Gradiva's father originated from Hanold's knowledge that Zoe Bertgang was the daughter of a respected teacher at the university, which can well be translated into classical terms as "temple-service." Finally, his fantasy transported her to Pompeii, not "because her quiet, calm nature seemed to demand it," but because no other or better analogy could be found in his science for his remarkable state, in which he became aware of his memories of his childhood friendship through obscure channels of information. Once he had made his own childhood coincide with the classical past (which it was so easy for him to do), there was a perfect similarity between the burial of Pompeii—the disappearance of the past combined with its preservation—and repression, of which he possessed a knowledge through what might be described as "endopsychic" perception. In this he was employing the same symbolism that the author makes the girl use consciously toward the conclusion of the story: "I told myself I should be able to dig out something interesting here even by myself. Of course I hadn't counted on making the find that I have." And at the very end she replied to Hanold's plan for their honeymoon with a reference to "her childhood friend who had also in a sense been dug out of the ruins again."

Thus in the very first products of Hanold's delusional fantasies and actions we already find a double set of determinants, a derivation from two different sources. One of these is the one that was manifest to Hanold himself, the other is the one which is revealed to us when we examine his mental processes. One of them, looked at from Hanold's point of view, was conscious to him, the other was completely unconscious to him. One of them was derived wholly from the circle of ideas of the science of archaeology, the other arose from the repressed childhood memories that had become active in him and from the emotional instincts attached to them. One might be described as lying on the surface and covering the other, which was, as it were, concealed behind it. The scientific motivation might be said to serve as a pretext for the unconscious erotic one, and science had put itself completely at the service of the delusion. It should not be forgotten, however, that the unconscious determinants could not effect anything that did not simultaneously satisfy the conscious, scientific ones. The symptoms of a delusion—fantasies and actions alike—are in fact the products of compromise between the two mental currents, and in a compromise account is taken of the demands of each of the two parties to it; but each side must also renounce a part of what it wanted to achieve. Where a compromise comes about it must have been preceded by a struggle—in this case it was the conflict we have assumed between suppressed erotism and the forces that were keeping it in repression. In the formation of a delusion this struggle is in fact unending. Assault and resistance are renewed after the construction of each compromise, which is never, so to speak, entirely satisfying. Our author too is aware of this, and that is why he makes a peculiar unrest dominate this stage of his hero's disorder, as a precursor and guarantee of further developments.

These significant peculiarities—the double motivation of fantasies and decisions, and the construction of conscious pretexts for actions to whose motivation the repressed has made the major contribution—will meet us often, and perhaps more clearly, in the further course of the story. And this is just as it should be, for the author has thus grasped and represented the unfailing chief characteristic of pathological mental processes.

The development of Norbert Hanold's delusion proceeded with a dream which, since it was not occasioned by any new event, seems to have arisen entirely out of his mind, filled as it was by a conflict. But let us pause before we enquire whether, in the construction of his dreams, too, the author meets our expectation that he possesses a deep understanding. Let us ask first what psychiatric science has to say to his hypotheses about the origin of a delusion and what attitude it takes to the part played by repression and the unconscious, to conflict, and to the formation of compromises. In short, let us ask whether this imaginative representation of the genesis of a delusion can hold its own before the judgment of science.

And here we must give what will perhaps be an unexpected answer. In fact the situation is quite the reverse: it is science that cannot hold its own before the achievement of the author. Science allows a gulf to yawn between the hereditary and constitutional preconditions of a delusion and its creations, which seem to emerge ready-made—a gulf which we find that our author has filled. Science does not as yet suspect the importance of repression, it does not recognize that in order to explain the world of psychopathological phenomena the unconscious is absolutely essential, it does not look for the basis of delusions in a psychical conflict, and it does not regard their symptoms as compromises. Does our author stand alone, then, in the face of united science? No, that is not the case (if, that is, I may count my own works as part of science), since for a number of years—and, until recently more or less alone[26]—I myself have supported all the views that I have here extracted from Jensen's *Gradiva* and stated in technical terms. I indicated, in most detail in connection with the states known as hysteria and obsessions, that the individual determinant[27] of these psychical disorders is the suppression of a part of instinctual life and the repression of

26. See Bleuler's important work, *Affektivität, Suggestibilität, Paranoia* and C. G. Jung's *Diagnostische Assoziationsstudien,* both published in Zurich in 1906.—[*Added* 1912:] Today, in 1912, I am able to retract what is said above as being no longer true. Since it was written, the "psychoanalytic movement" started by me has become widely extended, and it is constantly growing.

27. As contrasted, presumably, with a more general, inherited factor.

the ideas by which the suppressed instinct is represented, and soon afterwards I repeated the same views in relation to some forms of delusion.[28] The question whether the instincts concerned in this causation are always components of the sexual instinct or may be of another kind as well is a problem which may be regarded as a matter of indifference in the particular case of the analysis of *Gradiva;* for in the instance chosen by our author what was at issue was quite certainly nothing other than the suppression of erotic feelings. The validity of the hypotheses of psychical conflict and of the formation of symptoms by means of compromises between the two mental currents struggling against each other has been demonstrated by me in the case of patients observed and medically treated in real life, just as I have been able to in the imaginary case of Norbert Hanold.[29] Even before me, Pierre Janet, a pupil of the great Charcot, and Josef Breuer, in collaboration with me, had traced back the products of neurotic, and especially of hysterical, illness to the power of unconscious thoughts.[30]

When, from the year 1893 onwards, I plunged into investigations such as these of the origin of mental disturbances, it would certainly never have occurred to me to look for a confirmation of my findings in imaginative writings. I was thus more than a little surprised to find that the author of *Gradiva,* which was published in 1903, had taken as the basis of its creation the very thing that I believed myself to have freshly discovered from the sources of my medical experience. How was it that the author arrived at the same knowledge as the doctor—or at least behaved as though he possessed the same knowledge?

Norbert Hanold's delusion, as I was saying, was carried a step further by a dream which occurred in the middle of his efforts to discover a gait like Gradiva's in the streets of the town where he lived. It is easy to give the content of this dream in brief. The dreamer found himself in Pompeii on the day on which that unhappy city was destroyed, and experienced its horrors without being in danger himself; he suddenly saw Gradiva stepping along

---

28. See the author's *Sammlung kleiner Schriften zue Neurosenlehre,* 1906 [in particular the second paper on "The Neuro-Psychoses of Defence" (1896*b*)].

29. Cf. "Fragment of an Analysis of a Case of Hysteria" (1905*e*).

30. Cf. *Studies on Hysteria* (Freud, 1895*d,* with Breuer.)

there, and understood all at once, as though it was something quite natural, that since she was a Pompeian, she was living in her native town, and "without his having suspected it, living as his contemporary" [p. 12]. He was seized with fear on her account and gave a warning cry, whereupon she turned her fact toward him for a moment. But she proceeded on her way without paying any attention to him, lay down on the steps of the Temple of Apollo, and was buried in the rain of ashes after her face had lost its color, as though it were turning into white marble, until it had become just like a piece of sculpture. As he was waking up, he interpreted the noises of a big city penetrating into his bedroom as the cries for help of the despairing inhabitants of Pompeii and the thunder of the wildly agitated sea. The feeling that what he had dreamt had really happened to him would not leave him for some time after he had awoken, and a conviction that Gradiva had lived in Pompeii and had perished there on the fatal day was left over with him by the dream as a fresh starting-point for his delusion.

It is not so easy for us to say what the author intended with this dream and what caused him to link the development of the delusion precisely to a dream. Zealous investigators, it is true, had collected plenty of examples of the way in which mental disturbances are linked to dreams and arise out of dreams.[31] It appears, too, that in the lives of a few eminent men impulses to important actions and decisions have originated from dreams. But these analogies are not of much help to our understanding; so let us keep to our present case, our author's imaginary case of Norbert Hanold the archaeologist. By which end are we to take hold of a dream like this so as to fit it into the whole context, if it is not to remain no more than an unnecessary decoration of the story?

I can well imagine that at this point a reader may exclaim: "The dream is quite easily explained—it is a simple anxiety-dream, occasioned by the noises of the city, which were misinterpreted into the destruction of Pompeii by the archaeologist, whose mind was occupied with his Pompeian girl." In view of the low opinion generally prevailing of the performances of dreams, all that is usually asked from an explanation of one is that some external stimulus shall be found that more or less coincides with a piece of the

---

31. Sante de Sanctis (1899). [Cf. *The Interpretation of Dreams* (1900a), chapter 1, Section H, *Standard Ed.*, 4, 88ff.]

dream's content. This external stimulus to dreaming would be supplied by the noise which woke the sleeper; and with this, interest in the dream would be exhausted. If only we had some reason for supposing that the town was noisier than usual that morning! If only, for instance, the author had not omitted to tell us that Hanold, against his usual practice, had slept that night with his windows open! What a pity the author did not take the trouble to do that! And if only anxiety-dreams were as simple as that! But no, interest in the dream is not so easily exhausted.

There is nothing essential for the construction of a dream in a link with an external sensory stimulus. A sleeper can disregard a stimulus of this kind from the external world, or he can allow himself to be awakened by it without constructing a dream, or, as happened here, he can weave it into his dream if that suits him for some other reason; and there are numerous dreams of which it is impossible to show that their content was determined in this way by a stimulus impinging on the sleeper's senses.[32] No, we must try another path.

We may perhaps find a starting-point in the aftereffects left by the dream in Hanold's waking life. Up to then he had had a fantasy that Gradiva had been a Pompeian. This hypothesis now became a certainty for him, and a second certainly followed—that she was buried along with the rest in the year A.D. 79.[33] Melancholy feelings accompanied this extension of the delusional structure, like an echo of the anxiety which had filled the dream. This fresh pain about Gradiva does not seem very intelligible to us; Gradiva would have been dead for many centuries even if she had been saved from destruction in the year A.D. 79. Or ought we not to argue in this kind of way either with Norbert Hanold or with the author himself? Here again there seems no path to an understanding. Nevertheless it is worth remarking that the increment which the delusion acquired from this dream was accompanied by a feeling with a highly painful coloring.

Apart from that, however, we are as much at a loss as before. This dream is not self-explanatory, and we must resolve to borrow from my *Interpretation of Dreams* and apply to the present example a few of the rules to be found in it for the solution of dreams.

---

32. Cf. *The Interpretation of Dreams, Standard Ed.*, 4, 224.
33. See the text of *Gradiva* (15).

One of these rules is to the effect that a dream is invariably related to the events of the day before the dream.[34] Our author seems to be wishing to show that he has followed this rule, for he attaches the dream immediately to Hanold's "pedestrian researches." Now these had no meaning other than a search for Gradiva, whose characteristic gait he was trying to recognize. So the dream ought to have contained an indication of where Gradiva was to be found. And it does so, by showing her in Pompeii; but that is no novelty to us.

Another rule tells as that, if a belief in the reality of the dream-images persists unusually long, so that one cannot tear oneself out of the dream, this is not a mistaken judgment provoked by the vividness of the dream-images, but is a psychical act on its own: it is an assurance, relating to the content of the dream, that something in it is really as one has dreamt it;[35] and it is right to have faith in this assurance. If we keep to these two rules, we must conclude that the dream gave some information as to the whereabouts of the Gradiva he was in search of, and that that information tallied with the real state of things. We know Hanold's dream: does the application of these two rules to it yield any reasonable sense?

Strange to say, it does. The sense is merely disguised in a particular way so that it is not immediately recognizable. Hanold learned in the dream that the girl he was looking for was living in a town and contemporaneously with him. Now this was true of Zoe Bertgang; only in the dream the town was not the German university town but Pompeii, and the time was not the present but the year A.D. 79. It is, as it were, a distortion by displacement: what we have is not Gradiva in the present but the dreamer transported into the past. Nevertheless, in this manner, the essential and new fact is stated: *he is in the same place and time as the girl he is looking for.* But whence come this displacement and disguise which were bound to deceive both us and the dreamer over the true meaning and content of the dream? Well, we already have the means at our disposal for giving a satisfactory answer to that question.

Let us recall all that we have heard about the nature and origin of the fantasies, which are the precursors of delusions. They are substitutes for and derivatives of repressed memories which a re-

---

34. *The Interpretation of Dreams,* chapter 5, Section A, *Standard Ed.,* **4,** 165ff.
35. Ibid., **4,** 187 and 5, 372.

sistance will not allow to enter consciousness unaltered, but which can purchase the possibility of becoming conscious by taking account, by means of changes and distortions, of the resistance's censorship. When this compromise has been accomplished, the memories have turned into the fantasies, which can easily be misunderstood by the conscious personality—that is, understood so as to fit in with the dominant psychical current. Now let us suppose that dream-images are what might be described as the creations of people's physiological [i.e., nonpathological] delusions—the products of the compromise in the struggle between what is repressed and what is dominant which is probably present in every human being, including those who in the daytime are perfectly sound in mind. We shall then understand that dream-images have to be regarded as something distorted, behind which something else must be looked for, something *not* distorted, but in some sense objectionable, like Hanold's repressed memories behind his fantasies. We can give expression to the contrast which we have thus recognized, by distinguishing what the dreamer remembers when he wakes up as the *manifest content of the dream* from what constituted the basis of the dream before the distortion imposed by the censorship—namely, the *latent dream-thoughts.* Thus, interpreting a dream consists in translating the manifest content of the dream into the latent dream-thoughts, in undoing the distortion which the dream-thoughts have had to submit to from the censorship of the resistance. If we apply these notions to the dream we are concerned with, we shall find that its latent dream-thoughts can only have been: "the girl you are looking for with the graceful gait is really living in this town with you." But in that form the thought could not become conscious. It was obstructed by the fact that a fantasy had laid it down, as the result of an earlier compromise, that Gradiva was a Pompeian; consequently, if the real fact that she was living in the same place and at the same time was to be affirmed, there was no choice but to adopt the distortion: "You are living at Pompeii at the time of Gradiva." This then was the idea which was realized by the manifest content of the dream, and was represented as a present event actually being experienced.

It is only rarely that a dream represents, or, as we might say, "stages," a single thought: there are usually a number of them, a tissue of thoughts. Another component of the content of Hanold's dream can be detached, the distortion of which can easily be got rid of, so that the latent idea represented by it can be detected. This is a piece of the dream to which once again it is possible to extend the assurance of reality with which the dream ended. In the dream Gradiva as she steps along is transformed into a marble sculpture. This is no more than an ingenious and poetical representation of the real event. Hanold had in fact transferred his interest from the living girl to the sculpture: the girl he loved had been transformed for him into a marble relief. The latent dream-thoughts, which were bound to remain unconscious, sought to change the sculpture back into the living girl; what they were saying to him accordingly was something like: "After all, you're only interested in the statue of Gradiva because it reminds you of Zoe, who is living here and now." But if this discovery could have become conscious, it would have meant the end of the delusion.

Are we perhaps under an obligation to replace in this way each separate piece of the manifest content of the dream by unconscious thoughts? Strictly speaking, yes; if we were interpreting a dream that had really been dreamt, we could not avoid that duty. But in that case, too, the dreamer would have to give us the most copious explanations. Clearly we cannot carry out this requirement in the case of the author's creation; nevertheless, we shall not overlook the fact that we have not yet submitted the main content of the dream to the process of interpretation or translation.

For Hanold's dream was an anxiety-dream. Its content was frightening, the dreamer felt anxiety while he slept and he was left with painful feelings afterwards. Now this is far from convenient for our attempt at an explanation; and we must once again borrow heavily from the theory of dream-interpretation. We are warned by that theory not to fall into the error of tracing the anxiety that may be felt in a dream to the content of the dream, and not to treat the content of the dream as though it were the content of an idea occurring in waking life. It points out to us how often we dream the most ghastly things without feeling a trace of anxiety. The true situation, we learn, is quite a different one, which cannot be easily guessed but which can be proved with certainty. The anxiety in anxiety-dreams, like neurotic anxiety in general, corresponds to a sexual affect, a libidinal feeling, and arises out of libido by the process of repression. When we interpret a dream, therefore, we must replace anxiety by sexual excitement. The anxiety that originates in this way has—not invariably, but frequently—a selective influence on the content of the dream and introduces into it ideational elements which seem, when the dream is looked at from a conscious and mistaken point of view, to be appropriate to the affect of anxiety. As I have said, this is not invariably so, for there are plenty of anxiety-dreams in which the content is not in the least frightening and where it is therefore impossible to give an explanation on conscious lines of the anxiety that is felt.

I am aware that this explanation of anxiety in dreams sounds very strange and is not easy to credit; but I can only advise the reader to come to terms with it. Moreover it would be a very remarkable thing if Norbert Hanold's dream could be reconciled with this view of anxiety and could be explained in that way. On that basis, we should say that the dreamer's erotic longings were stirred up during the night and made a powerful effort to make conscious his memory of the girl he loved and so to tear him out of his delusion, but that those longings met with a fresh repudiation and were transformed into anxiety, which in its turn introduced into the content of the dream the terrifying pictures from the memories of his schooldays. In this manner the true unconscious content of the dream, his passionate longing for the Zoe he had once known, became transformed into its manifest content of the destruction of Pompeii and the loss of Gradiva.

So far, I think, it sounds plausible. But it might justly be insisted that, if erotic wishes constitute the undistorted content of the dream, it ought also to be possible to point at least to some recognizable residue of those wishes concealed somewhere in the transformed dream. Well, even that may be possible, with the help of a hint from a later part of the story. When Hanold had his first meeting with the supposed Gradiva, he recollected the dream and begged the apparition to lie down again as he had seen her do then.[36] Thereupon, however, the young lady rose indignantly and left her strange companion, for she had detected the improper erotic wish behind what he had said under the domination of his delusion. We must, I think, accept Gradiva's interpretation; even in a real dream we cannot always expect to find a more definite expression of an erotic wish.

---

36. "No, I didn't hear you speak. But I called to you when you lay down to sleep, and I stood beside you then—your face was as peaceful and beautiful as marble. May I beg of you—lie down once more on the step as you did then." (70.)

The application of a few of the rules of dream-interpretation to Hanold's first dream has thus resulted in making it intelligible to us in its main features and in inserting it into the nexus of the story. Surely, then, the author must have observed these rules in creating it? We might ask another question, too: why did the author introduce a dream at all to bring about the further development of the delusion? In my opinion it was an ingenious notion and once again true to reality. We have already heard that in real illnesses a delusion very often arises in connection with a dream, and, after what we have learned about the nature of dreams, there is no need to see a fresh riddle in this fact. Dreams and delusions arise from the same source—from what is repressed. Dreams are, as one might say, the physiological delusions of normal people. Before what is repressed has become strong enough to break though into waking life as a delusion, it may easily have achieved a first success, under the more favorable conditions of the state of sleep, in the form of a dream with persisting effects. For during sleep, along with a general lowering of mental activity, there is a relaxation in the strength of the resistance with which the dominant psychical forces oppose what is repressed. It is this relaxation that makes the formation of dreams possible, and that is why dreams give us our best access to a knowledge of the unconscious part of the mind—except that, as a rule, with the reestablishment of the psychical cathexes of waking life, the dream once more takes to flight and the ground that had been won by the unconscious is evacuated once again.

3

In the further course of the story there is yet another dream, which may perhaps tempt us even more than the first to try to translate it and insert it into the train of events in the hero's mind.[37] But we should save very little by diverging from the author's account and hurrying on immediately to this second dream; for no one who wishes to analyze someone else's dream can avoid turning his attention in the greatest detail to all the dreamer's experiences, both external and internal. It will probably be best, therefore, to keep

---

37. The last phrase in this sentence, which, in a slightly different form, has already appeared in the preceding paragraph, is an echo of the opening sentence of *The Interpretation of Dreams* (*Standard Ed.*, **4**, 1).

close to the thread of the story and to intersperse it with our glosses as we proceed.

The construction of the fresh delusion about Gradiva's death during the destruction of Pompeii in the year A.D. 79 was not the only result of the first dream, which we have already analyzed. Immediately after it Hanold decided on his journey to Italy, which eventually brought him to Pompeii. But, before that, something else happened to him. As he was leaning out of the window, he thought he saw a figure in the street with the bearing and gait of his Gradiva. In spite of being insufficiently dressed, he hurried after her, but failed to overtake her, and was driven back into the house by the jeers of the passersby. When he was in his room once more, the song of a canary from its case in the window of a house opposite stirred up in him a mood in which he too seemed to be a prisoner longing for freedom; and his springtime journey was no sooner decided on than it was carried out.

The author has thrown a particularly clear light on this journey of Hanold's and has allowed him to have a partial insight into his own internal processes. Hanold of course found himself a scientific pretext for his journey, but this did not last long. After all, he was in fact aware that "the impulse to make this journey had arisen from a feeling he could not name." A strange restlessness made him dissatisfied with everything he came across, and drove him from Rome to Naples and from there to Pompeii; but even at this last halting-place he was still uneasy in his mood. He was annoyed at the folly of the honeymooners, and enraged at the impertinence of the houseflies which inhabit Pompeii's hotels. But at last he could no longer disguise from himself "that his dissatisfaction could not be caused solely by what was around him but that there was something that sprang from himself as well." He thought he was overexcited, felt "that he was discontented because he lacked something, but he had no idea what. And this ill-humor followed him about everywhere." In this frame of mind he was even furious with his mistress—with Science. When in the heat of the midday sun he wandered for the first time through Pompeii, "the whole of his science had not merely abandoned him, but had left him without the slightest desire to find her again. He remembered her only as something in the far distance, and he felt that she had been an old, dried-up, tedious aunt, the dullest and most unwanted creature in the world." (55.)

And then, while he was in this disagreeable and confused state of feeling, one of the problems attaching to his journey was solved for him—at the moment when he first saw Gradiva stepping through Pompeii. Something "came into his consciousness for the first time: without being aware himself of the impulse within him, he had come to Italy and had traveled on to Pompeii, without stopping in Rome or Naples, in order to see whether he could find any traces of her. And 'traces' literally; for with her peculiar gait she must have left behind an imprint of her toes in the ashes distinct from all the rest."

Since the author has taken so much trouble over describing the journey, it must be worthwhile too to discuss its relation to Hanold's delusion and its position in the chain of events. The journey was undertaken for reasons which its subject did not recognize at first and only admitted to himself later on, reasons which the author describes in so many words as "unconscious." This is certainly taken from the life. One does not need to be suffering from a delusion in order to behave like this. On the contrary, it is an event of daily occurrence for a person—even a healthy person— to deceive himself over the motives for an action and to become conscious of them only after the event, provided only that a conflict between several currents of feeling furnishes the necessary condition for such a confusion. Accordingly, Hanold's journey was from the first calculated to serve the delusion, and was intended to take him to Pompeii, where he could proceed further with his search for Gradiva. It will be recalled that his mind was occupied with that search both before and immediately after the dream, and that the dream itself was simply an answer to the question of Gradiva's whereabouts, though an answer which was stifled by his consciousness. Some power which we do not recognize was, however, also inhibiting him to begin with from becoming aware of his delusional intention; so that, for the conscious reasons for his journey, he was left only with insufficient pretexts which had to be renewed from place to place. The author presents us with a further puzzle by making the dream, the discovery of the supposed Gradiva in the street, and the decision to undertake the journey as a result of the singing canary succeed one another as a series of chance events without any internal connection with one another.

This obscure region of the story is made intelligible to us by some explanations which we derive from the later remarks of Zoe Bertgang. It was in fact the original of Gradiva, Fräulein Zoe herself, whom Hanold saw out of his window walking past in the street (89) and whom he nearly overtook. If this had happened, the information given him by the dream—that she was in fact living at the same time and in the same town as he was—would by a lucky chance have received an irresistible confirmation, which would have brought about the collapse of his internal struggle. But the canary, whose singing sent Hanold off on his distant journey, belonged to Zoe, and its cage stood in her window diagonally across the street from Hanold's house. Hanold, who, according to the girl's accusation, had the gift of "negative hallucination," who possessed the art of not seeing and not recognizing people who were actually present, must from the first have had an unconscious knowledge of what we only learned later. The indications of Zoe's proximity (her appearance in the street and her bird's singing so near his window) intensified the effect of the dream, and in this position, so perilous for his resistance to his erotic feelings, he took to flight. His journey was a result of his resistance gathering new strength after the surge forward of his erotic desires in the dream; it was an attempt at flight from the physical presence of the girl he loved. In a practical sense it meant a victory for repression, just as his earlier activity, his "pedestrian researches" upon women and girls, had meant a victory for erotism. But everywhere in these oscillations in the struggle the compromise character of the outcome was preserved: the journey to Pompeii, which was supposed to lead him away from the living Zoe, led him at least to her surrogate, to Gradiva. The journey, which was undertaken in defiance of the latent dream-thoughts, was nevertheless following the path to Pompeii that was pointed out by the manifest content of the dream. Thus at every fresh struggle between erotism and resistance we find the delusion triumphant.

This view of Hanold's journey as a flight from his awakening erotic longing for the girl whom he loved and who was so close to him is the only one which will fit in with the description of his emotional states during his stay in Italy. The repudiation of erotism which dominated him was expressed there in his disgust at the honeymooners. A short dream which he had in his *albergo* in Rome, and which was occasioned by the proximity of a German loving couple, "Edwin and Angelina," whose evening conversation he could not help hearing through the thin partition-wall, throws a retrospective light, as it were, on the erotic drift of his first major dream. In the new dream he was once again in Pompeii and Vesuvius was once again erupting, and it was thus linked to the earlier dream whose effects persisted during the journey. This time, however, among the people imperiled were—not, as on the former occasion, himself and Gradiva but—the Apollo Belvedere and the Capitoline Venus, no doubt by way of an ironical exaltation of the couple in the next room. Apollo lifted Venus up, carried her out, and laid her down on some object in the dark which seemed to be a carriage or cart, since it emitted "a creaking noise." Apart from this, the interpretation of the dream calls for no special skill. (31.)

Our author, who, as we have long since realized, never introduces a single idle or unintentional feature into his story, has given us another piece of evidence of the asexual current which dominated Hanold during his journey. As he roamed about for hours in Pompeii, "strangely enough it never once recurred to his memory that a short time before he had dreamt of being present at the burial of Pompeii in the eruption of A.D. 79." (47.) It was only when he caught sight of Gradiva that he suddenly remembered the dream and became conscious at the same time of the delusional reason for his puzzling journey. How could this forgetting of the dream, this barrier of repression between the dream and his mental state during the journey, be explained, except by supposing that the journey was undertaken not at the direct inspiration of the dream but as a revolt against it, as an emanation of a mental power that refused to know anything of the secret meaning of the dream?

But on the other hand Hanold did not enjoy this victory over his erotism. The suppressed mental impulse remained powerful enough to revenge itself on the suppressing one with discontent and inhibition. His longings turned into restlessness and dissatisfaction, which made his journey seem pointless to him. His insight into his reasons for the journey at the bidding of the delusion was inhibited and his relations with his science, which in such a spot should have stirred all his interest, were interfered with. So the author shows us his hero after his flight from love in a kind of crisis, in a state of complete confusion and distraction, in a turmoil such as we usually find at the climax of an illness, when neither of the two conflicting powers has any longer a sufficiently superior strength over the other for the margin between them to make it possible to establish a vigorous mental régime. But here the author intervenes helpfully, and smoothes things out by making Gradiva appear at this juncture and undertake the cure of the delusion. By the power he possesses of guiding the people of his creation toward a happy destiny, in spite of all the laws of necessity which he makes them obey, he arranges that the girl, to avoid whom Hanold had fled to Pompeii, shall be transported to that very place. In this way he corrects the folly to which the young man was led by his delusion— the folly of exchanging the home of the living girl whom he loved for the burial-place of her imaginary substitute.

With the appearance of Zoe Bertgang as Gradiva, which marks the climax of tension in the story, our interest, too, soon takes a new direction. So far we have been assisting at the development of a delusion; now we are to witness its cure. And we may ask whether the author has given a purely fanciful account of the course of this cure or whether he had constructed it in accordance with possibilities actually present. Zoe's own words during her conversation with her newly married friend give us a definite right to ascribe to her an intention to bring about the cure. But how did she set about it? When she had got over the indignation aroused in her by his suggestion that she should lie down to sleep again as she had "then," she returned next day at the same midday hour to the same spot, and proceeded to entice out of Hanold all the secret knowledge her ignorance of which had prevented her from understanding his behavior the day before. She learned about his dream, about the sculpture of Gradiva, and about the peculiarity of gait which she herself shared with it. She accepted the role of the ghost awakened to life for a brief hour, a role for which, as she perceived, his delusion had cast her, and, by accepting the flowers of the dead which he had brought without conscious purpose, and by expressing a regret that he had not given her roses, she gently hinted in ambiguous words at the possibility of his taking up a new position.

This unusually clever girl, then, was determined to win her childhood's friend for her husband, after she had recognized that the young man's love for her was the motive force behind the delusion. Our interest in her behavior, however, will probably yield for the moment to the surprise which we may feel at the delusion itself. The last form taken by it was that Gradiva, who had been buried in A.D. 79, was now able, as a midday ghost, to exchange words with him for an hour, at the end of which she must sink into the ground or seek her grave once more. This mental cobweb, which was not brushed away either by his perceiving that the apparition was wearing modern shoes or by her ignorance of the ancient languages and her command of German, which was not in existence in her day, certainly seems to justify the author's description of his story as a "Pompeian fantasy," but it seems also to exclude any possibility of measuring it by the standards of clinical reality.

Nevertheless, on closer consideration this delusion of Hanold's seems to me to lose the greater part of its improbability. The author, indeed, has made himself responsible for one part of it by basing his story on the premiss that Zoe was in every detail a duplicate of the relief. We must therefore avoid shifting the improbability of this premiss on to its consequence—that Hanold took the girl for Gradiva come to life. Greater value is given to the delusional explanation by the fact that the author has put no rational one at our disposal. Moreover the author has adduced contributory and mitigating circumstances on behalf of his hero's excesses in the shape of the glare of the *campagna* sunlight and the intoxicating magic of the wine grown on the slopes of Vesuvius. But the most important of all the explanatory and exculpatory factors remains the ease with which our intellect is prepared to accept something absurd provided it satisfies powerful emotional impulses. It is an astonishing fact, and one that is too generally overlooked, how readily and frequently under these psychological conditions people of even the most powerful intelligence react as though they were feebleminded; and anyone who is not too conceited may see this happening in himself as often as he pleases. And this is far more so if some of the mental processes concerned are linked with unconscious or repressed motives. In this connection I am happy to quote the words of a philosopher, who writes to me: "I have been noting down the instances I myself experience of striking mistakes and unthinking actions, for which one finds motives afterwards (in a most unreasonable way). It is an alarming thing, but typical, to find how much folly this brings to light." It must be remembered, too, that the belief in spirits and ghosts and the return of the dead, which finds so much support in the religions to which we have all been attached, at least in our childhood, is far from having disappeared among educated people, and that many who are sensible in other respects find it possible to combine spiritualism with reason. A man who has grown rational and skeptical, even, may be ashamed to discover how easily he may for a moment return to a belief in spirits under the combined impact of strong emotion and perplexity. I know of a doctor who had once lost one of his women patients suffering from Graves' disease,[38] and who could not get rid of a faint suspicion that he might perhaps have contributed to the unhappy outcome by a thoughtless prescription. One day, several years later, a girl entered his consulting room, who, in spite of all his efforts, he could not help recognizing as the dead one. He could frame only a single thought: "So after all it's true that the dead can come back to life." His dread did not give way to shame till the girl introduced herself as the sister of the one who had died of the same disease as she herself was suffering from. The victims of Graves' disease, as has often been observed, have a marked facial resemblance to one another; and in this case this typical likeness was reinforced by a family one. The doctor to whom this occurred was, however, none other than myself; so I have a personal reason for not disputing the clinical possibility of Norbert Hanold's temporary delusion that Gradiva had come back to life. The fact, finally, is familiar to every psychiatrist that in severe cases of chronic delusions (in paranoia) the most extreme examples occur of ingeniously elaborated and well-supported absurdities.

After his first meeting with Gradiva, Norbert Hanold had drunk his wine first in one and then in the other of the two restaurants that he knew in Pompeii, while the other visitors were engaged in eating the main meal of the day. "Of course it never came into his head to think of the nonsensical idea" that he was doing it in order to discover in which of the hotels Gradiva was living and taking her meals. But it is difficult to say what other sense his actions could have had. On the day after their second meeting in the House of Meleager, he had all kinds of strange and apparently unconnected experiences. He found a narrow gap in the wall of the portico, at the point where Gradiva had disappeared. He met a foolish lizard-catcher who addressed him as though he were an acquaintance. He discovered a third hotel in an out-of-the-way situation, the "Albergo del Sole," whose proprietor palmed off on him a

---

38. Exophthalmic goiter.

metal clasp with a green patina as a find from beside the remains of a Pompeian girl. And, lastly, in his own hotel he noticed a newly arrived young couple whom he diagnosed as a brother and sister and whom he found sympathetic. All these impressions were afterwards woven together into a "remarkably senseless" dream, which ran as follows:

"Somewhere in the sun Gradiva was sitting, making a snare out of a blade of grass to catch a lizard in, and said: 'Please keep quite still. Our lady colleague is right; the method is a really good one and she has made use of it with excellent results.'"

He fended off this dream while he was still asleep, with the critical thought that it was utter madness, and cast around in all directions to get free of it. He succeeded in doing so with the help of an invisible bird, which uttered a short laughing call and carried off the lizard in its beak.

Are we to venture on an attempt at interpreting this dream too—that is, at replacing it by the latent thoughts from whose distortion it must have arisen? It is as senseless as only a dream can be expected to be; and this absurdity of dreams is the mainstay of the view which refuses to characterize dreams as completely valid psychical acts and maintains that they arise out of a purposeless excitation of the elements of the mind.

We are able to apply to this dream the technique which may be described as the regular procedure for interpreting dreams. It consists in paying no attention to the apparent connections in the manifest dream but in fixing our eyes upon each portion of its content independently, and in looking for its origin in the dreamer's impressions, memories, and free associations.[39] Since, however, we cannot question Hanold, we shall have to content ourselves with referring to his impressions, and we may very tentatively put our own associations in place of his.

"Somewhere in the sun Gradiva was sitting, catching lizards and speaking." What impression of the previous day finds an echo in this part of the dream? Undoubtedly the encounter with the elderly gentleman, the lizard-catcher, who was thus replaced in the dream by Gradiva. He sat or lay "on a sun-bathed slope" and he, too, spoke to Hanold. Furthermore, Gradiva's remarks in the dream

---

39. Cf. *The Interpretation of Dreams*, Standard Ed., 4, 103–4.

were copied from this man's remarks: viz. "The method prescribed by our colleague Eimer is a really good one; I have made use of it many times already with excellent results. Please keep quite still." Gradiva used much the same words in the dream, except that "our colleague Eimer" was replaced by an unnamed "lady colleague"; moreover, the "many times" in the zoologist's speech was omitted in the dream and the order of the sentences was somewhat altered. It seems, therefore, that this experience of the previous day was transformed into the dream with the help of a few changes and distortions. Why this particular experience? And what is the meaning of the changes—the replacement of the elderly gentleman by Gradiva and the introduction of the enigmatic "lady colleague"?

There is a rule in interpreting dreams which runs as follows: "A speech heard in a dream is always derived from one that has been heard or made by the dreamer in waking life."[40] This rule seems to have been observed here: Gradiva's speech is only a modification of the old zoologist's speech which Hanold had heard the day before. Another rule in dream-interpretation would tell us that when one person is replaced by another or when two people are mixed up together (for instance, by one of them being shown in a situation that is characteristic of the other), it means that the two people are being equated, that there is a similarity between them.[41] If we venture to apply this rule too to our dream, we should arrive at this translation: "Gradiva catches lizards just like the old man; she is skilled in lizard catching just as he is." This result cannot exactly be said to be intelligible as yet; but we have yet another puzzle to solve. To what impression of the previous day are we to relate the "lady colleague" who in the dream replaces the famous zoologist Eimer? Fortunately we have very little choice here. A "lady colleague" can only mean another girl—that is to say, the sympathetic young lady whom Hanold had taken for a sister traveling with her brother. "She was wearing a red Sorrento rose in her dress, the sight of which reminded him of something as he looked across from his corner of the dining room, but he could not think what. This remark of the author's gives us a right to regard her as the "lady colleague" in the dream. What Hanold could not recall were, it cannot be doubted, the words spoken by the supposed

---

40. Cf. *The Interpretation of Dreams, Standard Ed.*, 5, 418ff.
41. Ibid., 4, 320ff.

Gradiva, who had told him, as she asked him for the white flowers of the dead, that in the spring people give happier girls roses. But behind those words there had lain a hint of wooing. So what sort of lizard catching was it that the happier "lady colleague" had carried out so successfully?

Next day Hanold came upon the supposed brother and sister in an affectionate embrace, and was thus able to correct his earlier mistake. They were in fact a pair of lovers, and moreover on their honeymoon, as we discovered later when they so unexpectedly interrupted Hanold's third interview with Zoe. If now we are willing to assume that Hanold, though consciously taking them for a brother and sister, had immediately recognized their true relationship (which was unambiguously betrayed next day) in his unconscious, Gradiva's speech in the dream acquires a clear meaning. The red rose had become the symbol of a love-relation. Hanold understood that the couple were already what he and Gradiva had yet to become; the lizard catching had come to signify man catching; and Gradiva's speech meant something like: "Only let me alone: I know how to win a man just as well as the other girl does."

But why was it necessary for this penetration of Zoe's intentions to appear in the dream in the form of the old zoologist's speech? Why was Zoe's skill in man catching represented by the old gentleman's skill in lizard catching? Well, we can have no difficulty in answering that question. We guessed long ago that the lizard-catcher was none other than Bertgang, the professor of zoology and Zoe's father, who, incidentally, must have known Hanold too—which explains how he came to address him as an acquaintance. Let us assume, once again, that in his unconscious Hanold at once recognized the professor. "He had a vague notion that he had already had a passing glimpse of the lizard-hunter's face, probably in one of the two hotels." This, then, is the explanation of the strange disguise under which the intention attributed to Zoe made its appearance: she was the lizard-catcher's daughter and had acquired her skill from him.

The replacement of the lizard-catcher by Gradiva in the content of the dream is accordingly a representation of the relation between the two figures which was known to Hanold in his unconscious; the introduction of the "lady colleague" instead of "our colleague Eimer" allowed the dream to express Hanold's realization that she was wooing a man. So far the dream welded together ("condensed," as we say) two experiences of the previous day into one situation, in order to bring to expression (in a very obscure way, it is true) two discoveries which were not allowed to become conscious. But we can go further, we can diminish the strangeness of the dream still more and we can demonstrate the influence of his other experiences of the previous day on the form taken by the manifest dream.

We may declare ourselves dissatisfied with the explanation that has hitherto been given of why it was that precisely the scene of the lizard catching was made into the nucleus of the dream, and we may suspect that still other elements of the dream-thoughts were bringing their influence to bear in the emphasis that was laid on the "lizard" in the manifest dream. Indeed, it may easily have been so. It will be recalled [p. 22] that Hanold had discovered a gap in the wall at the point where Gradiva had seemed to vanish— a gap "which was nevertheless wide enough to allow a form that was unusually slim" to slip through. This observation led him in daytime to make an alteration in his delusion—an alteration to the effect that when Gradiva disappeared from his sight she did not sink into the earth but used the gap as a way of reaching her grave. In his unconscious thoughts he may have told himself that he had now discovered the natural explanation of the girl's surprising disappearance. But must not the idea of slipping through narrow gaps and disappearing in them have recalled the behavior of lizards? Was not Gradiva herself in this way behaving like an agile little lizard? In our view, then, the discovery of the gap in the wall contributed to determining the choice of the element "lizard" in the manifest content of the dream. The lizard situation in the dream represented this impression of the previous day as well as the encounter with Zoe's father, the zoologist.

And what if now, growing bold, we were to try to find a representation in the content of the dream of the one experience of the previous day which had not yet been exploited—the discovery of the third inn, the Albergo del Sole? The author has treated this episode at such length and has linked so many things to it that it would surprise us if it alone had made no contribution to the construction of the dream. Hanold went into this inn, which, owing to its out-of-the-way situation and its distance from the railway station, had remained unknown to him, to purchase a bottle of soda water to cool his heated blood. The landlord took the opportunity of displaying his antiquities, and showed him a clasp which he pretended had belonged to the Pompeian girl who had been found in the neighborhood of the Forum closely embraced by her lover. Hanold, who had never hitherto believed this often-repeated tale, was now compelled by a power unknown to him to believe in the truth of this moving story and in the genuineness of the find; he purchased the brooch and left the inn with his acquisition. As he was going out, he saw, standing in a glass of water in a window, a nodding sprig of asphodel covered with white blossoms, and took the sight of it as a confirmation of the genuineness of his new possession. He now felt a positive conviction that the green clasp had belonged to Gradiva and that she had been the girl who had died in her lover's arms. He quieted the jealousy which thereupon seized him, by deciding that next day he would show the clasp to Gradiva herself and arrive at certainty about his suspicion. It cannot be denied that this was a curious new piece of delusion; yet are we to suppose that no trace of it was to be found in his dream of the same night?

It will certainly be worthwhile to explain the origin of this addition to the delusion and to look for the fresh piece of unconscious discovery which was replaced by the fresh piece of delusion. The delusion appeared under the influence of the landlord of the "Sun Hotel" to whom Hanold behaved in such a remarkably credulous fashion that it was almost as though he had been given a hypnotic suggestion by him. The landlord showed him a metal clasp for a garment, represented it as genuine and as having belonged to the girl who had been found buried in the arms of her lover; and Hanold, who was capable of being sufficiently critical to doubt both the truth of the story and the genuineness of the clasp, was at once taken in, and purchased the highly dubious antique. Why he should have behaved in this way is quite incomprehensible, and there is nothing to suggest that the landlord's personality might offer us a solution. But there is yet another riddle about the incident, and two riddles often solve each other. As he was leaving the *albergo* he saw a sprig of asphodel standing in a glass in a window and took it as a confirmation of the genuineness of the metal clasp. How could that have come about? But fortunately this last point is easy to solve. The white flower was no doubt the one which he had given to Gradiva at midday, and it is perfectly true that something was confirmed by the sight of it in the window of the inn.

Not, it is true, the genuineness of the clasp, but something else that had already become clear to him when he discovered this *albergo* after having previously overlooked it. Already on the day before he had behaved as though he was searching in the two Pompeii hotels to find the person who appeared to him as Gradiva. And now, since he had so unexpectedly come upon a third one, he must have said to himself in his unconscious: "So *this* is where she is staying!" And added, as he was going out: "Yes, that's right! There's the asphodel that I gave her! So that's her window!" This then was the new discovery which was replaced by the delusion, and which could not become conscious because its underlying postulate that Gradiva was a living person whom he had once known could not become conscious.

But how did the replacement of the new discovery by the delusion take place? What happened, I think, was that the sense of conviction attaching to the discovery was able to persist and was retained, while the discovery itself, which was inadmissible to consciousness, was replaced by another ideational content connected with it by associations of thought. Thus the sense of conviction became attached to a content which was in fact foreign to it and this, in the form of a delusion, won a recognition which did not apply to it. Hanold transferred his conviction that Gradiva lived in the house to other impressions which he had received in the house; this led to his credulity in regard to the landlord's remarks, the genuineness of the metal clasp and the truth of the anecdote about the discovery of the embracing lovers—but only through his linking what he heard in the house with Gradiva. The jealousy which was already latent in him seized upon this material and the consequence was the delusion (though it contradicted his first dream) that Gradiva was the girl who had died in her lover's arms and that the clasp he had bought had belonged to her.

It will be observed that his conversation with Gradiva and her hint at wooing him (her "saying it with flowers") had already brought about important changes in Hanold. Traits of masculine desire—components of the libido—had awakened in him, though it is true that they could not yet dispense with the disguise of conscious pretexts. But the problem of the "bodily nature" of Gradiva, which pursued him all that day [pp. 20 and 23], cannot disavow its origin in a young man's erotic curiosity about a woman's body, even if it is involved in a scientific question by the conscious insistence on Gradiva's peculiar oscillation between death and life. His jealousy was a further sign of the increasingly active aspect of Hanold's love; he expressed this jealousy at the beginning of their conversation the next day and with the help of a fresh pretext proceeded to touch the girl's body and, as he used to do in the far-off past, to hit her.

But it is now time to ask ourselves whether the method of constructing a delusion which we have inferred from our author's account is one that is known from other sources, or whether, indeed, it is possible at all. From our medical knowledge we can only reply that it is certainly the correct method, and perhaps the sole method, by which a delusion acquires the unshakable conviction which is one of its clinical characteristics. If a patient believes in his delusion so firmly, this is not because his faculty of judgment has been overturned and does not arise from what is false in the delusion. On the contrary, there is a grain of truth concealed in every delusion,[42] there is something in it that really deserves belief, and this is the source of the patient's conviction, which is therefore to that extent justified. This true element, however, has long been repressed. If eventually it is able to penetrate into consciousness, this time in a distorted form, the sense of conviction attaching to it is overintensified as though by way of compensation and is now attached to the distorted substitute of the repressed truth, and protects it from any critical attacks. The conviction is displaced, as it were, from the unconscious truth on to the conscious error that is linked to it, and remains fixated there precisely as a result of this displacement. The instance of the formation of a delusion which arose from Hanold's first dream is no more than a similar, though not identical, example of such a displacement. Indeed, the method described here by which conviction arises in the case of a delusion does not differ fundamentally from the method by which a conviction is formed in normal cases, where repression does not come into the picture. We all attach our conviction to thought-contents in which truth is combined with error, and let it extend

---

42. Freud expressed this view at many points throughout the whole course of his writings. It appears, for instance, in the first edition of *Psychopathology of Everyday Life* (1901*b*), chapter 12, section C *(a),* and in *Moses and Monotheism* (1939*a*), chapter 3, part 2, section G.

from the former over the latter. It becomes diffused, as it were, from the truth over the error associated with it and protects the latter, though not so unalterably as in the case of a delusion, against deserved criticism. In normal psychology, too, being well connected—"having influence," so to speak—can take the place of true worth.

I will now return to the dream and bring out a small but not uninteresting feature in it, which forms a connection between two of its provoking causes. Gradiva had drawn a kind of contrast between the white asphodel blossoms and the red rose. Seeing the asphodel again in the window of the Albergo del Sole became an important piece of evidence in support of Hanold's unconscious discovery, which was expressed in the new delusion; and alongside this was the fact that the red rose in the dress of the sympathetic girl helped Hanold in his unconscious to a correct view of her relation to her companion, so that he was able to make her appear in the dream as the "lady colleague."

But where in the manifest content of the dream, it will be asked, do we find anything to indicate and replace the discovery for which, as we have seen, Hanold's new delusion was a substitute— the discovery that Gradiva was staying with her father in the third, concealed Pompeii hotel, the Albergo del Sole? Nevertheless it is all there in the dream, and not even very much distorted, and I merely hesitate to point to it because I know that even those of my readers who have followed me patiently so far will begin to rebel strongly against my attempts at interpretation. Hanold's discovery, I repeat, is fully announced in the dream, but so cleverly concealed that it is bound to be overlooked. It is hidden behind a play upon words, an ambiguity. "Somewhere in the sun Gradiva was sitting." We have quite correctly related this to the spot where Hanold met her father, the zoologist. But could it not also mean in the "Sun"— that is, Gradiva is staying in the Albergo del Sole, the Sun Hotel? And was not the "somewhere," which had no bearing on the encounter with her father, made to sound so hypocritically indefinite precisely because it introduced a definite piece of information about the place where Gradiva was staying? From my experience elsewhere of real dreams, I myself am perfectly certain that this is how the ambiguity is to be understood. But I should not in fact have ventured to present this piece of interpretative work to my readers, if the author had not at this point lent me his powerful assistance. He puts the very same play upon words into the girl's mouth when next day she saw the metal clasp: "Did you find it in the sun, perhaps, which produces things of this kind?" And since Hanold failed to understand what she had said, she explained that she meant the Sun Hotel, which they call "Sole" here, and where she had already seen the supposititious antique.

And now let us make a bold attempt at replacing Hanold's "remarkably senseless" dream by the unconscious thoughts that lay behind it and were as unlike it as possible. They ran, perhaps, as follows: "She is staying in the 'Sun' with her father. Why is she playing this game with me? Does she want to make fun of me? Or can it possibly be that she loves me and wants to have me as her husband?"—And no doubt while he was still asleep there came an answer dismissing this last possibility as "the merest madness," a comment which was ostensibly directed against the whole manifest dream.

Critical readers will now justly enquire about the origin of the interpolation (for which I have so far given no grounds) of the reference to being ridiculed by Gradiva. The answer to this is given in *The Interpretation of Dreams,* which explains that if ridicule, derision, or embittered contradiction occurs in the dream-thoughts, this is expressed by the manifest dream being given a senseless form, by absurdity in the dream.[43] This absurdity does not mean, therefore, that there is any paralysis of psychical activity: it is a method of representation employed by the dream-work. As always happens at specially difficult points, the author once more comes to our help here. The senseless dream had a short epilogue, in which a bird uttered a laughing call and carried the lizard away in its beak. But Hanold had heard a similar laughing call after Gradiva's disappearance. It had in fact come from Zoe, who with this laugh was shaking off the gloomy seriousness of her underworld role. Gradiva had really laughed at him. But the dream-image of the bird carrying off the lizard may have been a recollection of the earlier dream, in which the Apollo Belvedere carried off the Capitoline Venus.

There may still be some readers who feel that the translation of the situation of lizard catching by the idea of wooing has not been

---

43. *The Interpretation of Dreams, Standard Ed.,* 5, 444–45.

sufficiently well established. Some further support for it may be afforded by the consideration that Zoe in her conversation with her newly married friend admitted precisely what Hanold's thoughts about her suspected—when she told her she had felt sure that she would "dig out" something interesting in Pompeii. Here she was trespassing into the field of archaeology, just as he had trespassed, with his simile of lizard catching, into the field of zoology; it was as though they were struggling toward each other and each were trying to assume the other's character.

Here then we seem to have finished off the interpretation of this second dream as well. Both of them have been made intelligible to us on the presupposition that a dreamer knows in his unconscious thoughts all that he has forgotten in his conscious ones, and that in the former he judges correctly what in the latter he misunderstands in a delusion. In the course of our arguments we have no doubt been obliged to make some assertions which have seemed strange to the reader because of their unfamiliarity; and we have probably often roused a suspicion that what we pretended was the author's meaning was in fact only our own. I am anxious to do all I can to dissipate this suspicion, and for that reason I will gladly enter into more detail over one of the most delicate points—I mean the use of ambiguous words and phrases, such as: "Somewhere in the Sun Gradiva was sitting."

Anyone who reads *Gradiva* must be struck by the frequency with which the author puts ambiguous remarks into the mouths of his two principal characters. In Hanold's case these remarks are intended by him unambiguously and it is only the heroine, Gradiva, who is struck by their second meaning. Thus, for instance, when in reply to her first answer he exclaimed, "I knew your voice sounded like that" Zoe, who was still in ignorance, could not but ask how that could be, since he had not heard her speak before. In their second conversation the girl was for a moment thrown into doubt about his delusion, when he told her that he had recognized her at once. She could not help taking these words in the sense (correct so far as his unconscious was concerned) of being a recognition that their acquaintance went back to their childhood; whereas he, of course, knew nothing of this implication of his remark and explained it only by reference to his dominant delusion. On the other hand, the remarks made by the girl, whose personality shows the most lucid clarity of mind in contrast to Hanold's delusion, exhibit an *intentional* ambiguity. One of their meanings chimes in with Hanold's delusion, so as to be able to penetrate into his conscious understanding, but the other rises above the delusion and gives us as a rule its translation into the unconscious truth for which it stands. It is a triumph of ingenuity and wit to be able to express the delusion and the truth in the same turn of words.

Zoe's speech in which she explains the situation to her friend and at the same time succeeds in getting rid of the interrupter is full of ambiguities of this kind. It is in reality a speech made by the author and aimed more at the reader than at Zoe's newly married "colleague." In her conversations with Hanold the ambiguity is usually effected by Zoe's using the same symbolism that we found in Hanold's first dream—the equation of repression and burial, and of Pompeii and childhood. Thus she is able in her speeches on the one hand to remain in the role for which Hanold's delusion has cast her, and on the other hand to make contact with the real circumstances and awaken an understanding of them in Hanold's unconscious.

"I have long grown used to being dead." "To me it is right that you should give the flower of forgetfulness." (Ibid.) In these sentences there was a faint foretaste of the reproaches which broke out clearly enough later on in her final lecture to him, in which she compared him to an archaeopteryx. "The fact of someone having to die so as to come alive; but no doubt that must be so for archaeologists." She made this last remark after the delusion had been cleared up, as though to give a key to her ambiguous speeches. But she made her neatest use of her symbolism when she asked: "I feel as though we had shared a meal like this once before, two thousand years ago; can't you remember?" Here the substitution of the historical past for childhood and the effort to awaken the memory of the latter are quite unmistakable.

But whence comes this striking preference for ambiguous speeches in *Gradiva?* It is no chance event, so it seems to us, but a necessary consequence of the premises of the story. It is nothing other than a counterpart to the twofold determination of symptoms, insofar as speeches are themselves symptoms and, like them, arise from compromises between the conscious and the unconscious. It is simply that this double origin is more easily noticed in speeches than, for instance, in actions. And when, as is often made possible by the malleable nature of the material of speech, each of the two intentions lying behind the speech can be successfully expressed in the same turn of words, we have before us what we call an "ambiguity."

In the course of the psychotherapeutic treatment of a delusion or of an analogous disorder, ambiguous speeches of this kind are often produced by the patient, as new symptoms of the briefest duration; and it can happen that the doctor finds himself too in the position of making use of them. In that way it not infrequently happens that with the meaning that is intended for the patient's conscious he stirs up an understanding of the meaning that applies to his unconscious. I know from experience that the part thus played by ambiguity is apt to raise the greatest objection in the uninitiated and to give rise to the greatest misunderstandings. But in any case our author was right in giving a place in his creation to a picture of this characteristic feature of what takes place in the formation of dreams and delusions.

4

The emergence of Zoe as a physician, as I have already remarked, arouses a new interest in us. We shall be anxious to learn whether a cure of the kind she performed upon Hanold is conceivable or even possible, and whether the author has taken as correct a view of the conditions for the disappearance of a delusion as he has of those for its genesis.

We shall unquestionably be met at this point by an opinion which denies that the case presented by the author possesses any such general interest and disputes the existence of any problem requiring solution. Hanold, it will be said, had no alternative but to abandon his delusion, after its subject, the supposed "Gradiva" herself, had shown him that all his hypotheses were incorrect and after she had given him the most natural explanations of everything puzzling— for instance, of how it was that she had known his name. This would be the logical end of the matter; but since the girl had incidentally revealed her love to him, the author, no doubt to the satisfaction of his female readers, arranged that his story, a not uninteresting one otherwise, should have the usual happy ending in marriage. It would have been more consistent and equally possible, the argument will proceed, if the young scientist, after his error had been pointed out, had taken his leave of the lady with polite thanks and given as the reason for refusing her love the fact that he was able to feel an intense interest in antique woman made of bronze or marble, and in their origins if they were accessible to contact, but that he did not know what to do with contemporary girls of flesh and blood. The author, in short, had quite arbitrarily tacked a love story on to his archaeological fantasy.

In rejecting this view as an impossible one, we observe in the first place that the beginnings of a change in Hanold were not shown only in his abandoning his delusion. Simultaneously, and indeed before his delusion was cleared up, an unmistakable craving for love awakened in him, which found its outcome, naturally as it were, in his courting the girl who had freed him from his delusion. We have already laid emphasis on the pretexts and disguises under which his curiosity about her "bodily nature," his jealousy, and his brutal masculine instinct for mastery were expressed in the midst of his delusion, after his repressed erotic desire had led to his first dream. As further evidence of this we may recall that on the evening after his second interview with Gradiva a live woman for the first time struck him as sympathetic, though he still made a concession to his earlier horror of honeymooning couples by not recognizing her as being newly married. Next morning, however, he was a chance witness to an exchange of endearments between the girl and her supposed brother, and he withdrew with a sense of awe as though he had interrupted some sacred act. His derision of "Edwin and Angelina" was forgotten, and he had acquired a sense of respect for the erotic side of life.

Thus the author has drawn the closest link between the clearing up of the delusion and the outbreak of a craving for love, and he has paved the way for the inevitable outcome in a courtship. He knows the essential nature of the delusion better than his critics: he knows that a component of loving desire had combined with a component of resistance to it in bringing about the delusion, and he makes the girl who undertakes the cure sensitive to the element in Hanold's delusion which is agreeable to her. It was only this knowledge which could decide her to devote herself to the treatment; it was only the certainty of being loved by him that could induce her to admit her love to him. The treatment consisted in giving him back from outside the repressed memories which he could not set free from inside; but it would have had no effect if in the course of it the therapist had not taken his feelings into account and if her ultimate translation of the delusion had not been: "Look, all this only means that you love me."

The procedure which the author makes his Zoe adopt for curing her childhood friend's delusion shows a far-reaching similarity—no, a complete agreement in its essence—with a therapeutic method which was introduced into medical practice in 1895 by Dr. Josef Breuer and myself, and to the perfecting of which I have since then devoted myself. This method of treatment, to which Breuer first gave the name of "cathartic" but which I prefer to describe as "analytic," consists, as applied to patients suffering from disorders analogous to Hanold's delusion, in bringing to their consciousness, to some extent forcibly, the unconscious whose repression led to their falling ill—exactly as Gradiva did with the repressed memories of their childhood relations. Gradiva, it is true, could carry out this task more easily than a doctor: in several respects she was in what may be described as an ideal position for it. The doctor, who had no preexisting knowledge of his patient and possesses no conscious memory of what is unconsciously at work in him, must call a complicated technique to his help in order to make up for this disadvantage. He must learn how to infer with great certainty from the conscious associations and communications of the patient what is repressed in him, how to discover his unconscious as it betrays itself behind his conscious words and acts. He then brings about something like what Norbert Hanold grasped at the end of the story when he translated back the name "Gradiva" into "Bertgang." The disorder vanishes while being traced back to its origin; analysis, too, brings simultaneous cure.

But the similarity between Gradiva's procedure and the analytic method of psychotherapy is not limited to these two points—the making conscious of what has been repressed and the coinciding of explanation with cure. It also extends to what turns out to be the essence of the whole change—to the awakening of feelings. Every disorder analogous to Hanold's delusion, what in scientific terms we are in the habit of calling "psychoneuroses," has as its precondition the repression of a portion of instinctual life, or, as we can safely say, of the sexual instinct. At every attempt to introduce the unconscious and repressed causes of the illness into consciousness, the instinctual component concerned is necessarily aroused to a renewed struggle with the repressed powers, only to come to terms with them in the final outcome, often to the accompaniment of violent manifestations of reaction. The process of cure is accomplished in a relapse into love, if we combine all the many components of the sexual instinct under the term *love;* and such a relapse is indispensable, for the symptoms on account of which the treatment has been undertaken are nothing other than precipitates of earlier struggles connected with repression or the return of the repressed, and they can only be resolved and washed away by a fresh high tide of the same passions. Every psychoanalytic treatment is an attempt at liberating repressed love which has found a meagre outlet in the compromise of a symptom. Indeed, the agreement between such treatments and the process of cure described by the author of *Gradiva* reaches its climax in the further fact that in analytic psychotherapy too the reawakened passion, whether it is love or hate, invariably chooses as its object the figure of the doctor.

It is here that the differences begin, which made the case of Gradiva an ideal one which medical technique cannot attain. Gradiva was able to return the love which was making its way from the unconscious into consciousness, but the doctor cannot. Gradiva had herself been the object of the earlier, repressed love; her figure at once offered the liberated current of love a desirable aim. The doctor has been a stranger, and must endeavor to become a stranger once more after the cure; he is often at a loss what advice to give the patients he has cured as to how in real life they can use their recovered capacity to love. To indicate the expedients and substitutes of which the doctor therefore makes use to help him to approximate with more or less success to the model of a cure by love which has been shown us by our author—all this would take us much too far away from the task before us.

And now for the final question, whose answer we have already evaded more than once. Our views on repression, on the genesis of delusions and allied disorders, on the formation and solution of dreams, on the part played by erotic life, and on the method by which such disorders are cured, are far from being the common property of science, let alone the assured possession of educated people. If the insight which has enabled the author to construct his "fantasy" in such a way that we have been able to dissect it like a real case history is in the nature of knowledge, we should be curious to learn what were the sources of that knowledge. One of our circle—the one who, as I said at the beginning, was interested in the dreams in *Gradiva* and their possible interpretation—approached the author with the direct question whether he knew anything of such scientific theories as these. The author replied, as was to be expected, in the negative, and, indeed, somewhat brusquely. His imagination, he said, had inspired *Gradiva*, and he had enjoyed it; if there was anyone whom it did not please, let him simply leave it alone. He had no suspicion of how greatly it had in fact pleased his readers.

It is quite possible that the author's disavowal does not stop at this. He may perhaps altogether deny any knowledge of the rules which we have shown that he has followed, and he may repudiate all the purposes we have recognized in his work. I do not regard this as improbable; but if it is so, there are only two possible explanations. It may be that we have produced a complete caricature of an interpretation by introducing into an innocent work of art purposes of which its creator had no notion, and by so doing have shown once more how easy it is to find what one is looking for and what is occupying one's own mind—a possibility of which the strangest examples are to be found in the history of literature. Let every reader now make up his mind whether he is able to accept this explanation. We ourselves, of course, hold to the other view, the remaining alternative. Our opinion is that the author need have known nothing of these rules and purposes, so that he could disavow them in good faith, but that nevertheless we have not discovered anything in his work that is not already in it. We probably draw from the same source and work upon the same object, each of us by another method. And the agreement of our results seems to guarantee that we have both worked correctly. Our procedure consists in the conscious observation of abnormal mental processes in other people so as to be able to elicit and announce their laws. The author no doubt proceeds differently. He directs his attention to the unconscious in his own mind, he listens to its possible developments and lends them artistic expression instead of suppressing them by conscious criticism. Thus he experiences from himself what we learn from others—the laws which the activities of this unconscious must obey. But he need not state these laws, nor even be clearly aware of them; as a result of the tolerance of his intelligence, they are incorporated within his creations. We discover these laws by analyzing his writings just as we find them from cases of real illness; but the conclusion seems inescapable that either both of us, the writer and the doctor, have misunderstood the unconscious in the same way, or we have both understood it correctly. This conclusion is of great value to us, and it is on its account that it has been worth while to investigate by the methods of medical psychoanalysis the way in which the formation and the cure of the delusions as well as the dreams are represented in Jensen's *Gradiva*.

We would seem to have reached the end. But an attentive reader might remind us that at the beginning [p. 7.] we threw out an assertion that dreams are wishes represented as fulfilled and that we gave no proof of this. Well, is our reply, what we have described in these pages might show how little justification there is for trying to cover the explanations we have to give of dreams with the single formula that dreams are wish fulfillments. Nevertheless the assertion stands and can easily be proved too for the dreams in *Gradiva*. The latent dream-thoughts—we know now what is meant by them—may be of the most various kinds; in *Gradiva* they are "days' residues," thoughts that have been left over unnoticed and undealt-with from the mental activities of waking life. But in order for a dream to develop out of them, the cooperation of a wish (usually an unconscious one) is required; this contributes the motive force for constructing the dream, while the day's residues provide the material. In Norbert Hanold's first dream two wishes competed with each other in making the dream; one of them was actually admissible to consciousness, while the other belonged to the unconscious and operated from out of repression. The first was a wish, understandable in any archaeologist, to have been present as an eyewitness at the catastrophe in the year A.D. 79. What sacrifice would an archaeologist think too great if this wish could be realized in any way other than in a dream! The other wish, the other constructor of the dream, was of an erotic nature: it might be crudely and also incompletely stated as a wish to be there when the girl he loved lay down to sleep. This was the wish the rejection of which caused the dream to become an anxiety-dream. The wishes that were the motive forces of the second dream are perhaps less conspicuous; but if we recall its translation we shall not hesitate to describe them too as erotic. The wish to be taken captive by the girl he loved, to fall in with her wishes and to be subjected to her—for so we may construe the wish behind the situation of the lizard catching—was in fact of a passive, masochistic character. Next day the dreamer hit the girl, as though he was dominated by the contrary erotic current. . . . But we must stop here, or we may really forget that Hanold and Gradiva are only creatures of their author's mind.

Translated by James Strachey

12

Address to the Society
of B'nai B'rith

M ost honorable Grand President, honorable Presidents, dear
Brethren—

I thank you for the honors you have paid me today. You know
why it is that you cannot hear the sound of my own voice. You
have heard one of my friends and pupils speak of my scientific
work; but a judgment on such things is hard to form and for
a long while yet it may not be reached with any certainty. Allow
me to add something to what has been said by one who is both
my friend and the physician who cares for me. I should like to
tell you shortly how I became a B.B. and what I have looked for
from you.

It happened that in the years from 1895 onwards I was subjected
to two powerful impressions which combined to produce the same
effect on me. On the one hand, I had gained my first insight into
the depths of the life of the human instincts; I had seen some things
that were sobering and even, at first, frightening. On the other
hand, the announcement of my unpleasing discoveries had as its
result the severance of the greater part of human contacts; I felt as
though I were despised and universally shunned. In my loneliness
I was seized with a longing to find a circle of picked men of high
character who would receive me in a friendly spirit in spite of my
temerity. Your society was pointed out to me as the place where
such men were to be found.

That you were Jews could only be agreeable to me; for I was
myself a Jew, and it had always seemed to me not only unworthy

but positively senseless to deny the fact. What bound me to Jewry was (I am ashamed to admit) neither faith nor national pride, for I have always been an unbeliever and was brought up without any religion though not without a respect for what are called the "ethical" standards of human civilization. Whenever I felt an inclination to national enthusiasm I strove to suppress it as being harmful and wrong, alarmed by the warning examples of the peoples among whom we Jews live. But plenty of other things remained over to make the attraction of Jewry and Jews irresistible—many obscure emotional forces, which were the more powerful the less they could be expressed in words, as well as a clear consciousness of inner identity, the safe privacy of a common mental construction. And beyond this there was a perception that it was to my Jewish nature alone that I owed two characteristics that had become indispensable to me in the difficult course of my life. Because I was a Jew I found myself free from many prejudices which restricted others in the use of their intellect; and as a Jew I was prepared to join the Opposition and to do without agreement with the "compact majority."

So it was that I became one of you, took my share in your humanitarian and national interests, gained friends among you and persuaded my own few remaining friends to join our society. There was no question whatever of my convincing you of my new theories; but at a time when no one in Europe listened to me and I still had no disciples even in Vienna, you gave me your kindly attention. You were my first audience.

For some two thirds of the long period that has elapsed since my entry I persisted with you conscientiously, and found refreshment and stimulation in my relations with you. You have been kind enough today not to hold it up against me that during the last third of the time I have kept away from you. I was overwhelmed with work, and demands connected with it forced themselves on me; the day ceased to be long enough for me to attend your meetings, and soon my body began to rebel against a late evening meal. Finally came the years of my illness, which prevents me from being with you even today.

I cannot tell whether I have been a genuine B.B. in your sense. I am almost inclined to doubt it; so many exceptional circumstances have arisen in my case. But of this I can assure you—that you meant much to me and did much for me during the years in which I belonged to you. I ask you therefore to accept my warmest thanks both for those years and for today.

Yours in W.B. & E.[1]

SIGMUND FREUD

Translated by James Strachey

---

1. The abbreviation stands for '*Wohlwollen, Bruderliebe und Eintracht*', the motto of the order, which is translated "Benevolence, Brotherly Love, and Harmony."

13

A Difficulty in the
Path of Psychoanalysis

I will say at once that it is not an intellectual difficulty I am thinking of, not anything that makes psychoanalysis hard for the hearer or reader to understand, but an affective one—something that alienates the feelings of those who come into contact with it, so that they become less inclined to believe in it or take an interest in it. As will be observed, the two kinds of difficulty amount to the same thing in the end. Where sympathy is lacking, understanding will not come very easily.

My present readers, I take it, have not so far had anything to do with the subject and I shall be obliged, therefore, to go back some distance. Out of a great number of individual observations and impressions something in the nature of a theory has at last shaped itself in psychoanalysis, and this is known by the name of the "libido theory." As is well-known, psychoanalysis is concerned with the elucidation and removal of what are called nervous disorders. A starting-point had to be found from which to approach this problem, and it was decided to look for it in the instinctual life of the mind. Hypotheses about the instincts in man came to form the basis, therefore, of our conception of nervous disease.

Psychology as it is taught academically gives us but very inadequate replies to questions concerning our mental life, but in no direction is its information so meager as in this matter of the instincts.

It is open to us to make our first soundings as we please. The popular view distinguishes between hunger and love, as being the representatives of the instincts which aim respectively at the preservation of the individual and at the reproduction of the species. We accept this very evident distinction, so that in psychoanalysis too we make a distinction between the self-preservative or ego-instincts on the one hand and the sexual instincts on the other. The force by which the sexual instinct is represented in the mind we call "libido"—sexual desire—and we regard it as something analogous to hunger, the will to power, and so on, where the ego-instincts are concerned.

With this as a starting-point we go on to make our first important discovery. We learn that, when we try to understand neurotic disorders, by far the greater significance attaches to the sexual instincts; that in fact neuroses are the specific disorders, so to speak, of the sexual function; that in general whether or not a person develops a neurosis depends on the quantity of his libido, and on the possibility of satisfying it and of discharging it through satisfaction; that the form taken by the disease is determined by the way in which the individual passes through the course of development of his sexual function, or, as we put it, by the fixations his libido has undergone in the course of its development; and, further, that by a special, not very simple technique for influencing the mind we are able to throw light on the nature of some groups of neuroses and at the same time to do away with them. Our therapeutic efforts have their greatest success with a certain class of neuroses which proceed from a conflict between the ego-instincts and the sexual instincts. For in human beings it may happen that the demands of the sexual instincts, whose reach of course extends far beyond the individual, seem to the ego to constitute a danger which threatens its self-preservation or its self-esteem. The ego then assumes the defensive, denies the sexual instincts the satisfaction they desire and forces them into those bypaths of substitutive satisfaction which become manifest as nervous symptoms.

The psychoanalytic method of treatment is then able to subject this process of repression to revision and to bring about a better solution of the conflict—one that is compatible with health. Unintelligent opposition accuses us of one-sidedness in our estimate of the sexual instincts. "Human beings have other interests besides sexual ones," they say. We have not forgotten or denied this for a moment. Our one-sidedness is like that of the chemist, who traces all compounds back to the force of chemical attraction. He is not on that account denying the force of gravity; he leaves that to the physicist to deal with.

During the work of treatment we have to consider the distribution of the patient's libido; we look for the object-presentations to which it is bound and free it from them, so as to place it at the disposal of the ego. In the course of this, we have come to form a very curious picture of the original, primal distribution of libido in human beings. We have been given to assume that at the beginning of the development of the individual all his libido (all his erotic tendencies, all his capacity for love) is tied to himself—that as we say, it cathects his own ego. It is only later that, being attached to the satisfaction of the major vital needs, the libido flows over from the ego on to external objects. Not till then are we able to recognize the libidinal instincts as such and distinguish them from the ego-instincts. It is possible for the libido to become detached from these objects and withdrawn again into the ego.

The condition in which the ego retains the libido is called by us "narcissism," in reference to the Greek legend of the youth Narcissus who was in love with his own reflection.

Thus in our view the individual advances from narcissism to object-love. But we do not believe that the *whole* of the libido ever passes over from the ego to objects. A certain quantity of libido is always retained in the ego; even when object-love is highly developed, a certain amount of narcissism persists. The ego is a great reservoir from which the libido that is destined for objects flows out and into which it flows back from those objects. Object-libido was at first ego-libido and can be transformed back into ego-libido. For complete health it is essential that the libido should not lose this full mobility. As an illustration of this state of things we may think of an amoeba, whose viscous substance puts out pseudopodia, elongations into which the substance of the body extends but which can be retracted at any time so that the form of the protoplasmic mass is restored.

What I have been trying to describe in this outline is the *libido theory* of the neuroses, upon which are founded all our conceptions of the nature of these morbid states, together with our therapeutic measures for relieving them. We naturally regard the premises of the libido theory as valid for normal behavior as well. We speak of the narcissism of small children, and it is to the excessive narcissism of primitive man that we ascribe his belief in the omnipotence of his thoughts and his consequent attempts to influence the course of events in the external world by the technique of magic.

After this introduction I propose to describe how the universal narcissism of men, their self-love, has up to the present suffered three severe blows from the researches of science.

(a) In the early stages of his researches, man believed at first that his dwelling-place, the earth, was the stationary center of the universe, with the sun, moon, and planets circling round it. In this he was naively following the dictates of his sense-perceptions, for he felt no movement of the earth, and wherever he had an unimpeded view he found himself in the center of a circle that enclosed the external world. The central position of the earth, moreover, was a token to him of the dominating part played by it in the universe and appeared to fit in very well with his inclination to regard himself as lord of the world.

The destruction of this narcissistic illusion is associated in our minds with the name and work of Copernicus in the sixteenth century. But long before his day the Pythagoreans had already cast doubts on the privileged position of the earth, and in the third century B.C. Aristarchus of Samos had declared that the earth was much smaller than the sun and moved round that celestial body. Even the great discovery of Copernicus, therefore, had already been made before him. When this discovery achieved general recognition, the self-love of mankind suffered its first blow, the *cosmological* one.

(b) In the course of the development of civilization man acquired a dominating position over his fellow creatures in the animal kingdom. Not content with this supremacy, however, he began to place a gulf between his nature and theirs. He denied the possession of reason to them, and to himself he attributed an immortal soul, and made claims to a divine descent which permitted him to break the bond of community between him and the animal kingdom. Curiously enough, this piece of arrogance is still foreign to children, just as it is to primitive and primeval man. It is the result of a later, more pretentious stage of development. At the level of totemism primitive man had no repugnance to tracing his descent from an animal ancestor. In myths, which contain the precipitate of this ancient attitude of mind, the gods take animal shapes, and in the art of earliest times they are portrayed with animals' heads. A child can see no difference between his own nature and that of animals. He is not astonished at animals thinking and talking in fairy tales; he will transfer an emotion of fear which he feels for his human father onto a dog or a horse, without intending any derogation of his father by it. Not until he is grown up does he become so far estranged from animals as to use their names in vilification of human beings.

We all know that little more than half a century ago the researches of Charles Darwin and his collaborators and forerunners put an end to this presumption on the part of man. Man is not a being different from animals or superior to them; he himself is of animal descent, being more closely related to some species and more distantly to others. The acquisitions he has subsequently made have not succeeded in effacing the evidences, both in his physical structure and in his mental dispositions, of his parity with them. This was the second, the *biological* blow to human narcissism.

(c) The third blow, which is psychological in nature, is probably the most wounding.

Although thus humbled in his external relations, man feels himself to be supreme within his own mind. Somewhere in the core of his ego he has developed an organ of observation to keep a watch on his impulses and actions and see whether they harmonize with its demands. If they do not, they are ruthlessly inhibited and withdrawn. His internal perception, consciousness, gives the ego news of all the important occurrences in the mind's working, and the will, directed by these reports, carries out what the ego orders and modifies anything that seeks to accomplish itself spontaneously. For this mind is not a simple thing; on the contrary, it is a hierarchy of superordinated and subordinated agencies, a labyrinth of impulses striving independently of one another toward action, corresponding with the multiplicity of instincts and of relations with the external world, many of which are antagonistic to one another and incompatible. For proper functioning it is necessary that the highest of these agencies should have knowledge of all that is going forward and that its will should penetrate everywhere, so as to exert its influence. And in fact the ego feels secure both as to the completeness and trustworthiness of the reports it receives and as to the openness of the channels through which it enforces its commands.

In certain diseases—including the very neuroses of which we have made special study—things are different. The ego feels uneasy; it comes up against limits to its power in its own house, the mind. Thoughts emerge suddenly without one's knowing where they come from, nor can one do anything to drive them away. These alien guests even seem to be more powerful than those which are at the ego's command. They resist all the well-proved measures of enforcement used by the will, remain unmoved by logical refutation, and are unaffected by the contradictory assertions of reality. Or else impulses appear which seem like those of a stranger, so that the ego disowns them; yet it has to fear them and take precautions against them. The ego says to itself: "This is an illness, a foreign invasion." It increases its vigilance, but cannot understand why it feels so strangely paralyzed.

Psychiatry, it is true, denies that such things mean the intrusion into the mind of evil spirits from without; beyond this, however, it can only say with a shrug: "Degeneracy, hereditary disposition, constitutional inferiority!" Psychoanalysis sets out to explain these uncanny disorders; it engages in careful and laborious investigations, devises hypotheses and scientific constructions, until at length it can speak thus to the ego:—

"Nothing has entered into you from without; a part of the activity of your own mind has been withdrawn from your knowledge and from the command of your will. That, too, is why you are so weak in your defense; you are using one part of your force to fight the other part and you cannot concentrate the whole of your force as you would against an external enemy. And it is not even the worst or least important part of your mental forces that has thus become antagonistic to you and independent of you. The blame, I am bound to say, lies with yourself. You overestimated your strength when you thought you could treat your sexual instincts as you liked and could utterly ignore their intentions. The result is that they have rebelled and have taken their own obscure paths to escape this suppression; they have established their rights in a manner you cannot approve. How they have achieved this, and the paths which they have taken, have not come to your knowledge. All you have learned is the *outcome* of their work—the symptom which you experience as suffering. Thus you do not recognize it as a derivative of your own rejected instincts and do not know that it is a substitutive satisfaction of them.

"The whole process, however, only becomes possible through the single circumstance that you are mistaken in another important point as well. You feel sure that you are informed of all that goes on in your mind if it is of any importance at all, because in that case, you believe, your consciousness gives you news of it. And if you have had no information of something in your mind you confidently assume that it does not exist there. Indeed, you go so far as to regard what is 'mental' as identical with what is 'conscious'—that is, with what is known to you—in spite of the most obvious evidence that a great deal more must constantly be going on in your mind than can be known to your consciousness. Come, let yourself be taught something on this one point! What is in your mind does not coincide with what you are conscious of; whether something is going on in your mind and whether you hear of it, are two different things. In the ordinary way, I will admit, the intelligence which reaches your consciousness is enough for your needs; and you may cherish the illusion that you learn of all the more important things. But in some cases, as in that of an instinctual conflict such as I have described, your intelligence service breaks down and your will then extends no further than your knowledge. In every case, however, the news that reaches your consciousness is incomplete and often not to be relied on. Often enough, too, it happens that you get news of events only when they are over and when you can no longer do anything to change them. Even if you are not ill, who can tell all that is stirring in your mind of which you know nothing or are falsely informed? You behave like an absolute ruler who is content with the information supplied him by his highest officials and never goes among the people to hear their voice. Turn your eyes inward, look into your own depths, learn first to know yourself! Then you will understand why you were bound to fall ill; and perhaps you will avoid falling ill in future."

It is thus that psychoanalysis has sought to educate the ego. But these two discoveries—that the life of our sexual instincts cannot be wholly tamed, and that mental processes are in themselves unconscious and only reach the ego and come under its control through incomplete and untrustworthy perceptions—these two discoveries amount to a statement that *the ego is not master in its own house.* Together they represent the third blow to man's self-love, what I may call the *psychological* one. No wonder, then, that the ego does not look favorably upon psychoanalysis and obstinately refuses to believe in it.

Probably very few people can have realized the momentous significance for science and life of the recognition of unconscious mental processes. It was not psychoanalysis, however, let us hasten to add, which first took this step. There are famous philosophers who may be cited as forerunners—above all the great thinker Schopenhauer, whose unconscious "Will" is equivalent to the mental instincts of psychoanalysis. It was this same thinker, moreover, who in words of unforgettable impressiveness admonished mankind of the importance, still so greatly underestimated by it, of its sexual craving. Psychoanalysis has this advantage only, that it has not affirmed these two propositions which are so distressing to narcissism—the psychical importance of sexuality and the unconsciousness of mental life—on an *abstract* basis, but has demonstrated them in matters that touch every individual personally and force him to take up some attitude toward these problems. It is just for this reason, however, that it brings on itself the aversion and resistances which still hold back in awe before the great name of the philosopher.

Translated by Joan Riviere

14

The Great Man

How is it possible for a single man to evolve such extraordinary effectiveness that he can form a people out of random individuals and families, can stamp them with their definitive character and determine their fate for thousands of years? Is not a hypothesis such as this a relapse into the mode of thought which led to myths of a creator and to the worship of heroes, into times in which the writing of history was nothing more than a report of the deeds and destinies of single individuals, of rulers or conquerors? The modern tendency is rather toward tracing back the events of human history to more concealed, general, and impersonal factors, to the compelling influence of economic conditions, to alterations in food habits, to advances in the use of materials and tools, to migrations brought about by increases in population and climatic changes. Individuals have no other part to play in this than as exponents or representatives of group trends, which are bound to find expression and do so in these particular individuals largely by chance.

These are perfectly justifiable lines of approach, but they give us occasion for drawing attention to an important discrepancy between the attitude taken up by our organ of thought and the arrangement of things in the world, which are supposed to be grasped by means of our thought. It is enough for our need to discover causes (which, to be sure, is imperative) if each event has *one* demonstrable cause.[1] But in the reality lying outside us that is scarcely

---

1. Freud had made this point before in the third of his *Five Lectures* (1910a), *Standard Ed.*, 11, 38.—The fact of multiple causation was constantly insisted on by him from early times. See, for instance, chapter 4, section 1, of *Studies on Hysteria* (1895d), *Standard Ed.*, 2, 263.

the case; on the contrary, each event seems to be overdetermined and proves to be the effect of several convergent causes. Frightened by the immense complication of events, our investigations take the side of one correlation as against another and set up contradictions which do not exist but have only arisen owing to a rupture of more comprehensive relations.[2] Accordingly, if the investigation of a particular case demonstrates to us the transcendent influence of a single personality, our conscience need not reproach us with having by this hypothesis flown in the face of the doctrine of the importance of the general and impersonal factors. There is room in principle for both. In the case of the genesis of monotheism, however, we can point to no external factor other than the one we have already mentioned—that this development was linked with the establishment of closer relations between different nations and with the building up of a great empire.

Thus we reserve a place for "great men" in the chain, or rather the network, of causes. But it may not, perhaps, be quite useless to enquire under what conditions we confer this title of honor. We shall be surprised to find that it is never quite easy to answer this question. A first formulation—"we do so if a man possesses to a specially high degree qualities that we value greatly"—clearly misses the mark in every respect. Beauty, for instance, and muscular strength, however enviable they may be, constitute no claim to "greatness." It would seem, then, that the qualities have to be mental ones—psychical and intellectual distinctions. As regards these, we are held up by the consideration that nevertheless we should not unhesitantly describe someone as a great man simply because he was extraordinarily efficient in some particular sphere. We should certainly not do so in the case of a chess master or of a virtuoso on a musical instrument; but not very easily, either, in the case of a distinguished artist or scientist. In such cases we should naturally speak of him as a great poet, painter, mathematician or physicist, or as a pioneer in the field of this or that activity;

---

2. I protest, however, against being misunderstood to say that the world is so complicated that any assertion one may make is bound to hit upon a piece of truth somewhere. No. Our thought has upheld its liberty to discover dependent relations and connections to which there is nothing corresponding in reality; and it clearly sets a very high value on this gift, since it makes such copious use of it both inside and outside of science.

but we refrain from pronouncing him a great man. If we unhesitatingly declare that, for instance, Goethe and Leonardo da Vinci and Beethoven were great men, we must be led to it by something other than admiration for their splendid creations. If precisely such examples as these did not stand in the way, the idea would probably occur to us that the name of a "great man" is preferably reserved for men of action—conquerors, generals, rulers—and is in recognition of the greatness of their achievements, the force of the effects to which they gave rise. But this too is unsatisfactory and is entirely contradicted by our condemnation of so many worthless figures whose effects upon their contemporary world and upon posterity can nevertheless not be disputed. Nor shall we be able to choose success as a sign of greatness, when we reflect on the majority of great men who instead of achieving success have perished in misfortune.

For the moment, then, we are inclined to decide that it is not worthwhile to look for a connotation of the concept of a "great man" that is unambiguously determined. It seems to be only a loosely used and somewhat arbitrarily conferred recognition of an overlarge development of certain human qualities, with some approximation to the original literal sense of "greatness." We must recollect, too, that we are not so much interested in the essence of great men as in the question of the means by which they affect their fellowmen. We will, however, keep this enquiry as short as possible, since it threatens to lead us far away from our goal.

Let us, therefore, take it for granted that a great man influences his fellowmen in two ways: by his personality and by the idea which he puts forward. That idea may stress some ancient wishful image of the masses, or it may point out a new wishful aim to them, or it may cast its spell over them in some other way. Occasionally—and this is undoubtedly the more primary case—the personality works by itself and the idea plays a quite trivial part. Not for a moment are we in the dark as to why a great man ever becomes important. We know that in the mass of mankind there is a powerful need for an authority who can be admired, before whom one bows down, by whom one is ruled and perhaps even ill-treated. We have learned from the psychology of individual men what the origin is of this need of the masses. It is a longing for the father felt by everyone from his childhood onwards, for the same father whom the hero of legend boasts he has overcome. And now it may begin to dawn on us that all the characteristics with which we equipped the great man are paternal characteristics, and that the essence of great men for which we vainly searched lies in this conformity. The decisiveness of thought, the strength of will, the energy of action are part of the picture of a father—but above all the autonomy and independence of the great man, his divine unconcern which may grow into ruthlessness. One must admire him, one may trust him, but one cannot avoid being afraid of him too. We should have been led to realize this from the word itself: who but the father can have been the "great man" in childhood?[3]

There is no doubt that it was a mighty prototype of a father which, in the person of Moses, stooped to the poor Jewish bondsmen to assure them that they were his dear children. And no less overwhelming must have been the effect upon them of the idea of an only, eternal, almighty God, to whom they were not too mean for him to make a covenant with them and who promised to care for them if they remained loyal to his worship. It was probably not easy for them to distinguish the image of the man Moses from that of his God; and their feeling was right in this, for Moses may have introduced traits of his own personality into the character of his God—such as his wrathful temper and his relentlessness. And if, this being so, they killed their great man one day, they were only repeating a misdeed which in ancient times had been committed, as prescribed by law, against the Divine King and which, as we know, went back to a still more ancient prototype.[4]

If on the one hand we thus see the figure of the great man grown to divine proportions, yet on the other hand we must recall that the father too was once a child. The great religious idea for which the man Moses stood was, on our view, not his own property: he had taken it over from King Akhenaten. And he, whose greatness as the founder of a religion is unequivocally established, may perhaps have been following hints which had reached him—from near or distant parts of Asia—through the medium of his mother[5] or by other paths.

---

3. In German *der grosse Mann* means not only "the great man" but "the tall man" or "the big man."

4. Cf. Frazer, loc. cit.

5. The theory held at one time, that Akhenaten's mother, Queen Tiye, was of foreign origin, has been abandoned in view of the discovery of her parents' tomb at Thebes.

We cannot follow the chain of events further, but if we have rightly recognized these first steps, the monotheist idea returned like a boomerang to the land of its origin. Thus it seems unfruitful to try to fix the credit due to an individual in connection with a new idea. It is clear that many have shared in its development and made contributions to it. And, again, it would obviously be unjust to break off the chain of causes at Moses and to neglect what was effected by those who succeeded him and carried on his ideas, the Jewish Prophets. The seed of monotheism failed to ripen in Egypt. The same thing might have happened in Israel after the people had thrown off the burdensome and exacting religion. But there constantly arose from the Jewish people men who revived the fading tradition, who renewed the admonitions and demands made by Moses, and who did not rest till what was lost had been established once again. In the course of constant efforts over centuries, and finally owing to two great reforms, one before and one after the Babylonian exile, the transformation was accomplished of the popular god Yahweh into the God whose worship had been forced upon the Jews by Moses. And evidence of the presence of a peculiar psychical aptitude in the masses who had become the Jewish people as revealed by the fact that they were able to produce so many individuals prepared to take on the burdens of the religion of Moses in return for the reward of being the chosen people and perhaps for some other prizes of a similar degree.

Translated by Katherine Jones

ACKNOWLEDGEMENTS

Every reasonable effort has been made to locate the owners of rights to previously published works and the translations printed here. We gratefully acknowledge permission to reprint the following material:

Permission to quote from *The Standard Edition of the Complete Psychological Works of Sigmund Freud* has been given by Sigmund Freud Copyrights, 10 Brook Street, Wivenhoe, Colchester CO7 9DS, England, as well as by The Institute of Psycho-Analysis and by The Hogarth Press.
"Katharina." From *Studies in Hysteria*, by Josef Breuer and Sigmund Freud. Translated from the German and edited by James Strachey, in collaboration with Anna Freud, assisted by Alix Strachey and Alan Tyson. Published in the United States of America by Basic Books, Inc., by arrangement with the Hogarth Press, Ltd. Reprinted by permission of Basic Books, Inc., Publishers, New York.
"Letters to Fliess." From *The Origins of Psycho-Analysis: Letters to Wilhelm Fliess, Drafts and Notes, 1887–1902,* by Sigmund Freud. © 1954 by Basic Books, Inc. Reprinted by permission of Basic Books, Inc., Publishers, New York.
"The Method of Interpreting Dreams: An Analysis of a Specimen Dream." From *The Interpretation of Dreams,* by Sigmund Freud. Translated from the German and edited by James Strachey. Published by Basic Books, Inc. by arrangement with George Allen and Unwin Ltd. and the Hogarth Press, Ltd. Reprinted by permission of Basic Books, Inc., Publishers, New York.
"Infantile Sexuality." From *Three Essays on the Theory of Sexuality,* by Sigmund Freud. Translated and newly edited by James Strachey. Copyright © 1962 by Sigmund Freud Copyrights. Reprinted by permission of Basic Books, Inc., Publishers, New York.
"Freud's Psychoanalytic Procedure." "The Uncanny." "A Disturbance of Memory on the Acropolis." "Dreams and Telepathy." From *Sigmund Freud : Collected Papers, Volumes I–V.* Edited by James Strachey. Published in the United States by arrangement with the Hogarth Press Ltd. and the Institute of Psycho-Analysis, London. Reprinted by permission of Basic Books, Inc., Publishers, New York.
Excepted from *On Dreams* by Sigmund Freud, translated from the German by James Strachey, with permission of W. W. Norton & Company, Inc., 500 Fifth Avenue, New York, NY 10110. Copyright 1952 by W. W. Norton & Company, Inc., copyright renewed © 1980. All rights reserved.
Reprinted from *The Psychopathology of Everyday Life* by Sigmund Freud, Translated by Alan Tyson, Edited by James Strachey, by permission of W. W. Norton & Company, Inc. Editorial Matter Copyright © 1965, 1960 by James Strachey. Translation Copyright © 1960 by Alan Tyson.
"The Great Man." From *Moses and Monotheism* by Sigmund Freud, Translated by Katherine Jones. Copyright 1939 by Alfred A. Knopf Inc. and renewed 1967 by Ernst L. Freud and Anna Freud. Reprinted by permission of Alfred A. Knopf Inc.